Palgrave Debates in Business History

Series Editors
Bradley Bowden, Brisbane, QLD, Australia
Michael Heller, Brunel Business School, Brunel University, London, UK

Scholarship in business history often produced divergent opinions that seldom engage with each other. Business historians have continued their scholarly endeavors with little obvious concern to the popular discontents around them. This book series will foster debate among business historians, bring together a variety of opinions from around the globe to confront the key issues of our time with the intent of becoming a fulcrum of debate. The series will use a broad understanding of "business history" so that it brings together work that is currently operating in tandem with each other without ever engaging with each other: work from business and management history, social history, economic history, cultural history, labor history, sociology, and political history whose focus is societal rather than personal or narrowly institutional. The series will focus on the following current debates in the field: the nature of globalization; the nature of capitalism; the nature and effects of western civilization (particularly as relates to industrialization); the mediatisation of business; gender, class and identity; and business and shifts in wealth, power and inequality. Within these topics there is passionate dissension, creating an opportunity engage multiple perspectives.

Editors
Bradley Bowden, Griffith University, Australia
Michael Heller, Brunel University, UK

Associate Editors
Jeffrey Muldoon, Emporia University, USA
Gabrielle Durepos, Mount Saint Vincent University, Canada

Editorial Board
Bernardo Batiz-Lazo, University of Northumbria, UK
Arthur G. Bedeian, Louisiana State University, USA
Amanda Budde-Sung, US Air Force Academy, USA
Andrew Cardow, Massey University, New Zealand
Matteo Cristofaro, University of Rome, Italy
Sébastien Damart, Paris Dauphine University, France
Carlos Davila, University of the Andes, Colombia
Nick Dyrenfurth, Curtin Research University, Australia
Anthony M. Gould, University of Laval, Canada
Scott Hargreaves, Institute for Public Affairs, Australia
Albert Mills, Saint Mary's University, Canada
Jean Helms Mills, Saint Mary's University, Canada
Elly Leung, University of Western Australia, Australia
Jan Logemann, University of Göttingen, Germany
Mairi Maclean, University of Bath, UK
Vadim Marshev, Moscow State University, Russia
Patricia McLaren, Wilfrid Laurier University, Canada
Peter Miskell, Henley Business School, University of Reading, UK
Milorad Novicevic, University of Mississippi, USA
Andrew Popp, Copenhagen Business School, Denmark
Nimruji Prasad, Indian Institute of Management Calcutta, India
Michael Rowlinson, University of Exeter, UK
Stefan Schwarzkopf, Copenhagen Business School, Denmark
Philip Scranton, Rutgers University, USA
Grietjie Verhoef, University of Johannesburg, South Africa
James Wilson, University of Glasgow, UK

More information about this series at
https://link.springer.com/bookseries/16405

Philip Scranton

Business Practice in Socialist Hungary, Volume 1

Creating the Theft Economy, 1945–1957

Philip Scranton
Rutgers, The State University of New Jersey
New Brunswick, NJ, USA

ISSN 2662-4362   ISSN 2662-4370   (electronic)
Palgrave Debates in Business History
ISBN 978-3-030-89183-1   ISBN 978-3-030-89184-8   (eBook)
https://doi.org/10.1007/978-3-030-89184-8

© The Editor(s) (if applicable) and The Author(s), under exclusive license to Springer
Nature Switzerland AG 2022
This work is subject to copyright. All rights are solely and exclusively licensed by the
Publisher, whether the whole or part of the material is concerned, specifically the rights
of translation, reprinting, reuse of illustrations, recitation, broadcasting, reproduction on
microfilms or in any other physical way, and transmission or information storage and
retrieval, electronic adaptation, computer software, or by similar or dissimilar methodology
now known or hereafter developed.
The use of general descriptive names, registered names, trademarks, service marks, etc.
in this publication does not imply, even in the absence of a specific statement, that such
names are exempt from the relevant protective laws and regulations and therefore free for
general use.
The publisher, the authors and the editors are safe to assume that the advice and information in this book are believed to be true and accurate at the date of publication. Neither
the publisher nor the authors or the editors give a warranty, expressed or implied, with
respect to the material contained herein or for any errors or omissions that may have been
made. The publisher remains neutral with regard to jurisdictional claims in published maps
and institutional affiliations.

This Palgrave Macmillan imprint is published by the registered company Springer Nature
Switzerland AG
The registered company address is: Gewerbestrasse 11, 6330 Cham, Switzerland

ADVANCE COMMENTS ON BUSINESS PRACTICE IN SOCIALIST HUNGARY, VOLUME I

"In *Business Practice in Socialist Hungary, Volume 1*, Philip Scranton brings his keen sense for the theoretical and empirical aspects of business enterprise to the fascinating setting of Hungary's nascent socialist economy. Through a richly contextualized reading of some astonishing primary source documents, Scranton illustrates how capitalist and socialist organizations shared more characteristics than is widely acknowledged. Anyone interested in the challenges that face business enterprises—to say nothing of the contradictions between socialist visions and organizational realities—will cherish Scranton's insight and marvel at the tales and the toil he uncovers."

—Andrew Russell, *Dean, New York Polytechnic Institute; Co-director, themaintainers.org*

"Philip Scranton's new book, *Business Practice in Socialist Hungary, Volume 1*, brims with gritty archival detail and packs conceptual heft as it explores how managers and employees, farmers and peasants, party apparatchiks and party bosses, struggled – and fought – to build an economic system that 'worked, more or less' in newly socialist Hungary in the years following WWII. Centering the concepts of coping and maneuvering, Scranton reveals not only the limitations of strategizing and planning, already well-established, but also how, working from the bottom up, ordinary Hungarians developed creative workarounds that made the best of what was at hand, whilst frequently embracing shirking, resistance and theft, in order to meet the absurdities and cruelties they often faced. In doing so, they placed themselves at the heart of the development of this new economic system. Students and scholars of Hungarian and wider Soviet era economic history will find much to learn and enjoy in this deeply researched and tautly written book. But it has wider resonances and lessons. Once we begin looking for them, we will likely find coping and maneuvering somewhere at the heart of the constitution of all economic systems, even the most apparently smoothly humming capitalist machine."

—Andrew Popp, *Professor of History, Copenhagen Business School*

"Via this study of Hungary, Phil Scranton shows that socialist enterprises were not so simple as has been generally asserted. He looks at them both from top down and from bottom up, from the viewpoint of the government and the ministries and from that of the peasants and all the men and women who worked, traded or consumed. He sees how the choices made at the top prolonged the shock of World War Two and limited technological choices and learning processes. For years, the predatory behavior of the Russians and the constraints exerted by the government and the Party squeezed peasants especially, but in fact everyone. Instead of a socialist alliance of science and democracy, an economy of theft was born, often at the expense of the environment and nature. One of the many forms of the people's agency was to reciprocate such theft, through frauds, embezzlements, or stealing materials and goods. Civil society in general, technicians and engineers in particular, were creative and called for alternative strategies and regulations but their voices were turned aside – one source, among many, for the 1956 Revolt."

—Patrick Fridenson, *Ecole des Hautes Etudes en Sciences Sociales, Paris*

To Ginny, the light of my life

Preface: The Terrible Twelve—Core Tasks for Socialist and Capitalist Enterprises

Business historians have shown that creating and running an enterprise is both complicated and complex. It's complicated in that there are multiple tasks that have to be understood, planned for, juggled, and completed more or less simultaneously. It's complex because such actions intersect with those of others (competitors, suppliers, governments, financiers, workers, consumers) whose interests and goals business owners or managers imperfectly appreciate and whose initiatives compel them to make unanticipated, reflexive adjustments that can only be anticipated in part. Hence enterprises have to resolve concrete questions while moving forward, despite incomplete knowledge and considerable uncertainty. This is the case for small firms and large, as well as for companies operating in capitalist, communist, or colonial/developing world environments. Therefore, Patrick Fridenson and I identified a set of what we call "core tasks" for enterprises, issues that managers sought to address just about everywhere in the postwar world. Business practices are the ways in which this "addressing" materializes in projects, rules, routines, forms, evaluations, rivalries, alliances, and the like. We locate the set as "postwar" tasks because they arose in a specific era; a different set might well be needed for the mid-nineteenth century.

We acknowledge that this group is surely incomplete and that some elements overlap; thus we would welcome suggestions concerning additions and revisions. After what we would suggest are the foundational first three, the rest are unranked. In the chapters that follow, assessing business dynamics in socialist Hungary before the 1956 Revolt, these Tasks will serve as a background framework to link the elaborate interactions, initiatives, and flows sketched in the text with enterprises' unending necessity for identifying opportunities and solving problems.

Task 1. Defining the enterprise's purpose and methods of operations. What is this organization expecting to accomplish and how will it do this? What needs might its efforts satisfy? Are others already attempting this, and if so, how will this team do it better, cheaper, faster? Indeed, how will the actors learn that they are doing it better, cheaper, or faster? What do the actors know, and need to know, about the capabilities necessary to create and deliver their products and/or services? How much of what is needed for the job can they create in-house and how much can simply be bought from others? How best to evaluate those options?

Task 2. Securing and allocating resources. How much funding will the enterprise need to commence and continue its work? Where is this stream of resources to come from and on what conditions? What are the requirements for space, power, technology, expertise, and materials and what alternatives are available for acquiring them? How much time is needed to integrate and operationalize these inputs and who can guide this process? What provisions ought we make for conserving material resources (structures, infrastructures, technologies) through persistent, timely maintenance and repair? What human resources (e.g., workers, advisers, managers) are required for this range of operations and what practices will encourage their effective performance and retention (e.g., bonuses, benefits, profit-sharing)?

Task 3. Creating organizational structures and processes, identifying responsibilities, defining internal and external stakeholders, building competencies. How will the enterprise make decisions, set goals, coordinate its activities, and generate continuity in its operations? What options for each of these can be considered? To whom do responsible parties report, why, and with what possible consequences? How to define and reward/sanction excellence and failure? How will information be organized to flow through the enterprise and through business networks? Do managers emphasize creativity, participation, reliability, or responsiveness? If all four, in what proportions and how balanced?

Task 4. Establishing accounting and records management, defining relevance & rules/norms. How effectively to track what's happening, quantitatively, qualitatively, and discursively? What gets counted and analyzed and why? What data and documentation gets kept, why and where? How best to use these components of an organizational memory to adjust goals, spending, and activity? How to assure their cost-effective supply, flow, and processing?

Task 5. Installing purchasing and pricing practices. If the enterprise generates products, how do managers organize securing materials/components and determining an offering price to users (e.g., value chains, price matching, response to competition, state/regulatory settings)? If it provides services, what inputs must be secured to create them and how to determine user charges (comparables, negotiations, professional/regulated schedules)? In both cases, what incentives encourage systematizing these practices within and across enterprises?

Task 6. Inventing marketing and organizing distribution. Who are our likely customers or clients? How do we identify them and reach out with information, samples, or performance data that will encourage purchases? How much of our resources should be devoted to this work? What infrastructure can we employ to deliver our goods or services and at what costs? How can we differentiate our output from that of others in the same or similar field?

Task 7. Articulating external and internal relations. Outside the enterprise, to whom are we responsible and for what? What rewards or sanctions can be anticipated through links with government, regulators, associations, clients, competitors, communities, or professional networks? What benefits, information or value can we provide each group, beyond market transactions? Inside the enterprise, how best to establish productive relations with workforces, and to make critical decisions about full time, part time, and contractual labor? What codes, standards, and rule sets developed by outside entities (trade organizations, governments, scientific and technical bodies) inform, facilitate, and constrain structuring internal relations?

Task 8. Monitoring performance. Within the enterprise, how do we measure the effectiveness of what we are doing? To whom are managers and employees accountable and for what? This involves issues of benchmarking achievements, defining oversight, tracking emergent problems, plus attending to quality control and risk management. Again, what sanctions reach poor performers, and what policy changes might improve results? Conversely, what incentives do we devise to encourage excellence and what rewards are delivered when it is demonstrated? Also as financialization intensified on capitalist and socialist terrains, banks, state agencies and analysts tracked performance, making judgments which decisively affected access to credit, firm autonomy, and stakeholder confidence. How to frame policies to engage with these hazards?

Task 9. Encouraging learning, prospective and reflexive. As the technical and informational world is dynamic, how does the enterprise facilitate training, evaluate feedback, modify rules and routines to enhance its capabilities? What guidelines can be established to maintain both material and human resources? To what degree and at what cost should manager/worker education be formalized? What external organizations can be solicited to participate in this process and by what means? In what ways can the firm capture the value that a learning organization generates without losing the reliability that a systematized enterprise achieves?

Task 10. Planning for growth, crisis, conflict, innovation. What priority do we give to exploring the enterprise's current contexts and future possibilities? By what means do we select both the targets for such planning and the personnel to be involved (flexibility vs. hierarchy)? Given that "past performance cannot guarantee future returns," at what levels and in what domains might planning be most effective? Product development? Strategic resource allocation? Internationalization and/or diversification?

Task 11. Dealing with tensions between operations and innovation. Creativity is disruptive but operations can generate tunnel vision. Are we involved in an emergent or mature sector, and in either case, is ours an emergent or mature firm? What role does innovation play in the trade our enterprise inhabits? What costs and benefits would disruption bring? Or if stability, durability, or reliability are crucial, what implications does this have for operating practices and information uses? (This is germane to whether we sponsor special projects or not, to whether we diversify or not, to what kind of cost analysis we conduct, and to how much we emphasize R&D or applied science.)

Task 12. Assessing environmental relations. In production, what is the most cost-effective, lawful way to handle/recycle wastes from operations or surplus materials no longer used? What hazards, and perhaps resources, does our enterprise's activity present to that environment? Can we develop or adopt creative ways to conserve energy or minimize use of dangerous or scarce materials? What hazards and resources are present in the enterprise's broader material environments? In services, what aspects of the social and cultural environment need we closely consider as we establish principles and practices for operating effectively (e.g., gender, ethnic, class and age biases, racism, unvoiced assumptions)?

Complex and complicated indeed. To be sure, I will not be systematically tracing how business practices in Hungarian agriculture, commerce, infrastructure, and manufacturing link to each of the twelve tasks. Rather the tasks set out an array of bells that readers may occasionally ring when encountering empirical contrasts and resonances. Just one example for the moment. Take Task 7, "Articulating external and internal relations." Whereas a firm in France may have been responsible to shareholders and bondholders, government regulators, and perhaps consumers of its products, an enterprise in socialist Hungary was responsible to the nation's central planners, to a supervising sectoral ministry and to the Communist Party, whose officials possessed authority independent of the administration, but was certainly not beholden to consumers (or to victims of a toxic release). Doing business in response to this task was radically different in the two locales, and would change in different ways as lines of responsibility and options for action altered.[1] Moreover, external actors can, in both domains, profoundly influence the way business is done and how this changes. For example, survivors of Japan's Minimata fish poisonings successfully sought to limit the use of mercury in industrial and mining operations, given its dreadful environmental toxicity.[2] Similarly, Hungarian citizens complaining about pollution got nowhere: "Tell it to Stalin!"

Why offer such a collection? Surely most of this is pretty obvious, at least to business people and those who research their histories. Actually, not at all. Knowledge about how business and the economy work is extremely shallow in capitalist nations, as a 1984 Hearst Corporation survey of the American public documented.[3] Understanding what enterprises do and how they operate is thin even in financial markets, where vast sums are invested daily. As analyst John Kay explained recently:

> Anyone who comes from outside the financial sector to the world of trading is likely to be shocked by the superficiality of the traders' general knowledge... Fund managers and investment bankers deal in shares – or even buy and sell companies – with only a rudimentary understanding of the businesses involved or of concepts of business strategy. Many senior executives talk privately with contempt of the analysts who follow their company.[4]

Thus rather than restricting this work's potential readers to those already well-versed in business practicalities, the twelve tasks are sketched here so that all those embarking on this voyage to encounter *Business Practice in Socialist Hungary, Volume 1* appreciate in advance the questions that socialist businesses attempted to resolve.

Before venturing into that long-ago "everyday," a second contextual exercise needs to be deployed. This entails first reconstituting the historical and spatial landscape of Hungary's twentieth-century development and then, more specifically, the organizational and institutional environment within which enterprise and work took place in postwar Hungary. That's the job of the following two chapters.

New Brunswick, USA   Philip Scranton

NOTES

1. Resonances may also be identified. Writing of a reformed planning system (New Economic Mechanism, 1968), Geza Lauter noted: "the new role of the central plan in Hungary is not very much different from the role that 'Le Plan' plays in France. In both countries, the general long-range objectives include a high rate of economic growth, relatively stable employment, and technological advancements. Also the plans in both countries convey to managers a priority list of development objectives and define the various means through which such objectives can be achieved. Furthermore, managerial, professional and special-interest groups are asked to participate in the planning process through the presentation of ideas, proposals and constructive criticism" (Lauter, *The Manager and Economic Reform in Hungary*, New York: Praeger, 1972, 36).
2. Timothy George, *Minamata: Pollution and the Struggle for Democracy in Postwar Japan*, Cambridge: Harvard University Press, 2002.
3. Hearst Corporation, *The American Public's Knowledge of Business and the Economy*, New York: The Company, 1984.
4. John Kay, *Other People's Money: The Real Business of Finance*, New York: Public Affairs, 2015, 82–83.

ACKNOWLEDGMENTS

This study was developed without the aid of research grants or fellowships, in large part because its author is an emeritus professor no longer eligible for many funding opportunities. Yet financial support was hardly needed for the project, insofar as the vast archival collections used were wholly accessible online, without user fees or charges. However, I must express deep gratitude one more time to the Rutgers University Libraries, whose database subscriptions, extensive interlibrary loan services, and ever-responsive staff proved indispensable to the research process. It's been a decade since I left the University's teaching staff to focus on scholarship; and the Library system has continued throughout to ensure access to materials and support when things online don't function as expected. My deepest thanks to them all.

Unlike other monographs I've published, *Business Practice in Socialist Hungary, Volume 1* has not been previewed through papers/chapters offered in seminars and at conferences, thanks to the Covid pandemic and the cancellation of everything. A sizable chunk of early text was meant for a panel at the March 2020 Business History Conference in Charlotte, but the meeting essentially imploded in the face of rapidly spreading infections. Instead, I have shared documents and drafts with a number of colleagues whose responses and suggestions have been invaluable. They include my *ancien camarade*, Patrick Fridenson, of the Ecole des Hautes Etudes en Sciences Sociales, Paris, with whom I've been Zooming every two weeks for most of the last year, and my unindicted co-conspirators,

Prof. Lee Vinsel at Virginia Tech and Dean Andrew Russell at SUNY Polytechnic Institute, whose pioneering inquiries into the criticality of maintenance and repair were a source of inspiration. Prof. Andrew Popp of the Copenhagen Business School provided critical assessments at critical junctures, which I much appreciated. Prof. Howard Gillette, a fellow Rutgers emeritus historian, Dr. Roger Horowitz at the Hagley Museum and Library, and Prof. Daniel H. G. Raff of Wharton read and reacted to early sections, as did Dr. Ann Norton Green of the University of Pennsylvania. My sincere thanks to each and all of them.

Those of us who continue publishing late into our careers move past the decades when acknowledgments of (and apologies to) parents, children, cousins, pets, department chairs, computer repair-persons, et al. take their place in the brief comments preceding the main sections of a monograph. But we remain forever in debt to our spouses, the life-partners who suffer our grumbling, accept our minds often being elsewhere, and join fleeting celebrations at finding "the perfect source." In our life together, Virginia McIntosh has played each of those roles, and many more, over and again, superbly, for nearly forty years. This book is for Ginny, in profound gratitude.

CONTENTS

1 Introduction: Hungary—Geography, History, and Society to 1945 — 1
Hungary as Space and Economy — 4
From Defeat to Disaster: Politics, 1918–1945 — 9
The Path Ahead — 12

2 The Theft Economy: Occupation and Forced Industrialization — 19
The New Hungarian State: Organization and Plans — 23
Soviet Dominion in the Postwar Economy — 30
Structuring the Socialist Enterprise System — 34
The Story Arc, 1949–1956 — 39
A Note on the Forint — 43

3 Agriculture from Stalinism to the Revolt — 55
State Farms and Tractor Stations: Emulating Soviet Practice — 59
Private Farmers: Pressured and Evasive — 74
Toil and Trouble in the TSZs — 87
Conclusion — 97

4 An Unfinished Project: Constructing Socialist Construction — 111
The Ministry of Construction and Its Rivals — 114
In the Field: Construction Enterprises on the Job — 124
Chasing Bonuses: Enterprise Managers and Fraud — 131

xvii

xviii CONTENTS

Construction Workers: Living the Contradictions   134
Mega-Projects: The Budapest Subway and Sztálinváros   141
Conclusion   152

5 Socialist Commerce: Provisioning, Coping, Maneuvering, and Trading   165
Provisioning   166
Coping and Maneuvering   180
Trading   191
Conclusion   200

6 Hungary's Socialist Industrialization: A Snare and a Delusion   213
The Core: Heavy Industry   218
The Periphery: Light Industry, Handicrafts and Auxiliaries   246
Conclusion   262

7 The Revolt: Spontaneity, Repression, and Reaction   277

8 Afterword   293

Note on Sources   297

Index   301

LIST OF FIGURES

Fig. 1.1 Location of fuel sources with the borders of post-Trianon Hungary (dark line) and in territories previously part of the Kingdom (inside the exterior dotted line) (Creator: Pal Teleki (1879–1941), published 1923. *Source* https://archive.org/details/evolutionofhunga01tele Wikimedia Creative Commons) 5

Fig. 1.2 Wreckage of Budapest's Elizabeth Bridge, 1945 (Photographer unknown. *Source* FOTO:Fortepan—ID 60155: http://www.fortepan.hu/_photo/download/fortepan_60155.jpgarchivecopy Wikimedia Creative Commons) 13

Fig. 2.1 Hungary, counties map with county seats: www.mapsopensource.com/hungary-counties-map.html 20

Fig. 3.1 Driving a Hungarian-made Hoffher GS-35 tractor at a state farm, 1953 (Donor: Endre Baráth. *Source* FOTO: Fortepan—ID 7949, http://www.fortepan.hu/_photo/download/fortepan_14117.jpg, Wikimedia Creative Commons) 68

Fig. 4.1 Housing destruction in Central Budapest, 1945 (Donor: Dr. István Kramer. *Source* FOTO: Fortepan—ID 52083, http://www.fortepan.hu/_photo/download/fortepan_52083.jpg, archive copy, Wikimedia Creative Commons) 113

xx   LIST OF FIGURES

Fig. 4.2   Construction work on foundations for Budapest's TV tower, 1956 (Donor: Rádió és Televízió Újság. *Source* FOTO: Fortepan—ID 56321, http://www.fortepan.hu/_photo/download/fortepan_56321.jpg, Wikimedia Creative Commons)   127

Fig. 4.3   Budapest Subway construction, 1952 (Donor: UVATERV. *Source* FOTO: Fortepan—ID 91594, http://www.fortepan.hu/_photo/download/fortepan_91594.jpg, Wikimedia Creative Commons)   143

Fig. 4.4   Construction of the Sztálinváros port, 1952 (Donor: UVATERV. *Source* FOTO: Fortepan—ID 91581, http://www.fortepan.hu/_photo/download/fortepan_91581.jpg, archive copy, Wikimedia Creative Commons)   148

Fig. 5.1   Dunakapu Square Market, Györ. 1950 (Donor: Tamás Konok. *Source* FOTO: Fortepan—ID: 28215. http://www.fortepan.hu/_photo/download/fortepan_43687.jpg, Wikimedia Creative Commons)   173

Fig. 5.2   Batthyány Square Market Hall, Budapest District 1, 1952. The hall, built in 1900, could accommodate nearly 700 stalls in its 3000 m^2 of floorspace (Donor: UVATERV. *Source* FOTO: Fortepan—ID 1094. http://www.fortepan.hu/_photo/download/fortepan_3972.jpg, archive copy, Wikimedia Creative Commons)   174

Fig. 6.1   MEH scrapyard with Mercedes truck tire being repaired, 1951 (Donor: Építész. *Source* FOTO: Fortepan—ID 15,086, http://www.fortepan.hu/_photo/download/fortepan_23439.jpg Wikimedia Creative Commons)   222

Fig. 6.2   Ganz 424 steam locomotive and tender, 1963 (Donor: Gyula Simon. *Source* FOTO: Fortepan—ID No. 70604. https://commons.wikimedia.org/w/index.php?search=MAV+424+locomotive&title=Special:MediaSearch&go=Go&type=image. Wikimedia Creative Commons)   232

Fig. 6.3   Ganz four-unit railcar at Henderson, Argentina, on its final run before retirement, 1977 (Photographer: Carlos Pérez Darnaud. *Source* Plataforma 14, https://upload.wikimedia.org/wikipedia/commons/3/33/Tren_estacion_henderson.jpg Wikimedia Creative Commons)   235

Fig. 7.1	Stalin's head on a Budapest square, 24 October 1956 (Photographer: Robert Hofbauer. *Source* FOTO: Fortepan—ID 93004, https://commons.wikimedia. org/wiki/File:1956_a_budapesti_Szt%C3%A1lin-szobor_ elgurult_feje_fortepan_93004.jpg, Wikimedia Creative Commons)	280
Fig. 7.2	"Russians Go Home!" In a Budapest shop window, October 1956 (Photographer: Gyula Nagy. *Source* FOTO: Fortepan—ID 24794, http://www.fortepan.hu/_photo/ download/fortepan_40202.jpg, archive copy, Wikimedia Creative Commons)	282
Fig. 7.3	Soviet Tank clearing a Budapest street Barricade (Photographer: unknown. *Source* Central Intelligence Agency, https://www.flickr.com/photos/ciagov/811398 0088/in/set-72157631830870415/, Wikimedia Creative Commons)	283
Fig. 7.4	Food deliveries in Budapest's District 13, November 1956 (Donor: Gyula Nagy. *Source* FOTO: Fortepan—ID 24837, http://www.fortepan.hu/_photo/download/fortepan_ 40245.jpg, archive copy, Wikimedia Creative Commons)	286

LIST OF TABLES

Table 4.1	Distribution of forced labor by sector, December 1952	140
Table 6.1	Machine tools at Ganz Railway, Machinery, Electrical, and Shipbuilding, 1948	231

CHAPTER 1

Introduction: Hungary—Geography, History, and Society to 1945

When agriculture is referred to, both Hungarians and foreigners involuntarily are reminded of the seemingly infinite expanse of the Great Hungarian Plain (Alföld). In reality, however, more than half of agricultural production in Hungary is conducted in hilly woodland country.
—György Lakos (1963)[1]

Farmer Imre Egyed in Dióskál owns 15 acres of land and lives as if it were 1930. He is not interested in anything but farming... He does not read newspapers or books and has no radio. He grew 60 quintals [6 tons] of cereals without the help of machines, because to him mechanical agricultural work does not seem genuine work... After having disposed of his obligations to the state [3 tons sold for ca. 6000ft], he prefers to stockpile the [rest]. If pressed, he would sell the cereal in other villages at prices 80 to 100 forints per quintal above the fixed official prices [+40-50%, yielding ca. 10,000ft]... He has a very well kept vineyard and a wine-cellar where 25 to 30 hectoliters [2500-3000 litres] of several-years-old wine are stored up. Out of the sale of the wine he could pay his taxes for five or six years.
—*Zalai Hirlap* (23 September 1960)[2]

[At the Wilhelm Pieck Railway Plant in Györ,] there was no production devoted to the making of spare parts; however, all items that were rejected were salvaged for spare parts. In the area where I worked all the transmissions were inspected before shipment... about one in four was rejected and the parts used for spare parts. Most of the rejected transmissions were

© The Author(s), under exclusive license to Springer Nature Switzerland AG 2022
P. Scranton, *Business Practice in Socialist Hungary, Volume 1*, Palgrave Debates in Business History,
https://doi.org/10.1007/978-3-030-89184-8_1

no different from the ones that passed the inspection. All of the so-called spare parts were sent to Budapest.[3]

"A system that worked, more or less." Thus did Czech economist Radoslav Selucký describe the political economies of Central European socialism at the close of the 1960s. Gaps between plan and performance remained obvious in all the "people's republics"; since the mid-1950s, reformers in Hungary, Poland, and Czechoslovakia had undertaken repeated drives toward decentralizing authority, reducing bureaucracy, and fostering initiatives among workers and managers in the service of "building socialism." Yet as Selucký concluded in 1970 (two decades before the Bloc's meltdown), planners, Party officials, and enterprise leaders, proved "incapable of finding a positive solution to any of the basic problems."[4] Although the socialist states gradually improved education and training, food and consumer goods supplies, and community health/nutrition (while reducing pre-war inequalities), efficiencies in using capital, materials, and equipment were elusive, technological advances lagged Western achievements, housing shortages persisted, and planned coordination among firms and agencies disappointed, as did the quality of goods and services. Post-1989 analyses of "what went wrong" have abounded, in what specialists call the "transitology" literature.[5] Yet among scholars, embracing capitalism has often meant dismissing socialism, or employing it as a foil for declinist narratives.

This study will attempt something different: to recount and in part reconstruct the lived experience of Hungarian enterprises (plus managers. workers and farmers), moving forward in two volumes from the late 1940s to the late 1960s, thereby reconstructing what "worked, more or less." These organizations and individuals could not envision the system's eventual demise, but instead worked to manage life and labor within it. At the time, Western writers and visitors often flattened descriptions of everyday socialism into the monochrome routines of a totalitarian society.[6] By contrast, what may be most memorable about the tales related below is the pervasive diversity of the initiatives, improvisations, evasions, and compromises Hungarians enacted, despite material, organizational, and political constraints flowing from the perennial disarray that top-down central planning spawned. The opening epigraphs signal this shift in perspective—from presuming uniformity to documenting diversity. For example, observers and planners focused on Hungary's vast

Alfold plains, ideal for employing agricultural machinery (like comparable terrains in the USSR and the US), overlooked the other half of the rural landscape—almost seven million acres of cropland distributed across hills and valleys and on terraced mountainsides, interspersed with orchards and vineyards—utterly unsuited to "modern" mechanized sowing and harvesting.[7] "Modernizing" agriculture demanded a varied array of projects, not a single big idea.

Comparable diversity was also evident at the family level: amid the campaign for rural collectivism, patriarch Imre Eyged ruled his Zala County farm and family as a personal fiefdom, "as if it were 1930." Plainly rejecting all things socialist and most things modern or mechanized, he sought the best market prices for his grain, built his wine-cellar into a savings account, and lived independently. Although characterized as a relic of a bygone era, Eyged had evidently been left to his own devices despite the national crusade to bring private farmers and their land into agricultural cooperatives (TSZs).[8] Organizers ignored him as an unlikely cooperator, but did recruit several hundred thousand comparable (and usually less wealthy) farm families whose dogged independence differed only in degree from his, and generated continuing trouble for co-op directors, Party leaders, and local officials.

Diversified on an industrial scale, the Wilhelm Pieck railway equipment complexes[9] had had a distinguished history before their nationalization. Founded in 1896, the Hungarian Railway Carriage and Machine Works (MVG) fell under Austrian control a decade later, returning to Magyar hands only in 1935 when its Viennese owners, facing bankruptcy, sold their shares to the more stable RIMA Ironworks, a company also started under the Austro-Hungarian Empire.[10] Bombed five times during World War II, MVG's Győr plant suffered nearly 50 percent destruction, then was stripped by "the plundering troops of the Red Army [who] took possession of the raw materials and finished products... that were still disposable."[11] A decade later, with no priority given to manufacturing spare parts for their products, managers improvised by "rejecting" and disassembling finished transmissions to supply components to Budapest warehouses. Such situations were not uncommon in socialist manufacturing, echoing conflicts in the TSZs, in construction, and in trade, which together suggest that Hungary's path to progress was not just rocky, but strewn with boulders.

Having set the stage for enterprise dramas, the task now is to build a theater around it, first in spatial terms—scanning the geography of

4   P. SCRANTON

a newly-independent nation after World War I's bitterly-received settlement, then along a temporal axis—summarizing Hungary's historical trajectory from the dispiriting end of one great war to the final spasms of another. With this framework in place, the Introduction will close by offering the customary preview of the chapters to come.

HUNGARY AS SPACE AND ECONOMY

The creation of modern Hungary was involuntary and traumatic, a spatial event trailing the collapse of the Austro-Hungarian Empire and the Dual Monarchy. Separated from Austria by an October 1918 parliamentary resolution, the Hungarian Kingdom found that regions nominally under its control ignored directives from Budapest, announcing breakaways toward self-determination (e.g., Czech lands to the north, Croatia to the south). As republican and revolutionary politics surged, formal treaty-making plodded along in France. Adjoining the Versailles settlement with Germany, Great Britain, France, Italy, and the United States concluded four other agreements (1919–1920), which reorganized Central Europe and recognized republican Turkey as the Ottoman Empire's successor. One of these, the Treaty of Trianon, confirmed the fragmentation of Imperial Hungary[12]; over 70% of its former territory and 60% of its population would belong to other states: Czechoslovakia, Romania, Yugoslavia, and Austria. Worse, the severed territories held some 3.4 million ethnic Hungarians, half of them located in Romania, now to be governed from Bucharest.[13]

Recovering these lost lands and communities fueled irredentist politics in Hungary during the interwar decades, overshadowed, to be sure, by Germany's more successful maneuvers to absorb Austria and the Sudetenland in Czechoslovakia.[14] Yet the *economic* losses to Hungary (Fig. 1.1) were just as, or more, crippling. The Kingdom once had 35 million acres of arable land and 17 million acres of pastures and meadows; the Republic held just 13.5 million acres of farmland (39%), only a quarter of the prior grazing areas and just twelve percent of some 21 million forested acres. Over half of the Kingdom's "factories and industrial plants" resided in nations other than Hungary, as did all its mines for precious metals, copper, and salt, four-fifths of its iron ore resources, and two-thirds of public roads and railways.[15] These shifts fundamentally transformed

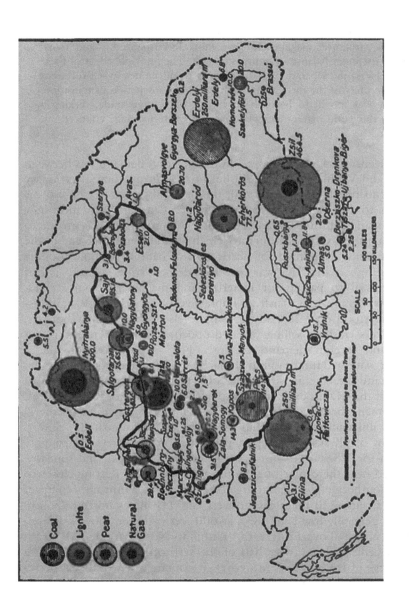

Fig. 1.1 Location of fuel sources with the borders of post-Trianon Hungary (dark line) and in territories previously part of the Kingdom (inside the exterior dotted line) (Creator: Pal Teleki (1879–1941), published 1923. *Source* https://archive.org/details/evolutionofhunga01tele Wikimedia Creative Commons)

the conditions of economic life. The relative importance of the various industries remaining within the country's new boundaries changed the economic structure, making Hungary more industrialized... and transforming the inner balance of industry as well. The principal effect of these changes [was] the separation of the country from the nearly self-sufficient economic unity of the former Monarchy; without any period of transition, Hungary was forced to become dependent on foreign trade, seeking a place on the world market to replace its secure internal trade connections, now lost.[16]

Disaster ensued. Finance and credit crumbled as banking ties between Budapest and Vienna frayed, as did links to Germany, long a secondary source for loans. By February 1920, the national currency (the crown) had fallen to one-eighth of its 1914 value. Cut off from most raw materials, manufacturing floundered; whereas "agriculture was unable to recover from the disorganization into which it had fallen by the end of the war." As farming accounted for nearly 60% of national income (double manufacturing's share), this was especially demoralizing, as exports had become crucial to paying for materials and machinery from abroad. Recovery was gradual, but far from impressive—by the 1929 peak, industrial output stood only 25% above 1914 levels within the new borders. Then markets crashed, selling prices dropped, tariffs rose to punishing heights, and foreign demand cratered. For a resource-poor, trade-dependent nation, Hungary initially faced a brutal Depression decade. Bilateral trade agreements with Hitler's Germany and Mussolini's Italy in 1934 eased the strains, exchanging exported foodstuffs for manufactures. Soon Germany became "Hungary's most important trading partner," forging an unbalanced relationship which the Reich dominated.[17]

In terms of physical geography, post-Trianon Hungary was roughly the size of the US state of Indiana (ca. 36,000 sq. miles), and similarly, was located near the center of a continental land mass. Resting closer to Europe's southern edges than to its northern shores, Hungary's compact territory ran just 220 miles east-to-west and 118 miles north-to-south. Its land is generally low-lying, 85% at 600 feet or fewer above sea level, only two percent above 1200 feet.[18] Within its Northern ridges, Western hills, and central plains (over half of the territory), Hungary offers "a great variety of landscapes." Moreover, it contains "a wealth of species in the natural vegetation, the soil covering has a mosaic-like character, and the climate is extremely changeable."[19] Thus deer hunting in the northern ranges went hand-in-hand, however awkwardly, with cultivating rice in southern wetlands, another confirmation of Hungary's ecological diversity.[20] "Changeable" climatic conditions followed weather currents flowing in from the Atlantic, the Mediterranean, and the mountains (Alps and Carpathians).

> The Atlantic effects can cause cool summers with abundant precipitation and mild, foggy winters; the continental effects can cause dry, cloudless weather with hot summers and cold winters, and the Mediterranean systems may bring about early spring, hot and dry summers and a rainy autumn and winter season. In general, these effects alternate within short periods... Solar radiation is abundant and its duration moderate. The average number of the sunny hours is about 2,000 per year... The vegetation growing period of eight months provides abundant solar energy for annual crop cultures.[21]

New Hungary also straddled the central basin of the Danube River, Europe's longest at 1800 miles, ample water being supplied from its Alpine tributaries accompanied by periodic, severe flooding. The Danube bisects the capital city before flowing south through the Great Plain and into the Balkans.[22]

As for economic geography, post-Hapsburg Hungary's chief remaining mineral resource was huge deposits of "brown coal" or lignite, the lowest quality in BTU terms and the smokiest. Alongside its forests, the country's most important economic asset remained "the varied and fertile soil cover." Soil research dating to the nineteenth century demonstrated agriculture's durable vitality and its diversity, for "often a number of different soil types occur[red] in a small area," triggering complicated land uses. They included fertile black Chernozem in the Great Plains (five feet thick in places), lime-rich Rendzina in once-forested districts (along with other forest variants), bog soils, meadow soils, sandys and alluvials (along rivers), alkali soils (e.g., clay-infused Solonetz), plus many sub-types.[23] The World War I settlement little changed Hungary's customary agricultural relations and practices. In 1895 nearly half the arable land was held in large parcels, 150 acres or more (a third of it in estates spanning more than 1500 acres), accounting for just one percent of all properties. Forty years later the proportions were virtually identical, whereas the percentage of the rural landless had risen (from 54 to 72%). Although tractors and power threshing machines began to populate Plains grainlands in the

1920s, the Depression stalled their diffusion: horses and oxen retained central roles. "For the most part, agricultural technique was based on traditional implements and simple machines. Though on average there was one plow for every holding, most of the small peasant plots lacked even that much equipment... Hoeing, harvesting, and other operations were performed almost entirely by hand."[24] Although the interwar years brought expansion of market gardening near Budapest and smaller cities and a surge in orchard plantings, the nation's output of grain crops overfilled the domestic market, yielding price-taking in export trades. Sadly, its commercial livestock activity "presented an even sorrier picture," failing to attain 1913 peaks by 1938, a quarter century later.[25]

Empire-era manufacturing development had been more dynamic, but reorienting post-1920 industry was "burdened with inherent contradictions." Before 1914, investment in consumer-goods capacity (e.g., textiles, household goods) had been modest, because much of "domestic consumption was covered by imports," whereas the Kingdom's technologically more intensive sectors (e.g. machinery, electrical) had been heavily export-oriented. Tariffs proliferated in the 1920s, creating diverging incentives. Now Hungary's textile industry could meet just 25% of domestic needs; thus "the transplantation of many formerly Austrian or Czech textile mills to Hungary" proceeded steadily. Spindles for making cotton yarn, for example, grew sixfold, 1921–1929, to 193,000 (wool, fourfold), reducing imports from 86% of all fabrics in 1921 to half by decade's end. At the other extreme, sophisticated food processing and metalworking establishments, many in Budapest, finding once-profitable export markets blocked, could not attain prewar production levels and faced substantial unused capacity.[26] Budapest, long the Kingdom's center, emerged in the 1890s as a major modern metropolis, with extensive transport, financial, and trade connections to other European cities. It dominated the region, particularly through a hub-and-spoke pattern of railways and roads; commerce and communication from the hinterlands flowed into, through, and only then, beyond Budapest.[27] After Trianon, over half of Hungary's "industrial population" lived and worked in the capital district, where 15% of the nation's citizens resided. Between the wars, the city's industrial centrality "increased considerably,"[28] a trend that continued well into the socialist decades. One report affirmed that:

> Budapest contains not only the largest industrial complex in the country but perhaps the most intricate and heterogeneous in all of Eastern Europe.

In no other European socialist state does the capital city dominate national industry as completely as Budapest does.... Moreover, the Hungarian metropolis concentrates a greater percentage of the nation's employment in *every* branch of manufacturing than the capitals of the other socialist countries and Austria do. [It] is especially dominant in market-oriented metropolitan-type industries that demand skills (communications equipment, pharmaceuticals, printing and publishing...).[29]

Hungary had no "second cities" like Chicago in the US or Lyon in France. Instead, the administrative seats of its 19 counties (*megyek*) served as local anchor points. After 1945, when Budapest reported nearly 1.6 million residents, only three other cities had populations greater than 100,000: Debrecen (Hadjú-Bihar county), Miskolc (Borsod), and Szeged (Csongrád).[30]

Decentralization, a recurrent goal in postwar policy-making, remained elusive.

From Defeat to Disaster: Politics, 1918–1945

Several weeks before the 11 November 1918 Western Front armistice, the Austro-Hungarian Empire began disintegrating. In a rapid sequence from October 27–31, Czechs, Slovaks, Croatians, Romanians, and Ukrainians seceded, just as the Austrian National Assembly voted to create a constitutional republic. Amid a soldiers' rebellion, the Budapest parliament, led by Count Mihály Károlyi, a pacifist and one of the region's wealthiest aristocrats, severed ties with Vienna on November 1 (the Aster Revolution), then proclaimed a Democratic Republic on the 16th, once Charles IV abdicated as Hungary's King. Károlyi tried to cooperate with the victorious Allies so as to defend Imperial borders, but this proved fruitless; armed forces from the emergent republics were already seizing territory. By spring 1919, desperate Budapest leaders transferred power to a coalition of socialists and communists. The latter launched the Hungarian Soviet Republic on March 21, with Béla Kun as People's Commissar for Foreign Affairs. Hopes rose for Bolshevik support against the Paris peacemakers, but this did not materialize. Instead, in early April the Big Four sent to Budapest diplomats led by South African General Jan Smuts. Smuts carried a non-negotiable proposal to obstruct further military incursions and delineate new Hungarian borders surrounded by a neutrality zone. Kun's team sought to bargain for a better deal, without result or response; rejecting discussions, the Smuts delegation simply left the city.[31]

Military actions by the Romanian army commenced in mid-April, the Czechs soon joining the drive to unseat Kun's Soviet. Reportedly, to drive out the invaders, "half the working population of Budapest enlisted in the newly-formed Hungarian Red Army," staffed by former Imperial officers, Meanwhile, with quiet French support, counterrevolutionary Hungarian forces began coalescing in a southern city, Szeged. The anti-Bolsheviks gathered several thousand veterans, many exiled from lost Transylvanian lands, into a National Army, led ironically by a former Admiral in the now-vanished Royal Navy—minister of war Miklós Horthy. Although Kun's Red Army drove back the Czechs and occupied much of Slovakia by late May, telegrams from Paris soon announced Hungary's official boundaries and demanded troop withdrawals. Demoralized, Kun's forces complied, undermining the Soviet's support; within weeks the communist government unraveled. The Romanian Army occupied Budapest in August amid mass hysteria. By fall 1919, "blame for the defeat and dismemberment of the nation was placed on [the] communists and the Jews who had played an important role in the 1918 revolution and made up more than half of the people's commissars in the Bolshevik government." Horthy's National Army occupied western counties not under Romanian control, deploying a "White Terror," slaughtering thousands of leftists, Jews, workers, and "poor peasants." Romanian battalions began withdrawing in November under pressure from the US and Britain, who then recognized another coalition government which set parliamentary elections for January 1920.[32]

As the Big Four blocked Emperor Carl's return to his thrones, the Budapest Parliament selected Admiral Horthy as an administrative place-holder, a Regent who could serve as chief of state until the Western Powers relented. As so often in Hungary, things did not turn out as planned. When Carl arrived unannounced in the capital (26 March 1921) to demand his restoration, Horthy rebuffed him, likely fearing renewed Allied interventions and/or uprisings were Carl welcomed. A second appearance in October led only to humiliation; Hungary expelled Carl "on a British gunboat down the Danube." He never returned, and Horthy's regency lasted until 1944, when he suffered a comparable humiliation at the hands of German and Hungarian Nazis. In the meantime, Hungarian politics oscillated between conservative and far right policies, guided during the 1920s by prime minister Count István

Bethlen, "Horthy's most trusted advisor." Bethlen secured a modest territorial recovery through an Entente-supervised plebiscite in the western Sopron district, returned to Hungary after the balloting. As well, he arranged Hungary's admission to the League of Nations, providing both a voice in international policy debates and potential access to foreign loans that could cover mandated reparations and stabilize state finances. The Party of Unity, an alliance of wealthy landowners, businessmen, the lesser aristocracy, civil servants, and army officers, anchored Bethlen's regime. The Party dominated the National Assembly well into the next war, but "allowed the small opposition parties, supported primarily from Budapest and the urban Jewish middle class, to operate freely." To offset potential extremism, Bethlen also restored Parliament's upper house in 1926, a vaguely-syndicalist body representing conservative interest groups (law, universities, churches, aristocracy, public officials) serving ten-year terms to insulate them from political vogues. At least one observer concluded that "the upper house was to become a guardian of Hungary's liberal heritage during World War II, opposing anti-Semitism and National Socialism."[33]

The Great Depression brought Bethlen down; having no solutions to the lengthening crisis, he resigned in August 1931. An interim government stumbled into 1932. While university graduates shoveled snow for food, leading politicians "were ready to accept any government that promised to restore order." Their (and Horthy's) fateful choice in October as prime minister, Gyula Gömbös, had been key to organizing the National Army in the early 1920s, but also once led a radical group of military anti-Semites and had envisioned a one-party state. "Unlettered and inexperienced" in politics, Gömbös openly sought to emulate Mussolini. He visited the Duce a month after his appointment, and on returning, gave a rousing balcony speech to massed Budapest crowds. In June 1933, he became the first foreign statesman to meet with Hitler, but the Führer brushed aside his proposal to reverse Trianon. Gömbös next worked to consolidate a hard right block in the Assembly, succeeding by 1935. As Hungary fell ever more under German influence, anti-Jewish manifestations escalated, led by local Nazi formations (which became Ferenc Szálasi's Arrow Cross Party), and by "radicalized youth" seeking to drive Jews out of universities and the professions. After Gömbös's death in 1936, a series of short-term prime ministers alternately banned and championed Hungary's fascists. Parliament passed its first "Jewish

Law" in summer 1938, creating local occupational "chambers" to regulate the proportion of Jews "in most of the liberal professions." The ugliness ran much deeper, however.[34]

Once war commenced, Horthy initially sought neutrality, even admitting defeated Polish soldiers to the country, a "gesture likely to be regarded by Germany as unfriendly." Yet his and the hard right's resolute irredentist goals cemented support for Berlin, as a series of land grabs to restore "Greater Hungary" had to have Hitler's assent. Thus, although Horthy banned Arrow Cross, forcing it underground, Hungary joined the Nazi invasion of Yugoslavia in 1941, then declared war on the Soviet Union, a fatal step. In spring 1944, impatient with the slow pace of Nazification, German forces invaded Hungary, installing a government which revived Arrow Cross. The latter's reign of terror initiated Hungary's Holocaust, with well over a half-million Hungarian Jews exterminated (ca. 430,000 at Auschwitz). Indeed, Adolph Eichmann, who visited Budapest to supervise the transports, commented on the "dazzling speed" with which the summer roundups were executed. By October Horthy recognized that Germany's fate was sealed and reportedly arranged a cease-fire with the Soviets, but Szálasi quickly displaced him to become the wartime nation's final Leader. By year's end Russian armies surrounded Budapest, then systematically destroyed their German and Hungarian antagonists, along with much of the city (Fig. 1.2), crushing a "racist nationalism" that had stoked hatred and promoted revenge for a quarter century.

Soviet occupation commenced with widespread looting and mass rapes, confirming many Hungarians' disdain for and suspicion of all things Russian and Communist. Surviving and returning Jews, however, largely viewed the USSR as a force for liberation (indeed, many joined the Party). Painfully, residual anti-Semitism blended with popular anti-Communism rather readily, as the victors imposed their will on defeated, resentful Hungarians.[35]

THE PATH AHEAD

The following chapters will trace the development and operations of business enterprises in postwar Hungary from the years of reconstruction through the immediate aftermath of the 1956 Revolt, which toppled a deeply despised government only to be overwhelmed by Russian military intervention. The study commences amid wartime ruins and Soviet

Fig. 1.2 Wreckage of Budapest's Elizabeth Bridge, 1945 (Photographer unknown. *Source* FOTO:Fortepan—ID 60155: http://www.fortepan.hu/_photo/download/fortepan_60155.jpgarchivecopy Wikimedia Creative Commons)

occupation and will briefly review the maneuvering that led to Communist dominion in 1948, the excesses of Stalinist rule, its partial rejection after 1953 and the deep fractures which generated the 1956 uprising and a second Soviet invasion. Throughout, deep hostility to the regime persisted, manifested in widespread illicit economic activity, necessarily covert given the diligence and cruelty of state security forces modeled on the Soviet secret police. Chapters 3 through 6 review business activity in four domains: agriculture, construction, commerce, and manufacturing, focusing on the first wave of agricultural collectivization (and its troubles), projects for rebuilding infrastructure, housing, and industrial capacity, challenges of supplying an impoverished population while managing compulsory exports, and deploying investments in heavy industry, all in the context of multiple, top-down reorganizations set in motion first by

14 P. SCRANTON

sectoral imbalances and then by Stalin's demise. Chapter 7 will sketch the convulsive 1956 revolt, its business impact, and the implications of the Kádár government's initial programs.

NOTES

1. Gyorgy Lakos, "The First Two Years of Two New Cooperative Farms," *New Hungarian Quarterly* (hereafter NHQ), No. 12 (1963): 150.
2. *Zalai Hirlap* (Zala News), 23 September 1960, 3, Joint Publications Research Service Report No. 7083, 19 December 1960, 27 [hereafter JPRS].
3. CIA Information Report, "The Machine and Railway Equipment Plant," Magyar Györ, 27 June 1957, 3 (Confidential, CIA-RDP81-01043R000900160004-7) [hereafter, CIAIR].
4. Radoslav Selucký, *Czechoslovakia: The Plan That Failed*. London: Thomas Nelson, 1970, 10.
5. See Eszter Bartha, *Alienating Labour: Workers on the Road from Socialism to Capitalism in East Germany and Hungary*, New York: Berghahn Books, 2013, Introduction.
6. For a report from Budapest acknowledging and amending this portrayal, see Jack Raymond, "Hungarians Lack Fear of Regime," *New York Times*, 18 September 1955, 10. Raymond noted that "the lack of inhibition in complaining appeared to the visitor to be completely out of joint with reports one heard of th[is] Iron Curtain country." To be sure, the "lack of fear" in 1955 was a substantive change from the general anxiety that dominated the high Stalinist years, 1949–1953.
7. Of 9.5 million cadastral yokes of arable land (13.5 million acres), 4.74 million CYs lay in the Alfold plain, 3.55 million in the hilly lands "West of the Danube," and the remaining 1.2 million in more mountainous "Northern Hungary." See *Statisztikai tájékoztató*, Budapest: Hungarian Statistical Office, 1950, excerpted and translated in CIA, Information from Foreign Documents, "Industrial and Sociological Statistics for Hungary," 17 August 1951, 1 (Confidential, CIA-RDP80-00809A00600400724-3) [hereafter CIAIFD]. See also László Simon, "Some Problems of Intensive Agriculture in Hungary," in *Geographical Types of Hungarian*

Agriculture, István Asztalos, ed., Budapest: Akadémiai Kiadó, 1966, 18–31.

8. *Termelőszövetkezetek* (TSZ) = agricultural producers' cooperatives. For official views of this process, see Ernő Czimadia, *Socialist Agriculture in Hungary*, Budapest: Akadémiai Kiadó, 1977, Ch. 1; Resző Nyers, *The Cooperative Movement in Hungary*, Budapest: Pannonia, 1963; and András Hegedűs, *The Structure of Socialist Society*, New York: St. Martins, 1977, Part Two: Changes in Rural Society.

9. So named to honor the first President of the German Democratic Republic (1949–1960). Additional name changes followed in later decades.

10. *The Economist*, 58 (27 October 1900): 1505. The RIMA firm was founded in 1881 at Salgótarján (Nógrád County): see Réka Várkonyi-Nickel, "Revisiting Enterprise Politics in Interwar Hungary: The Case of the Rimamurány–Salgótarján Iron Works Co.," *Metztek* 7:4(2018): 151–66. https://doi.org/10.18392/metsz/2018/4/9.

11. Pál Germuska and János Honvári, "The History of Public Vehicle Production in Győr from 1945 Until 1990," in *Industrial Districts and Cities in Central Europe*, Edit Somlyódyné Pfeil, ed., Győr: Universitas-Győr, 2014, 131–35.

12. Steven B. Vardy, "The Impact of Trianon on Hungary and the Hungarian Mind: The Nature of Interwar Hungarian Irredentism," *Hungarian Studies Review* 10:1(Spring 1983): 21–42. The other treaties were Saint Germain (re Austria), Neuilly (Bulgaria) and Sevres (Ottoman) [https://www.theworldwar.org/learn/peace/treaties (accessed 19 October 2020)].

13. Balint Hóman, et al., *Hungary: Yesterday and Today*, London: Grant Richards, 1936, 32–33.

14. Irredentism revived after the socialist period and remains a feature of the current Orban government's aspirations. See Steven B. Vardy, "The Trianon Syndrome in Today's Hungary," *Hungarian Studies Review* 24:1–2(1997): 73–79; Kate Maltby, "Victor Orban's Masterplan to Make Hungary Greater Again," *The New York Review of Books*, 3 June 2020, https://www.nybooks.com/daily/2020/06/03/viktor-orbans-masterplan-to-make-hungary-greater-again/ (accessed 21 October 2020).

15. Hóman, *Hungary*, 32–33.

16. I. T. Berend and G. Ranki, *Hungary: A Century of Economic Development*, Newton Abbot: David and Charles, 1974, 93–94.
17. Ibid., 95–122. In the last prewar years, Germany absorbed over half of Hungary's exports and provided over half of its imports, effectively "a monopoly position in foreign trade" (122).
18. György Enyedi, *Hungary: An Economic Geography*, Boulder, CO: Westview, 1976, 61.
19. Ibid., 3.
20. György Majtényi, "Between Tradition and Change: Hunting as Metaphor and Symbol in State Socialist Hungary," *Cultural and Social History* 13 (2016): 231–48; Eugene Keefe, et al., *Area Handbook for Hungary*, Washington, DC: GPO, 1973, 243–44; also https://www.indexmundi.com/agriculture/?country=hu& commodity=milled-rice&graph=production (accessed 21 October 2020), which shows Hungarian rice output at 28,000 metric tons in 1960, rising to over 40,000 MT in the early 1970s.
21. Enyedei, *Hungary*, 68–69.
22. Máton Pécsi, *Geomorphological Regions of Hungary*, Budapest: Akadêmiai Kiadó, 1970.
23. Enyedei, *Hungary*, 86–90.
24. Berend and Ranki, *Hungary*, 126–29.
25. Ibid., 130–31. The calculations use post-Trianon boundaries for both dates.
26. Ivan Berend and Györgi Ránki, *The Hungarian Economy in the Twentieth Century*, London: Croom Helm, 1985, 55–56. Of course, 193,000 spindles was not a huge number comparatively; individual large mills in western Europe and the USA ran 100,000 or more spindles at this time. The US had ca. 28 million cotton spindles in 1919.
27. Lászlo Fodor and Iván Illés, "Problems of Metropolitan Industrial Agglomeration: The Budapest Case," *Regional Science Association Papers* 28(1968): 65–82; John Lukacs, *Budapest 1900: A Historical Portrait of a City and Its Culture*, New York: Grove Press, 1994.
28. By 1930, Budapest employed 60% of Hungary's factory workers. Györgi Enyedi, "Economic Policy and Regional Development in Hungary," *Acta Oeconomica* 22(1979): 113–25.

29. Leslie Dienes, "The Budapest Agglomeration and Hungarian Industry: A Spatial Dilemma," *Geographical Review* 63 (1973): 356–77.
30. https://en.wikipedia.org/wiki/Demographics_of_Hungary (accessed 27 October 2020). During its alliance with Nazi Germany, the Hungarian state acquired and annexed several segments of its "lost lands," particularly from Yugoslavia, such that by 1944, Budapest administered over 30 districts. This did not last, as the Allies restored the Trianon borders almost entirely by 1947.
31. https://en.wikipedia.org/wiki/Mihály_Kálrolyi (accessed 30 October 2020); Deborah Cornelius, *Hungary in World War II*, New York: Fordham University Press, 2013, 9–11, 19–21; Tamás Révész, "Post-war Turmoil and Violence (Hungary)," *1914–1918-Online International Encyclopedia of the First World War*, Ute Daniel, Peter Gatrell, Oliver Janz, Heather Jones, Jennifer Keene, Alan Kramer, and Bill Nasson, eds., Berlin: Freie Universität Berlin, 2019-08-05. https://doi.org/10.15463/ie1418.11396. Charles IV, King of Hungary, was also Charles I, Emperor of Austria. He died in exile in 1922.
32. Cornelius, *Hungary*, 21–25; Thomas Sakmyster, "From Habsburg Admiral to Hungarian Regent: The Political Metamorphosis of Miklós Horthy, 1918–1921," *East European Quarterly* 17:2(1983): 129–148. The Royal Navy had been transferred to Yugoslavia, as were Imperial ports in Croatia. Intense debates have emerged about the contours of Hungarian anti-Semitism. See, for example, Veronika Lehotay, "Measures of Deprivation of Freedom in the Horthy-Era, with Special Regard to Anti-Jewish Laws," unpublished Ph.d., Faculty of Law, University of Miskolc, 2012; L. Péter, "A Debate on the History of Hungary between 1790 and 1945," *Slavonic and East European Review* 50(1972): 442–47; István Deák, "Review of Corneilus, *Hungary in World War II*," *Holocaust and Genocide Studies* 27(2013): 500–2. Paramilitary groups joined the White Terrorists (See Béla Bodó, "Paramilitary Violence in Hungary After the First World War," *East European Quarterly* 38[2004]: 129–72).
33. Salkmyster,"From Habsburg Admiral," 143–44; Cornelius, *Hungary*, 32–42. See also T. Sakmyster, "István Bethlen and Hungarian Foreign Policy," *Canadian-American Review of*

Hungarian Studies 5:2(1978): 3–16; Mária Ormos, "The Early Interwar Years, 1921–1938," in *A History of Hungary*, Peter Sugar and Péter Hanák, eds., Bloomington: Indiana University Press, 1990, 319–38; and CIA, National Intelligence Survey, *Hungary: Politics*, March 1973, 2–3 (Secret, CIA-RDP01-00707R000200110039-1).

34. Cornelius, *Hungary*, Chaps. 2 & 3; Bernard Klein, "Anti-Jewish Demonstrations in Hungarians Universities: 1932–36: István Bethlen vs Gyula Gömbös," *Jewish Social Studies* 44:2(1982): 113–24; Sakmyster, "Bethlen"; Omos, "Early Interwar Years"; Nandor Dreisziger, *Hungary's Way to World War II*, Astor Park: Danubian, 1968; Andrew Janos, "Nationalism and Communism in Hungary," *East European Quarterly* 5(1971): 74–102.

35. Cornelius, *Hungary*, Chaps. 8 & 9; Thomas Sakmyster, "Miklós Horthy, Hungary, and the Coming of the European Crisis, 1932–41," *East Central Europe* 3(1976) 220–32; Gabor Baross, *Hungary and Hitler*, Astor Park: Danubian, 1970; Loránd Tilkovsky, "The Late Interwar Years and World War II," in *A History of Hungary*, 339–55; David Cesarani, ed., *Genocide and Rescue: The Holocaust in Hungary*, London: Berg, 1997; https:// en.wikipedia.org/wiki/The_Holocaust_in_Hungary (accessed 4 November 2020); Randolph Braham and Scott Miller, eds., *The Nazi's Last Victims: The Holocaust in Hungary*, Detroit: Wayne State University Press, 1998; Robert M. Bigler, "Heil Hitler und Heil Horthy! The Nature of Hungarian Racist Nationalism, 1919–1945," *East European Quarterly* 8(1974): 251–272; Nándor Dreisziger, eds., *Hungary in the Age of Total War, 1938–1948*, New York: East European Monographs, 1998, esp. Krisztián Ungváry, "The Second Stalingrad: The Destruction of Axis Armies at Budapest," 151–68. For short stories which vividly capture Budapest under and after the early 1945 siege, see Tibor Déry, *The Portuguese Princess and Other Stories*, Evanston: Northwestern University Press, 1987. Also, it was in Budapest that Raoul Wallenberg used his Swedish diplomatic credentials to issue "protective passports" that saved many Jews from the Auschwitz convoys. See Ingrid Carlberg, *Raoul Wallenberg*, London: MacLehose, 2017.

CHAPTER 2

The Theft Economy: Occupation and Forced Industrialization

Budapest, her beauty shattered, is slowly emerging from the war's wreckage. Buda is a collection of gaunt, granite skeletons overlooking the Danube. Pest, on the east side of the river, is a heap of rubble... There is a shortage of food and fuel. The situation is bad, and the prospect [is] that more than 75 percent will be cut from this year's harvests. There is a great fear... of what next winter may bring (Fig. 2.1).
—*New York Times*, 27 June 1945[1]

The work of reorganization and rehabilitation started... without any administrative measures on the part of the central authorities. Though production was seriously hampered by shortages of equipment and labor, restoring of productive capacity and elimination of economic chaos was achieved by the private initiative of the administrators of industrial plants, as well as of the workers... The National Bank of Hungary, with the consent of the Government, granted credits very freely to reorganize and re-equip industrial plants. With these funds... industry was able to adapt itself to new conditions.
—CIA Information Report, 4 October 1948.[2]

Hungary is certainly the most troubled of all the European states subject to the USSR. Its population is overwhelmingly hostile to the Communist government, and is apathetic and uncooperative toward the economic program. The economy has been dislocated by unrealistic plans and by

© The Author(s), under exclusive license to Springer Nature Switzerland AG 2022
P. Scranton, *Business Practice in Socialist Hungary, Volume 1*, Palgrave Debates in Business History,
https://doi.org/10.1007/978-3-030-89184-8_2

19

incompetent management.... The standard of living of the people is generally low and in the urban areas, except for the privileged, is substantially below prewar levels. There is a very considerable number of black market dealers who obtain much of their merchandise as a result of widespread pilfering by workers. Agricultural machinery has thus far had little effect because of poor maintenance [and] lack of spare parts... Factories are badly planned and some of them are left unfinished.[3]
—CIA National Intelligence Estimate, 29 March 1955

The above reports draw sharp contrasts: massive destruction and gnawing dread transformed into vigorous reconstruction vs., a decade later, pervasive apathy, incompetence, and theft. By the 1950s, enthusiasm had ended for reviving the economy and repairing wartime damage, estimated at US$4.3 billion (five years of GDP in the 1930s[4]). Communist activists who had spent the war years in the USSR accompanied the Red Army's conquest, aiming to establish a Stalinist people's democracy; but in the ensuing elections, the Party claimed just 17% of the vote. Rural Hungarians favored the Smallholders, whose leader, Zoltán Tildy, became

Fig. 2.1 Hungary, counties map with county seats: www.mapsopensource.com/hungary-counties-map.html

the Hungarian Republic's first President in 1946.[5] After the Communists worked steadily to augment their forces (with Mátyás Rákosi as the Party's General Secretary and Imre Nagy as Minister of Agriculture, then Interior), several years of "political and economic pluralism gave way to five years of growing Stalinist terror (from 1948 to the spring of 1953), followed by three years of gradual decompression called the New Course (1953-56) that culminated in a short-lived nationalist, anti-Soviet uprising in October 1956 – an uprising whose echoes resonated worldwide for decades to come".[6]

An overview of the tumultuous postwar decade now heads our agenda, with special attention to the organizational landscape, to Soviet occupation and dominance, and to the Party's efforts to erect a socialist system through headlong industrialization. Glaring deficiencies in this project propelled revisions after Stalin's death (1953), revisions that exposed splits within the ruling cadres, just as citizens, students, intellectuals, and journalists began launching sharp critiques of the costs and consequences Sovietization had generated.[7] Then, drawing on contemporary first-person accounts and a trove of archival sources, succeeding chapters will survey business practices through 1956 in what one might regard as Hungary's "theft economy."

From top to bottom, stealing permeated "socialist" economic activity, both as metaphor and as behavior.[8] The occupying Soviets stole systematically, initially using "trophy brigades" to lay claim to entire factories, masses of machinery, artworks and artifacts, and trainloads of industrial and agricultural products. The USSR then reaped reparations harvests from Magyar producers (with output values calculated at exchange rates favoring the Soviets), closing the circle with takeovers of all German-owned enterprises, accompanied by "50-50" joint operations of Hungary's "iron and steel industry, oil wells and oil refineries, power plants, chemical plants, factories for the manufacture of agricultural, electrical and other machinery, shipping on the Danube, and air and road transport."[9] All the while, Red Army divisions stationed in Hungary were provisioned at no cost to the Soviets; although their numbers soon dropped, US agents in Budapest estimated the expense for 1946 at $50 million.[10] Simultaneously, another macro-theft, a hyperinflation worse than Germany's 1923 crisis triggered by the Soviet exactions, made the national currency (the *pengo*) worthless, destroyed the savings of the middling classes, wiped out creditors assets, and led to workers being paid in foodstuffs.[11]

For its part, the Rákosi People's Democracy systematically stole from its citizens, both to satisfy the Soviets and to provision the nation while funding investments in heavy industry, bureaucracy, and state security (the AVH[12]). Control agencies compelled farmers to deliver sizable shares of field harvests, orchard and vineyard produce, and livestock, either without compensation or at painfully low prices. In tandem, they routinely hiked property taxes, so as to force family farmers to "donate" their land toward forming rural cooperatives. In Budapest, the state confiscated the apartments, homes, and villas of middling to upper class families, relegating them to work in agriculture, mining, or forestry, in order to offer residences to the growing mass of ministerial employees and enterprise officials. Administrators next shrank workers' purchasing power through a double squeeze: earnings reductions combined with food and clothing price hikes, accompanied by intense exhortations to increase production.[13]

If grand theft was the leitmotif for those building socialism, little wonder that everyday Hungarians picked up the theme and worked variations on it: fraud, embezzlement, bribery, smuggling, accounting fiddles, price deceptions, short weighing, fake certificates of quality (and qualifications), and falsified plan outcomes. As a railway maintenance engineer explained: "A special feature of the Satellite states is... that they have to strive in all their functions to serve the bottomless appetite of the Soviet Union. In consequence, a People's Democratic State is conducting a *robber economy*, not only with regard to the material resources of the country, but also with regard to the work power. The exploitation is far more thorough and achieved [at] a far higher degree than ever before."[14] György Faludy, an editor imprisoned during the high Stalinist period, provided examples from farm, factory, and commercial settings:

> Gyűmért, the fruit exporting agency, made [compulsory] contracts with the peasants, agreeing to buy up all their perfect Jonathan apples for four forints per kilo. [However, peasants] could sell their leftover bad apples for eleven forints on the free market. The result was that the next year, the peasants used no insecticides, so that all their crop was worm-eaten. This enabled them to sell all of their fruit on the free market for a higher price. There were two kinds of factories: those where the workers could steal and those where they could not. If they were unable to steal anything, they produced rejects, or threw away tools in order, at least, to destroy. I had a friend who had a job as a truck guard, from which he was fired because he refused to steal. At Közért [a retail chain], the employees sold

short weight and stole the rest. When the members of the employees' families came in, they bought half a kilo's worth of goods and received ten kilos.[15]

If the Soviets' appetite was "bottomless," so too was the resourcefulness of the citizenry in frustrating the Russians and in subverting the Party's socialism. *The New York Times*' C. L. Sulzberger summarized the situation by 1953: "There is no doubt that factory production has mounted impressively. But the output of goods is generally shoddy, prices are too high in terms of real wages, and a major share of the national output is disappearing eastward to the Soviet Union."[16] All true, but closer to the ground, the clash between incompetence and improvisation in the theft economy was vivid, visible, and quietly visceral.[17]

THE NEW HUNGARIAN STATE: ORGANIZATION AND PLANS

During the first three postwar years, a coalition republican government guided Hungary's reconstruction. Officially led by the Smallholders Party, which held a Parliamentary majority, the state became increasingly dominated by prominent Communists. Following the much criticized 1948 elections, marred by extravagant fraud in absentee balloting, the Workers' Party gained political control, dismissed its former partners, installed a centralized administration, and began to replace state-supported capitalism with Stalinist socialism. Several rounds of nationalizations in industry, mining, banking, and commerce swelled the roster of state-controlled enterprises, which joined longstanding pre-war monopolies (e.g., tobacco, long-haul railways). A series of transformative events marked 1949: replacement of the Supreme Economic Council by the National Planning Office, initiation of compulsory agricultural deliveries at low, fixed prices, and in August, confirmation of a new, socialist constitution.[18]

As the formal mechanism confirming Hungary's Sovietization, the constitution proved operationally a fraud, guaranteeing freedoms of speech, assembly, worship, and "liberty of conscience," none of which the Rákosi regime respected. In fact, officials never accepted the constitution "as an effective limitation on the power of the government." Though its phraseology echoed basic Western commitments, there was "neither a constitutionally established system of checks and balances nor a separation of governmental powers. Provisions that appear to support the principles of popular sovereignty, democratic government and civil liberties ha[d] little significance" in the absence of any enforcement provisions. Putting into effect the constitutional framework relied on the Party apparatus, commanded by its First Secretary in consultation with the Central Committee and protected by state security forces. Actually, political leaders ruled through decrees establishing priorities and practices, which the Parliament duly ratified. Yet even the Party was subordinated to the state apparatus.

> Basing its pervasive role on a vague constitutional provision, the party dictates the functions of government, formulates national policy, and supervises the implementation of that policy without any system of direct popular checks... Despite the primacy of the party's position, however, *the government is the principal avenue* through which the party's control over the nation is manifested.[19]

One consequence of this dualism was "duplicate bureaucracies," sizable Party organizations ostensibly guiding and supervising state agencies. Paramount among all agencies was the Council of Ministers, "the actual focal point of the government and its clearing house for the collection of information, implementation of policy, and solution of problems which filter up from the individual ministries." Though the ministry roster unsurprisingly included Finance, Defense, Health, and Interior,[20] it is noteworthy that nine of them centered on economic planning, development, and control: Agriculture, Construction, Foreign Trade, Domestic Trade, Heavy Industry, Light Industry, Metallurgy and Machine Industry, Labor, and Transport.[21]

The National Planning Office anchored yet another parallel structure, devising resource allocations and investments for the people's economy. Initially, an intermediate agency served as its liaison to the Council of Ministers, but this was dissolved in 1952. Thereafter, while periodically communicating with the Council, the Office's six "general departments" (economics, finance, labor, technical development, material allocation, and investments) worked independently to "draw up the plans for the entire economy." The Office's "industrial departments" closely matched the economic ministries, which consulted intensively with them through the phases of plan formation. After preliminary drafts, sent down the ladder for comments, came back up for review of recommended changes, Planning forwarded the final version to the Council for confirmation.[22]

State Ministries were sidelined within this process. Ministerial "general departments" kept in "close contact" with those of the Planning Office, as their "directorates" remained responsible for plan execution— "the direction of productive activity." Lower down the hierarchy were "trusts" (clusters of similarly-oriented firms), multi-unit enterprises, and finally individual plants, factories, and workshops. This structure reflected manufacturing categories, but analogies existed for agriculture, commerce (trade), and construction.[23] National planning missions necessitated an enormous staff, tens of thousands in Budapest alone, mirrored by huge Ministry bureaucracies and somewhat less bloated Party contingents.[24]

The planning process, "protracted" and intricate, comprised three nested sets of targets and allocations: long term (three to five years), annual, and quarterly plans. Hungary's first Five Year Plan not only detailed general economic objectives, but also prescribed specific goals, e.g., "how many work clothes, motorcycles and motion pictures should be produced during the period." This did not work as expected: "Because of numerous and extensive modifications," the individual targets routinely had to be "forsaken." Yearly plans, appreciably more relevant for enterprise managers, had diminished impact due to persistent delays. They commonly arrived late, in March or April of the plan year, not the previous fall, and were "frequently modified" thereafter. In one memorable case, "six Hungarian construction trusts... received their yearly plans for 1954 on January 21, 1955; [this] is not exceptional." Thus managements chiefly relied on quarterly plans, which if late in arriving were simply copied from the previous year's version. The system's internal practices were at fault:

> The [revised] plan approved by the Council of Ministers proceeds through six stages before it reaches the enterprise level. The counter-plan prepared by [each] enterprise travels along the same route (if modification of the ministry's plan has also been made necessary), and as a last step, the newly-approved version of the plan descends by the same stages back to the enterprise. As an example of the time needed, the second version of the 1954 plan for the Ministry of Heavy Industry was transmitted to the ministry from the Planning Office on October 9, 1953 and the plans of the enterprises were approved in March and April of 1954.[25]

One consequence of this organizational complexity was that enterprises could (and did) receive overlapping, competing, or contradictory directives from the Party, from one or more Ministries, and from the Planning Office. All issued "guidance," both to firms and agencies, in tremendous volume. As planner Béla Balassa reported, one "county received 1,338 regulations and decrees from the Ministry of Agriculture in the first four months of 1954, while another county received 5,400 regulations and directives from the Ministry of Domestic and Foreign Trade in 1953." In addition, the Ministries, the Party and state security all had surveillance and investigation units ("controls"), whose visits were as dreaded as they were inevitable. "The Conveyor factory in Budapest was audited and inspected 1,500 times in the course of a year; in the Mirelite deep-freezer factory, several controllers investigated tramway tickets for three days to see whether those marked for official use had been used on Sundays." Overall, as János Kornai noted, skillful managers learned which orders could be ignored, which could be played off against one another, and which demanded close attention.[26]

Other consequences of bureaucratic complexity, information overload and uncertainty, percolated from the bottom upward. Ministries, statistical agencies, and planning units constantly required factories, state farms and producer cooperatives to generate reports, as did research institutes, design centers, and the national railways. So many forms had to be filed that managers were suspected of completing them without ascertaining actual conditions. Security services also contributed tens of thousands of surveillance assessments to the flood, while Party functionaries added their independent, often conflicting observations. Reviews and estimates poured into multiple administrative headquarters which simply could not process, organize, summarize, and synthesize such masses of data and text.[27] The result was systemic incoherence, featuring duplication, inconsistent numbers, and conflicting narratives—some released by Party newspapers for the public; others, not necessarily more reliable, used for internal decisions. Ambitious targets, often based on soft information, were not met, infuriating the leadership. For example, in food supply, as the Agriculture Ministry recounted:

> 1950 was the year of the first major crisis in Hungarian agriculture. The first symptom was a grave meat shortage. To shake things up, the director and deputy director of the Meat Industry Center were executed. In the further search for scapegoats, they then got onto sugar. We had signed

contracts for 200,000 holds [280K acres] of sugar beets in that year. The planning board drafted their plans on the basis of an estimated 1.6-1,7 million ton beet crop. The actual crop turned out to be 1.1-1.2 million tons. They had made export commitments [based on] the higher estimate, and as these commitments had to be met, a shortage developed on the home market.

That fall, Rákosi personally phoned the ministry's Contractual Crops office, but the chief was absent. Told about the call on his return, "he went pale as a sheet." The head of state, believing the staff had sabotaged the plan, demanded a report in 48 hours. Were it unsatisfactory, a visit from state security would follow. Agency managers

> concluded that the only hope of a way out was to be brutally frank and tell him... that the whole agricultural policy of the government is rendering our work impossible. I drafted 180 lines, referring quite [directly] to the artificially created labor shortage on the land, the perpetual organizational reshuffles, and the unwillingness of the peasants to produce because of the insecurity of their future. I said, and could prove, that we did provide seed and fertilizers in time and that we could do no more.

Grumbling, Rákosi accepted their conclusions. No arrests ensued, instead he fired the Crops director.[28] Nothing was done, however, to remedy the information system's weaknesses.

State security functions rested nominally within the Interior Ministry, but through 1953 the AVO, State Security Section [later renamed the AVH (State Security Agency)], was responsible directly to First Secretary Rákosi and his closest colleagues. Acknowledged as "the most detested and feared of the police organs," the AVH occupied the former headquarters of the Nazi-allied Arrow Cross Party and readily welcomed fugitive fascists into its ranks.[29] Created early in 1945 by a Communist resistance group centered around Gábor Péter, then confirmed "by Ernö Gerö, the highest ranking Hungarian appointee of the Russian NKVD,[30]" the AVO settled in at 60 Andrássy Street and commenced purchasing adjoining properties, "automobiles and other equipment." Reportedly,

> while the country as a whole was in financial ruin... the secret source of funds for this expansion was traced to 14 trunks of looted gold treasure buried by fleeing Arrow Cross Party members in a cellar on Szent István Boulevard. The location of this treasure was communicated to the political

police as a part of a deal for leniency toward a former Arrow Cross Party leader who had been condemned to death by the People's Court.[31]

Soon Budapest's resident NKVD General introduced Péter to János Kovács, sent from Moscow to organize the AVO "into an offensive weapon" for the Party. Kovács designed a comprehensive surveillance system with 17 "subdivisions," infiltrating domestic and foreign politics, all ministries and large enterprises, church, youth, and social organizations. Agents conducted street observations, supervised passport control, and offered bodyguard services for state and Party leaders. To fill posts in this sprawling apparatus, Kovács evidently summoned "14,760 former lower-ranking Arrow Cross Party men... Almost an equal number were taken from the internment camps. All of them were then coerced into becoming informers."[32]

Separated from the Interior Ministry in 1950, the AVO "became a completely independent agency" (hence the name change) and soon welcomed the Defense Ministry's Border Guard under its span of control. Thereafter there were "two distinct service branches in the organization: the interior police, called 'blue' AVH from the color of the uniform, and the border guard, or 'green' AVH." No AVH officer reported to any local or national police branch; quite the reverse, as "the regular police organization is paralleled by independent AVH agencies which keep watch over and control the national police." By 1954, the divisions were politically reshaped, following the death of Lavrentiy Beria, master of Stalin's state security empire. This reworking clustered its 17 units into four offices (Administration, Executive Group, Special Agencies and auxiliaries) and reconfigured their assignments functionally. Sections now existed for "political interrogation and punishment," "penal institutions," counterintelligence, ciphers, couriers, and the control of foreigners. In another organizational parallel, "interrogation and punishment" operated "branches dealing with agriculture, industry, trade, mining, religion and travel." Spatially, the AVH established "18 provincial district offices" outside Budapest, each of which had "its own special armed unit," mostly platoon size (ca. 50 troops), but two in the capital and several others reached battalion size (ca. 1000). Their main charge when mobilized was "to suppress all mass demonstrations." The Border Guard's nine district commands numbered an estimated 18,000 agents and the blue AVH about 32,000 in 1954.[33]

The AVH deployed unlimited state power to deny employment to "class enemies," to gather evidence on incompetence in agencies and enterprises, to arrest and compel confessions from those identified as dangers to Party and nation, and to imprison and punish such criminals, who were often sentenced without trial. Its network of informers relayed (sometimes invented) tales of theft, embezzlement, or disrespect of Party leaders and policies, leading to dismissals or worse, middle-of-the-night arrests.[34] The AVH anchored the 1951–1952 deportations, hauling thousands of urban home-owners to rural locations, thus liberating their properties for government use. Its agents compiled lists of likely targets, secured administrative consent, then tasked local police with rounding up the deportees and delivering them to AVH transport. Apart from some food and clothing, all family possessions had to be left behind.[35] Many others were deported because of their personal histories. Béla Balassa, whose father was a Horthy-era army officer, was caught in one of these sweeps and shipped to a farm in eastern Hungary. He later commented acidly: "There followed three months of working in the cotton fields, [on] a crop that represented a misuse of land in Hungary's climactic conditions."[36]

More grimly, the AVH increasingly governed the regime's internment camps, detention centers, and forced labor sites, also placing surveillance teams in penal institutions operated by other sections of the administration.[37] Consistent with the theft economy, AVH supervisors at convict labor mills and farms commonly withheld "a part of the output for sale on the black market," whereas central office staff "lined their pockets through the sale of passports." Such graft was not merely tolerated at the top but "encouraged," as once-tolerated stealing could later serve as "formal grounds for trying and jailing [an officer] whenever... they wished to get rid of him." Reports of both crude abuse and sophisticated torture of those confined spread widely and were repeatedly confirmed during and after the '56 revolt, when AVH staff were assaulted nationwide (and at times murdered). Though popular contempt for the Rákosi government had many origins, pervasive fear of the AVH generated deep mistrust and resentment.[38]

Soviet Dominion in the Postwar Economy

From the outset, "Moscow's rule was rejected by the Hungarian people. The Soviets wanted control; popularity did not matter." Hungarians' reactions also did not matter; the power disparity between the triumphant Soviets and the defeated Magyars was beyond measure. The Russians promptly set the agenda for long-term economic exploitation: demanding food for troops, plus coal and fodder, exacting reparations (including entire factories, as well as future production from restored plants and farms), seizing enterprises with German roots and taking half-shares in others owned by Hungarians, and concluding trade agreements employing heavily favorable exchange rates.[39] To frame a context for these practices, revisiting the wartime destruction the Horthy regime sustained may be helpful.

A 1946 report by Budapest's Central Statistical Office provided loss estimates for agriculture, industry, construction/transport, and commerce. For livestock, between 1942 and 1945, 1.4 million cattle, half a million horses, 3.5 million pigs, and 1.4 million sheep vanished from rural precincts, respectively, 58, 59, 75, and 83% of pre-war farm animals. Their total value, conservatively: US$300 million. Some were surely slaughtered for consumption and not replaced; whereas others were either shipped to unknown destinations, killed during combat, or fell to disease or starvation as provisioning systems collapsed. Crop losses accounted for another US$200 million, about three-quarters of a year's national harvest. Agricultural equipment fared somewhat better. Although 275,000 "farm wagons were destroyed," 85% of tractors and 80% of threshing machines survived. Aggregate industrial losses neared US$400 million, a third in "machine production," alongside many tens of millions in textiles, mining, food, and chemicals. As for ruined buildings and transportation facilities, the Office estimated the toll at US$800 million, one-third in besieged Budapest, where four of every five structures had been destroyed or damaged. Thousands of bridges had also been bombed or dynamited, including the most traveled Danube crossings. Railways accounted for 80% of all transport losses, ca. US$600 million, including 1,300 locomotives, 4,000 passenger cars, and 45,000 freight cars. Impassible roads and highways topped all other categories in value; investments of US$1.6 billion would be required to repair or replace them. Nor was Hungary's National Bank immune; its assets shrank dramatically. Indeed, the nation's entire reserve of precious metals exited: "27,500 kg. of gold and 232,000 kg. of silver."[40] A British observer summarized:

> At the end of the second war the greater part of the industrial equipment lay in ruins or was so badly damaged that for some time it was incapable of production. Agriculture suffered similarly. It was deprived of the greater part of its livestock, tools and machinery. The communication system was destroyed to such an extent that even neighboring districts remained completely isolated from each other… [Such] damage… together with the large scale removal of Hungarian property by the retreating Germans and the systematic dismantling of industrial establishments and removal of millions worth of all kinds of public and private property by the Red Army were the main causes of the complete economic collapse.[41]

Into this morass drove Stalin's "trophy brigades," aiming to identify and tag Hungarian property that could be extracted as compensation for Horthy's Nazi alliance.[42] The "specifications of equipment and commodities to be shipped to the USSR by Hungary as reparations" appear in a remarkable, 96-page document from 1945. Its 112 sections are memorable for their scope and level of detail; clearly, knowledgeable engineers and technicians complied them, having taken a rapid yet thorough survey of still-operational facilities. For example:

> Specification No. 1: Complete equipment of the Hatvan electric power plant [Heves county] with transformers, laboratories, and technical documentation. The equipment includes six steam boilers of 65 atmospheric pressures and 56-70 tons steam output per hour, and three 34,000 kw and one 5500 kw turbo-generators. Requirements include all equipment located within or outside of the power plant. Delivery must be all inclusive in all details to assure reassembly and operation of the power plant at full efficiency as a complete single unit.
>
> Specification No. 26: Equipment from the Budapest Gamma optical and mechanical works with electric motors, laboratory equipment, and documentation. [This] includes one 750mmx600x1500, one 700x550x500, and one 500x750x1000 "Heracut" electric furnaces for the drying of lenses, as well as [the] complete lathe [shop], automatic milling machine, apprentice, machine tool, repair and preparation shops.
>
> Specification 57/A: Complete automatic telephone exchanges, each for 3,000 lines, suitable for expansion to 10,000 lines. Equipment includes spare parts for 5 years operation, cable, 3,000 receivers and coin stations, complete set of operating and regulating instruments, an extra set of

instruments and parts for regulation and repair work, and complete technical descriptions, together with maintenance calendar for each automatic exchange. All equipment must conform to Soviet specifications.[43]

Soviet demands for agricultural products were similarly comprehensive, though perhaps fanciful in 1945, given the fractured state of rail transport. They included 660,000 tons of wheat, 14,000 tons of "ground corn," and 2,500 tons of alfalfa [known as lucerne]. How these figures were determined is unknown, but the team identified both goods for immediate consumption (5,000 tons of slaughtered hogs, 180,000 tons of bacon, 2,000 tons of beans) and for near and long-term futures, viz.:

> 3,000 tons of clover seed, 2 tons of tomato seed, 2 tons of watermelon seed, 50 tons of beet seed, 165 tons of onion seed, 160 tons of carrot seed, and 20 tons of cucumber seed. [As well,] 3,850,000 phylloxera-resistant American grapevines, 55,000 European grapevines, 7500 kg of flower seeds, 61,600 various fruit tree saplings (peach, almond, apple, etc.), 21,500 rose trees and other saplings; all to be delivered by 14 January 1946.[44]

Whereas industrial asset stripping is well documented,[45] it is difficult to imagine how shipping diverse agricultural goods could have been managed, as they would have to have been gathered from disparate places, packed, stored, and assembled for rail transit, a herculean task.

Competition from the occupying forces for logistical resources and supplies was significant, too. In the last three quarters of 1945, "the Soviet Army ordered 64,500 tons of flour, 23,000 tons of beef, 91,000 tons of oats and 173,000 tons of hay, which would have stretched public supply even if the Soviets had been willing to pay for the shipments, which was not the case." From October through December, the Red Army "requisitioned 40,000 tons of coal and 25,000 cubic meters of wood as well." Nothing changed in 1946, as military demands in June and July included "3,000 tons of meat, 800,000 eggs, 645 tons of milk," as well as tons of butter, spices, fresh fruits and vegetables." Unable to consume everything, the Russians exported much of the non-perishable goods to the West, "since they regarded them as war booty."[46] Military confiscations dropped with the repatriation of Soviet troops to the homeland—a 90% decline (to 100,000) by mid-1948.[47] Other asymmetrical relations soon took their place, accompanying the appointment of Russians to oversight and policy positions in virtually every significant Hungarian organization.

The formal Peace Treaty (February 1947) fixed reparations payments to the Soviet Union at US$200 million, US$166 million "to be delivered in industrial goods," the residual to come from agricultural produce, "such as cereals, seeds, livestock, oil, oil products,[48] hides, etc." The plants and machinery confiscated in 1945 were to be deducted from the industrial account, whence arose the next big steal. The Russians assessed the seized assets at just US$36 million, whereas outside observers suggested as a "most moderate estimate," a figure above US$300 million. Another fiddle arose when, for the remaining US$130 million of yet-to-be-manufactured industrial goods, the USSR established its calculations "in terms of U. S. dollars at the 1938 price level." Adopting rates from a decade earlier yielded values "no more than 40 percent of present (1947) world prices," increasing Hungary's liabilities by 150%—to nearly US$400 million. Of course, "to the victor...", but the economic effects of these extractions were dire, as "at present (1947) more than half of Hungary's industrial production goes for reparation purposes. It is hard to imagine how her industry, with its reduced capacity and its damaged, insufficiently repaired, worn out and already partially obsolete machinery will be able to meet the demands confronting its different branches."[49]

To inform those at the other end of the pipeline, USSR trade managers published a 1948 catalog for Russian purchasing agents documenting the "range of items produced by Soviet machine-building and electrical engineering enterprises in Hungary," and listing firms "which accept orders for manufacture of special items from drawings and specifications." This "handbook" offered 31 sections, including "cable products, high-voltage equipment, electrical machinery, rectifiers" and 27 other categories of goods which could be secured from 28 Budapest factories, such as Hungarian Siemens, Telefunken, and Haas and Somogyi Special Steels.[50]

These plants were among at least fifty German-owned enterprises the occupiers seized, companies identified using a 1942 National Bank roster of firms authorized to export profits to the Reich. The Russians shortly expanded that cluster to include businesses with minority German shareholding. In consequence, "the Soviets took the most meaningful parts of what remained of Hungarian light and heavy industry."[51] An array of new ventures ensued: joint enterprises half owned by USSR ministries, trade agreements with advantageous price levels,[52] and most invasive, Russian military, political and managerial personnel installed in top positions at Hungarian firms and agencies. In their thousands, such "advisers" and "directors" populated every level of governance and operations: e.g.,

34   P. SCRANTON

a representative of the Soviet Five Year Plan Office "attached" to its Budapest counterpart; cotton expert Andrei Skoblykov similarly placed at the Agriculture Ministry; Ivan Altomare directing processed food exports from the Light Industry Ministry; or Andrei Ragyanski heading the Hungarian Air Association. Soviet engineers served as Directors-General at aluminum refining plants, at textile mills, and even at the Miskolc barbed wire factory.[53] In the Almásfüzitő bauxite refinery,

> their prime interest is management. A general manager who is a technician himself, has a staff of three to four Soviet technicians to assist him. They all [help] in the development of the aluminum industry. From 1946 [initially] the caliber of Soviet technicians was only mediocre, [although] these technicians are better paid than the Hungarians. The Soviet officials have cars of their own, receive free lodging and have two large stores similar to US [army] post exchanges where they can purchase food and beverages. There is no need for them to do any shopping in Hungarian stores.[54]

A staff roster for Budapest's Meszhart Shipping Company illuminates the extensive penetration by Russian managers, even in far-from-critical trades. A 1946 joint venture in Danube water transport, within and beyond Hungary, Meszhart branched out to river excursions in 1952. Among its 33 administrators (in 14 divisions), just five were Soviets, but they occupied all the key posts: General Manager, Chief Engineer, Navigation Division Chief, Company Accountant, and Planning Department Head. The highest post a Hungarian held was Deputy [General] Manager.[55] As everywhere, such officials ranged from oppressive and interfering to relaxed and diffident, but they *were* everywhere and were *everywhere* resented.

STRUCTURING THE SOCIALIST ENTERPRISE SYSTEM

Entire forests have been transformed into monographs and essay collections documenting and analyzing the 1990s transitions (or returns) to capitalism in Central Europe and the (former) Soviet Union.[56] Little comparable investigation has focused on the 1940s transitions *to socialism*, generally understood as forced adoptions of Soviet principles and practices, managed by Moscow-trained cadres, and accepted, however grudgingly, by subject populations. But surely such a sketch is oversimplified. From the outside and the top down, it may seem plausible, but from the inside looking out, creating socialist institutions that worked was a far more contingent and uncertain project, even when Soviet experts transferred tested Soviet models. Party leaders promoting and directing the economic transition may have learned their lines well, but had to contend both with Hungarians who resented what was happening and with Party members and supporters who had no clue what to do, first, next and thereafter. Nationalizing enterprises did not produce rapid absorption of socialist priorities, approaches to decision-making, or planning routines, whether management was retained from the capitalist era or was newly selected. Propaganda about proletarian power and the glories of industrialization could not nourish factory workers' families; indeed, households' standards of living steadily decayed after 1949.[57] The challenge facing those "building socialism" in Hungary was to transform postwar chaos into competence, reluctance into resilience, and rivalry into cooperation. That challenge was not well met.

On the ground, at least five fault lines hazarded Hungary's socialist enterprise system. First, the whole program was designed, imported, and supervised by the despised occupiers—not an advantage. Next, although a host of new institutions had to be created, the supply of competent bureaucrats, managers, auditors, and planners to staff them was meager at best. In part, this valorized the widespread appointment of Russians to key positions. (As well, many "bourgeois" white collar workers and business staff had emigrated or had been war/Holocaust victims.) Third, the rush to industrialize did not magically make thousands of experienced machinists, electricians, molders, or draftsmen materialize; instead, after minimal training, one-time rural workers filled factory positions, gradually learning by doing. Moreover, the mass of the population, rural and urban, had no knowledge or understanding of socialist ideology, terminology, and institutions, nor much interest in them.[58] (Indeed, few knew much about capitalism, either, but they were at least familiar with key features: markets, fluctuating prices, competition.) Last, the state secured obedience and coordination initially through threats, coercion, and terror, rather than through incentives, education, and open communication. Vast power disparities between state institutions and citizens meant overt resistance or rebellion was foolish, but the regime's all-stick-and-no-carrot tactics reliably generated indifference and evasion. It was in this unappealing environment that, during the late 1940s, the Rákosi team moved systematically to restructure Hungarian enterprises, accepting Moscow's guidance although not following Soviet practice scrupulously.[59] Brief sketches of the organizational landscape at the war's end and the sets of new institutions the Party state sought to install will suggest how vast was the job of configuring operable socialist enterprises in agriculture, construction and transport, commerce and manufacturing.

Before World War II, half of Hungary's arable land had been held in middling and great estates (hundreds to thousands of acres) and much of the rest in family farms (20–50 acres). An extensive 1945 reform, the broadest in Europe, appropriated church and company landholdings, dissolved most of the estates, and conjured up hundreds of thousands of mini-farms (under 10 acres) transferred to once-landless rural laborers. The new proprietors leaned toward subsistence agriculture, as they lacked sufficient equipment, capital and connections to attempt market operations. Roughly 40% of the 7.6 million confiscated acres remained in government hands, gradually being reconfigured chiefly as "state farms" (models for large-scale mechanization and modernization) but also as producer co-ops (in which families would collectively sow, till, and harvest, securing high yields to provision industrial/mining districts and cities).[60] At the outset of Party rule, however, "the hostility of the Hungarian peasantry to collective farming was so well known to the leaders of the Communist Part that they avoided the topic." Technology to support new and veteran farmers lay in a growing network of Soviet-style Tractor Stations (221 in 1949), whose monopoly in equipment purchasing assured that "the mechanization of Hungarian agriculture was resolved exclusively through the use of state-owned large machines." Private threshers and tractors were eventually confiscated, making all co-ops and individual farms dependent on rented technologies.[61] Such centralization resonated with the state's goal of managing agriculture so as to achieve full collectivization in due time, with sufficient surpluses spun off along the way to sustain non-farm populations and to provide exports earning hard-currencies that covered payments for machinery and materials from the West. These ambitious targets would not be easily met.

In construction and transport, Hungarian enterprises before 1949 were a mélange of private firms and state agencies. The Army, the state railways (MAV) and several state agencies sustained in-house construction units, as did some industrial corporations, taking on military projects, extending/replacing tracks, or building new production facilities. A host of smaller private firms handled home building and renovations, while countryside construction and repairs often involved family do-it-yourself projects. Meanwhile, MAV dominated rail freight and passenger transportation, including Budapest commuting, although narrow gauge private tracks did serve many mines and factories. Road hauling remained largely short-distance and horse-drawn; in urban areas, private trucking had a local clientele. Only Budapest operated a full transit system with trams, buses, and a one-line subway serving the Pest side of the Danube (1896). The socialist transformation little affected transport at first; however, once roadways were rebuilt, a state trucking agency displaced most private operations. The organization of construction, however, altered substantially. Rapid industrialization called for major construction investments in plant and facilities, transportation, and electric power supply and transmission. To facilitate these projects, the state created not only a Ministry of Construction (for major public works), but also construction units within other ministries (e.g., Heavy Industry, Mining). At the same time MAV retained its construction/repair units, as did the military. Nonetheless, housing authorities contracted with private, licensed builders to erect apartment blocks; and families and co-ops continued to work with smaller enterprises and individual craftsmen, often illegally. This crazy-quilt set-up triggered fierce, behind-the-scenes rivalries among ministries for funding, materials, skilled labor, logistics, and planning priorities, while the smaller players competed on the margins for supplies and reliable workers.[62]

Pre-communist commerce resembled that in Western Europe. Outside state purchasing for its monopolies and the military, private, often-family businesses carried on wholesaling and import-export functions which the Trianon territorial losses had substantially altered. Small cities like Miskolc and Szeged, once regional centers for agricultural commission sales, now stood quietly near Hungary's borders. The capital's earlier "dynamism" stalled, though the density of Budapest retail shops did compare favorably with that of Vienna or Munich. The total number of stores grew nationally, but this was not a good sign. It resulted from

> unfavorable postwar economic conditions, which prompted many who were unable to make a secure living in other ways to open little shops... The plethora of tiny shops was, however, not [just] an indication that the retailing system was well-developed, but also that it was over-extended and old-fashioned. Outside the capital, retail stores remained small, backward and undifferentiated.[63]

In Party theory, traders were unproductive parasites. Therefore, the state upended commercial networks through nationalizations of city department stores and wholesalers, denial of goods supplies to small shops, and consolidation of foreign and domestic trade under state agencies, including monopolized agricultural purchasing. To perform service trades like tailoring or home repair required membership in artisan cooperatives or special licenses. Thousands of stores closed permanently, with their properties requisitioned by the state, to be replaced by retail food chains like Közért,[64] known for shortages and surly staff, and rural consumers' cooperatives (FCC), which, being outside the capital, remained "backward" and undersupplied with needed factory-made goods. Still, as before, farmers hauled their surpluses (after required deliveries to state purchasing) to town and city markets for public sale, usually at higher-than-official prices that irregularly provoked raids by state "controllers." And, as before, unlicensed (illegal) craftsmen undertook home, tool, clothing, shoe, and watch repair everywhere, ignoring the state's lowball price schedules.

Manufacturing firms also converted to wholly new organizational forms after a series of nationalizations and state-sponsored startups. As noted, the Soviets took control of most heavy industrial firms, which had co-located in Budapest or clustered in eastern or western industrial cities. Major investments in expanded metal and chemical production capacity for large-scale "ministerial" firms followed, despite the insufficiency of Hungarian raw material supplies, other than bauxite for aluminum. Though also "ministerial," light industry plants (textiles, leather, clothing, printing) languished, many firms still operating with turn-of-the-century equipment. Meanwhile construction materials suppliers, scattered across the landscape, ran low-tech works located close to sources of heavy, low-value inputs (clay, stone, timber). The First Five Year Plan offered little to them.

As well, in Budapest and provincial industrial districts, small auxiliary workshops long thrived by taking on specialty jobs for leading metal, machine, electrical, or chemical enterprises. At first, the socialist state starved them for materials and many closed—some reviving by unlawfully taking off-the-books jobs. By 1950, finally recognizing their key roles in smoothing production, the state initiated a shop companion to its farm co-ops, the KTSZ,[65] enlisting craftsmen by trade to serve both consumer and manufacturing needs. "Extensive" KTSZs used hand labor and simple equipment to turn out both cheap and high-fashion shoes, clothing, and jewelry, plus combs, brushes, and small tools; "intensive" versions did tool and die work, precision metal-cutting and grinding, or fine cabinetry, employing more sophisticated technologies and often hard-to-get materials.[66] Last, a group of producers (and builders) operated under the supervision of authorities in each county, undertaking repairs (appliances, vehicles) and services (painting, carpentry), doing home handwork (pillows, knit goods, embroidery), or making local market goods (kitchen furniture, baskets).[67] In the perennial struggles for materials and supplies, they were at the end of the queue. "Ministerial" enterprises always had a higher priority, while battling among themselves for preference. Completely out of view, by the way, were yet other manufacturers producing military goods (arms, ammunition, vehicles), much of it for the USSR. Presumably, they had first call on all available inputs.

THE STORY ARC, 1949–1956

The Rákosi regime dominated Hungary from 1949 through 1953, overseeing successful completion of the reconstruction-centered Three Year Plan (1947–1949) and the launch of the First Five Year Plan (1950–1954), which favored funding heavy industry while seeking "the integrated development of all branches of the economy." Within months, the Korean War's outbreak triggered a sudden change: "to enhance war production, the USSR intervened radically in the management of Hungary's national economy," increasing output targets in "bauxite, alumina, aluminum, iron and steel." Unsurprisingly, these demands overwhelmed enterprises, yielding "considerable delays in production" and a failure to fulfill the "augmented" goals. Boosting outputs would have required rapid increases in coal and electricity supplies, which could only be achieved thorough long-term investments. Rákosi found this hard to swallow, and in early 1952, when announcing great advances during the Plan's first two years, he conceded that the coal sector missed its 1951 target "and production continues to lag this year." However, it proved useless to urge that enterprises maximize machine utilization, economize on materials and expenses, and make certain that outputs "meet export standards." By autumn 1953, "for all practical purposes, the Five Year Plan – that is, economic planning on a national scale – ha[d] been scrapped." Companies operated "only on the basis of temporary instructions," although "feverish preparations [were] being made with a view to opening up new sources of energy."[68]

Rákosi's political situation also eroded after Stalin's March 1953 demise. Although "surrounded by a cult of adulation," his regime fell out of favor with Moscow for overreaching with show trials and AVH "terror tactics," which even Beria called "inadmissible and intolerable." As "the large number of mostly unjustified sentences seemed to threaten the stability of the system," the Soviet leadership "reprimanded" Rákosi in June.[69] Resigning as prime minister in favor of his deputy, Imre Nagy, a former agriculture minister who "had not been implicated in the purges," Rákosi nonetheless retained his post as Party First Secretary. Nagy quickly announced significant shifts, asserting that "our economic policy, though aimed at building socialism, fails to apply the fundamental economic law of socialism: a constant rise in the population's standard of living." To achieve this:

> Consumer goods production would be encouraged at the expense of heavy industry which had hitherto been given preferential treatment. Collective farmers were to be allowed to leave the agricultural cooperatives and take their own property with them. He also promised a revision of judicial practices which had offended "Socialist law," along with the closure of internment camps and an end to arbitrary police methods.[70]

Much of this was accomplished through decrees and policy proclamations, but the Stalinists soon fought back shrewdly to derail Nagy's "New Course." Popular reception of the promised changes was enthusiastic, but led to unanticipated consequences. Discipline in factories and building sites slipped badly; absenteeism increased noticeably and output slumped. In rural districts, canceling fines for private farmers' deficient compulsory deliveries brought widespread suspension of all deliveries. A decree increasing co-op members' family garden plot sizes triggered the abandonment of work on collective fields. Within weeks, Rákosi and his "old course" allies commenced efforts "to slow the implementation of the program."[71] By November 1953, the scope of the opposition became clear—arising not just from the First Secretary's own Political Committee, but also from the National Planning Office and the "Ministries for Heavy and Light Industry, Heavy Machine Construction and for the Iron and Steel Industry."[72]

Nagy, controlling the Party Central Committee and its newspaper, defended prioritizing consumer goods and agricultural development; but rural households understood his policy changes as ending the era of tight control. By January 1954, Deputy PM András Hegedűs reported that 180,000 TSZ members had withdrawn from coops, roughly 40% of the mid-1953 total. Worse, 2.5 million acres "lay untilled, although the country was short of food." Yet by fall the tilt toward light industry had taken effect, with "entire factories... switched away from heavy industrial production to the output of consumer goods." By year's end after "rationalization measures," overstaffed heavy industrial plants would dismiss a quarter million workers. Those discharged retained access to health care and family allowances for six months, also receiving four weeks discharge pay, but this was a feeble response. The New Course began to retreat,

> accompanied by a deluge of confessions that the Hungarian economy is now in extremely bad shape. Industrial production is said to be "stagnant," agricultural production "insufficient," and reserves have apparently almost been depleted. "We were day dreaming chasing cotton growing, while in the meantime our wheat production became so poor that it is almost unparalleled in our history," *one broadcast said*. The effort... to improve living conditions is now admitted to have failed substantially.[73]

Consistent with the 1955 CIA assessment opening this chapter, a New York college student visiting Hungary in summer 1954, found "the most outspoken resentment against the Government."

> I spoke with hundreds of persons. I found not one who was not thoroughly disgusted with the Communist Government. Their grievances are mostly economic... "They laugh at the bourgeois," a railway conductor told me. "I'll tell you a secret," he moved closer and whispered in my ear. "The bourgeois were better, because the bourgeois paid. The Communists only promise." He pointed to his tattered uniform.[74]

What was not a secret was that Nagy's project was falling apart. Attempting to stimulate farm output, in late 1953 his administration had reauthorized public market sales by "private agricultural producers and traders." This incentive had been insufficient, as had the tandem re-licensing of "private small scale industry and retail trading." Also, such steps caused "concern" in Moscow, suggesting backsliding toward capitalist practice.[75] More troubling, they did not work as planned, and news of that failure had widely circulated. By early 1955 their effect had been

42   P. SCRANTON

to intensify the resistance of the peasants, who are withholding delivery of their products and, in anticipation of further concessions, are refusing to pay taxes. The regime has been unable to keep its promise to increase food supplies for factory workers. Morale and production in the factories have declined correspondingly. In some cases officials responsible for crop collections have conspired with the peasants to frustrate the regime's production plans, *according to stories appearing in the Hungarian press.*[76]

Such fraud was not unusual in Stalinist Hungary, but for it to be documented in newspaper reports and to have planning failures announced on the radio was remarkable.

Rákosi and his colleagues returned to power in April 1955, restoring earlier commitments to "forcing heavy industry" that Nagy had sidelined. Signs of this reversion were evident in January, when the often-outspoken Zoltán Vas, head of the Council of Ministers Secretariat, was suddenly demoted to the "weightless" post of Deputy Minister of Foreign Trade. In an October 1954 speech, Vas had described the plan for making Hungary a center of steel production as a "megalomaniac swindle."[77] Clever, but no longer suitable a few months later as the Stalinist orthodox reassumed power. András Hegedűs replaced Nagy as Prime Minister, a favor Nagy would briefly reciprocate during the 1956 revolt.[78] In the interim the Party stripped Nagy of his offices and terminated his membership, assigning him responsibility for all failed policies. Yet two things of significance resulted from the New Course experiment. First, Stalinism revived was not Stalinism as before. The prisons were not refilled; coercing the peasants continued, but the AVH receded from view. As the *New York Times* observed: "The difference in the political climate is perhaps best indicated by the fact that Mr. Nagy, although he lost his job, kept his liberty and is still in Budapest."[79] Second, in 1955 citizens and journalists no longer cringed before the Party state. Western visitors reported "that contempt for the regime rather than fear of it is the dominant feeling of the majority of the Hungarian people with whom they spoke." The *Times'* Jack Raymond related his contacts with Budapest workers and shopkeepers. Of one shoemaker, he noted:

Without knowing who the visitor might be, he responded quickly to questions about business. He complained about taxes, about economic regulations in general, and about the regime. The lack of inhibition in complaining appeared to the visitor completely out of joint with reports one heard of th[is] Iron Curtain country and the presence everywhere in Budapest of people in uniform.[80]

His colleague John MacCormac echoed such sentiments when discussing daily newspapers:

The Communist press is loud with complaints about inadequacies. It publishes acrid comment about shoes that don't match, textile colors that run, stockings that disintegrate or summer clothes offered for sale in winter, not to speak of adulterated food.... [Such] liberty as Hungarians enjoy – and they actually enjoy far more than one would imagine – comes from their apparent ability to finagle their way among a multitude of official ordinances.[81]

Finagling the rules was a crucial skill in the theft economy; building socialism was wholly beside the point.

A Note on the Forint

Throughout the socialist era, Hungary's currency unit was the *forint*, which succeeded the Horthy-era *pengo* after the postwar hyperinflation and is still in use today. Like other Bloc currencies it was not freely convertible into capitalist Marks, Francs, Pounds, or Dollars. Formally, 11.8 forints equaled US$1, a rate that continued in force through 1967,[82] but such rates were generally of no interest to workers and consumers. That rate also makes value comparisons from forints to dollars more gestural than sensible. It's important to recognize that prices and wages in Hungary were set arbitrarily by state agencies and that the relation between earnings and consumption was thus also artificial, in the sense that none of them was regulated by market tests in which price balances supply and demand. However, in the theft economy, the official exchange rate for forints was irrelevant when import-export transactions were involved or when illegal imports, like razor blades or silk scarves, were being traded. In the first case, state agencies could not trade Hungarian goods for Western machinery at 11.8 ft per USD equivalent value of the imported items, but instead, due to their lack of financial leverage (and the often marginal quality of what they were offering) had to ship 20, 30, or 40 forints worth of, say, fruit preserves for each USD worth of a Swiss textile loom. The Soviets also overvalued the ruble when cutting comparable deals, so Hungary's official rate was fungible indeed. On the black market, similar devaluations of the forint took place. In some cases, deals for prized imports were made only in US currency, so local buyers had to secure actual dollars at whatever rate illicit traders demanded, usually more than double the state's 11.8. Where purchases could be made with forints, place- and goods-specific multipliers lowered the forint's purchasing power, though evidently moreso with fine silks than with shaving accessories.

These issues were, however, tangential to all-domestic transactions. There the challenge was stretching incomes to manage consumption within a system of fixed state pricing that made housing cheap, public services (transit, health care, education) cheap or free, but many necessities like food and clothing expensive relative to earnings. Thus it's crucial to get a sense of what one or a thousand forints could buy and by extension what a monthly budget might look like for a manager or a worker. (Farm life took shape mostly outside this sphere, centering on seasonal and annual returns.) A female bus conductor, age 30, reported that her 1956 base income was 630 ft/month, which rose to 900 when overtime and her share of direct ticket sales were added, then shrank to 780 once taxes, dues, insurance, and the forced "Peace Loan" to the state were deducted. Her husband, a bus driver, earned 1300 ft/mo, taking home 1000–1100, the couple's income summing to over 1800 ft. Their apartment cost a modest 280 ft/mo, but food and clothing were expensive—three days pay for a kilogram of salami, a month of his salary for a pair of "custom-made boots," needed because the state store shoes "were of a very inferior quality." Only by skimping on food could they afford the occasional film or theater ticket (about 3–10 ft).[83] Incomes for those at the peaks of the administrative or managerial hierarchy were appreciably, but not enormously, larger—a senior bank official received 3,000 ft/mo, a ministry director perhaps 5,000, enterprise directors 3,000 or more, chief engineers, ca. 2500 and the Budapest opera orchestra conductor, 6,000. This meant few restrictions on food purchasing, but a man's Csepel bicycle and a baby carriage each cost 1,000; a second-quality worsted wool suit, 1,350–2,000; and ordinary men's shoes, 400. These not-so-expensive shoes "creaked like hell," but a pair of custom made were twice the price or more.[84] Converting forint prices into dollars is not terribly revealing (a baby carriage cost US$84 in 1955, while a month's rent was $24), except when looking at large sums invested in construction or manufacturing. In consequence, such conversions are usually avoided in the following chapters.

NOTES

1. A. J. Goldberg, "Budapest Now a City of Sweepers," *New York Times*, 27 June 1945, 7.
2. CIA, Information Report, "Foreign Holdings in Hungary," 4 October 1948 (Confidential, CIA-RDP82-00457R001900410007-3), 3.
3. CIA, National Intelligence Estimate, 12.5-55, "Current Situation and Probable Developments in Hungary," 29 March 1955 (Secret, CIA-RDP79R01012A005400040004-6), 1,4.
4. "Economic Losses of Hungary During the War," *Hungaria*, Munich, 13 March 1953, 1 (CIA translation, Unclassified, CIA-RDP80-00809A000700170298-2).
5. Jörg Hoensch, *A History of Modern Hungary, 1867–1994*, Harlow: Longman, 1996, 174–76.
6. Charles Gati, "From Liberation to Revolution, 1945–1956," in *A History of Hungary*, Peter Sugar and Péter Hanák, eds., Bloomington: Indiana University Press, 1990, 368–83.
7. Cold War scholars use the term Sovietization to designate the compulsory copying of Russian policies and practices, here reinforced by Soviet military, technical and political personnel overseeing Hungary's principal agencies and enterprises. See, for one example, Zsuzsanna Varga, *The Hungarian Agricultural Miracle? Sovietization and Americanization in a Communist Country*, London: Lexington Books, 2021.
8. In Hungary, theft involved not just property, but time, space, categories, and ideas, including devious maneuvers concerning quotas, costs, and profits.
9. John MacCormac, "Hungary Viewed as Loser in Pact," *New York Times*, 25 September 1945, 9.
10. Idem., "Hungary Hopeful on Stabilization," *New York Times*, 23 April 1946, 10.
11. Pierre Siklos, *War Finance, Hyperinflation and Stabilization in Hungary, 1938–1948*, New York: St. Martins, 1991; "Inflation Becomes Nightmare in Hungary," *New York Times*, 4 April 1946, 4.

12. *Államvédelmi Hatóság*, the political police.
13. For detailed analysis of the immediate postwar years, see Eric Roman, *Hungary and the Victor Powers, 1946–1950*, New York: St. Martins, 1996. For discussion of early state planning, see Béla Balassa, *The Hungarian Experience in Economic Planning*, New Haven: Yale University Press, 1959.
14. Columbia University Research Project on Hungary (CURPH), Interview No. 562, August 1957, 8, Open Society Archives, Budapest, HU OSA 414-0-2-333 [emphasis added]. Accessible at https://catalog.osaarchivum.org/?f%5Bdigital_collection%5D%5B%5D=CURPH+Interviews+with+1956+Hungarian+Refugees.
15. CURPH, Interview No. 506 (György Faludy), July 1957, 33–34, HU OSA 414-0-2-304
16. C. L. Sulzbereger, "Economic Program Chains Hungarians," *New York Times*, 23 June 1953, 12.
17. The pervasiveness of comparable behavior in the postwar USSR has been documented and analyzed in two recent studies: James Heinzen, *The Art of the Bribe: Corruption Under Stalin, 1943–1953*, New Haven: Yale University Press, 2016, and Juliette Cadiot, *La société des voleurs: Propriété et socialisme sur Staline*, Paris: Editions EHESS, 2021.
18. Nigel Swain, *Hungary: The Rise and Fall of Feasible Socialism*, London: Verso, 1992, 42–43; Ivan Berend and György Ránki, *Hungary: A Century of Economic Development*, Newton Abbot: David and Charles, 1974, 188–89.
19. CIA National Intelligence Survey, *Hungary: Government and Politics*, 1973, 6–8 (Secret, CIA–RDP01-00707R000200110039-1) [Emphasis added].
20. The Interior Ministry exercised policing functions, as is common in Europe, rather than overseeing public lands, natural resources and national parks, as is the American approach. See https://www.doi.gov/about (accessed 11 January 2021).
21. CIA, *Hungary: Government*, 9–11.
22. In 1950, the Industrial department's divisions were Mining, Metallurgy & Heavy Industry, Electrical, Materials and Construction, Lumber, Textiles, Leather, Chemicals, and Agricultural Machines. Director Zoltán Vas (1949–1953) added a Labor department. The Office's 17 core units also included departments for Finance, Military, Construction, Materials, Trade, and Communications, along

with Culture, Statistics, Control, and Press. The military unit worked on "strict secrecy" rules. See CIA, "Planning Office of the Hungarian Government," 3 February 1950, 1–3 (Confidential, CIA-RDP82- 00457R004200360001-9).

23. Balassa, *Economic Planning*, 56–58.

24. In the late 1940s, the Workers' Party expelled many thousands of members who had joined in the postwar rush.. Poorly schooled in Marxism-Leninism and (rightly) suspected of opportunism or closet nationalism, they were purged in order to achieve tightly-disciplined and politically reliable forces to push nationalization, collectivization, and collective obedience. At a minimum the results were mixed. In a second purge following the '56 revolt, Hoensch estimates that ca. 90 percent of the Party's 900,000 members were dismissed. See Martin Mevius, *Agents of Moscow: The Hungarian Communist Party and the Origins of Socialist Patriotism, 1941–1953*, Oxford: Oxford University Press, 2005, Ch. 10, and Hoensch, *History of Modern Hungary*, 226.

25. Balassa, *Economic Planning*, 59–62. In exile after 1956, Balassa completed a doctorate at Yale, the basis for the book cited, then became a Johns Hopkins professor and consulted with the World Bank on development economics.

26. Ibid., 85. Such administrative overkill was a core finding of János Kornai's 1957 dissertation, translated into English and published two years later: *Overcentralization in Economic Administration: A Critical Analysis Based on Experience in Hungarian Light Industry*, Oxford: Oxford University Press, 1959.

27. During the 1956 revolt, rebels broke into Budapest state security headquarters and were amazed to find entire rooms stacked with unprocessed reports, neither evaluated nor filed (CURPH Interview No. 626, 1957, HU OSA 414-0-2-320. The respondent was a historian invited to assess this information trove in the uprising's first days; he soon relocated to Britain).

28. CURPH Interview No. 606, 10-12, HU OSA 414-0-2-344.

29. Paul Ignotus, "The AVH: Symbol of Terror," *Problems of Communism* 6 (September–October 1957): 19–25; CIA, *Hungary: Government*, 44–45. The Party also initially welcomed the "little Arrow-Cross people," workers and peasants whose "compromised political records" assured their obedience to directives (21).

30. *Naródnyy Komissariát Vnútrennikh Del* (People's Commissariat for Internal Affairs), the Soviet secret police.
31. Arthur Garamvölgyi, "The Story of the AVO," *Nyugati Hirnök* (Western Herald), Nos. 5–6, St. Cloud, France, 1950, 1–2 (Restricted, CIA-RPD 80-00809A000600300264-5). *NH* (1947–1952) was an émigré journal sponsored by remnants of displaced centrist and peasant parties. Waves of postwar emigrants created a diverse exile press, much of it in Latin America and the UK under the control of ex-Nazis. See Robert Major, "The Hungarian Emigrant Press," *Journalism Quarterly* 32(1955): 205–8.
32. Garamvölgyi, "Story," 3; László Borhi, *Hungary in the Cold War, 1945–1956*, Budapest: Central European University Press, 2004, 207.
33. CIA Information Report, "The Position of the AVH," 14 June 1954, 1–4 (Secret, CIA-RDP80-00809A0005004\820146-6) [hereafter CIAIR]. Border Guard training was hazardous, as it regularly included work clearing mine fields laid down in the 1940s by Hungarian and German forces [CIA Information Report, "AVO Border Guard Training and Duty," 27 March 1957, 3 (Confidential, CIA-RDP80T00246A000700210001-0)].
34. A classic bit of Hungarian black humor captures this neatly. God is checking through his ledgers and discovers that a Hungarian who was supposed to have departed this life had been overlooked. So he calls up the Grim Reaper and assigns him the task of fetching this laggard. Grumbling all the way about the extra work, the Reaper goes to the man's house well after midnight and bangs on the door. The farmer comes downstairs in his robe and asks "Who's there?" "Death," says the Reaper. "Oh, fine," comes the reply, "I thought it might be the secret police."
35. Józeph Hegedűs and Ivan Tosics, "Housing Classes and Housing Policy: Some Changes in the Budapest Housing Market," *International Journal of Urban and Regional Research* 7(1983): 467–94; "Class Deportations Resumed in Hungary," *New York Times*, 29 November 1951, 3; "Hungarian Tells of New Terrors," Ibid., 9 August 1952, 3; George May, "Behind the Curtain in Hungary," Ibid., 15 March 1953, SM 10.
36. Béla Balassa, "My Life Philosophy," *American Economist* 33:1(Spring 1989): 13–23. Balassa was able to relocate to his

parents' farm in the west, where he worked for 18 months in fields and forests and in construction, until the first Nagy regime revoked deportations. See also "Forced Labor in Hungary," *Neue Zuercher Zeitung*, 26 October 1952, CIA Information from Foreign Documents, 5 February 1953 (unclassified, released 25 October 2011, CIA-RDP80-00809A000700100442-9).

37. Barbara Bank, "The Hungarian 'Gulag,' 1945–53," in *NEB Yearbook 2016–2017*, Réka Kiss and Zsolt Horváth, eds., Budapest: Committee of National Remembrance, 2018, 87–120.

38. Ignotus, "The AVH," 21–23. Borhi reports that Rakosi's brother Zoltán Bíró asserted that in 1953 over a half million "hostile elements" still remained in Hungary, in a population of less than 10 million. Beria indicated that before 1953, 1.5 million had been "subjected to legal proceedings" (*Hungary in the Cold War*, 211).

39. Bothi, 139–84.

40. "Economic Losses of Hungary," 1–3. Ironically, the National Bank did indirectly assist recovery, as it approved stacks of loan applications in 1945–1946, just as the pengo hyperinflation gathered momentum. Those who had borrowed soon repaid their loans in devalued currency, while keeping the machinery or materials purchased with this financing. See William Bomberger and Gail Makinen, "The Hungarian Hyperinflation and Stabilization of 1945–1946," *Journal of Political Economy*, 91 (1983): 801–24. The gold reserves had been "carried away by Germany," but US forces discovered them in Austria and returned them to Budapest (about US$60 million worth). See J.A.S., "Hungary's Post-War Economic Difficulties," *The World Today* [Royal Institute of International Affairs] 3(1947): 353–63.

41. J.A.S., "Hungary's Post-War," 354.

42. Most academic discussion of Soviet trophy hunting has concerned art and collectibles, some of which have been restored to Hungary. See Konstantin Akinsha, "Stalin's Decrees and Soviet Trophy Brigades," *International Journal of Cultural Property* 17:2(2010): 195–216, and Jennifer Otterson, "Art Restitution in Hungary," unpublished seminar paper, Columbia University, 2011, which focuses on "trophy books," particularly an early modern religious library removed to Gorky (accessed via Google Scholar, 14 January 2021).

43. Ő Armá, "Hungarian Reparations Deliveries to the USSR in 1945," Enclosure to Report No. R-87-50, ID688588, Budapest, 24 July 1950 (Confidential, CIA-RDP32-00039R000200020060-2). From internal evidence, this document evidently passed through the Allied Control Commission to the US Army, which forwarded it to Washington. On these commissions, one per conquered country, see "Allied Control Councils and Commissions," *International Organization* 1(1947): 162–70. On Hungary's ACC, see David Reynolds, "The Roots of Communist Hungary in the Allied Occupation – The Allied Control Commission of Budapest, Parts I-IV," *Hungarian Review*, 11 (January, March, May and July 2020): unpaginated (accessed 15 January 2021).

44. 'Hungarian Reparations Deliveries," 12. I suspect that the 3.8 million "phylloxera-resistant American grapevines" was a typo, as it's several orders of magnitude larger than the "55,000 European grapevines" following.

45. Laszlo Borhi, "The Merchants of the Kremlin: The Economic Roots of Soviet Expansion in Hungary," Working Paper No. 28, Cold War International History Project, Woodrow Wilson International Center for Scholars, June 2000 (accessed 15 January 2021).

46. Borhi, *Hungary in the Cold War*, 145–46.

47. CIAIR, "Soviet Troops in Hungary," 9 June 1948 (Secret, CIA-RDP82-00457R001500990003-8).

48. Oil here refers to sunflower oil; "oil products" to seed cake (for fodder). Hungary was a major producer of both.

49. J.A.S., "Hungary's Post-War," 357–58; John MacCormac, "Hungarians Fear Soviet Wants All," *New York Times*, 18 October 1945, 8; Albion Ross, "Hungary to Slash Living Standards," Ibid., 28 June 1946, 6. For the administration of these provisions, see CIA Intelligence Report, "Hungarian Reparations," 2 February 1948 (Secret, CIA-RDP82-00457R001300130006-4).

50. Y. Burman, ed., "Products of Soviet Machine-Building and Electrical Engineering Enterprises in Hungary," Budapest 1948, translated 1951 (Secret, CIA-RDP80-00809A000600380181-9).

51. Borhi, *Hungary in the Cold War*, 158–59. Most of these "were sold back to the Hungarian state at a hefty price" in 1952. (159) CIA assessed that Stalin "returned about 500

units (!) of Soviet-administered German assets… to consolidate Soviet holdings in Hungary, streamline their administration, and discard unprofitable enterprises." CIAIR, "Return of Soviet Administered German Assets," 25 July 1952 (Secret, CIA-RDP82-00457R013100340005-8) Reportedly, workers objected to these returns because "Russian supervisors are interested chiefly in comfortable living and passable production rates," whereas Hungarian Communist foremen "were stricter than Soviet managers" in pushing for higher output.

52. Albion Ross, "Hungary's Trade Shifts to Soviet," *New York Times*, 28 May 1947, 10; C. L. Sulzberger, "Soviet Trade Grip on Hungary Shown,' Ibid., 5 May 1948, 13. Borhi, *Hungary in the Cold War*, 161–74.

53. CIAIR, "Russians Holding Influential Positions in Hungary," 22 September 1951 (Secret, CIA-RDP82-00457R008400370002-1). For a 1953 list of Russian technicians continuing to manage "returned" firms, see CIAIR, "Soviet Technicians in Hungary," 23 June 1953, 1–3 (Secret, CIA-RDP80-oo810A001500800001-6).

54. CIAIR, "Positions of Soviet Advisors and Technicians," 25 June 1953, 1 (Secret, CIA RDP82-0047R000300100003-3). The plant was in northern Komárom County along the Danube, which forms the border between Slovakia and Hungary.

55. CIAIR, "Members of the Management of the Meszhart Shipping Company," 14 December 1953 (Secret, CIA-RDP80-00810A003100620008-1). Meszhart closed in 1954, supposedly due to "a lack of resources."

56. See Valerie Bunce, "Should Transitologists Be Grounded?" *Slavic Review* 54(1995): 111–27; and Jordan Gans-Morse, "Searching for Transitologists," *Post-Soviet Affairs* 20:4(2004): 320–49.

57. About 80% of the 358 CURPH interviews included a section on postwar consumption conditions through 1956. Universally, factory and farm responders noted sharp declines in food and clothing provision after 1949. Exiles who had held high posts in ministries and Party institutions did not, however, confront the oft-reported choice between buying food and clothing.

58. The Party had few adherents in the countryside; its strongholds were in Budapest and outlying industrial or mining districts, as the 1945 election results indicated.

52   P. SCRANTON

59. For example, the configuration of socializing agriculture sharply diverged from Russian models. See Varga, *Hungarian Agricultural Miracle*, Ch. 2.

60. Berend and Ranki, *Hungary*, 185–87. This transfer involved over a third of the nation's arable lands; over 600,000 families received land, including the landless and those already holding fewer than seven acres. Midsize private farms were not affected at this stage.

61. Varga, *Hungary's Agricultural Miracle*, 37–44. State farms had their own machinery, but could secure harvest supplements and repairs and overhauls from tractor stations, as needed.

62. Balassa, *Economic Planning*, 81–87, 145–58.

63. Berend and Ranki, *Hungary*, 145. The FIRE sector was similarly regarded. The Rakosi government consolidated finance/banking and insurance into national-scale agencies, and real estate transactions became bureaucratic functions, whether among firms or between the state and households.

64. Acronym of *Községi Élelmiszerkereskedelmi Rt* (Municipality Food Trade Joint-Stock Company).

65. *Kisipari Termelöszövetkezet* (Small Industrial Producers' Cooperative).

66. Gábor Kertezi, "Two Types of Development of Small-Scale Industry in Hungary," *Acta Oeconomica* 28:1/2(1982): 71–86.

67. CIA, Information from Foreign Documents, "Hungary Authorizes Local Councils to Direct Enterprises," Tanácsok [Council], Budapest, 15 October 1950 (Confidential, CIA-RDP80-00809A000600370734-6) [hereafter CIAIFD].

68. CIAIR, "Economic Planning: Metallurgy, Aluminum and Power Production," 29 October 1953 (Secret, CIA-RDP80-00810A002700440003-1); *Szabad Nep*, Budapest, 13 & 15 January 1952 (Restricted, CIA-RDP80-00809A000700060150-7). These issues of power and materials were well understood. The Hungarian Academy of Sciences published an 841-page report on them in 1951. For a summary, see CIAIFD, "Problems of Material and Power Supply in Hungary," Budapest, 1951, 1–24 (Confidential, CIA-RDP80-00809A000700160189-4).

69. Bothi, *Hungary in the Cold War*, 205, 213.

70. János Rainer, "The New Course in Hungary in 1953," Working Paper 38, Cold War International History Project, Woodrow Wilson Center, Washington, DC, June 2002, 26; Hoersch, *History*

of Modern Hungary, 211–12. Rainer concludes that nearly 16,000 persons were released from prisons, over one-third of those held ("New Course," 46).

71. "Hungary Puts Brakes on Her New Program," *New York Times*, 25 July 1953, 3; John MacCormac, "Hungary Is Short of Bread Grains," Ibid., 28 October 1953, 6; Rainer, "New Course," 39–41.

72. John MacCormac, "Old Guard Scored by Hungarian Reds," *New York Times*, 7 November 1953, 4.

73. "Hungary Farmers Quit Cooperatives," *New York Times*, 13 January 1954, 6; "Hungary Aids Jobless," Ibid., 10 October 1954, 5; Harry Schwartz, "Hungary Turning to Light Industry," Ibid., 31 October 1954, 6 (emphasis added); Dana Adams Schmidt, "Dilemma on Food Plagues Hungary," Ibid., 19 January 1955, 6.

74. Andrew Meisels, "Open Resentment Found in Hungary," *New York Times*, 10 October 1954, 5.

75. Rainer, "New Course," 49–50.

76. Schmidt, "Dilemma on Food," 6 (emphasis added).

77. https://hu.wikipedia.org/wiki/Vas_Zoltán_(politikus) (accessed 25 January 2021); John MacCormac, "Hungary Reverts to Basic Industry," *New York Times*, 26 January 1955, 10; Idem., "Satellite Events Heralded Change," Ibid., 9 February 1955, 10; Hoensch, *History of Modern Hungary*, 214.

78. Nagy replaced Hegedus on 26 October 1956; his second PM term ended with the 4 November Soviet invasion.

79. John MacCormac, "Rákosi Restores Hold on Hungary," *New York Times*, 25 October 1955, 5.

80. Harry Schwartz, Hungarian Shift Tied to Failures," *New York Times*, 10 March 1955, 2; Jack Raymond, "Hungarians Lack Fear of Regime," Ibid., 18 September 1955, 10.

81. John MacCormac, "Once Gay Budapest Now Dull," *New York Times*, 6 November 1955, 27.

82. https://arfolyam.iridium.hu/en-US/USD/1960-05 (accessed 17 July 2021).

83. CURPH Interview No. 74-F, July 1957, 26–29, HU OSA 414-0-2-73.

84. RFEFR, "Prices and Wages," 23 July 1955, HU OSA 300-1-2-60354.

CHAPTER 3

Agriculture from Stalinism to the Revolt

"Grumbling against the regime and general dissatisfaction with political and economic conditions were constant. The Hungarian peasantry sabotaged compulsory planned deliveries wherever it could. Where there was a possibility to avoid control, as for example in the raising and harvesting of corn, the government was never able to achieve more than a 70% completion of its crop delivery program."
—Analyst, Central Bureau of Statistics, Budapest, 1948–1955[1]

"There was also sabotage in connection with compulsory deliveries.... The local council chairman wanted to take away our hogs. A policeman came with him but we knew him well. My father hit the local council chairman over the head with a pitchfork. No criminal proceedings were launched against him and even our hogs remained at home."
—Son of a Szabolcs County farmer/shoemaker, 1957.[2]

"This year's spring sowing will require extraordinary efforts to make up for the consequences of last year's drought and mismanagement. Mistakes worse than any since the liberation made by the Ministry of Agriculture and subordinate officials have aggravated the situation."
—Imre Nagy, 23 February 1953[3]

"Given equal advantages and equal conditions of production, the individual peasant holdings would clearly outstrip... the collectives or State Farms... [I]n spite of the disadvantages under which they operate, the

© The Author(s), under exclusive license to Springer Nature Switzerland AG 2022
P. Scranton, *Business Practice in Socialist Hungary, Volume 1*, Palgrave Debates in Business History,
https://doi.org/10.1007/978-3-030-89184-8_3

55

gross production of the individual peasants per hectare is higher than that of the collectives."
—RFE Background Report, 1958[4]

Farming has long been one of the most intricate and contingent of economic practices. So many things can go wrong across the months from sowing to harvest and many more reversals may occur before human, animal, or industrial consumption proceeds. In Hungary's diverse landscape, soils, seed quality, weather, and water all varied widely, periodically, and unreliably. A hailstorm in a vineyard or an orchard invaded by pests could devastate a year's output, negating the husbandman's labors. Keeping livestock healthy was a perennial challenge; even tiny bees could be menaced by yet-tinier mites. Moreover, agricultural knowledge was spatially situated—social, historical, and local, not universal and timeless, pragmatic not scientific. Some of it was sedimented practice, infused with religious customs and cultural rituals. In mid-century Hungary, only a fraction of agricultural knowledge was "modern." Although veterinarians and soil chemists had been carefully trained since Hapsburg times, they had not penetrated far into rural districts.

The animating agricultural illusion of the postwar decade was that Sovietization would transform Hungary's "backward" practices into an engine for socialist development, delivering vast surpluses to non-farm populations while filling export trade requirements. Revenues from state purchasing would enable farm households to discard outdated traditions and participate in socialist consumption. Electrification, tractors, and efficient machinery would elevate standards of living and reduce the average "socially necessary labor time"[5] for production, thereby releasing surplus rural dwellers for industrial employment. Producer cooperatives (TSZs) would integrate planning and organizational capabilities with up-to-date agricultural science, using farm labor effectively and reducing waste while steadily raising yields. The smooth linearities and interdependencies of these expected relationships should have sounded warning bells, but did not. Their symmetries contrasted sharply with the lived experience of farming, its irregularities, particularities, and uncertainties. State actors finessed the sharp differences in scale and condition between Hungary and the Soviet Union, on whose processes they modeled their expectations. Planners also ignored the tragedy forced collectivization brought to the USSR's pre-war history.

3 AGRICULTURE FROM STALINISM TO THE REVOLT   57

Implementing a program for socializing agriculture brought two rationalities into direct confrontation. Hungary's farmers understood what they were doing and how to go about it, although their approaches differed by location and production orientation (for field crops, seasonal vegetables, orchards and vineyards, livestock, industrial crops [sunflowers, sugar beets], deployed in various combinations). They recognized that some crops demanded ongoing labor (corn and sugar beets need hoeing) and others did not (wheat, rye) and that, while some animals governed human routines (milk cows, particularly), others not so much (pigs, sheep). Farmers' situational knowledgeability entailed accepting risks (weather, prices) and limitations (matching plantings to available labor). Such unsystematic, practical rationality was unacceptable in planners' view, precisely because of its localism, sustainability, lack of ambition, and routines without supervision, and consequently, the absence of collective goals and strategies. To supersede such approaches, the state would mobilize socialist rationality to transform great estates into high-productivity model farms and would foster cooperatives in which households would pool their land, allocate crops wisely to increase yields and work collectively to build socialism. The state would fund capital improvements, provide trained agronomists and administrators, and guarantee crop purchases. Households would share fairly in year-end profits, although ministries would subsidize deficits, if necessary. Who could not leap at such opportunities?

This head-to-head clash between the promised and the practiced is mischaracterized, however, when simplified into an unequal contest between state initiative and peasant resistance. In a modernist context privileging innovation and progress, the state stands as a prime mover, its targets dismissed as "backward." Yet from the actors' situated perspectives, the unfolding struggle proved more spiky and contingent, with strategies enacted on both sides. The state undertook a forcible reconfiguration of rural production, based on a host of homogenizing assumptions (e.g., holdings could readily be merged and cultivated with tractors; co-ops would be more profitable than household farms). To do so, it created a cluster of organizations, agents, and sanctions/rewards, using its bureaucratic power to compel compliance. This is all well documented in the literature, contemporary and scholarly. Not so obvious were the coping strategies devised by rural folks responding to the state's collectivizing tactics. Robert Chia and Robin Holt explained this with precision:

The key point... is that strategy and consistency of action can emerge non-deliberately through a profusion of local interventions directed toward dealing with immediate concerns. These local coping actions may actually give rise to a strategic consistency even in the absence of prior specified goals. In other words, attending to and dealing with the problems, obstacles and concerns confronted in the here and now may actually serve to clarify and shape the initially vague and inarticulate aspirations behind such coping actions with sufficient consistency that, in retrospect, they may appear to constitute a recognizable 'strategy.' *We often act and react knowing what we do not want*, rather than in response to any predefined goals.[6]

Indeed, farmers persistently acted to reject, deflect, or undermine the socialist project, knowing what they did not want. Their tactics, which James Scott memorably described as "weapons of the weak," involved "sabotage, foot-dragging, evasion, false compliance, pilfering, feigned ignorance, and slander."[7] These and other maneuvers (e.g., fraud) surfaced routinely in construction, commerce, and manufacturing as well. Appreciating this dynamic is central to understanding both the recursive emergence of Hungary's theft economy, as well as the deployment of state agents' reciprocal deceptions and brutalities.

Agricultural enterprises fell into three classes during the Stalinist decade: state farms, independent (private) farms, and producer cooperatives (TSZs). As late as 1952, Hungary's 500 state farms occupied just 12% of all arable land, household farms 74%, and co-ops, numbering 4,500 after diligent campaigning, about 14%.[8] As state farms and their allied machine tractor stations (MTS) exemplified and anchored collectivization, exploring their operations will be the initial task here. Because individual land holders were the greatest obstacle to achieving that project, their activities and the collectivizing pressures they endured will frame the chapter's second topic. State-supported TSZs and their initiatives to meet plan targets and generate efficiencies will anchor the closing section. Together, these three groups illuminate the persistent contingencies and disappointments attending efforts to establish socialist agriculture. Before 1956, the cohort of state farms stabilized in the high 400s, private lands gradually diminished, but TSZs waxed, waned, and waxed again. When Imre Nagy relaxed state controls in 1953 (despite local officials' fierce opposition), several hundred thousand co-op members withdrew, demanding the return of their land (and equipment, in some places). Consequent on Nagy's dismissal, Party and agency operatives cajoled and coerced former members to rejoin, an effort still under way when the revolt shattered every sort of plan. In 1955, a UK observer summarized: "The production of the State Farms, which are short of skilled technicians and labour, remains unsatisfactory. A large proportion of the agricultural co-operatives, despite their recent reform, still produce less than the individual peasants. [Moreover,] only 51% of the tractors ordered had been delivered by October 1954."[9] Such problems and shortcomings persisted.

STATE FARMS AND TRACTOR STATIONS: EMULATING SOVIET PRACTICE

State farms came in many sizes and shapes, ranging from smallish 3,000 acre establishments to the huge Eger complex (Heves county), sprawling across a quarter million acres of plowland, meadows, vineyards, and forests. Under the supervision of the State Farms and Forests Ministry (a different agency oversaw TSZs and private farms), each was "an independent community with its own administration, including such things as an agricultural machinery center, dairies, a stock raising division, a poultry division, grocery stores, taverns, a physician, and police guards." At 26,000 acres in 1953, Borsod county's sizable Putnok enterprise, operating near the Slovak border, represented "a typical example." Including several villages featuring the local "grocery, clothing and spirits stores" along with the police post, it was operated by a nine-person team, headed by the Farm Manager. His eight colleagues included an agronomist, the Party Secretary, a bookkeeper/quotas manager, a paymaster, a tractor and equipment supervisor, and staffers responsible, respectively, for crops, livestock and commerce.[10] Putnok's workers included both permanent and temporary employees, the latter often holding renewable annual contracts. According to an Institute of Economic Research publication, Hungary's state farms employed just over 50,000 permanent workers in 1951 and about a thousand more in 1954. Among them, 13% were administrators, 12% "animal breeders," eight percent in technical/industrial jobs, and the other two-thirds, field workers.[11]

The former agronomist at the Csobokapuszta farm (Borsod) estimated that by 1956 some 300,000 men and women staffed state farms nationally, 250,000 of them likely as short-term hires, some from villages near the complexes, but many "from quite different areas of the country."

His farm's 300–400 temporaries earned 14 forints per day in 1950 (by 1956, 32), from which 8 forints was deducted for room and board—three unimpressive meals a day and bunks in rooms holding 8–10 men. Permanent hands received 450–600 forints per month (1949–1950), a rate increased to 700–800 by 1956. Such modest earnings were a bit illusory, however, because "in the average family of the agricultural workers, both parents and two kids worked, each of them receiving a pay."[12] To attract and hold employees, management distributed state farm workers' earnings twice monthly in cash. As well, the state reportedly exempted their income from taxation and kept enterprise shops well supplied with goods at prices discounted from official levels.[13] Overall, socialist-era state farms extended the reach of the Horthy-era "treasury estates," which had specialized in horse breeding, in horticulture and seed supply, or in improving livestock lineages. While those activities continued, new farms were also tasked with hosting experimental projects and with "ensuring provision of necessary food supplies to the non-farming population." These proved difficult goals, because acreage expanded faster than investment funds for construction, housing or irrigation, because political "vigilance" led to dismissal of veteran experts as untrustworthy "class aliens," and because their replacements often lacked experience with local conditions.[14]

The sources of disappointment were multifarious and not often acknowledged or addressed. Here we can consider just three: (1) Ministry interference, indifference, and incompetence, (2) planning blunders, and (3) the joys of everyday stealing. When, after Csobokapuszta's agronomist consolidated postwar confiscations with other scattered parcels recently "donated" to the state farm, he traveled to the capital in February 1949 to consult on planting options, so as to design its initial crop distribution.

> To my great surprise I found that the ministry in Budapest [had] established the area for each plant that should be cultivated by the state farms, and the central plan disregarded the local conditions of land and climate. At Csobokapuszta we had to grow a certain area with soya beans. The climate was good for soya beans; however, we did not have the necessary migratory labor force... The representatives of the state farm could not change the central plan... Of course, it was impossible to keep [to] such a plan, because in a rainy month we used fewer working days [than allotted], in another month we needed more than anticipated.[15]

3 AGRICULTURE FROM STALINISM TO THE REVOLT 61

Early that summer, the agronome encountered ministerial indifference as he tried to determine how managers could best allocate work time for a new crop.

> I had to give instructions to my workers to hoe 1600 square ells of sugar beets [equal to 1 hold/yoke or 1.4 acres]. There were no norms concerning this work. I tried to [contact] the central office of the state farms in Budapest by phone, but I could not reach them. Finally I sent a special delivery letter to Budapest asking about the norms. No answer came,... I received the norms about the end of August, a long time after the work had been done. Then it turned out that the norms were not good. [They] prescribed that one worker should hoe 100 ells of sugar beets [daily – about 6,000 ft^2]. This was no good, since I had only girls to work on that job, who made not more than 50-60 square ells a day. [Were men available] one man would need 16 days to hoe one yoke and during that time the weeds would have grown up and he would have to start his work all over again.

Committed to uniformity, Budapest would not permit state farm leaders to "solve the problem of workers on a local basis," even though "the central office could never handle such problems."[16]

As for ministerial incompetence, one need look no farther than the Hegyeshalom state farm in Györ, near the Austrian border. With 5,200 holds (7,300 acres) and 400 employees in 1952, the farm operated three units, one for fattening pigs, another supplying milk (200 cows), and a third devoted to field crops. Construction teams were also building a "grain store" sufficient to hold "600 metric tons." Yet, as a former tractor driver explained, the enterprise "has been unable to fulfill its prescribed work and production plan and will continue to be unable todo so because of lack of implements, farm machinery, and manpower." Although Hegyeshalom had priority access to tractors from the local MTS for plowing and harvest, the ministry's failure to provide adequate equipment for everyday tasks (or additional employees) meant that the farm had to fall back on traditional field practices. Even when workers "put in 12 to 14 hours of work daily," sometimes including Sundays, reaching plan targets proved impossible.[17] Of course, the targets could not be adjusted, nor could sufficient tools for the job be expected.

Planning blunders involving state farms included technology and labor supply, as above, but two additional, vivid cases concern agricultural efforts to overcome Hungary's thin resources of industrial materials.

62 P. SCRANTON

Between 1949 and 1955, the Agriculture Ministry and several special project agencies experimented at research institutes and on state farms with new crops for industrial processing (*koksagyz*, cotton, kenaf, jute, ramie, and yucca), as well as for human and animal consumption (rice, peanuts, tea, and black sesame seeds).[18] In September 1950, the Council of Ministers decreed that, synchronizing with expanded manufacturing, "industrial crops, especially fibers, will be increased by 61 percent" in 1951. Accordingly, agriculture minister Ferenc Erdei transferred one of his protégées to a just-formed vegetable rubber enterprise, "because they needed an agricultural organizational expert to start off the great and glorious experiment in rubber growing in Hungary."

> The idea was to introduce, following the Russian example, the growing of *koksagyz*, a rubber bearing plant whose roots are supposed to contain 2% natural rubber. This plant ought to be sown in February, but as the enterprise was set up far too late, and [as] they did not want to wait until 1952, they ordered a trial seeding for August... it failed to germinate. For the next season, the seed from Russia did not arrive until early in April. We hastily distributed it and it was sown on 6000 hold [8500 acres]. On 5000 hold, there was no growth at all. On 1000, the roots yielded 0.45% rubber instead of the forecast 2%.

The Soviets next delivered 10 million forints worth of seed for the 1953 plan year, "for which we had to pay." Shortly, the whole 30-million-forint project was canceled, having generated just "400 pounds of rubber" from thousands of acres of public lands and thousands of hours of wasted labor.[19] The project director was swiftly transferred to a parallel enterprise promoting cotton production.

A CIA informant assessing the cotton project's decay by 1954 noted: "Cotton growing in Hungary has no past whatsoever, and according to results to date, it has no future. That cotton is grown at all in Hungary is one of the inexplicable Soviet orders which... has baffled economic experts." Greenhouse plantings in winter 1948 had led to experimental outdoor trials on 600 holds [850 acres] during 1949, "with the assistance of 1400 specially assigned farmers." Unfavorable weather delayed the harvest "catastrophically;" the fields delivered only 300 kg/hold, a third below the expected yield.[20] Even so, at a conference reviewing experiences thus far, Soviet cotton expert Andrei Skoblykov "cited examples among state farms" where this performance "was surpassed." Deputy

Minister Mihály Keresztes argued that both state farms and TSZs could profit from cotton plantings, and in closing, Minister Erdei asserted that cotton had become "essential for the development of Hungarian agriculture as a whole."[21] Not actually.

The core miscalculations centered on seed, greed and weather. Initially, "a highly competent old seed man, Ferenc Schüller was in charge. He relied on Bulgarian seed, which seemed capable of being acclimatized to Hungarian conditions." Even while pressing for rapidly increasing the cotton acreage, the top brass "felt it improper to rely on other than Russian seed." This led to the cotton debacle of 1953–1954, once the weather factor came to the fore.

> Cotton matures in 210 days, and it needs 150 sunny days. In Hungary, these conditions are fulfilled in two out of every ten years. In other words, cotton only succeeds in Hungary when [very dry] weather is disastrous for other crops. Such a year was 1951; cotton yielded 300 kg/hold on an area of 50,000 holds [70,000 acres]. The enthusiasm of the planners caught fire and they set an acreage target of 100,000 holds for the 1953 season.[22]

Schüller rejected such grandiosity and was both fired and drummed out of the Party, replaced by Skoblykov, who "became Hungary's cotton dictator." An agronomist from Barayna explained:

> They insisted we raise cotton. We had no competent people to direct it, no workers to raise it, no machinery, no understanding, inadequate soil; in one word no requirements were there. But the ministry [set] a uniform pattern for the whole country and issued idiotic rulings. If absurd orders were challenged one was told this is political, it must be carried out, no opposition will be tolerated.[23]

An economist from the National Bank often visited rural loan/investment clients and experienced this directly. When inquiring into one enterprise at Karcag (Szolnok), he requested a look at its cotton fields. His hosts drove him to an area featuring only healthy weeds.

> I said: "You won't get any cotton on this field." The president of the farm agreed with me... He said that the production plan received from the District Council insisted that his collective plant one hundred holds [140 acres] of cotton. They planted the cotton, but it froze. Then they

tried to get permission from the Council to plant corn instead, but the Council insisted they plant cotton again on the same land. They followed the order, but didn't even bother to hoe the cotton, knowing that it would freeze anyway.[24]

Getting to 100,000 holds was problematic in two additional ways: it colonized land previously used for more valuable crops (onions, paprika) and for fodder (corn); and it pushed the boundary of the cotton districts northward into areas known for sustained summer rains. The result was "invariably a total failure."

> In both 1952 and 1953, the autumn was wet, and the average cotton yield was under 200 kg/hold, with the proportion of immature [unopened] pods being over 50%! The cotton spinning industry had a horrible time; they were in tears and flatly stated that it is impossible to use Hungarian-grown cotton. The picking, too, was a horrible task; school children and army troops had to be commandeered to do it.[25]

Another planning omission became evident after the harvest: "Hungary did not possess any machinery for cleaning cotton," i.e., cotton gins. Thus in 1952, the No. 65/5 Construction State Enterprise rapidly erected a three-story processing plant in the Great Plain (Alfold) near Hódmezővásárhely (Békés). Animated by Soviet machinery, the operation "is fully mechanized, has its own repair shop and a large-sized sulfuric acid tank, needed for the treatment of cotton seeds," which were soon shipped to "all state farms."[26] This coordination came too late, however, as the 1953 collapse brought the "cotton craze" to an end.

> For 1954, the acreage was reduced to a few thousand hold, the Budapest Head Office was quietly liquidated, and the headquarters were shifted to Hódmezővásárhely, where there was a large cotton gin. By now [1957] there is only experimental production at a few state farms... One reason for the more complete failure of cotton in Hungary that should have been the case was the bustle and helter-skelter methods of the Russians – they would not give us a chance to breed the Bulgarian seed.[27]

Once again, seed grain from Russia, "ordered in 1954," arrived and had to be accepted. "Due to the fact that it couldn't be used for anything else, it was fed to the fish."Once again, having managed two shipwrecks, the project director moved on, this time to "the firm organizing and maintaining the annual Agricultural Exhibition and Fair."[28]

Stealing, cheating, embezzling falsifying, and deceiving were key skills in the Party state and well documented in state farm practices. One general manager, noting that state farm employees generally were economically better off than TSZ members, added:

> But in both cases, the workers try to supplement their pay through stealing. One chief shepherd of the state farms, who had 3,000 sheep under his care, stole every day a van load of wheat for his own cattle. If we take into consideration the stealing, the workers of the state farms made as much money as the industrial workers of the city. That was one of the main reasons why they stayed in the countryside and did not move into the city.[29]

Elsewhere, the fiddle concerned chemical fertilizer. When an agricultural supply agency was instructed to deliver 150 quintals (15 tons) of artificial fertilizer to a state farm, "those who loaded the wagons put in only 80 or 100 quintals, but got paid for the 150 ordered." Those delivering the chemicals to the fields furthered the fraud, because they got paid according to the amount the paperwork said they had spread. "There was no actual plot between the people involved. There was just an agreement to go along with this, because both sides gained."[30]

Another farm director reported cheating on a grander scale, when a Hungarian dairy enterprise entered a "socialist competition" for milk production, a political cousin of Stakhanovitism in mines and factories, with a similar Russian operation.

> In this particular case, the whole county 'pitched in' – they kept changing the cows. Extra feedings took place and the fodder for this noble purpose was taken away from the allotments of the collective farms. During the competition, the quantity of milk was determined on the basis of a trial milking which took place once a month... no milking took place Wednesday evenings [before the trial], so that Thursday morning production would be considerably increased.[31]

Delaying milking assured impressive results on trial days, but, as anyone familiar with dairying knows, at the cost of a miserable night for the cows. Elsewhere, as a clerk at an "experimental dairy" near Sopron (Györ) reported, the low wages paid "resulted in a high percentage of thefts," which management tended to overlook.

> The amount of dairy products stolen was really fantastic. Each worker was allowed one liter of milk per day in addition to his wages. The result was that instead of one liter, everybody took at least a can [2L]. It was in the interest of the entire dairy that this should be allowed. That is why people got away with it. Milk had a greater value than money and therefore people were willing to work for lower wages.[32]

Heavy and more durable items also walked away. Harvesting combines built in Hungary, "copies of an old American type produced 20 years ago," failed to cut stalks close enough to the ground, wasting both grain and straw. They had a second deficiency: "the motor of the combine is the same as the engine of the Csepel [vehicles]. Consequently people steal the engine parts... and every year before the season starts, the combines have to be overhauled and the missing parts replaced."[33] A state farm manager, later Supervisor of Department Chiefs at the Ministry of Agriculture, summarized the national situation, which had "created serious worries for Imre Nagy."

> Everybody cheated: the factory manager and the unskilled worker as well, and the whole nation was educated on corruption... If a farmer needed any type of construction material, he also stole. Cheating became a moral act. In his own case, lying started when he advised two or three of his employees not to admit that they were so-called class aliens. Lying became an everyday necessity.... When it came to fulfill the prescribed plan, everybody cheated: the plant manager, the chief engineer, the Party secretary, the workers.[34]

As enterprises, state farms undertook an array of core tasks to upgrade the capabilities of Hungarian agriculture, but could not gather sufficient financial, organizational and technical resources to fulfill them. They fared badly as sites for Soviet-promoted crop experiments, yet became notable locations for theft and fraud, given their workers' generally modest earnings.

Theft and deception were also routine at Machine Tractor Stations, which first must be introduced as technical and political organizations supporting agricultural modernization. The initial cohort (the 100th opened in December 1948) targeted supporting private farmers, including land reform beneficiaries, through leasing tractors and machinery. That plan changed sharply in 1949: as in the USSR, tractor stations became the technical arm for building socialist agriculture, focusing on TSZs and state farms while restricting or denying access to independents.[35] Their initial tractors were war survivors; of 10,000 at work in 1944, only 6,000 "old models" remained by 1947. Beyond those destroyed, "all the better tractors had been confiscated by the Russians." Thus building Hungarian tractors was a priority in the late 40s, notably the G-35 Hoffher model (Fig. 3.1) assembled in Budapest, using machinery scrounged from the Manfred Weiss and Lang plants. Although the Hoffhers soon became "pretty much obsolete," production continued at about 3,000/yr, a third of them exported. By 1956, MTSs also relied on light, 22-hp Czech Zetors ("the best adapted to Hungarian conditions") and heavy-duty 55-hp Soviet tractors ("can be used in Hungary for certain works of cultivation only").[36]

A typical early station held ten or more tractors, an equal number of plows, five "barrows" for hauling grain or fertilizer, two threshing machines, and many traditional horse-drawn plows (25–30), barrows (12), and sowing machines (12). Each also had an "auxiliary tractor with trailer for repairs" to fetch disabled units and return them to the station, which operated "a complete repair kit for tractors." By 1951, Hungary regained the 10,000 tractor mark, with state farms operating 40% and MTSs 60% of the fleet; five years later there were 24,000, roughly half at the stations, where total employment neared 20,000. Rates charged for plowing, sowing, and harvesting varied by the clients' political status; TSZs received a 30% discount on the fees charged private farmers. Each of the over 300 stations served "10 or 12 villages," but this created problems. Considerable time (and gasoline) was wasted in traveling from one site to another, and supervision of the drivers was impossible.[37] A one-time state farm manager complained that initially,

> there were many abuses and wrongdoings in the operation of these stations. The whole organization was set up in a rush. Most of the machines were confiscated [from estates], then collected in improvised buildings which were sometimes demolished by the first storm. There was not a single station housed in an adequate building... The machinery, naturally, deteriorated quickly. There were no expert personnel to do necessary repairs. When the season came, there were hardly any good machines available.[38]

Fig. 3.1 Driving a Hungarian-made Hoffher GS-35 tractor at a state farm, 1953 (Donor: Endre Baráth. *Source* FOTO: Fortepan—ID 7949, http://www.fortepan.hu/_photo/download/fortepan_14117.jpg, Wikimedia Creative Commons)

A 1951 report was unsparing: MTS equipment's extraordinary wear and tear derived from "bad servicing" and Party "competitions" promoted to boost productivity. For years, "the quality of the tractor stock... degenerated and did not improve until... 1954," when purchasing resumed. Sadly, many replacements were "the wrong type"; instead, MTSs needed "all purpose tractors and other machinery," so as to mechanize hoeing field crops like corn and sugar beets. Specialized accessories were also scarce—nationally in December 1953 just 43 potato-planting machines, plus only 30 potato harvesters. Management credentials were just as thin; just one percent of MTS directors and 11% of chief engineers were "graduate engineers," whereas nearly half of directors and district agronomists had completed only secondary school or an MTS training course.[39] Overall, a state farm agronomist concluded that the mechanization of agriculture was "a strange mixture of large-scale plans and miserable local failures."[40]

Another dubious MTS practice, deep plowing, also duplicated Russian methods[41]; it was implemented on state farms, but overusing it was a mistake.

> On shallow soils, deep plowing kills the humus – Hungarian soil science was very highly developed before the war, and we knew perfectly well where deep plowing was advantageous and where not. Under the Soviet system, deep plowing is the general order of the day, and since evasion of this order counts as punishable sabotage of the people's economy, agriculturalists can do little to prevent the resulting damage to the land.[42]

Substantial damage likewise was an unintended consequence of the poorly coordinated construction program rolled out to remedy the sorry conditions at the first MTS sites. Plans for several hundred new, much larger stations floundered amid complaints about the farm acreage lost to their construction and the failure to arrange for electricity and water supplies. Overall, "a person outside of Hungary cannot possibly visualize the chaos existing in connection with the construction work of such tractor stations. These were originally planned to be complete in 3–4 years. But as the years pass, the plans are constantly being changed, and not a single station, was, in fact completed [by mid-1953]."[43]

Finally, MTS administration was complex, both bureaucratic and politicized. The core staff included a general manager, his deputy, a personnel chief, an agronom, a technical manager, a supplies keeper, and several

70   P. SCRANTON

repair mechanics, along with a separate political division headed by the Party secretary. The chief agronomist at a large station (60 tractors) concluded:

> A tractor station is basically an excellent idea, but the domestic type of it [in Hungary] is over-bureaucratized, irrational and ineffective. In relation to the investment involved, it is not successful. Due to political aspects... [managers] never worried about productivity. It was a planned-loss operation. However, the station couldn't fully fill the work-needs of the outside, completely apart from whether it was to be a paying proposition.[44]

At the onset of Party rule, stations were "primarily political organizations" pushing mechanization, featuring "many low quality... new agronomists" turned out by agricultural schools. They offered too-often-erroneous advice to farmers, but "once he was fooled, the peasant lost confidence in agronomists as a breed." Technical supervision was feeble, delegated to "repair mechanics" until 1954, when "engineers were assigned to tractor stations." Worse,

> the equipment left much to be desired. With the exception of three or four stations (out of eighteen in [Baranya] county), none had mechanical plow sharpeners. This is very hard work if done by hand. Our resources were limited, our tools were few and there was no replacement for lost equipment. Generally our [machinery] was coarse, huge, and heavy... Sheds were built at the stations, but there was not enough room for all the equipment. Much was outside, year-in, year-out, either because it was not needed or because we preferred to keep the iron machinery outside, which only rusted, while wooden equipment would rot.[45]

Self-interest and fraud were woven into MTS relationships with the TSZs they ostensibly served and with the ministry that supposedly supervised them. Stations concluded annual service contracts with producer cooperatives, in which the TSZs were the dependent party.

> The station had to meet its production quota... The idea was to mechanize as much of the work as possible. Often the TSZs' horse teams were not used, but they were obliged to use our machinery. In the case of early spring seeding, for instance, the work is easier done with a team of horses, but we forced our contract on them. At the same time, our machinery was busy just then and sometimes the work wasn't done until it was too

late. This was also true for weeding... The individual peasant smallholder never had the advantages of the special machinery services, aside from the plowing and other soil work which was forced on him regardless. But he never had any help for harvesting.[46]

Equipment was so generally in poor condition and parts in such short supply that stations relied on stripping defunct tractors to keep their brethren going. As a Budapest machine designer explained: "There was a depressing lack of spare parts. This led to cannibalism; the people at an MTS would [even] dismantle a new machine and use the parts so obtained to repair other machines."[47] Russian-made tractors were especially vulnerable, as "broken parts are irreplaceable." Reportedly, the parts famine put seven of 11 Stalinets models at a Győr MTS out of commission and a number of its Hungarian tractors would not work, as their "run-down batteries" could not be replaced. Desperate situations led to desperate measures. In 1953:

> panicky directors of MTSs which have been unable to repair tractors because of a lack of spare parts have taken matters into their own hands. Knowing that no help is forthcoming from the ministry, and afraid of being branded reactionary, the directors are sending their supply men directly to the machine factories. Armed with bacon, sausage, wine, etc., the supply men approach the workers and offer to trade food for spare parts.

When the Red Star Tractor Plant's Budapest Party unit learned of these exchanges, "laborers working for the barterers, rather than completing the plan," they barred the supply men's entry.[48]

An MTS chief engineer elaborated: All the stations had a number of "black tractors," which had been "officially turned in as decrepit, but actually kept [for parts] while some junk was handed" to the scrap yard. "Our tractor station once traded a time-punch clock in," instead of a tractor. Baranya county workers applauded this deal because thereafter they "spent long minutes in the morning signing in with pen and pencil." Both off-the-books and broken equipment could pose problems when ministerial inspectors visited to document each station's machinery inventory. Therefore, once district directors established the assessors' itinerary, MTC managers concealed their wrecks and arranged a technology rotation: equipment in working condition "was borrowed from station to station [and] returned after the inspection." At times, tractors would go missing "for a larger part of the summer," having been appropriated by

Party officials or the military or abandoned at a TSZ. After fall harvests, MTS staff began "to look for them. Sometimes they were found under haystacks, buried, or in ditches." Deceiving the state in order to meet quotas and secure bonuses for work completed "was an art form in itself. Work sections, land areas were switched back and forth between quarterly quotas or allocated land, but as a result we always pepped up our norms and quotas."[49] A Pest county chief engineer was on the same wavelength; in 1955, he noted, we "managed to break even (This was a result of juggling accounting-wise [the] damages done deliberately or involuntarily to machinery, so the ruined machines were not charged against the station's budget.)."[50] Local folks did secure one unanticipated benefit from the Baranya station, however. The state provided its director with both a motorcycle to travel around the district and repair facilities to keep it running. "So, everybody's private motorcycles were repaired with equipment requisitioned for this. As a result the annual repair bill for [my] motorcycle equaled the price of a new one."[51]

Tractor drivers were a perennial source of enterprise concern. There were, it seems, never enough of them, despite vigorously promoted training courses. Planners fretted that the most mechanically inclined graduates migrated from MTSs to factories where they could earn more,[52] but those staying on the job sought means to plump their pay packets, too. An engineer's view:

> The tractor drivers were paid by the acre, which told on the quality of the work and on the life of the implements. They would turn at the end of the furrow without lifting the implement out [of the ground], who led to many breakages. The drivers were often hostile and deliberately mishandled the machinery, or, out of resentment, they would say about a perfectly suitable machine that "we just cannot use it here" – they just would not take the trouble to learn...[53]

Of course not. Nobody was paying them to develop new skills; time spent figuring out how to use unfamiliar machinery simply meant fewer acres cultivated and lower earnings. Moreover, in the battle to achieve quotas, "cheatings were in order – in order to reach the norms, which were very high. For instance, when a [client] ordered a deep plowing, he was given a shallow one."[54] This may not have been all bad, given the damage from deep plowing, but the charge for "deep" was still assessed.

3 AGRICULTURE FROM STALINISM TO THE REVOLT 73

Ministries changed the norm system every year, pushing for greater productivity per tractor. Early on, tractor drivers occasionally fought back. When the ministry announced new norms in October 1951, drivers in Békés and Csongrád counties and in the Sopron district of Györ refused to work, claiming the targets "were impossible to reach." Over a dozen were arrested.[55] The alternative was either to cheat the clients and skimp the work to reach targets or to compensate for reduced earnings through theft, deception, and illegal activity. Rushing to meet their acreage assignments, drivers ignored "the quality of the work... The furrows are not straight and there is always a space between them which is an excellent place for the weeds." As for option two, "tractor operators accept so-called black or illegal work and pocket the income."[56] The Pecs chief engineer provided other examples:

> To steal state property was not considered a crime. The tractor drivers stole tractor parts, tarpaulins, in other words, anything that could be moved... Cheating was commonplace at tractor stations... It was hard to fulfill the prescribed hoeing and seeding [norms]. So, the tractor driver made a deal with the peasant; it was agreed that the tractor driver will [only] plow the peasant's land, while the peasant verified [falsely] that the working hours spent... included the hauling of fertilizer and/hoeing. This way the peasant benefited by having to pay less and the tractor driver... could show that he could produce more than his prescribed norm. The peasant [still] had to pay extra for the hauling of fertilizers; however the rate for this was cheap... The tractor driver's cheating resulted in benefits to everybody involved. He received a bonus, the tractor station fulfilled the plan, and thus the leaders also received bonuses.[57]

One Szeged (Csongrád) worker, after reporting the arrest of a Party secretary whose illegal takings allowed him to build his own home, added: "Even more stealing went on at the tractor stations. Even the newspapers wrote about it."[58] Even the newspapers...

By summer 1955, at least at Györ's Kapuvár MTS, such a system as there was, was on the verge of falling apart. Demand for TSZ spring plowing had waned; with new regulations, co-ops had begun to acquire machinery, while "the individual farmers think it a point of prestige to never let the tractors come to their fields." As a result, "the driver's wallet remains empty." One announced he was quitting, but management exercised its authority not to allow this. He "had to stay, with the hope that at the time of harvest, he would earn what he needs for the winter." When earnings did not cover the 400 ft advance drivers received monthly, MTS officials demanded return of the difference. The drivers refused, but the sums were deducted on the next payday.

> On these days, there is a "revolutionary" mood among the workers. "It is hair-raising what one hears on a payday." The workers abuse the tractor station and its leaders; they complain about the unbearable conditions which prevent them from looking for work at places where there would be more work and more money to earn... It is small wonder that the men avoid work whenever there is a chance for it... The tractor drivers summoned for repair work spend the day sleeping beneath the threshing machines. [Others] appeared at the tractor station in the morning, had their labor sheet signed, and afterwards crept over the fence and returned only at the end of official working hours.

Managers ceased to demand discipline "because they would not be obeyed... and open coercion would only aggravate the situation."[59] For those with eyes to see, the cracks were everywhere.

Private Farmers: Pressured and Evasive

At mid-century, 3.2 million Hungarians worked in agriculture, 93% of them on private farms, occupying over 80% of arable land and generating "92 percent of the chief crops collected by the state." Among them, some 650,000 individuals and families had benefited from the postwar land reform, a group about equally divided between estate laborers and smallholders already owning a few acres. In general their plots were inadequate to sustain market agriculture; roughly a third of new owners also held wage-earning jobs, others (ca. 100,000) soon contributed their acreage to newly formed TSZs, not uncommonly under pressure from Party and district officials. More significant as mini-enterprises were 600,000 family farms ranging from five to 20 holds (7–28 acres), with fields, pastures, orchards, and vineyards totaling 5.8 million holds (8.1 M acres).[60] Another 100,000 farms were larger; the state classified their owners as "kulaks," a punitive term borrowed from the USSR, identifying those who hired labor for land, livestock, or orchard/vineyard duties. In Hungary, this class included those (1) with 25+ holds (35+ acres); (2) with smaller properties but raising animals or owning tractors; (3) with market gardens; or (4) using land to supply another occupation (e.g., butchers, millers). Continuing confiscations that had started with the nobility and gentry, the state sought to erase kulaks by targeting them with sharply higher taxes and prosecutions for infractions otherwise tolerated, refusing them use of MTS equipment or access to chemical fertilizers, and reportedly deporting several thousand families to labor camps in 1951–1952.[61]

Understanding two dynamics associated with private farming is essential to appreciating the independents' conflictual relations with the Party state. First, the government committed to enlarge the scope of rural producer cooperatives[62] by recruiting family landholders and their holdings. This project included several collectivization campaigns before the Revolt: "building socialism" drives in 1948–1949 and 1950–1951 and a restoration effort in 1955–1956, following mass departures during Nagy's tenure. The first surge drew "100,000 families" into 2,500 generally small co-ops; the second added 2,000 more TSZs; these gains by 1953 reduced the independent farms' share of working lands to 61%. However, the second dynamic, land abandonment, undercut the first. Rather than enter TSZs, thousands of former farm laborers left their undersized plots to seek jobs in towns and cities. Thousands more "kulaks" walked away or were deported. Moreover, as taxes and demands for compulsory crop deliveries rose, thousands of "middle peasants" threw in the towel. The state now owned these territories, but had little capacity to do anything productive with them. Such "so-called 'reserve' lands were actually abandoned lands, for which no tenants could be found."[63] The people who could have re-animated them had departed, while Hungary's investment capital had flowed chiefly into heavy industry. Vacant land produced no grain; tons of fruit rotted in orphaned orchards. According to an agronomist: "The state-owned lands were actually ownerless. They were neglected and no one cared." His own Baranya county lacked resources to revive thousands of "useless" acres.[64] At a crucial June 13, 1953 Moscow conclave, which coincided with upheavals in East Berlin, Lavrentiy Beria urged the Budapest leadership to pay "more attention to agriculture. Then there would not be 750,000 holds (1+M acres) of abandoned land (10% of all arable land). There would not be a situation in which peasants leave agriculture and move to industry." Premier Gyorgy Malenkov also complained that "there is data that shows that the income of producer cooperative members is below that of individually-farming middle peasants."[65] Perhaps private farmers could not thrive, but they had persisted and were outperforming the TSZs. How was this possible?

First, as with the abandoned lands, the Party state simply could not impose its will and redesign agriculture. It had neither the personnel, nor the funds, nor the expertise to force crops out of silent fields.[66] Unlike factories, where surveillance and control were feasible, if difficult, small farms spread across scores of administrative districts presented an insuperable management-from-above problem. Still, neither state nor society could function without the crops private farmers raised, though the tax regime and practices commandeering harvests arguably sought to drive them out of business. Second, ironically, state squeezes reinforced many families' determination to hold on, no matter what—working harder and farming more intensively to meet compulsory deliveries, devising evasive tactics or scamming the system through bribery and fraud. Third, TSZs, the socialist alternatives to family-based agriculture, were not functioning well. Progress toward modernizing and mechanizing Hungarian agriculture seemed glacial. In the mid-50s, the nation could not afford to have private farming fade away.

Compulsory deliveries were the coercive face of the state's public stance emphasizing rural voluntarism. One household farmer, whose summer 1951 quotas from her 1.2 acre plot were two tons of grain, 1.5 tons of potatoes and 800 kg of hay, received in payment just about enough to "cover the taxes on my property." Police then visited twice to search for hidden grain and finding none, promised to return. "This is our peaceful life," she wrote. "The most remarkable fact is that we have to surrender everything 'voluntarily.'"[67] Such rhetoric and practices were readily applied in other situations. For instance, a soldier and a TSZ member visited another farmer that summer, asking him "to offer his potatoes voluntarily to the Army."

> If the farmer refuses, they search his place and take away not only all the potatoes they can find, but also any new clothing they may come across. The presumption is, of course, that the farmer sold his potatoes on the black market and bought clothes with the money thus realized. The price paid for the potatoes is 1.5 ft/kg., even though the market price stands at 8.3 ft. In the case of eggs and meat, a farmer must give 34 eggs for each hold and 4.5 kg. of meat. If he is unable to meet these quotas, he must pay a sum equal to the black market price for the missing balance.[68]

The gaps between forced purchase prices, state buyers' contract prices for surpluses, the state's selling price to companies and consumers, and the open market price were key to the compulsory delivery system, as well as to farmers' disgust with its exactions. They opened spaces for the state to steal from farmers and consumers alike and, to a degree, for farmers' evasions.

Paying land taxes was a separate obligation. A Békés farmer who twice had refused to join a local TSZ decided to sell two of this three horses to cover a new tax bill. Local officials in Kevermes regarded him as a troublemaker because his reluctance encouraged others to remain independent. On October 8, 1951 he took the horses "to market," where two council members told him to sell them to the TSZ, not to other private farmers. He declined, as he was seeking the highest price. Not receiving an acceptable offer, he returned home.

> Next morning, two policemen came and "investigated" at his house. They "found" two automatic weapons... and he was arrested. The same afternoon his horses were taken away by the TSZ. His other belongings were removed the next day. His wife and three children are still in Kevermes without money while the "guilty" peasant was taken to Makó [70 km. distant]. A delegation of peasants tried to intervene... on his behalf.

One local councilman proclaimed it useless to "champion" such a criminal and sent them away. Hostility to the authorities grew so intense "that policemen never go in the street alone after dark."[69] In such cases, as a Sopron farmer noted: "peasants thus bullied and intimidated were compelled to choose the road the people's educators [Party activists] wanted them to choose; to 'voluntarily' enter and become members of the TSZ cooperatives." Those refusing risked seeing their possessions "being sold at public auction. The process was simple enough: the free peasants were so overburdened with all sorts of taxes and forced deliveries that they simply could not pay any longer."[70]

Taxes were entwined with compulsory deliveries in roughly the following way. Three land-based levies required payments in the early 1950s: the wheat field tax, the land tax in kind and the land tax in currency. The wheat field tax was calculated as 10 kg of grain per hold times each hold's rating on the "golden crown" quality scale (from 10 to 40).[71] A 20-crown (average quality) field would owe 200 kg/hold, for example—two tons of grain for a 10-hold plot. Being a tax, this "was to be delivered to a government warehouse... for which no compensation was paid." Second, the land tax in kind was calculated as 80% of the wheat field tax; in the example, another 1.6 tons of grain. For this there *was* compensation, but only at 0.60 ft/kg; here, 960 ft for a 10 hold, 20-crown quality plot's second delivery. Finally, the cash tax added 15 ft/hold times the crown value, here 3,000 ft [10 holds × 15 ft × 20].[72] All this applied only to independent farmers; and in this case, the tax bill alone for ten holds would come to about 11,500 ft/yr.[73]

For compulsory deliveries, a second set of ratings, the "point scale," fixed each private farm's obligation, "after having taken into consideration the producer's economic status (size of the land, quality of the soil, number of cattle, etc.). It established "for each particular property," a delivery target expressed in an accounting "currency," the "wheat-kilogram," which set a common value scale for crops, livestock and their products, and wine. Thus, classified according to their gold crown ratings, farms had to deliver an assortment of products whose total value matched their "wheat-kilogram" (WK) assessments. The values attached to material goods suggested their relative economic significance and perhaps the labor time to create them. Ten liters of milk earned 10 WK, but 10 liters of wine accounted for 116 WK. Ten kilos of either pork or poultry chalked up 100 WK, but the same weight in beef, just 75. Given this required point target, the farmer "could deliver his quota in the produce he chose, that is, in whatever suited him best."[74]

Of course, the state set the price schedules, the third element in the scheme. As a district Delivery Office collector explained, the state paid (in 1956) 80 ft for a quintal (100 kg) of wheat. "The free market price was 200-600 ft," depending on quality. For barley and oats, just 60 ft/q., yet the market rate was 200-500 ft/q. Agents credited pork at 5.6 ft/kg, but "its free market price was 20-28 ft, [and] at the butcher's you bought it for 30-32 ft." Lowball prices for compulsory purchases provided the state with huge margins, not shared with workers and consumers, as retail prices indicated. Indeed, non-farm citizens blamed peasants for high food costs, imagining them to be living in luxury (a few were, but not legally).[75] A Budapest planning engineer calculated the cash-grab implicit in state price setting. Until a 1953 increase, private farmers delivered each quintal of wheat at 60 ft; once milled this yielded about 72 kg of white flour, which state millers sold to bakeries and retailers at 4.80 ft/kg, a sixfold multiple. "The state made an even greater profit if the wheat was made into bread. Out of the 72 kilos of flour, 150 kilos of bread would be made, which at the current prices [3 ft for a one kg loaf] meant 450 forints" income for an initial expenditure of 60 ft. "The other expenses involved in making bread were negligible."[76] Multiplied by millions of quintals, grain profits amounted to a tidy sum.

Revenues from markups such as these sustained the state's industrial and construction investment programs, while exported farm goods, raw, or processed, partially covered trade deficits within the Bloc or brought in hard currencies from the West. Nonetheless, our Somogy county collector "hated and despised" his work, claiming that, except for the AVH, "the greatest outrage in Hungary [was] the way the peasants had been exploited." His office had an inside staff of five ("the bureaucracy was unbearable... useless, hairsplitting"), and four field operatives:

> I had to collect every day the delivery reports of 56 communities on the phone and then to compile them and send the report to the county office. I did this three days during the week and then for two days I had to go to the country to control [supervise/inspect] the administration there and to propagandize the delivery among the peasants.

His lack of enthusiasm was apparent; then summertime promotional "campaigns" stretched his daily work to twelve hours or more. Given the legal cheating that deliveries embodied, it is doubtful that country people warmly received him. Nor were his thrice-weekly reports on deliveries likely welcomed by county bureaucrats; hundreds of companion accounts from other collection districts accompanied them. State agencies were often critiqued for being overstaffed, but the torrent of information kept most everyone busy six days a week. "I couldn't have taken days off anyway," the collector whined, "because the work would have piled up so much that I would never have been able to catch up with it."[77]

How did private farmers cope with the web of constraints that the Party state had spun? Those who refused to fold their tents and join TSZs focused instead on making money, evading regulations, securing help from sympathetic officials and neighbors, and defrauding the state, tactics which resonate with Chia and Holt's notion of "strategy without design" and with an American diplomat's diagnosis. Reporting from Debrecen in 1953, he judged that Hungarians "are masters of passive resistance, especially the peasants," a posture which seemed, in his view, "to suit the Hungarian temperament."[78] First, consider earning cash, mostly legally. One Baranya agronomist noted: "When compared to the situation before the war, the Hungarian peasant lives now in a money economy, the peasant with eight holds does a great deal of trading." He continued:

80   P. SCRANTON

All the peasants tried to find ways in order to make money. For example, their milk production is very important, in spite of the fact that they have to deliver so much feed to the state. I know of many cases where the peasant bought [replacement] cattle feed for money and his milk production was still lucrative. They tried to make money out of poultry or out of fruit orchards and in such a way the economy of the individual peasant became very intensive in the last few years... [He also] has the freedom to go to the market place of a nearby city and sell his fruits and vegetables there.[79]

Ministry regulations provided for market sales once required deliveries were complete. Purportedly, market prices would match those on state schedules, but this was not often the case. A Csongrád dance band musician reported that "on the open markets, the prices were always somewhat higher than... in the government stores," but "one could obtain everything all the time" in markets whereas the stores had "periodic shortages."[80] In the capital's lively food halls, university students supplemented their tiny stipends by working Saturdays and Sundays loading/unloading carts and trucks, earning "about 100 forints each weekend" thereby. Until December 1951, farmers also sold restricted goods (fodder, grain) "on the black market in order to be able to acquire the money necessary for taxes."[81] Price gouging was not unknown. Farms near Debrecen had to sell the state 30 eggs/hold, for which they received 5.4 ft in total. The state shop resold these at 2 ft each (60 ft, a 1,000% margin), so in city markets peasants charged 3–5 ft each for their surplus eggs. "They were right for selling them for more and the others were also right for being angry with them for it," a local official concluded.[82] Reportedly, collectors also had a powerful lever to force villages to catch up in delivering deficient products (e.g., poultry, milk): they could bar all farmers in the district from selling such goods in cities until delinquencies were cleared.[83] Other strategies could generate legitimate and borderline cash flows to independents. Many tried "to find some other work outside of their farms. [They] do carting, work for state farms, for certain cooperatives, or at construction in a nearby city." When the state sought to reduce imports by raising the price for sheared wool, "all the peasants tried to acquire a few head of sheep." But once this became "a good business," agents reduced the price paid, perhaps unintentionally increasing the mutton supply.[84] In Szentpéterfa (Vas), private farmers sent sons off to factory work or road building, so they could bring home all (or most) of their earnings to cover cash taxes. During harvests, family members would work for TSZs "in order to earn the wheat" for the farm's deliveries. One Szolnok man cut a quietly illegal deal with a neighbor:

> The only way I could continue to keep my eight holds of land and could continue to comply with the delivery regulations was by going halves in regard to an additional six holds with someone else. I would like to mention in this connection that if you did this officially then you were responsible for the compulsory delivery in regard to your half [of the crops]. However, if you made an unofficial deal with the landowner, then you would get one half of the whole produce... for the labor you put in... The compulsory deliveries in such a case would have to be discharged by the landowner from the other half of the produce. Because of this you naturally made such deals only with owners of fertile land.

This tactic was satisfying because on the extra acreage, one could sow crops promising the best market profits, not what the Ministry mandated under a revised post-1953 system. "People didn't like to be told what to produce and how large an area had to be sown for a certain type."[85]

In 1953, the incoming Nagy administration recognized that Rákosi's Stalinist approach to collections had generated discontent; but it did not discard the process, reorganizing it instead. First, state decrees "erased penalties applied that year to individual farms" that had not met delivery quotas and also canceled a portion of the fines assessed—a concession valued at 680 million forints. Additional measures permitted renting land (up to 25 holds), cleared a path toward repossession of abandoned plots, and reduced delivery requirements by a quarter or more.[86] However, soon after, to farmers' dismay "a new collection system was started." Before 1954, as noted above, private farmers could meet their annual requirements with any combination of outputs that reached their assigned WK unit total. But "this will not necessarily be the best thing for the state, too; on the contrary, the state will get too much of some kinds of agricultural products and not enough of others."[87] Hence, specific quantities of grains, meat, and/or milk and eggs were evidently assigned to each producer, though their total value was less than before the reform. The Szolnok sharecropping tactic represented an evasive, if enterprising response to this restructuring.

Other sorts of evasions were ubiquitous, but here only two can be outlined, one regarding vineyards and the other, barter. Hungary had long been renowned for its wines, the glories of Tokaj and the vigor of Egri Bikavér (Bull's Blood) celebrated throughout the Empire and beyond.[88] The Party state had little patience for vintages and "terroir;" its monopoly enterprises, Abofor (purchasing) and Monipex (export), dominated a trade in bulk varietals. In fall 1951, Abofor sent agents to wine districts "to register all barrels and other containers in order to prevent... hiding and withholding wine." Monipex had created seven standard wine grades to set prices for foreign sales, chiefly at the time to the Soviet Union.[89] To avoid selling wine or grapes at ruinous prices, vineyarders either pressed their harvests privately for home consumption or carefully sold quantities "without the knowledge of the authorities." One family near the western border had owned vines inside Austria which after 1949 became inaccessible. Thus, they bought local grapes sufficient for 100–150 liters of wine and gathered enough blackberries for 10–15 liters of fruit brandy, processed "secretly at home." More ambitious and hazardous were the practices of a former Horthy-era border guard in Debrecen. Refusing "to work for the Communists," he lived off the produce of his three-hold vineyard, quietly selling his wine for 12 ft/liter (vs. 17 ft/l, a 1952 state price).[90] Vineyards producing lower quality wine sold it "illegally... for 5 ft a liter. The state bought the wine for 0.9 ft and resold it for 18–20 ft." In a Vas village, administrators took over the tavern and raised wine prices to 30 ft/liter. Thereafter, local folks went to the tavern only for beer, getting "their wine at the different houses. In the houses, you could buy better wine and much cheaper."[91]

More dramatic and decisive was the decision to abandon or wreck plantings. The Baranya agronomist summarized:

> When the vineyards' tax value was raised to five times that of regular land, the peasants started destroying their vineyards. I myself destroyed my own vineyard secretly for I couldn't afford to keep it. At the same time there was a strong government campaign for vine-planting... In the famous Villány wine district, there are perhaps 300 acres of excellent vineyards. Of this maybe three or four acres are well-tended today (1956). The rest is used for raising corn or fattening pigs.[92]

Elsewhere in the county, with grain being requisitioned at a fraction of its state retail or free market price, families used it as currency to pay for spare parts or inputs to construction. "If we wanted material to repair the house, we were forced to pay for it with grain," one peasant complained.

On the other hand, it was surely useful that "instructions sent from Pecs," the county seat five km distant, "lost their force just like a cup of water [poured] into the desert sand."[93] Illegal bartering could not be impeded.

Cooperation with friends and undisciplined officials (like those ignoring Pecs' directions) could prove crucial for circumventing state practices; but like selling wine on the quiet, it depended on trust and carried risks, especially when it bordered on or strayed into fraud.

> Most people in [my Hadjú-Bihar] village helped each other out when needed. The threshing machine was supervised by a man from the village who would record that eight quintals had been threshed when actually it had been 15, and the farmer could keep the difference. The veterinarian helped circumvent the cattle delivery quota, because [if] he gave a certificate that a cow was with calf, then the delivery collector didn't take it.[94]

When deficiencies occurred, even the collectors might try to deflect state sanctions:

> A transfer brigade took away everything it could find if a delivery quota was not fulfilled… They brought in gypsies who had to remove everything from the house if the quota was not fulfilled in three days. This system was begun in 1955-56, in spite of the promises of Rákosi and Imre Nagy that the farmer would not have to worry about the bailiff in his yard… Even the delivery collectors couldn't bear to see the situation, and when they knew that the transfer brigade was coming, they told the farmers to take the cattle out into the woods to save it.[95]

More often aid from officials was less dramatic. In Vas's Szentpéterfa, a "good local council chairman" confronted Party activists pushing private farmers to contribute their holds to a TSZ. He explained that, before the war, many villagers had migrated to America. "They had become rich and consequently everyone had relatives" there. If the pressure were kept on, local people would simply cross the border and the Atlantic, leaving the land vacant. The Party men withdrew; "this was how everybody was able to keep his land."[96] A statistical officer who traveled the Hadjú-Bihar county countryside "to control and inspect" boasted (in exile): "I was able to help the people. I did not denounce all of the irregularities and countless false data I found in the declarations of all enterprises, although the supplying of false information was punishable by six months to five years imprisonment. Nobody went to jail because of me."[97]

By no means were state agents so circumspect generally, especially when fraud was involved. Whereas in Hadjú-Bihar, cheating had benefited only the farmers, an attempt to duplicate the thresher under-weighing scheme didn't succeed. In Szolnok, the difference between the recorded total and the actual weight was divided between the landowner and the weigher, who then faced the challenge of selling quite a lot of grain. "After the Communists found out about this practice, they tracked down the violators." Thenceforth, only "trusted" agents handled the process.[98] In such circumstances, independents were helpless. One summer, private farmers near Sopron learned that:

> all harvested grain was to be delivered to a place designated by the authorities, to be threshed there. The produced quantities were secretly weighed and government inspectors supervised the entire operation. We realized only later what the purpose of this unusual procedure was. The produced quantities, as recorded by the threshing inspectors, became the basis on which the forced deliveries were later calculated. Many a person in the village attempted to bribe the inspectors. But informers were already at work, and 36 farmers were shortly arrested.[99]

Bribery could work more effectively within agencies, in closed-door meetings. Petitions to reduce compulsory quotas due to drought or disasters were routinely ignored, unless "the person involved gave one of the officials a considerable bribe."[100] The traveling statistician admitted:

> Bribery was general. A friend of mine was the assistant to the director of the department of harvesting. He always had plenty of money, although his salary was low. There were 6,000 farmers in Debrecen without including the collectives. This man helped the peasants with setting up their quotas. The Hungarian peasants are clever like no one else. They knew how to [evade] every Communist regulation. Every time they came into the city, they would play dumb in the offices.[101]

Fraud also went more smoothly when you partnered with a state employee. For instance, one lawful way for private farmers to bypass collections was to cut a deal with a buyer for a food processing plant. One such person worked for a conserve factory near Budapest. Until 1956, he circulated among regional villages to secure purchasing agreements.

If they made contracts with us, then they didn't have to hand their products in to the government. They preferred to make contracts with us, because [we] were much more lenient than the government supervisors. I always underestimated the possible crop of a certain field, so that the peasant, having more [yield] than he made contract for, was able to sell the remaining crops on the free market, and was grateful to us buyers, and divided with us his profit.[102]

Defrauding state quotas was more direct, but depended on collectors with a blind eye. "Everyone in the village managed to to deliver produce of the worst possible quality," a farmer's son noted:

They mixed water with the milk... or else, they removed the cream from it. A peasant who owned four pigs would report that he owned only two. If he slaughtered two pigs, he reported that he slaughtered one, so that he had to pay delivery on one pig only. The peasants in the village managed to thresh [some of] their grain by hand before the harvest, because then the delivery collector could not supervise the amount harvested. One could even cheat at the threshing machine by removing the crop from the machine without weighing it.[103]

A butcher in Ajak (Szabolcs-Szatmár) prospered "from 1951 onwards... by illegally buying and slaughtering livestock which he sold on the [local] black market." He favored young calves whose owners "told the authorities" that they had been born prematurely and died. He also butchered healthy pigs but bought diseased animals or carcasses to deceive inspectors, claiming they had been intended for compulsory deliveries. His ability to carry on illicit livestock processing for years was doubtless aided by the fact that his "best customers included... the director of the state store, the wives of the local Party president and secretary, a secret police lieutenant, a police corporal and the village's two police informers."[104]

Among private farmers, stealing from one another was plainly wrong, but theft from "kulaks," collectors, state farms, MTSs, or TSZs, or buying items others appropriated from them was not. Often, "the peasant had to steal his own produce and crops, also his farm animals."[105] The son of a displaced peasant outlined the moral landscape: "There were certain thefts which were not considered crimes by others.... In the village it was not considered a crime to steal from a kulak... The children of the poor peasants... believe that it is not a crime to steal from the gardens of the kulaks, or to break their windows."[106] And so it was at an orchard near Budapest in 1952. The owner caught two women who had taken 20 kg of apricots from his trees and "turned them over to the police." No charges followed because the women "were considered people in need;" ignoring their own analysis, the police kept the apricots "to consume."[107] On a private Békés farm, compulsory deliveries had so cramped a family's resources that, embarrassingly, "we even had to buy our own bread." To bake at home, "sometimes we managed to steal a little grain from our own granary [diverting it from the collections] and illegally ground it under somebody else's name. But we had to keep the flour at our friend's house." Eventually that household, designated as kulaks, saw its assets devoured by taxes to the point that "we lived on what we could steal."[108]

Yet sometimes a moral balance could be restored, as proved the case in Baranya:

> One old peasant kept stealing clover regularly from the TSZ fields and [other] peasants began to watch him. When they had proof, they came to me [the agronomist]. I once visited him and... told him to stop. I suggested he do some work in exchange... for the common good. He immediately did it and was happy about it, as were the other peasants. The party secretary who heard of this kept quiet. People had a general sense of commiseration and tried not to hurt each other.[109]

A displaced farmer from the Sopron area concluded: "Stealing is one of [the people's] democracies life-saving institutions. The slogan is: He who does not steal, perishes. About 20 percent of all the goods in circulation is stolen property... What we steal now – Hungarians say – will not come into the hands of the Russians. And how true it is." The son of a forester put it concisely: "To steal from a thief is not a sin."[110]

In a 1957 London interview, a former planner from the Hungarian National Bank identified the critical fracture point in the state's relationship with private farming.

> There was a constant contradiction in the regime's peasant policy and this problem has not yet been solved. 60 to 70 percent of the peasantry consists of independent farmers even today, and if these independent farmers are dissatisfied then they won't work, whereas if they are satisfied they refuse to enter the collective farms. In the Hungarian papers this problem is treated with self-contradictory and grotesque whining. They would like

the peasant to produce more, but they would also like to prove that independent farming is uneconomical and no good, thus forcing the peasant into the TSZs.[111]

Private farmers cooperated with the government only when coerced, only when no alternatives beckoned. Under Rákosi and Nagy, the state had refused the option of Soviet forced collectivization, confiscating crops and letting the laggards starve,[112] and thus generated a contradiction, not a solution. Meanwhile, the much-promoted TSZs had troubles of their own.

TOIL AND TROUBLE IN THE TSZS

The village of Vajdácska nestles in a northern Borsod county valley a few kilometers from the Slovakian border. Long a source of emigrants to North America,[113] the settlement endured repeated visits in the late 1940s by activists urging its 2,000 remaining residents to join producer cooperatives. "Most of them refused to listen; still fewer agreed… Finally in 1950 the Party managed to establish the Petőfi Collective." When one of the founders discovered that this TSZ "was not what he imagined, he left it," returning only after his son, an Army lieutenant, implored him to do so. Although its properties included a 350 hold farm (500 acres) whose owner had died recently, the co-op did not thrive. Others among the original 25 members (chiefly former estate workers) shared the founder's dissatisfaction. "They earned little money, received bad food, and had to pay fines when they failed to fulfill the norms. Consequently, one after another, they took the first opportunity to get away and took jobs as hired laborers at the State farm in Várhomok." Matters worsened steadily.

> At the beginning of December 1952, the potatoes and sugar beets were still lying in the fields, as a result of mismanagement and insufficient manpower. The [Party] solved this problem by ordering all the inhabitants of Vajdácska to collect potatoes in the fields – an attempt which failed because the soil was already frozen, making digging practically impossible. Then [they] ordered out a tractor, which broke down after half an hour. The potatoes were still in the fields in January.[114]

Why such a miserable outcome? Clearly Petőfi's members had delayed unearthing acres of potatoes and sugar beets. This was backbreaking stoop labor, never eagerly approached. Clearly as well, in freezing conditions the MTS tractor couldn't handle the job either. Yet, the observer who profiled this village and its co-op laid its faults at the feet of TSZ officials and Council leaders. Petőfi's chairman had been chosen for Party loyalty, not for his knowledge of farming practices. His daughter, 22 and barely literate, served as the office clerk, "assisted" by a former notary public "dismissed" for unreliability. The Council's Economic Department chief, a one-time shoemaker, had "not the faintest idea about agriculture" and issued bizarre orders, "heartbreaking for a conscientious farmer."[115] Too many agricultural administrators were just incompetent.

Consider for a moment that the Party state managed to create, nation-wide, over 4,000 TSZs between 1948 and 1953. Each one of these elected a chair to provide overall guidance, or accepted one whom Party officials designated. Each needed an agronomist to manage planning and organize the year's labor, equipment use, and seed/fertilizer orders. Each also required a bookkeeper or accountant to track funds, produce, and work completed, as well as to draft reports for district or county supervisors. Given that agriculture was the First Five Year Plan's step-child, where were these 12,000 capable staffers to come from? The answer: From the Party faithful, from hastily arranged training courses, and from Horthy-era white collar retreads—not a promising cohort. TSZ enthusiasts had templates for organizing Hungarian variants of Soviet *kolkhozes*, but often proved inept when challenged to put them into effective operation.

Agricultural producers cooperatives took three forms: Types I, II, and III, ascending from temporary to permanent commitments.[116] In the first, a general "growers' group," households "pooled, without losing possession, their land, animals, and agricultural tools" (on an area limited to 120 holds), working together, especially in spring, and distributing the results according to the output of their individual fields. As benefits, Type I members received a 20% reduction in delivery quotas and taxes, were immunized against stock seizures if quotas could not be met, and could access one-year, interest-free loans to cover any shortfalls. Operating costs were apportioned according to the acreage owners allotted to the project: "to produce a single crop on a consolidated parcel of land." Party men distrusted Type I associations, however, regarding them as "hiding places for individual farmers." Type II, the "average distribution" group, could range up to 200 holds and involved joint sowing, cultivating, and harvesting of areas members selected for the project, with returns again distributed on the basis of each household's share of the land used, but calculated according to the average output of the entire operation. Type IIs also offered more benefits than Type Is (e.g., five-year no-interest loans, lower taxes). Type III, the "joint producer cooperative group," was the Party's favored arrangement—all land, tools, and livestock had to be permanently contributed, with their use thereafter determined by TSZ officials and a members' general assembly. The state pledged to supply investment funds, fertilizer, machinery, and expertise. Its regulations apportioned shares of annual profits: 75% for labor inputs (recorded as "work units") and 25% calculated in proportion to the acreage donated. As well, over several years, cash compensation would be paid for the land contributed. After ownership transfers, members had no land taxes and received household "garden plots" (up to 1.5 holds/2 acres), often exempt from delivery demands.[117] So logical and orderly, but also so many moving parts, so many promises, so much that could go wrong.

Several substantial problems gradually surfaced. One Ministry study demonstrated that, of those entering co-ops in 1949, sizable numbers had retained private farmland for their use. In the north, more than half, in the east, perhaps a quarter, in the west 30%, and in the center and south, roughly two-thirds of members held onto household plots averaging five holds [7 acres]. This did not demonstrate confidence in the new system. Second, the pace of entry was much slower than anticipated. By mid-1952, despite squeezing private farmers financially amid years of relentless propagandizing, Hungary's 4,000 TSZ groups controlled just 18% of the nation's arable land.[118] This did not demonstrate efficacy in transforming agriculture. Third, evidence was growing that TSZ members tended to slight essential collective tasks which earned work units, in order to focus on cultivating their household plots intensively, tending livestock, and selling their surpluses in urban free markets, which earned money right away. The work units' value was uncertain until the year-end accounting, whereas cash from market transactions was immediately available.[119] This choice did not demonstrate a commitment to building socialism.

To initiate a Type III co-op, averaging about 800 holds [1,100 acres] in 1950, organizers needed to gather and amalgamate dozens of adjacent farms and eliminate barriers between them to form the open fields conducive to mechanical plowing and harvesting. Carving state farms out of pre-war estates already devoted to large-scale grain production was a fairly straightforward process, as was dividing parts of such *latifundia* into "dwarf farms" in the postwar land reform.[120] But for the mass of Hungary's land, held by "middle peasants," the process was more complicated. Before 1945,

> in many villages, small farms ha[d] been divided, mostly by inheritance, into tinier strips of land. These strips, sometimes only a few yards wide, are often at great distances from each other. The farmer has to transport his plow, his fertilizers, his seed and himself from one end of the village fields to the other. The amount of labor wasted through this procedure is considerable. [To consolidate,] each little bit of land has to be carefully evaluated, and the little strips exchanged between farmers.

When unification was attempted, arbitration was usually required, at times leading to "long legal suits." Yet, inasmuch as farmers "wasted" 30% of rural workdays trudging among parcels, consolidation was "an indispensable feature of any land reform."[121]

This spatial situation severely complicated assembling a Type III TSZ, as the acreage contributed often lay in fragments scattered across the landscape. Even where holdings consisted of continuous fields, it did little good to secure participation by, say, a dozen of a district's thirty households. The patchwork land-quilt resulting from partial success would resemble a collage of village strips, just on a larger scale. In neither case would tractors be of much value. This obstacle accounts for propaganda celebrations of new "socialist towns," where under heavy pressure the entire population signed up for cooperative membership, bringing all their fields and pastures into the fold at once. Unfortunately for the TSZ project, after an organizing triumph at Túrkeve (Szolnok) was reported directly to Rákosi in 1951:

> a third of the members who had been violently forced to join either never worked for the producer cooperative or left it after a few months to work in industry. Cegléd [Pest] too became a "socialist town" using similar methods: there a number of the Great Stalin Producer Cooperative members were put on the membership list "by copying names from the cemetery headstones, while others never showed up... after signing the membership forms."[122]

If this mass processing approach seemed ineffectual, what was to be done?

One substitute strategy was "commasation," a practice that involved mandatory, systematic land exchanges, so as to create large, contiguous state-managed fields. According to a Baranya agricultural specialist:

> The first great wave... began in the fall of 1949. At that time, the main aim of the Communist policy was to establish those large tables of land which lent themselves to estate cultivation in state farms and cooperatives. Consequently the lands of such [enterprises], which were in many small parcels, were now commasated and the land of individual farmers lying in between was exchanged. [This] did not take into account the individual wishes of the peasants. They received an exchange property for their former landholdings; however, the exchange was carried out in a way that gave birth to many grievances. The exchange property was usually of poorer quality and was [in] some distant part of the community.

In some areas, between 1950 and 1953, every farmer lost parcels to TSZ consolidations, in return receiving peripheral and marginal land. Described as an "act of terror," this practice drove some households to join TSZs, "rather than accept the exchange property." Economist Béla Balassa estimated that nearly 13 million acres were "regrouped" through commasation, "almost 60 percent of agricultural land."[123]

A Sopron farmer confirmed the details. Once the Ministry declared a local program for rational co-op development, decrees ordered that "the best quality land in the immediate proximity of the village, if possible, is to be expropriated as the TSZ site."

> If a non-TSZ member happened to have a property within the borders of the proposed TSZ's domain, that property was taken away from him and he received another piece of land, not necessarily of equal value, at a different locality. Very often the land received was very far away and of inferior quality. The land taxes of the affected peasant remained the same, however, irrespective of his new property's gold crown value. He continued to be taxed on the basis of the old land's value, as if nothing had happened.[124]

This tax maneuver was a scam of genius, deepening the theft economy. The state acquired fertile terrain at no cost, land on which co-op members would not be taxed, yet tied the former owners to that land's gold crown rating, assuring an ongoing tax flow. That the replacement property was inferior in potential crop yields, thus lower in crown rating and tax liability, was irrelevant. "As if nothing had happened," indeed.

The son of a Békés middle peasant family was very precise about what did "happen." At the war's end, his family had roughly 21 holds, in two parts. The state confiscated the larger piece, 16 holds, in 1949, after categorizing the family as "kulaks," and transferred it to a TSZ. "Our land" about one km away from the village, was "beautiful good soil with orchards and domestic animals." The exchange plot, also 16 holds, was "bare sand" located 15 km from town. "From this time on we couldn't make a living. My father left the land alone and tried to work for other farmers." Three years later, "everything my father had was taken for taxes. When he left his land, we had about 65,000 ft in tax arrears." By 1956, his wife having died of diabetes, the father served "as a doorman in a large state company."[125] A Ministry commercial officer added:

> It is necessary to understand what is meant by "consolidation" today. Suppose the regime succeeds in having a TSZ formed in a village, embracing 30 or 40 peasants with bits of land here and there. Now these bits and pieces dispersed all over the place have to be consolidated. An arbitrary area equal to the sum of the individual holdings is marked out somewhere, generally on the best land of the village, and those [independent] peasants whose lands happened to be in that area are "commasated" with the outlying bits of those who have entered the TSZ. This is usually a disastrous deal... In fact, the threat of "consolidation" is one of the most potent means of forcing reluctant peasants into the TSZs. The other means is discriminatory taxation.[126]

Once established, TSZs' performance ranged from excellent to "grotesque," the term of art a central banker selected. He often visited rural districts and toured co-ops which had received credits from Budapest, with his area manager arranging an agenda.

> When I visited Tapolca [Veszprem], I told the branch representative to take me to two collectives, to the best and to the worst of the district. The best was a pleasant, attractive, fairly small collective farm of four to five hundred holds [560-700 acres], concentrating on vineyards and cattle. The president was an intelligent farmer. One received a very pleasant impression here, a feeling of cooperation, of socialist building in the best sense of the word. At the worst collective farm, we didn't find a single soul on the

collective lands at 4:00 pm, although it was spring. The members of the farm were all working their own land.[127]

Administrators soon classified TSZs as good, average or weak—good meaning profitable, average meaning breaking even, more or less, and weak indicating annual deficits, failures to meet plan targets, and misman-agement. Though proportions varied,[128] roughly a third of all co-ops ranked as week and about a sixth as good. Weak TSZs necessitated state subsidies in order to continue, so the Ministry paid special attention to them, sending advisers, pushing staff to augment skills through courses, and if all else failed, merging them with middling TSZs or other weak enterprises to increase scale and perhaps improve performance.[129]

Planning screwups were especially galling. The TSZ at Mosonszen-tjános (Győr) had a very rocky 1951, despite filing a full "working plan" in January. "When the time came for an increased amount of work to be executed, all plans were simply thrown to the wind." Brigade team work was in shambles. Repeated hoeing of sugar beet fields was ignored, resulting in "very poor [yields] for soil of this quality." The second mowing of the pastures "was never accomplished," seriously reducing the fodder supply, a task crowded out by requirements to deliver grain and beets on time. Worse, after sowing 55 holds (77 acres) of *baltacim* (purple hay), members left it to rot, only "three cartloads" being reaped. The Party Secretary had helped with spring tasks, "but by the time fall came, he worked no more," yet credited himself with scores of fraudulent work units (as did the President's wife). Members kept quiet, as "to remark about it would have meant a great deal of trouble."[130] The Party daily complained that fall about bad behavior by TSZ leaders and members who exhibited poor discipline, disregarded work schedules, ignored deadlines and instructions from above, and condoned "illegal labor migration."[131] István Rács later argued that, during the Nagy opening,

> it became known how ineffective, inefficient and at times irrational were the agricultural production methods applied on the collective farms… The collectives were more often than not mismanaged and they compared unfavorably to private holdings in every respect. Some of this agricultural impotence I have seen myself; there was for example an orchard, 60 holds of peaches [84 acres]. The leadership of the collective decided to cut the trees because they simply did not know how to cultivate them.[132]

Mosonszentjános, exemplifying a weak co-op's struggles, needed year-end budget supplements to continue operating. By 1956, the total state subsidy to TSZs had reached four billion forints annually [ca. $350 million at official exchange rates]. Something had gone very wrong.[133]

Organizationally, every TSZ had an operating manual, an "institutional code, as prepared by the government," supplemented by an annual plan matching crops to territories, specifying capital investments, and detailing construction projects. According to these mandates and the plan, the "population was split into small operational groups called brigades, each consisting of some 7–10 people, and each responsible for performance of some specialized activity." A Party member was supposed to head each brigade, though frequently there were too few to go around. Brigades, assigned to work "from 7 o'clock in the morning till 6 o'clock in the evening," focused, for example, on cultivating vegetables or managing livestock. Grain sowing and harvesting brought all hands to bear "on a compact territory of the domain, sliced out for this purpose." Machinery for field work came from the MTSs, though not always reliably, despite the co-ops' priority access. TSZs had to follow "centralized directives. Every single detail was prescribed to them, and the directives had to be carried out. The trouble was that this centralized planning did not take into consideration local peculiarities of soil, climate, etc. The various farm activities were improperly and poorly executed."[134] Members regularly shirked tasks that private farmers would have seen as undesirable, but unavoidable. At a Sopron TSZ, after a field of hay was cut, "they did not have the men to work as haymakers, and both the hay and lucerne [alfalfa] remained out in the fields, unattended, and becoming rotten and useless."[135] "Not having the men" was all too common, for several reasons.

In that Sopron co-op, many members were "older people, 50 years old and older. The young folk preferred to go and work in the factories, rather than enter the collectives."[136] This drained agriculture of the labor force necessary to make TSZs effective, even as industries welcomed the newcomers. At Lentikápolna (Zala), not far from the Slovenian border, the local TSZ "should actually be called the 'old people's home', for... every able and young member left to work in other villages."[137] Second, households joined co-ops tactically, enrolling the family head, but not his wife or children, or alternatively, the wife and perhaps a grandparent but not the father. This selectivity facilitated maximizing earnings: only members were required to labor on collective lands and stock-raising properties. The non-member spouse might take a job in town or tend the household's chickens or pigs; young adults joined construction teams, took up casual labor (loading rail cars, carting), or secured factory or commercial positions in the county seat, coming home periodically. (Such sojourners were known for Monday late arrivals, returning from their villages, and for disappearing during harvests.[138]) By committing their material assets to the TSZ, households ended the delivery squeezes, the tax grind, the inspections, and the propaganda campaigns. By excluding a portion of their labor resources, however, they preserved opportunities to "make money" and reduce uncertainty. As well, each "TSZ member continued to steal, whatever and as much as he could, to round out his actual compensation."[139] One tactic, widely adopted—"they cut down their wheat when it was still green... and used it as animal fodder."[140] A state ethnographer finessed the entire issue a few years later. Regrettably, he wrote, "many members do not yet sufficiently feel that the communal farm is their own. They may on several occasions even pilfer from it, as the former estate laborers did from the landlords."[141] Such commentary confirms the wisdom of heavily discounting official versions of agricultural conditions.

A critical resource in members' quest for cash was the TSZ-allotted "household plot;" it anchored the central theft in TSZ operations—stealing time from the state, not materials or goods, so as to maximize private yields. Derived from Soviet practice, yet politically explosive, these mini-farms supported family self-provision in TSZs and supplied open markets (and state purchasers) with fresh milk and eggs, meat, fruits, vegetables, and in some cases, wine. Limited to one hold, they expanded (illegally) and contracted (legally) in the tug of war between private initiative, administrative pragmatism and Party orthodoxy. Analogous to private farmers, TSZ members drawing substantial revenues (one milk producer reaping 3,000 ft/month) skimped on time commitments for common lands and livestock. Yet, official moves shrinking their plots to force greater reliance on shared earnings generated anger, stimulated evasions, brought threats of member walkouts, and depleted needed produce flows to town markets.

Practices and conditions varied considerably. According to a Baranya commentator:

> The size of peasant backyards is limited by law to one hold. This is the land the peasant spends all his effort on, and he tries to circumvent the

one hold ruling by putting land in a son's name and [in] many other ways. So he has two or three holds and all his efforts are spent on this land, for he pays no taxes on this land nor does he have contribution obligations on this backyard. Thus the rest of the [TSZ] land is neglected.[142]

An agronomist from the same district added:

Originally every member of the cooperative was supposed to received a household plot of one hold. But now the extent of this plot has been decreased in many case to half a hold or even less. The members of the cooperative work really hard on their household plots, doing there either fruit growing or dairy farming in order to get some cash.[143]

In Györ, by contrast, delivery requirements remained and plot locations changed each year:

All TSZ members also had a small homestead to themselves, amounting to a maximum of one hold per family, for which they delivered 2 kg of eggs and 2.5 kg of poultry per year to the government. This land, the location of which varied yearly, was theirs to use as they pleased. The assignment of the homestead land was accomplished every year by throwing [dice]. If one was lucky, he got fertile land; others, less fortunate, were assigned arid territory. The brigade leaders could choose their own land.[144]

Whatever the local rules, household plots were the glue that kept TSZ members in place. Party conservatives reflexively attacked these "residues of capitalism," but planners realized that they, like private farmers, could not be dispensed with.

At the summer 1953 outset of the Nagy administration, agricultural specialists of all stripes appreciated that the TSZ project was not going well. Central Committee member Reszó Nyers later admitted that the state had tried to go too far, too fast with collectivization: "a swift pace which was unrealistic." Yet Nagy's elimination of requirements and restrictions, particularly creating an opening for TSZ members' withdrawal, threatened to unravel the whole system, or so believed the post-Stalin orthodoxy. Rákosi loyalists stepped in to block this, insofar as possible, by asserting that those leaving could take neither land nor tools with them. Yet, tallies of co-op membership suggested these obstacles weren't convincing. (There was, after all, a great deal of untilled land available for leasing.) Permissions to leave were delayed for months, and in reply, TSZ members apparently "refused to plant cooperative land," estimated at a million holds.[145] Co-ops of all types had reported ca. 375,000 members in June 1953, just before the leadership shift, and ca. 225,000 in December 1954, some months before Nagy's April 1955 dismissal. Over the next 18 months, the Rákosi team conducted an all-hands campaign to restore memberships and revive dormant or discontinued TSZs. This paid dividends rapidly, as over 100,000 individuals returned to co-op membership (which rose to ca. 350,000) and some 600 TSZs re-commenced operations.[146]

Yet dissatisfaction continued; in August 1956 the state acknowledge essentially "a stoppage in collectivization, if not a decrease in the number of collectivized peasants." Prime Minister András Hegedűs allowed that "measures have to be taken to give the working farmers more interest in production... to make the pioneer work of the cooperatives easier." He pledged long-term 1% construction loans and an end to central bank deductions from TSZ accounts "for credits extended." The Party daily still scolded: "there are villages where some people misinterpret the Party's policy... They believe that... it is permissible to flaunt the laws, to cheat the people's state and to fail to comply with surrender obligations."[147] Exactly so, and two months later, the October Revolt tore the lid off rural discontent. By the end of the year, nearly a quarter million Hungarians abandoned TSZs, according to Resző Nyers' data, with the remaining 119,000 members closely matching the December 1950 total, six years earlier.[148] Back to square one.

Conclusion

Unlike its heavy industry drive, frequently regarded as successful if inappropriate, Hungary's poorly funded and badly administered agricultural policies and practices proved deeply inadequate on at least three fronts. First, the state's obsession with centralized uniformities and resistance to contradictory information meant that plans and programs were doomed from their starting blocks. Like so much else, the farm system only "worked, more or less." Second, mountains of propaganda failed to convince family-centered rural actors of socialism's promise; their eyes told them they were being manipulated and stripped by mandates, restrictions, and incompetence. Third, widespread distrust, combined with agencies' arbitrariness, authorized, and deepened the theft economy in the countryside. "He who does not steal, perishes." The Nagy team's rethinking was inadequate to the scale of the defects. "It was in agriculture, where the greatest gains were planned and needed, that the "New Course" most conspicuously failed," a U.S. analysis judged. Critical to this result was "the failure of the regime to win the support of the peasants. Even the additional concessions made during 1954, including further cancellation of tax arrears, failed to generate confidence."[149] A later assessment, filed ten days after the Soviets crushed the 1956 Revolt, argued that agricultural disappointments indeed stemmed from weak investment "in buildings, implements, fertilizer, insecticides, and soil and crop improvement." But more salient was that "the independent peasants" had rejected the regime. They "have been unwilling to invest in their strips of land because they are uncertain of holding the same place permanently," fearing compulsory land exchanges when TSZs were formed. Moreover, "the entire system of crop collection has forced peasants to enter the cooperatives."[150] The combination of high taxes and robbery in delivery prices provided them "little incentive to farm the land productively." On the whole, Hungarian agriculture was decaying, not advancing. Despite swaths of Budapest being in ruins once again, with Soviet dominion re-asserted, the business of agriculture would have to change substantially if building socialism in the countryside was to have meaning and substance.

NOTES

1. Columbia University Research Project on Hungary (CURPH), Interview No. 62-M, 44, HU OSA 414-0-2-60 (Full text available online at Open Society Archivum. https://catalog.osaarc hivum.org/?f%5Bdigital_collection%5D%5B%5D=CURPH+Int erviews+with+1956+Hungarian+Refugees).
2. CURPH Interview No. 79-M, 30, HU OSA 414-0-2-78.
3. Quoted in Johan MacCormac, "Hungary Seen Facing Crop Crisis," *New York Times*, 4 April 1953, 5.
4. A. Sz, "Intersectional Comparison of Yields, Production and Income in Hungarian Agriculture," Radio Free Europe Background Report, 9 August 1958, HU OSA 300-8-3-9610, 1. The Report covers the period 1938–1955 (Online access to full text at Open Society Archivum. https://catalog.osaarchivum.org/? f%5Bdigital_collection%5D%5B%5D=RFE+Information+Items& f%5Blanguage_facet%5D%5B%5D=English&f%5Brecord_origin_

facet%5D%5B%5D=Digital+Repository&f%5Bsubject_geo_facet% 5D%5B%5D=Hungary).

5. A key concept in Marxist economics, regarding the calculation of value. See https://en.wikipedia.org/wiki/Socially_necessary_lab our_time.

6. Robert C. H. Chia and Robin Holtw, *Strategy Without Design: The Silent Efficacy of Indirect Action*, Cambridge: Cambridge University Press, 2009, 5 (emphasis added).

7. James Scott, *Weapons of the Weak: Everyday Forms of Peasant Resistance*, New Haven: Yale University Press, 1985. Quote from https://en.wikipedia.org/wiki/Weapons_of_the_Weak (accessed 3 August 2021). Outsiders were well positioned to read the resistance in such behavior. A British writer touring still-colonial Vietnam in 1950 noted: "The Vietnamese people, described by early travelers as gay, sociable and showing a lively curiosity where strangers were concerned, have now withdrawn into themselves... they are utterly indifferent. It is as if a general agreement has been reached that this is the best way of dealing with an intolerable presence" (Norman Lewis, *A Dragon Apparent: Travels in Cambodia, Laos and Vietnam*, London: Jonathan Cape, 1951, 26–27).

8. Zsuzsanna Varga, *The Hungarian Agricultural Miracle?*, London: Lexington Books, 2020, 41, 59.

9. F.F., "The 'New Line' in Hungary: Politics and Economics under the Nagy Government," *The World Today* 11:1(January 1955): 27–40, quote from 35.

10. CIA Information Report, "Independent Farming and Agricultural Cooperatives," 13 May 1953, 4–5 (Secret, CIA-RDP80-00810A001100010004-4), [hereafter CIAIR].

11. CIA, Information from Foreign Documents, "Statistics on Manpower Employees on State Farms in Hungary," 11 March 1955 (unclassified, CIA-RDP80-00809A000700240055-3), [hereafter CIAIFD]. The technical and industrial workers maintained and repaired equipment, undertook small-scale construction, and produced articles needed for operations (e.g., small tools, parts).

12. CURPH Interview No. 443, 14–16, HU OSA 414-0-2-264. Only in "shopwindow" farms, visited by touring foreigners, did temporaries have individual rooms (16). Netting 22 forints/day

would provide temporaries with 550 forints, in cash, for a 25-day work month, ample funds for cigarettes and Saturday night drinking or for sharing with families at home. In families, working teenagers received less than an adult males' monthly rate, as did women. Still, with four earners, a permanent family could realize upwards of 1800 forints monthly.

13. CIAIR, "Independent Farming," 5. At an undetermined number of state farms, holding on to workers was not an issue, as they were staffed by prisoners and deportees. See RFE Field Reports: "Persecution—Expulsion," 11 July 1951, HU OSA 300-1-2-2204, [hereafter RFEFR], for "former ministers, bankers, civil servants" doing field labor at a state farm, and "The Bernátkút Prisoners' Farm," 21 December 1951, HU OSA 300-1-2-12940, for prisoners in Feher county, and in Bacs, "The Harta Judicial Agricultural Enterprise," 4 March 1952, HU OSA 300-1-2-16513.

14. Varga, *Agricultural Miracle*, 40–42. See also Kenneth Murray, *The Agricultural Situation in Eastern Europe, Part IV: Hungary*, Washington, DC: Foreign Agricultural Service, US Dept. of Agriculture, March 1960, 6, 16–20.

15. CURPH 443, 4.

16. Ibid., 6–7. Land measurements in Hungary were usually framed in cadastral yokes or holds, the equivalent of 1.4 acres in US terms, or 0.6 hectares in the metric system.

17. RFEFR, "Conditions in Mosonszolnok," 7 February 1952, 1, HU OSA 300-1-2-15162. A clerk at the Mosonoszolnok SF (Györ) concurred: "We had a great many problems here. One of them was that the Council of Ministers promised needed machinery but we did not receive it." CURPH Interview No. 203, 23. HU OSA 414-0-2-180.

18. CIAIFD, "Cultivation of Rice, Industrial Crops in Hungary," 19 May 1953 (Restricted, CIA-RDP80-00809A000700110206-9). [Translated newspaper articles] *Koksagyz* is a species of dandelion whose roots yield a variant of natural rubber; kenaf is an Asian fiber plant; and yucca, a perennial from the Western hemisphere, offers fibrous leaves which can be processed for use in making rope and coarse textiles (Multiple Wikipedia entries, accessed 9 February 2021).

3 AGRICULTURE FROM STALINISM TO THE REVOLT   101

19. CURPH Interview No. 606, August 1957, 12–13, HU OSA 414-020-344. See also CIAIFD, "Extend Cultivation of Kok-Sagyz in Hungary," 1 April 1952 (Restricted, CIA-RDP80-00809A000700050446-0). Both the US and the USSR planted large acreages of koksagyz during WWII, when Asian rubber supplies were blocked. The Russians claimed to have drawn 200 kg/hectare from its roots (https://en.wikipedia.org/wiki/Taraxacum_kok-saghyz, accessed 9 February 2021).
20. CIAIR, "Cotton Production in Hungary," 25 February 1954, 1 (Confidential, CIA-RDP81-01036R000100120064-8).
21. CIAIFD, "Urge Growing More Cotton in Hungary," *Magyar Mesőgazdaság* (Hungarian Agriculture), 16 February 1951 (Confidential, CIA- RDP80-00809A000600400032-1).
22. CURPH 606, 13–14. Another fire also affected the Békés cotton harvest in 1951, when a large shed holding one state farm's entire crop burned on the night of 2 November. Once "two empty kerosene cans were found" a few meters from the blaze, the bitter rivalry between the farm director and a man he had refused to appoint as Party Secretary came to light. The latter had torched the barn, hoping the director would be blamed (RFEFR, "Big Fire in Békés State Farm," 22 November 1951, HU OSA 300-1-2-11327).
23. CURPH Interview No. 406, 13, HU OSA 40\14-0-2-237.
24. CURPH Interview No. 528, 11–12, HU OSA 414-0-2-322.
25. Ibid., 14–15. To get to the 100,000 hold level, state agents contracted with TSZs and private farmers, as state farms could not offer additional lands. The CURPH respondent estimated that only a third of these cotton planters broke even or earned a profit on their costs of production, whereas had they planted onions they could expect an income of 15,000 ft/hold, not counting costs and taxes, of course. That was state-sponsored "crowding out" in spades. CURPH 443 confirms that "the Hungarian cotton was of such a poor quality that finally the whole plan was given up" (49).
26. CIAIR, "Cotton Production in Hungary," 2.
27. CURPH 606, 16.
28. CURPH Interview No. 402, 13, HU OSA 414-0-2-233. This respondent was the chief engineer of an MTS near Pecs (Baranya). See also CURPH 606, 16. Anticipating the next topic, our

intrepid project manager noted of his third job that "there was much deliberate falsification of statistics and the tilting in favor of the Socialist sector, although despite all measures favoring the Socialist and repressing the private sector, private peasant yields were still higher..." (16).

29. CURPH 443, 15.
30. CURPH Interview No. 226, 90, HU OSA 414-0-2-202. Respondent was the son of an independent farmer.
31. CURPH Interview No. 615, 44–45, HU OSA 414-0-2-350.
32. CURPH 203, 20.
33. CURPH 443, 17–18. Dismantling machines to steal parts also took place in mining. At Várpolata (Veszprem), two Soviet-made coal cutting machines were the target. "First, various parts disappeared... then each lost one of its seven motors, and finally the blades disappeared." Repair plant managers were "extremely puzzled because "all that remained of them was a heap of scrap metal." CIAIFD, "Dismantle Coal Cutters," *Szabad Ifjusag* (Free Youth), 17 July 1953 (Confidential, CIA-RDP80-00809A000700160245-1).
34. CURPH 615, 44. Staff members from bourgeois or noble backgrounds would be (and were) dismissed once their family histories became known. Creating false biographies could assist in job retention, but it often failed.
35. Varga, *Hungarian Agriculture*, 42–44.
36. CIAIR, "Hungarian Tractor Stations," 9 March 1951, 1–2 (Confidential, CIA RDP82-00457R007000470009-8); CURPH Interview No. 414, 40, HU OSA 414-0-2-245.
37. CIAIR, "Hungarian Tractor Stations"; CURPH 414, 40–42.
38. CURPH Interview No. 109, 84, HU OSA 414-0-2-136. His last job before leaving for the US (to join his brother) was in the State Statistical Office for Fruits and Vegetables. There, "we dealt with true figures, not those published in the papers and other propaganda materials. These data were handled as classified material and weren't available [outside] the highest government circles." The Party did not interfere with their calculations.
39. CIAIFD, "Development of the MTS in Hungary, 1954," *Statisztikai tájékoztató*, No. 4, Budapest, 1954, 1–6 (unclassified, CIA-RDP80-00809A000700240072-4). Potato harvesters dig into the ground mechanically, bring up both potatoes and

3 AGRICULTURE FROM STALINISM TO THE REVOLT 103

soil, shake off the soil and convey the potatoes into a bin or an accompanying truck. The savings in field labor is immense.

40. CURPH 443, 25.
41. See Jan Pryblyla, "Problems of Soviet Agriculture," *Journal of Farm Economics* 44(1962): 820–36.
42. CURPH 606, 17.
43. RFEFR, "Trouble in Construction of Tractor Stations," 21 July 1953, HU OSA 300-1-2-33515. For more on this, see Chapter 4.
44. CURPH 406, 12.
45. Ibid., 14–15.
46. Ibid., 36.
47. CURPH Interview No. 603, 18, HU OSA 414-0-2-337. CUPRH 443 noted that parts shortages arose because "the factories manufacture whole tractors only, but no parts, according to the 5-Year Plan." No bonuses were included for making parts, so parts weren't made (41).
48. CIAIFD, "Barter Food for Tractor Parts," *Hungaria*, Munich, 27 March 1953 (CIA-RDP80-00809A000700110585-8).
49. CURPH 406, 36. See also CURPH 402, 28–29.
50. CURPH 402, 11.
51. CURPH 406, 36–37.
52. CURPH 443, 41.
53. CURPH 603, 18.
54. CURPH 402, 14.
55. RFEFR, "Tractor Drivers Protest Against Increased Labor Norms," 11 October 1951, HU OSA 300-1-2-8752.
56. CURPH 443, 41–42.
57. CURPH 402, 27–28.
58. CURPH Interview No. 524, 37, HU OSA 414-0-2-318.
59. RFEFR, "Conditions and Personalities at the Kapuvár Machine and Tractor Station," 22 October 1955, HU OSA 300-1-2-63251.
60. Teréz Kovács, "Rural Development in Hungary," Discussion Paper No. 34, Center for Regional Studies, Hungarian Academy of Sciences, Pécs, 2001; Péter Kovács, "Middle Peasantry Developing into Kulak Class in Hungary," *Társadalmi Szemle* (Social Review), February 1951, 1–2 (Confidential, CIA-RDP80-00809A000600400052-9). *TS* was the Party's theoretical journal.

61. John MacCormac, "Hungary Pushes 'Kulaks' Off Land," *New York Times*, 19 April 1949, 3; Kovács, "Middle Peasantry"; https://en.wikipedia.org/wiki/Kulak (accessed 15 February 2021); CIAIR, "Independent Farming and Agricultural Cooperatives," 13 May 1953, 3 (Secret, CIA-RDP80-00810A 001100010004-4). See also RFEFR, "Morale and General Mood," 11 June 1951, HU OSA 300-1-2-589, on rural deportations.
62. There were also town and city producer cooperatives, chiefly of craftsmen, dressmakers, et al., the *Kisipari Termelőszövetkezet* or KTSZ.
63. CURPH 606, 17.
64. CURPH 406, 16.
65. RFEFR, "Living Standards and the Economy of Hungary," 7 September 1953, 2–3, HU OSA 300-1-2-38539; Varga, *Hungarian Agriculture*, 71. Estimates of abandoned land ranged far higher, however. In a December 1953 speech to the Central Committee András Hegedűs indicated that "2,500,000 acres of Hungary's land lay untilled" (*New York Times*, 13 January 1953, 6). A state farm agronomist estimated the 1953 figure at 2 million holds or 2.8 million acres (CURPH 443, 31). Such levels represent over a quarter of all arable land.
66. The Ministry divided farmland into six classes in order of "preference in equipment, seed, fertilizers and machinery." TSZs were at the top, followed by state farms, then private farms. Below two categories of "reserve" lands (abandoned and never tilled) was "kulak land" (CURPH 406, 17).
67. RFEFR, "Morale," 11 June 1951.
68. RFEFR, "Requisitioning of Potatoes in Hungary," 6 June 1951, HU OSA 300-1-2-428. Another 1951 account of a 72-year old Pest widow's requirements can be found at RFEFR, "Poor Peasant Woman's Delivery Plight," 15 October 1951, HU OSA 300-1-2-8891. Though half of her property was a vineyard and the rest rocky soil, in addition to 200 liters of wine, she was also ordered to provide corn, wheat, chickens, eggs, potatoes and lard, most of which she would have had to purchase at market rates (e.g., 110 ft/kg for lard).
69. RFEFR, "A Peasant Sells His Horse," 23 October 1951, HU OSA 300-1-2-9519.

3 AGRICULTURE FROM STALINISM TO THE REVOLT   105

70. CURPH Interview No. 155, 73, HU OSA 414-0-2-171.
71. The unit of land quality measurement in Hungary was a "golden crown" scale, ranging from 10 to 40. Below 15 is weak; 15–25 average; 25–35 good; above 35 very good (E. Hamza and K. Miskó, "Characteristics of the Land Market in Hungary at the Time of the EU Accession," *Agricultural Economics—Czech* 57:4(2007): 161–66). Fields often had different ratings within a farm, of course. This scale apparently dated to the Imperial era.
72. CURPH 155, 7–9; CURPH Interview No. 215, 71, HU OSA 414-0-2-192.
73. This presumes a state selling price for grain at 2.4 ft/kg, and is aimed to be more exemplary than accurate. In the early 50s, for comparison industrial workers' annual earnings ranged from 7 to 10,000 forints, after deductions.
74. CURPH 215, 65–68. The respondent in this case had been a clerk in the Food Deliveries Department of Somogy county, responsible for determining forced collections and supervising their acquisition. Separate from the interview, he drafted a nine-page document, "The Agricultural Collection System in Hungary," which is priceless.
75. CURPH Interview No. 26-M, 15, HU OSA 4145-0-2-20. Respondent was the son of a farmer with 35 holds who restocked in 1946 after the Russians seized all his livestock, was then declared a kulak, so that his cattle and pigs were again appropriated. Once the Nagy government relaxed controls in 1953–1954, he restocked for a third time (12).
76. CURPH Interview No. 243, 39–40, HU OSA 414-0-2-217. See also CURPH Interview No. 46-M, 16, HU OSA 414-0-2-42. Consumers regularly complained about the low quality of Hungarian bread, a result of export agencies' practice of sending high quality wheat abroad, either to the USSR or in exchange for Western machinery and hard currency. Bad bread thus resulted from conscious state policy. See RFEFR, "Budapest Citizens Shocked by Bad Quality of Bread," 10 December 1952, HU OSA 300-1-2-28631.
77. CURPH 26-M, 19–20.
78. Chia and Holt, *Strategy without Design*; RFEFR, "Morale and Passive Resistance," 11 November 1953, HU OSA 300-1-2-41802. See also CIA Intelligence Memorandum, "Changes in the

Agricultural Policies of the European Satellites During 1953," 12 April 1954, 14 (Secret, CIA-RDP79T00935A000200320002-6).

79. CURPH 443, 27. Technically, buying fodder was banned, as like grain it was a state monopsony, but illicit supply channels from state farms and TSZs to private farms did operate.

80. CURPH Interview No. 12-M, 19, HU OSA 414-0-2-5.

81. CURPH Interview No. 21-M, 25–26, HU OSA 414-0-2-15. As of December 1, 1951, surpluses of restricted goods could be sold in public markets, after compulsory quotas had been met. Respondent also knew people who traded in smuggled Austrian watches, brought in by crews of Danube ships, purchased in Budapest for ca. 400 ft and sold in provincial towns for 600–700, far less than the official price of 1200. This was risky, as anyone caught could spend "4 to 10 years" in prison (26).

82. CUPRH 203, 15.

83. CURPH Interview No. 80-F, 21, HU OSA 414-0-2-80. The frequency with which this was done is unknown.

84. CURPH 443, 26–28.

85. CURPH Interview No. 474, 8, HU OSA 414-0-2-287.

86. Varga, *Hungarian Agriculture*, 72–73.

87. CURPH 215, 65–66.

88. Alex Liddell, *The Wines of Hungary*, London: MITCH, 2006.

89. RFEFR, "Communists Making Preparations to Skim Off Record Vintage," 19 October 1951, HU OSA 300-1-2-9228.

90. CURPH 226, 38; CURPH 46-M, 27–28; RFEFR, "Latest Prices of Various Articles in Hungary," 12 December 1952, HU OSA 300-1-2-28606.

91. CURPH Interview No. 25-M, 1957, 20. HU OSA 414-0-2-19; CURPH Interview No. 461, July 1957, 8.

92. CURPH 406, 16–17. Villany, located in Baranya county, has once again become a source of quality red wines.

93. CURPH Interview No. 72-M, 22, 31, 33. HU OSA 414-0-2-71.

94. CURPH Interview No. 565, 41, HU OSA 414-0-2-336. Respondent lived 38 km south of Debrecen.

95. Ibid., 42. Interviewees repeatedly blamed gypsies (Roma) for performing this ugly task.

96. CURPH 461, 3.

97. CURPH 46-M, 31.

98. CURPH 474, 9.

99. CURPH 155, 9–10.
100. CURPH 12-M, 28.
101. CURPH 46-M, 40.
102. CURPH Interview No. 136, July 1957, 33–34, HU OSA 414-0-2-163. As this description suggests, respondent was something of a slimy character, also detailing frauds which he was involved as a competitive diver and in construction projects.
103. CURPH 226, 88–89.
104. RFEFR "Illegal Slaughtering and the Sale of Meat in Ajak," 9 April 1955, HU OSA 300-1-2-56987.
105. CURPH Interview No. 33-M, 30, HU OSA 414-0-2-28.
106. CURPH 26-M, 20.
107. CURPH 33-M, 31.
108. CURPH Interview No. 82-M, 11, 24, HU OSA 414-0-2-82.
109. CURPH 406, 29.
110. CURPH 155, 57; CURPH 25-M, 13.
111. CURPH Interview No. 508, 13, HU OSA 414-02-322.
112. Anne Applebaum, *Red Famine: Stalin's War on the Ukraine*, New York: Doubleday, 2017.
113. Estimates of 1848–1945 immigration to the US run between 600,000 and 1 million, plus over 50,000 to Canada before 1956. After the Revolt about 75,000 of Hungary's 200,000 exiles relocated to North America.
114. CIA, Security Information, "Agricultural Conditions and Communist Officials in the Village of Vajdácska," 1953 (Confidential, CIA-RDP83-00423R000700660001-1), An agronomist confirmed that private farmers produced more potatoes and sugar beets per hold than TSZs (CURPH 442, 19). A poet and revolutionary hero (1848), Sándor Petőfi symbolized Hungarian nationalism.
115. Ibid., 2; John MacCormac, "Hungary to Create Farm Collectives," *New York Times*, 1 July 1948, 6.
116. A fourth form, specialized co-ops, also existed, but does not seem to have thrived. These enterprises focused on particular tasks, like cattle breeding, seed development, or orchard management. See Resző Nyers, *The Cooperative Movement in Hungary*, Budapest: Pannonia, 1963. Only Type IIIs had a legal existence as enterprises; Type Is represented working agreements, not independent entities (CURPH 606, 20).

117. CIAIR, "Independent Farming and Agricultural Cooperatives, 5–8; Varga, *Hungarian Agriculture*, 44–45, 50. A Ministry of Agriculture analyst indicated that Type II co-ops were rare, a "paper category" (CURPH 606, 20).

118. Varga, *Hungarian Agriculture*, 46, 60.

119. CIAIR, "Agricultural Collectives," 26 June 1952, 2 (Secret, CIA-RDP80-00809A000600020178-9). The complexity of the accounting system needed to track and value work units too often overmatched TSZ bookkeepers, adding to members' distrust (CURPH 443, 36).

120. See for example CURPH 474, 5–6.

121. George Kiss, "Landed Estates and Peasant Farmers in Hungary," *The Scientific Monthly* 54(1942): 461–66. *TSM* was a publication of the American Academy for the Advancement of Science, succeeded in 1957 by *Science*.

122. Varga, *Hungarian Agriculture*, 58. See also CIAIR, "Agricultural Collectives," 2.

123. CURPH 443, 30–31; CIAIFD, "Order Land Unification," *Szabad Nép*, 25 July 1951 (Confidential, CIA-RDP80-00809A000700010594-0); and Béla Balassa, "Collectivization in Hungarian Agriculture," *Journal of Farm Economics* 42(1960): 35–51. See also Idem., *The Hungarian Experience in Economic Planning*, New Haven: Yale University Press, 1959, 256–57.

124. CURPH 155, 80. See also CURPH 474, 6 and CURPH 528, 10.

125. CUPRH 82-M, 11.

126. CURPH 606, 23–24. See also Balassa, "Collectivization," 45 and Ferenc Erdei, "The Socialist Transformation of Hungarian Agriculture," *New Hungarian Quarterly* 15(1964): 3–28—commasation discussed at 13–14. An agronomist confirmed that tractors could not be used on properties remaining in "strips" (CURPH 443, 24–25).

127. CURPH 528, 11.

128. One observer argued that few Borsod county TSZs were not running deficits by the mid-1950s (CURPH 25-M, 22).

129. CURPH 152, 46–48. In 1960, 1300 of 3000 co-ops had weak ratings (Lewis Fischer and Philip Uren, *The New Hungarian Agriculture*, Montreal: McGill, 1973, 41). By 1964, 1200 weak TSZs were counted, and 800 "goods" out of 3500 total (Gyula

Varga, "A Cooperative Village," *New Hungarian Quarterly*, No. 19 (1964): 16–34.
130. RFEFR, "Strange Results of the Production Cooperative of Mosonszentjános," 6 February 1952, HU OSA 300-1-2-15101.
131. CIAIFD, "Call for Stricter Discipline," *Szabad Nép* (Free People) 10 November 1951 (Restricted, CIA-RDP80-00809A-000700050013-0).
132. CURPH 152, 22–23. Similarly in Szabolcs-Szatmar, a local council could not secure boxes for shipping apples from area orchards, so rather than start a box-making workshop, they ordered the trees cut down (CURPH Interview No. 439, July 1957, 61–62, HU OSA 414-0-2-260).
133. CURPH 443, 35.
134. Ibid., 23.
135. CURPH 155, 81–84.
136. Ibid., 82.
137. RFEFR. "Life in Lentikápolna," 16 April 1953, 1, HU OSA 300-1-33520.
138. RFE Background Report, "Building Industry and Construction in Hungary before the Revolution," 15 February 1957, 24, HU OSA 300-8-3-3211.
139. CURPH 155, 84. Also CURPH 443, 45–46.
140. CURPH 152, 406.
141. Imre Katona, "Trends in the Transformation of the Hungarian Peasantry," *New Hungarian Quarterly*, No. 4 (1960): 3–27, quote at 15.
142. CURPH 406, 17.
143. CUPRH 443, 37–38.
144. CURPH 115, 84–85.
145. CIAIFD, "Hungary—Agriculture, Food Supply," 14 July 1954, 17 (Confidential, CIA-RDP80-00809A000700190181-9).
146. Nyers, *Cooperative Movement*, 64, 169; Varga, *Hungarian Agriculture*, 82–83.
147. RFEFR, "Agricultural Measures—Background," 16 August 1956, HU OSA 300-8-3-3036. See also RFEFR, "Creeping Resistance of Hungarian Farmers," 8 November 1955, HU OSA 300-1-2-60803, which reports that co-ops in Szabolocs-Szatmar

110 P. SCRANTON

county were neglecting root crop hoeing, members being "reluctant to work," reportedly a part of a 'widespread "go slow" movement.'
148. Nyers, *Cooperative Movement*, 169. Some of the missing TSZ members surely had gone into exile.
149. CIA, National Intelligence Estimate, 12.5-55, "Current Situation and Probable Developments in Hungary," 29 March 1955, 4 (Secret, CIA-RDP79R01012A005400040004-6).
150. CIA, Intelligence Memorandum, "Problems of the Hungarian Economy," 13 November 1956, 9 (Secret, CIA-RDP79T00935A0004001700020\-1).

CHAPTER 4

An Unfinished Project: Constructing Socialist Construction

The balance of supply and demand in a planned economy occurs in offices where a few people unaware of the real effects of their authoritarian plan become the supreme judges of the destinies of all producers and consumers... From this source of authority plans lead further down to smaller bodies, splitting unrealistic averages into still smaller averages, according to [rules] born in offices which, when they reach the enterprise level, have little resemblance to the conditions of actual life.
—Rudolf Bićanić, 1957[1]

A Hungarian who was the friend of a domestic employee of a Western diplomat did some work in the house of this diplomat on a private basis. He declined payment for the materials used, explaining they had cost him nothing, since he had stolen them from the factory where he worked. When the diplomat looked surprised, the man explained: "I make only 575 forints a month. I could not live on that, so I must sell things which I take from the factory. There is nothing wrong with this because everybody does it."
—RFE Field Report, 1952[2]

There was a longstanding dispute between the ministries over whether only the Ministry for Construction or other ministries as well should have construction enterprises under their jurisdiction... Finally in 1955, the Council of Ministers resolved the problem by deciding that construction enterprises should be operated solely by the Ministry of Construction

© The Author(s), under exclusive license to Springer Nature Switzerland AG 2022
P. Scranton, *Business Practice in Socialist Hungary, Volume 1*, Palgrave Debates in Business History,
https://doi.org/10.1007/978-3-030-89184-8_4

and (for the purpose of road and railroad construction) by the Ministry of Transportation. But the other ministries did not give up their building firms for many months and... finally established enterprises under false names... in order to continue construction activity.

—Béla Balassa, 1959[3]

Construction, like agriculture, experiences seasonal ups and downs; projects depend on the weather, which can halt work or wreck an effort well begun. Local conditions matter intensely; in both sectors, understanding soil characteristics is crucial. Both building and farming are complex, involving a variable mix of assumptions and contingencies, which make outcomes uncertain and underdetermined, despite best-laid plans. However, construction is a polar opposite to agriculture in other, equally-significant ways. Where agriculture exemplifies what "settled" means, construction materializes in a series of site-specific projects; when one is completed, everyone moves to other places and other tasks. Although farmers *cycle* back and forth between fields, orchards, gardens, and barns, building trades workers and supervisors *migrate* across space, even when they work in just one city. The spatial fixity of Hungary's private farms and TSZs brought rural actors to confront much the same resources and challenges annually, whereas construction projects' spatial inconstancy forced designers and operations managers recursively to attack problems that might be familiar but were rarely the same. Indeed, errors in presuming sites' similarities or in choosing appropriate construction materials and methods could trigger rude and expensive surprises. In industrializing Hungary, although agriculture was key to feeding the non-farm workforce and in delivering organic raw materials, construction was literally foundational to building socialism, first in remedying war damage, then in knitting together transportation, communication, and power supply networks, and finally, through Five Year Plans and special initiatives, in creating the heavy industrial capacities Cold War anxieties necessitated—mines, steel mills, chemical plants, factories for machinery and electrical goods. Under Stalinism, construction was a very big deal, and as such, generated perpetual contests over resources, authority, performance, and rewards.

The dynamics of building centered on, but were not confined to, Budapest's Ministry of Construction (MC). In cooperation with the Investment Bank and the National Planning Office, this huge agency

4 AN UNFINISHED PROJECT: CONSTRUCTING SOCIALIST CONSTRUCTION 113

Fig. 4.1 Housing destruction in Central Budapest, 1945 (Donor: Dr. István Kramer. *Source* FOTO: Fortepan—ID 52083, http://www.fortepan.hu/_photo/download/fortepan_52083.jpg, archive copy, Wikimedia Creative Commons)

designed, financed, and erected Hungary's principal public works—factories, power stations, dams, and canals. Other ministries and directorates sponsored specialized construction units, for instance the military, the state railways (MAV), road builders (and maintainers), and the Ministry of Agriculture (rural projects at state farms, TSZs and MTSs).[4] Counties and principal cities, especially the capital, sponsored a lower stratum of builders, supervised by MC and targeting public service capacities (schools, hospitals, offices) and the sector's stepchild—housing. Perhaps a quarter of Budapest's 300,000 dwellings had suffered war damage or destruction (Fig. 4.1); although most were repaired or replaced by 1949, overcrowding was persistent. Fearing atomic war, state policy called for building new factories in provincial cities. Although housing their incoming workforces was essential, ministerial allocations for apartment blocks proved chronically inadequate.[5] Last, small, private construction firms had long been elements of town and village business communities. Increasingly organized as "builders' cooperatives," they continued to serve local needs, including those of individual families seeking new housing (or repair/expansion).[6]

This chapter will chiefly review practices in planning and executing large-scale projects by ministerial departments, construction trusts,[7] and enterprise units. These organizations dominated construction nationally (except for home building, more than half of which was handled by local companies).[8] Projects generally looped back and forth through four intersecting phases after official authorization: design, finance, contracting, and construction. Other initiatives interfered with and complicated job completion: reorganizations of agencies or lines of responsibility, drives to standardize designs or modernize technologies, conflicts over labor and materiel, negotiations to extend deadlines, demands for plan adjustments and redesigns, and accounting manipulations to assure bonuses. After reviewing the Ministry's structure and activities, visiting several "ordinary" works-in-progress will illuminate construction's instability and disorderliness, as will a review of managerial practices and the industry's workforce. Throughout the range of project scales, opportunities for unauthorized or unlawful behavior abounded, stretching from swiping tools and lumber form worksites to the executive-suite fiddles known as "plan fraud." Closer attention to two mildly-bizarre mega-projects will follow: the Budapest Subway (which failed) and the Sztálinváros [Stalin Town] steel complex along the Danube (which succeeded, more or less, eventually). Scaling up from single-site building to a multidimensional grand scheme was a non-linear exercise. The necessary coordination and collaboration intensified as interdependencies increased, as did occasions for mangled connections and missed deadlines. One example: To promote rapid industrialization, the state created seven "new socialist towns" in the 1950s[9]; in each case, for production to commence, rail, road, power, water, housing, storage, and communications systems had to be configured and integrated. Rarely did coordinating these components go smoothly.

The Ministry of Construction and Its Rivals

Consistent with Soviet principles, the ministry practiced "one man management." Its director regularly reported to Rákosi's Council of Ministers about all activities—political, technical, project planning and execution, finance, and material supply. The State Control Center (later, Ministry of State Control) exercised parallel oversight, as did the Finance Ministry's Auditing Department. Appropriately, "every department, directorate and building firm had its own chief who was directly responsible to the minister." Deputy ministers were to control their realms "in every detail"; yet staff members could directly approach the minister, Lajos Szjiártó, who held "weekly reception hours during which anyone could go and talk with him." Several times annually the deputies and minister met to address problems in planning or organization and to evaluate each unit's successes and failures.[10] The agency's three divisions were Administration (personnel, legal, budget, maintenance), Theoretical (accounting, labor, statistics, planning, technical), and Production. The first two were "not in direct touch with firms"—that was Production's task. Its six sections "immediately directed and controlled the firms within their spheres of authority," which were: (1) "carrying out works" for large/medium-scale industry, along with public and residential buildings; (2) installations; (3) transport; (4) mechanization; (5) planning (at enterprise levels); and (6) raw materials production (brick, tile, cement, glass, concrete, stone, lumber, hardware, et al.).[11] Of course, effective directing and controlling was the key organizational challenge—at times a nightmare.

Building trade workers headed each production division; though their appointments initially reflected Party activism, most did attend the "Red Academy (higher education for promoted worker cadres)" and/or evening technical classes. In practice, "the director was merely the political leader... The technical leader was the chief engineer, the economic one the chief accountant. The director himself dealt only with personnel and political matters; the rest was done by section heads and expert *rapporteurs*." Chief engineers routinely held university degrees and often were not Party members; chief accountants had similar profiles. Beyond tracking and reporting deficits and profits, accountants, through both scheduled and "unexpected" site visits, supervised subordinate firms' management of wages, technology, and resources.[12] A former deputy minister judged that, despite "great difficulties," especially being pressed to handle a "senseless and forced building program" for rapid industrialization, the ministry "functioned relatively well." Still,

> there was a considerable shortage of technical experts. Some firms, for example that of county Szolnok, had as late as 1955, only one qualified

116 P. SCRANTON

engineer. Building, including constructions costing several million forint, was carried out by former master builders, foremen, or stone masons. Some of the men employed had no [professional] qualifications at all, yet were taken on, especially by provincial firms... There was a shortage of suitable machinery and equipment, particularly scaffolding.

Significantly, MC's minister, believing that construction was a technical field, sought "to bring together the best experts, which meant putting aside party and political considerations." In response, Party leaders, who (correctly) "attacked the Ministry as being the gathering place of capitalist and reactionary elements," nominated "politically reliable people" wherever possible. As both politically- and technically-well-trained officials were in short supply, this conflict continued, even as the organization's overall competence increased. In the two years preceding the Revolt, MC units finally began to meet or exceed profit targets—through improved performance supplemented by accounting manipulations.[13]

Another ongoing struggle, which the third epigraph highlights, involved rivalry among ministries over controlling construction projects, and by extension, competition among enterprises, even within the same ministry, for materials, tools, transport, manpower, and housing. For instance, an August 1954 survey showed that one county's current allocations (200 million forints) funded nearly 800 construction projects, the three dozen largest commanding 70% of the budget. What likely vexed MC managers was that these projects originated from *thirteen* ministries. The twelve others, in decreasing order of contract values, were: Agriculture, City and Town Economy, Produce Collection, Education, Light Industry, Metallurgy and Machines, Food, Internal Commerce, Health, Transport, Culture, and Heavy Industry. Formally, MC controlled less than ten percent of total expenditures (19 m ft); but because some ministries did not have captive construction units, MC enterprises wound up undertaking work valued at 73 million (37%). Ministries *with* building units (Agriculture, Metallurgy, Transport) handled jobs amounting to 65million (a third). The remaining 30% fell to local council enterprises, building co-ops, specialist firms, and craftsmen.[14] The Ministry of Construction had installed "one-man management"; but in practice the boundaries of what could be managed were vague and shifting, even if crystal clear on paper. The chair of the State Committee on Industrial Organization observed: "It is often said that excessive centralization has been the principal fault of the methods applied so far. In reality the

4 AN UNFINISHED PROJECT: CONSTRUCTING SOCIALIST CONSTRUCTION   117

central decisions have not been effective at all... [Instead] many elements of anarchy have appeared."[15]

One source of that anarchy was the profusion of planning offices serving ministries and agencies, mostly in Budapest. In addition to the MC's IPARTERV (Industrial Construction, 1000 employees, six divisions), they included separate institutions for City Planning, Public Building, Agricultural Construction, Power Plant Planning, Foundries, Military, Machinery Planning, Communications, and Chemical Plant Construction. Overall,

> the system of the planning offices is extremely bureaucratic with general chaos reigning. For example, if a planning office writes a letter to another planning office [in the capital], the answer usually never arrives earlier than three weeks. There is a constant quarrel among the planning offices; if something goes wrong then one office will blame another.

Additional design resources could be found outside the ministries, as private architects operated on construction's fringes. Offices bulging with work could contract with a qualified external individual to draft plans at less than half the internal cost and reliably "prepared for the date required."[16] A subtle variant, devised to augment staff earnings, involved deception by designers who would announce that no one in the firm could address a particular problem.

> In such cases, the architect in question will report to his superior about his elderly uncle, who... since his retirement has specialized in that one line. He promptly brings along his "uncle," who receives the assignment. The architect then carries out the work at home in the evenings. The "uncle" returns at the given date with the completed plan, and receives the money. After deducting 10 percent thereof, he turns the money over to the architect.

Perhaps not anarchy, but fraud certainly. MC banned both practices in summer 1952; but such private work continued, though "having become illegal, [it] is more dangerous."[17]

One strategy to control construction projects would be for MC to take charge of sectoral supply chains. This may be why the Ministry of Building Materials, created in 1952, was folded into the Ministry of Construction (June 1953), so that MC could (in theory) govern access to essential supplies. Its Directorate for the Manufacture of Raw Materials stood as an "intermediary" between producers and building firms, so as to guide flows and prevent leaks. This did not prove feasible, because brick and tile works, cement plants, and sawmills were scattered across rural districts, just like farms. Control from Budapest was impossible without placing resident agents at every production site. It was also obstructed by firms and projects adopting a Soviet practice to evade interference—employing a *tolkach* or "pusher," a person who used any means necessary to secure "certain favors to which a firm or individual is not legally or formally entitled," here "the procurement of materials." Although project plans specified the type and volume of inputs to be used, on-time deliveries, in correct quantities and at agreed prices, were far from reliable. As Balassa noted, "the method of physical allocation cannot ensure avoidance of discrepancies between... supply and demand. [Hence] an informal system of material procurement will necessarily develop."[18]

For instance, to influence deliveries for their immense steel plant project,

> the Construction Trust of Sztálinváros in 1956 stationed a group of pushers, consisting of about twelve or fifteen people, in the capital, and the enterprises [within] the trust employed two to three agents for the same purpose. There was a permanent fight between the Ministry of Construction and the trusts and enterprises which did not have their main offices in the capital, since the Ministry repeatedly forbade [locating] pushers in Budapest. These orders have never been carried out; the trusts and enterprises changed the location of the material expediters rather than discontinue their activity.

Firms lodged pushers in private apartments, or added them to staff rosters at Budapest area construction sites, as an ongoing "game of 'hide and seek' developed between the ministry and its enterprises."[19] Enterprises got value for the money spent on expediters, as securing materials "outside official channels" avoided "interruptions in production costing millions in production value," often at an "insignificant cost." Pushers bypassed regulations to "create and maintain good relations with the suppliers." In consequence, materiel producers produced inputs above their own plan's quotas (doing extra work) or illicitly transferred them from allocations to other projects.

4 AN UNFINISHED PROJECT: CONSTRUCTING SOCIALIST CONSTRUCTION 119

[T]he material expediters are highly specialized and have been working in their fields for years. Their methods consist of friendly persuasion, recompense in products manufactured by the enterprise in question, offering target bonuses, and in some cases, outright bribery. Some pushers work for more than one firm and enjoy a considerable income, paid under various disguises.[20]

Ministry of Construction leaders could hardly complain that subordinate units were ignoring their rules and requirements, for, like other agencies, they also "carried out only those [state] decrees which were in harmony with their interests." Along the way, they had cheerfully boosted the administrative staff's share of MC's total workforce from 10–12% in 1949 to 37% (of a larger force) by 1955, surely suggesting bureaucratic empire-building. When both the regime and the Party pressed ministries to reduce office headcounts (1954), MC and other agencies dismissed thousands of "non-productive" staff, then quietly re-hired most of them, reclassified as "productive"—"a process called 'hiding'." Relabeling roughly six percent of the ministry's workforce satisfied the reduction demand without disturbing operations.[21]

Conflicts between ministries and enterprises stemmed from the latter's dependence on plans which the former created. To be sure, in response to the ministry's preliminary scheme, firms sent their own draft programs up the ladder for consideration; but after negotiations, the agency had the final say. Ministries controlled enterprises' managerial appointments, had major input into labor availability, and together with the Planning Office and Investment Bank, authorized "the allocation, planning, financing and supervision of investments." However, effective oversight from afar was unusual. "The problem of information is of utmost importance in physical planning," Balassa wrote. Reports ministries demanded from below flooded in, but planners rarely had sufficient time to digest and translate them into program elements, so as to meet deadlines for plan dissemination and implementation. Building enterprises thus improvised, responding to persistent delays in information flows.

> During 1950-52, technical plans were prepared mostly parallel to construction itself. In 1953, among 182 large investment projects under construction, 85 did not even have a project outline and the situation has not greatly improved.... In 1955, only 10 big investment projects out of 250 possessed completed technological plans. Finally in 1956, 60 percent of the projects lacked completed documentation.

These shortcomings led to further chaos and delay, as completed but wrongheaded plans had to be altered in order commence work. Hence, in 1955 alone "18,000 modifications were made of the technological plans of 4,300 investments."[22] Project managers and enterprise executives thus regularly acted independently of, sometimes in opposition to, ministerial direction and supervision, even as their firms fought one another over labor, materials, and equipment.

Before considering projects on the ground, several other issues deserve attention. First, one party to these interactions is missing thus far—the clients—the plant managers, power-grid engineers, and regional housing authorities a finished project would eventually serve. As potential users paying a fraction of the costs, they had little voice, other than to complain, until they took charge of the results (when distressing discoveries might well surface). Ministry planners determined what new factories were essential, where an electrical station best fit national needs, which cities or towns deserved new apartments, although they did respond to local or enterprise pressure.[23] The MC selected each project's design bureau (the client had no input), and shunned securing multiple cost estimates as that wasted precious time. Within the planning and funding agencies, however, some officials did have "voice": careerists scheming to open bright futures for themselves. These staffers sought "jobs as managers in the new enterprises at a considerably higher salary than that enjoyed at the directorate. Consequently they have favored the establishment of new factories instead of the reconstruction of old ones, and have tried to locate the enterprises in Budapest, where they lived."[24] Such ambition was a key reason why repair and rehabilitation funding proved hard to secure.

Other agency employees just wanted to retain their positions. Like the MC's rehired "non-productive" staff, they stayed hidden, for they had "bad kaders"—personnel files which documented individual and family histories marking individuals as politically unreliable, thus fit only for manual labor. Having owned a business or served the Horthy government, or having been associated with right-wing or even social-democratic politics disqualified thousands from employment consistent with their training and experience. Tales abounded of former gentry tilling lands they once possessed or cashiered air force officers repairing radios.[25] Even so, construction ministries, trusts, and enterprises, following Minister Szijártó's lead, had few qualms about employing such subversives in order to get technical work done right.[26] At Budapest's Hydraulic Trust, which specialized in excavations and bridge-building, technical chief and Party member Julius Gossler was "said to be secretly harboring scores of non-Communists and outright enemies of the regime." At the Borsod Regional Construction Trust, which designed and built highway bridges and steel plant components, chief engineer Ladislas Selmeczi played an analogous role. As "the real head of the organization," he used his Party credentials to protect "a number of 'subversives' from arrest by vouching for their loyalty and claiming their indispensability."[27] The secretary to a construction firm's deputy chief engineer had a similar experience: "I was only kept on because I was an extremely good worker. I took part in all the national shorthand and typing contests, in which I won several prizes for the company, so... in spite of being called 'politically unreliable,' I was never dismissed."[28] A draftsman at IPARTERV, the design center for industrial and agricultural projects, added detail and context:

> Such bureaus were the haven of the politically unreliable. Out in industry, life was harsh, people were sent to prison because they could not run the machinery without spare parts, or because they were given impossible tasks. Needless to say, the first to go to prison were the politically unreliable. On the other hand, life in a designing bureau was quite safe, working conditions were quite pleasant, and the fulfillment of given tasks depended only on one's individual ability and industry.[29]

During her 1950 interview for a draftsman's place at Budapest's sewerage agency, a young married woman reported "crying hysterically." She desperately needed the job but knew she wouldn't get it "because of my middle class background... and all the damaging circumstances of our family." "Immensely relieved," the section chief calmed her and replied: "'Well, you are a reactionary then!' He assured me that I would certainly get the job since they were only afraid they would be sent some AVH informer, that they meant to protect the quiet and peace of the office." She was hired; several years later, a bridge engineer she worked for on loan invited her to join an urgent project, the Budapest Subway. Her untrustworthy family no longer proved a problem, and the subway project doubled her previous salary.[30] Meanwhile, a county-level builder's financial officer reported that "my subordinates were all reactionaries (ex-officers, former civil servants, a former monk), not experts, but trying the best they could, helping me as least as much as I could help them."[31]

122   P. SCRANTON

One forestry specialist identified a broader, collective, strategy-without-design process among the Hungary's "community of engineers," undermining the regime's socialist project.

> It is thanks to the community of the Hungarian engineers that the middle-aged Hungarian intelligentsia, which was sentenced to destruction by the regime—both men and women—have survived in comparative safety. Example: in the wide regions of Tiszántúl, where the deportees from Budapest and other cities were settled, the technical jobs were filled [by] them at the newly-built great power stations of Tiszalök, Tiszapalkonya, and Tiszántúli Távvezeték, and the water engineering projects, at the forestry engineering, which has worked on the reforestation of the Great Plain, the office of engineers of Road and Railroad Planning and Leveling in Tiszántúl, and this was the work of engineers alone. In this way, many thousands of these unfortunate people have been accepted into the frames of state enterprises and as such, they could trickle back with time to their original place of living.[32]

This was truly a remarkable phenomenon, suggesting a quiet counter-force to the mass displacement of the urban technical bourgeoisie and the even quieter acquiescence of Party secretaries at their new enterprises.[33] The Tisza projects turned out remarkably well, also. "The power station at Tiszalök is in my mind a very good and useful investment of the Communist system," a Budapest construction engineer remembered.

> It represents a dam in the river of Tisza, which is supposed to serve the canalization of the Hortobágy[34] and supply water to the rice fields there. I think the problem was successfully solved. It was a good project, well carried out... [This] gives me the idea that one must not ridicule all the investments made by the Communists. Similarly, I think that the power station at Tiszapalkona is a very good and useful job. It made possible the electrification of villages in a large part of the country... The situation nowadays is that there are very few villages along the Tisza without electric lights.[35]

Other groups, however, strove to defraud state bureaucracies, as at the state electrical planning office, which designed power systems for industrial facilities. An engineer who worked there from 1952 to 1956 explained the scheme. Of the office's 250 employees, only eight were credentialed engineers, assisted by two dozen technicians and a hundred or more men and women at drafting tables. Another hundred dealt with

4 AN UNFINISHED PROJECT: CONSTRUCTING SOCIALIST CONSTRUCTION   123

administrative matters, many of them Party members in make-work jobs. The pivot for the fraud was a record-keeping convention, the "engineer hour," a specific number of which was attached to each design job by the "norm secretary," a Party man with whom the technical staff "haggled" continuously. Accumulating sufficient engineer hours yielded full pay plus bonus awards, ideally with a minimum of work.

> Finally one of the engineers wanted to put [the engineer hour] on a scientific basis and he worked out a mathematical formula to compute the norm... It was a long and difficult formula which had a factor of complexity which was taken on its square. The formula looked very scientific indeed and few norm secretaries had the necessary mathematical knowledge to understand it. As a result this formula worked to the advantage of the engineers who really knew something. The engineers of the old guard like myself who had a good private practice could easily over-fulfill the norms and did not overstrain themselves.[36]

Using the sham formula to inflate the "engineer hours" in design jobs both assured earnings and left plenty of time for consulting, for reading technical literature (English and German texts translated first into Russian, then into Hungarian), or for devising further scams. To wit: when in 1954, "the ministry decided that the flour mills should be electrified,"

> our office received orders to prepare the plan for electrification of 30 mills within one month. The norm was 400 engineer hours for each of the mills, [totaling] 12,000 engineer hours for one's credit... What I did was that I prepared a master plan and my draftsmen copied it ten times with insignificant alterations. Then I prepared another master plan which was copied ten times again; working rather easily I was able to prepare the plans... just before one great Communist holiday. I got a prize and a money award for my work and... I fulfilled my norms for half a year or more.

Of course, the plans were terrible, "as they did not take into consideration the local conditions," something building firms complained about bitterly. But it really didn't matter very much because the whole electrification project stalled and was shelved.[37]

Defrauding the bonus system was incredibly easy, he continued. When charged with drafting a factory plan, the engineer prepared two, "a very

124   P. SCRANTON

expensive one and a cheaper one," then argued that adopting the latter generated such immense savings that he merited an award. He plotted regularly with colleagues to milk the bonus cow: "It is true that this whole premium business was nothing but cheating, but it meant a lot of work and time for us. Sometimes I wasted a whole day in conference with the other engineers, bosses, and the other members of the premium committee to determine how much we saved and how much premium we could claim." The ministry tried to counter with directives to increase planning production quotas, but never seemed able to outmaneuver the schemers. From exile, this designer summarized: "The state wanted to cheat the people and the people, the state. How could you work under such circumstances?"[38]

In the Field: Construction Enterprises on the Job

Once plans were in hand (complete or not), firms had to commence building something. Although the process often was riddled with conflict, construction moved forward. For instance, by late 1950 1,378 war-damaged bridges had been repaired, though several major spans crossing the Danube and the Tisza had not.[39] Much of Budapest's wrecked factory stock had been demolished and reconstructed, including a full restoration of the vast Ganz Electrical Works that added a "six-story high motor manufacturing plant." Yes, the Soviets had dismantled and shipped away several Hungarian power stations, but construction of substitute facilities anchored a national electrification program expected to modernize agriculture and disperse manufacturing outside the capital. Older stations' generators had deteriorated during decades of inadequate maintenance, so installing replacement equipment also was a priority, as was wiring country villages, despite a shortage of power-line poles. Rehabilitating mines to provide electricity stations with coal (while reinforcing railways' capacity to deliver it) would, in turn, provide rising electrical output for industrialization. In this context, the state acknowledged that Hungary had too few construction professionals and that the skilled worker supply could not meet demand. Thus by 1950, it announced programs for an "academy of construction engineering" and for programs training construction foremen and draftsmen, optimistically aiming to add 1,000 "technical experts" and 6,000 workers within two years. Eventually, despite the lumbering bureaucracies, postwar enterprises did complete construction work of durable significance.[40]

4 AN UNFINISHED PROJECT: CONSTRUCTING SOCIALIST CONSTRUCTION   125

Individual success stories are not hard to locate. The Borsod Regional Construction Trust (BRCT), responsible to the Ministry of Transport, began working on manufacturing-related jobs after completing repairs on wrecked highway bridges northeast of the capital. Seeing an opportunity, the Ministry of Heavy Industry tried to capture the Trust, but Transport "refused to relinquish its hold on this organism and... succeeded in resisting all efforts... to take it over." During the early 1950s, BRCT was particularly active in the Diósgyőr steel works expansion, dedicating 6,000 workers to a series of jobs. First, by tapping into the Sajó river (20 m ft), it completed a "large waterworks and aqueduct," ending "the chronic water shortage which for some decades had plagued the plant." Then it set the foundations for a new smelter "in record time," relocating a huge gas storage unit in order to clear the site. Work gangs from many of the "27 other state trusts... active in and around the plant" completed the project in spring 1952. BRCT also routinely laid "concrete and steel bases for large units of machinery" and cooperated in constructing three open hearth furnaces using Hungarian cement and DDR technologies. Meanwhile its companion Hydraulic Trust undertook a three-year project to carve out an underground munitions plant in Nógrád county, employing 3,000 workers to complete the excavations and installations by early 1952.[41]

Budapest's specialty painting and whitewashing enterprise served an array of state construction firms (never private projects), scattering its 3500 workers and 170 apprentices ("of whom 70 are girls") across the city region. It adopted the time-saving, two-coat Soviet method, replacing Hungary's traditional three coats, and, given privileged access to materials and colorants, marginalized independent decorators. Big jobs finished in 1951 included six, three-story buildings to house army officers, four police and one military barracks, lodgings at the Kossuth Military Academy, workers' retirement homes in the suburbs, and "other work" near the Lake Balaton vacation complex (135 km southwest). Workers judged their piece-rate quotas as fair, although wasting supplies was constant, especially by apprentices. As so often, "the only materials not wasted are those which the painters set aside in order to steal them."[42]

From the workers' viewpoint, construction provided some truly excellent jobs. Beginning in 1952, members of an MC experimental drilling squad traveled the nation testing soils ahead of project start-ups. They were "practically the first explorers. At that time, nobody knew anything about soil-testing regarding weight-carrying capacity." Thus the group developed and documented an important process, which when successfully used, could prevent building collapses and financial losses. Helpfully as well, their Budapest bosses could not directly monitor their work.

> The Head Driller was a former intellectual who always established the percentage of our fulfillment for us, and how much work it was reasonable to do before we were working for nothing. For, if we made better [than the] norms, the Company would have raised our norms, which is what happened later anyway, with reference to our [improved] skill. This way, it happened that we didn't work more than three days a week because we finished our necessary output within that time.

Realizing that increasing earnings wasn't feasible within the system, as income was easily tracked, they voted to increase their leisure. Management initially rated erecting a soil-drilling tower at 120 work hours; but the eight-man team handled the job in a single day, using 64 work hours. "The remaining 56 hours were free for us."

> We usually made an agreement, my colleagues and I, when we would get up in the morning and when we would finish work. We didn't have set hours. Nobody told us how many hours to work daily... I cooked for myself and, for instance, when I was in Budapest, I bought two geese or a big piece of porkmeat, broiled it, and put it in lard... and took it with me. This way I could assure a little better food for myself.

Visiting officials eventually learned about the tower fiddle and reduced the erecting allowance to 40 hours. Not a problem: "we became such experts that we made three towers in a day," taking just over 20 work hours apiece. At that point (1956), MC gave up squeezing the rate and just paid the team for whatever work it reported.[43]

Other workers stumbled into good jobs. A political prisoner released in 1956 unwittingly secured an ideal post helping construct a television transmission tower on Budapest's Széchenyi Hill (Fig. 4.2). To his surprise, everyone was competent: "Even the skilled workers knew their business." Superiors were "quick to praise good work and to denounce anything done wrong," and his foreman cheated on his team's piecework reporting to assure good earnings. "He told us if he were strict in computing our wages, we would not be getting half as much as we were getting."[44] Whether managing the job from the inside out or simply

Fig. 4.2 Construction work on foundations for Budapest's TV tower, 1956 (Donor: Rádió és Televízió Újság. *Source* FOTO: Fortepan—ID 56321, http://www.fortepan.hu/_photo/download/fortepan_56321.jpg, Wikimedia Creative Commons)

faking performance reports, rejecting ministerial rules could create or preserve good work within a poorly-designed system.

Trying to enforce those rules could also create somewhat decent jobs. Two "bad kader" staffers traveled frequently to worksites. One, a draftswoman at a bridge-erecting firm, usually worked in the office, staying late when urgent work piled up. But regularly "I had to travel," sometimes hundreds of miles a week, using the company motorcycle "to collect the Building journals and check on the labor schedule."[45] The other, refused entry to a civil engineering course because his father had worked in commerce, found a place in an agricultural construction unit as "assistant construction manager."

He was responsible for the actual building process [and] directed the foremen. He had to supervise the work on ten, at least ten, usually twelve, fourteen, even sixteen building projects at once. His [Szeged] office was in the center of a 50-kilometer area. He traveled by motorcycle which belonged to the firm for which he was working. The firm... belonged to the state, of course... None of his superiors actually let him feel that he had to fear anything, but he didn't feel at ease talking with them.[46]

The construction projects similar supervisors monitored numbered in the thousands annually (remember the 800 simultaneously in process in one county); only three can be reviewed briefly here—building tractor stations (MTS), setting up a city's central bakery, and converting a palace for university functions. As noted earlier, Hungary's first MTSs were of modest scale (20 or so tractors), but in 1951, the Ministry of Agriculture commenced a project for 200 much larger facilities (60–100 tractors). Both the current stations and the MA's planning and building work had already been "severely criticized by the press." Complaints mounted about the Stations' "poor efficiency, stressing that too many tractors [we]re still idle and thus delay sowing." Building bigger stations might help, but the first phases hardly seemed promising. Standard plans had been drafted, ostensibly to conserve scarce capital; but cheap reinforced concrete pillars, built on-site, "frequently broke" due to insufficient load-bearing capacity. A second trouble spot: unlike early stations needing only six to eight contiguous holds of land (9–12 acres), the new designs required 24 holds (35 acres) each, reducing the arable land supply. Worse, coordination between builders and other enterprises faltered badly. Late in 1951, contractors discovered that many "of the partly-finished and already-operating tractor stations would not receive electricity for years to come." Transformers were unobtainable and the power cables installed were inadequate and had to be replaced. Moreover, the larger stations included "8–10 twin houses" for drivers and mechanics; but as arrangements for water supply had been overlooked, "neither the bathrooms nor the toilets could be used." Last, some of the new buildings just "collapsed because of faulty calculations and deficient construction."[47]

A surveyor involved with MTS site selection explained why the state chose to enlarge the stations, taking three times as much land than before. "Soviet advisers" directed the new program, as they intended the MTS facilities to serve as "tank repair shops in case of war." The demand for "30–40 acres of ground" stemmed from a requirement that buildings

4 AN UNFINISHED PROJECT: CONSTRUCTING SOCIALIST CONSTRUCTION   129

be dispersed "against possible air attack." The location pattern seemed "irrational," until one realized that military priorities were the paramount consideration. "The committee always had a silent Russian member, who paid no attention to the discussion, but whose word decided the location in the end." In consequence,

> very few MTS were projected for the North, Northeast and East of the country. They appeared to be heavily concentrated in the West, Southwest and South [near Austria and Yugoslavia]—their density was quite absurd in the Southern third of the territory between the Danube and the Tisza. This openly revealed a plan to have a large number of tank bases for a possible attack against Yugoslavia.

After Stalin's death, "the strategic obsession became less strong," Hungarian engineers could argue for plan modifications, for repairing rather than demolishing existing buildings, and for reducing construction costs (something "nobody cared about").

> On the occasions when I ventured to point out the wastefully large scale, I was told that "Socialist enthusiasm knows no bounds." In fact, most of the MTS were only half completed, water mains were laid down in the grounds without being connected to any water supply. Sewage mains were built without any provision for sewage disposal. These MTS... were also supposed to be nuclei of "agro-towns." Only the best would be good enough for them, for example, bitumen [asphalt] access roads were planned, gravel roads would not do, but since there were no resources to build elaborate roads, no access roads were built at all.[48]

Blending agricultural, military and regional planning goals, when combined with insufficient funds and weak coordination, invited failure.

A bakery project by Borsod's county-level building enterprise did not fare as well as the BRCT steel plant work discussed above. Grumbling about poor quality bread had become customary in Hungary's socialist age. Authorities often blamed aged ovens, rather than the low-grade grain reserved for domestic consumers. Replacing ancient bakehouses with modern facilities was the obvious solution. Thus the industrial city of Ozd learned in 1953 that it would soon benefit from a new central bakery, capable of turning out five thousand one-kilo loaves daily, when opened in a year or so. A visitor to the chosen site reported regretfully that "in April 1954, only the outer walls had been completed." None of the

130   P. SCRANTON

ten ovens for the proposed bakeroom had been installed; indeed tiling its walls was only half completed. In the unfinished storeroom, no windows had been inserted and "six somewhat worn-looking Hungarian machines for sieving flour" occupied its floor space. When a second enterprise took over the job, it committed 100 workmen to finishing construction. Managers promised foremen large premiums for rapid progress; but set the bar so high that they "often gave false returns for the work done" so as to secure the bonuses. (When fakery was uncovered, the firm fined workers, not foremen.) Still, success proved elusive. Builders installed a 3m × 4m storeroom door (9′ by 12′) in the wrong spot; hence a whole wall had to be rebuilt. Four trucks were available to transport materiel to the site (one always on the fritz), but they frequently sat idle "because no building material was available." When supply halts persisted, the firm laid off its construction brigades at half pay. Thin wage packets surely stimulated the disappearance of such materials as were on hand: "Although the building site was watched at night by an old man, thefts were frequent. All sorts of building materials, even already built-in material, were stolen.. Wooden balustrades, water taps and tiles found a ready black market. Tiles sold... for 50 forints per 100."[49]

Comparable illegalities occurred at a prestigious Budapest project as well, reported by an unskilled laborer.

> Bribery and graft were tremendous. I remember when the royal palace was reconstructed to be made a so-called university city. A tremendous amount of old and new building materials was stolen. Everybody cheated, from the director of the factory for the building materials to the last mason. If somebody needed a certain amount of bricks for some building or reconstruction, one just went to a building contractor. The contractor asked [for] a much larger amount of bricks for the construction he was doing and sold, for a good price, the amount which he did not need.[50]

Thus was the materials delivery system repurposed. If small builders could not purchase bricks or mortar from state agencies, they opened another door instead, suborning willing construction managers to over-order supplies and retail them "for a good price." Once ministries understood what was going on, they under-filled incoming materials requests, which both stalled projects that had not inflated their orders and enhanced the role of enterprise "pushers" scouring the nation for loose bags of cement. For instance, at Veszprem County's Inota power station project, carpenters used sturdy lumber to set frames for pouring concrete slabs. Yet regularly they requisitioned four to six long boards for each frame, rather than one or two. "The boards disappeared from night to night. On the other hand, one could regard this as a constructive result in that villages surrounding the "great construction of socialism" contain the most new peasant cottages, built from excellent materials and with healthful [designs, constructed] of course from the material "removed" from the site." The engineer relating this tale quoted a local worker: "Why should it be a crime to defraud public institutions or state companies, if it is true that everything belongs to us?"[51]

CHASING BONUSES: ENTERPRISE MANAGERS AND FRAUD

Construction workers could make tools and materials disappear. Truck drivers could do hauling on the side for cash. Foremen could report higher-than-actual team performances to keep everyone's earnings up. But managers pushing paper and spinning numbers were best positioned to exploit the construction sector for individual and collective gains. The chief means to this end was manipulating enterprise bonus programs which rewarded technical and executive staff. Other fraudulent maneuvers could boost incomes, moves like substituting lower grade materials and embezzling the price difference, creating imaginary staff members and pocketing their pay,[52] or subcontracting for unneeded services and enjoying the kickbacks. The problem with these ventures was that AVH informers or ministry auditors might ruin the game, leading to long prison sentences.[53] Chasing bonuses was far safer, a version of insider trading that stretched regulations rather than broke them. As Béla Balassa explained, under capitalism many managers try to maximize profits, rewarding themselves and owners, but in socialism, the state appropriates all profits. "The principle of rational behavior, however, implies a maximization process in the socialist firm as well; here it takes the form of the maximization of bonuses."[54]

One driver in the bonus chase was relatively-low Hungarian technical and managerial salaries. About 1955–1956, a qualified engineer would earn ca. 1600 ft/month, a chief accountant perhaps 1800, and a company director 2500. Such sums could support a fairly comfortable life, but one without the little luxuries such persons cherished—good wine, opera tickets, quality clothing, travel, a motorbike. Reliable bonus payments made such items and experiences affordable; in key sectors like construction they maxxed out at 75% of staff salary bases. Engineers, for example taking home 19,000 ft/yr (16,000, after 15% in taxes and deductions) could add 14,000 in bonuses, nearly doubling the net income. Though the upper limits were not often reached, typical bonuses in construction varied from 35 to 50%, in this example, 6600–9500 ft/yr. With a custom made suit running over 2000 ft, and opera tickets 30–50 ft, a hefty bonus payment could seriously augment a family's consumption. Unsurprisingly, "bonuses have actually become a quasi-permanent part of the managers' income. They regard them as an intrinsic part of the salary."[55] A civil engineer directing water projects reported his unit regularly overtopped plan targets (115–140%), which triggered the 75% rate. To his 2400 ft/mo. base, the company added "1500–1750 forints bonus, totaling approximately 4000 forints per month." As a result, "he had a completely filled wardrobe (12 suits, 5 coats, 6 trousers, 40 shirts, 14 pair of shoes, 50 pairs of socks)."[56]

In construction, the up-to-75% formula included 25% for meeting output goals and 50% for passing profit targets (the maxima varied by sector). In 1956,

> a two percent bonus was paid for every one percent overfulfillment of the production plan above 100 percent (the maximum being 25 percent for a 112.5 percent plan fulfillment); a ten percent bonus was paid for fulfilling the profit plan, and an additional five percent for every one percent increase in profits until 50 percent was reached.

Measuring was done quarterly; by recording profits four percent above plan for a three-month period, technical and managerial staff could reap a 25% bonus. Nine percent extra profit generated the 50% add-on. Earlier, bonuses had been based on output only, with the result that "enterprises squander[ed] resources, endeavoring to fulfill the production target at all costs." This "fetish" had troublesome consequences: "production of unwanted commodities, deterioration of quality... juggling production records between periods and actual falsification of production data." Thus, building the profit motive into the equation, at double the earlier rates for passing output targets, should incentivize cost- and waste-consciousness. This failed to materialize; firms followed "the direction of least resistance," achieving cost savings by further reducing quality, hiking prices, or fiddling records to pack losses into one quarter and profits into the other three.[57]

For example, MC's largest Hungarian construction trust, employing about ten percent of the ministry's workforce, responded casually to profit-based bonuses. Executives "concluded that not much could be done by way of reducing costs, and that efforts should be concentrated on raising prices and improving billing."At the firm level, builders conducted "lengthy discussions" to assess the likely profitability of proposals, trying (not always successfully) to reject unpromising jobs, like constructing "farm buildings scattered over a large area – which notoriously meant incurring a deficit." Accounting maneuvers proved magnetic as well; when one company's first quarter 1955 returns surpassed the 112.5% profit maximum, it simply "reserved a part of its actual production for the next quarter," in effect as insurance against a disappointing spring. Another head accountant admitted that, frustrated by the "incredible confusion" consequent on poor technical staff and contradictory regulations, he became illegally creative. "To save the firm, I engaged in 'plan fraud' on a considerable scale, not by overstating our output, but by overstating planned cost and then 'saving' some of it. Eventually I got the firm out of the red by this means."[58] In these games, the chief accountant was pivotal, becoming "a sort of business manager who has ideas for raising prices... and through manipulation of the balance sheets, tries to show the figures needed to obtain the desired amount in bonuses." Extended quarterly meetings among technical and managerial staff led to agreement on the necessary adjustments in reports to the supervising trusts.

> If the modifications are to be concealed from the ministry, a secret document may be signed to make the director and the chief engineer the accomplices of the chief accountant. In some enterprises, two balance sheets are drawn up; the official balance sheet is presented to the supervising ministry and is the basis of bonus payments; the secret balance sheet contains the true figures.

Trust officials were not immune to assisting enterprises in reaching bonus-authorizing levels, inasmuch as their own bonus packages depended on profitable operations by their subordinate companies.[59]

Such were the variants of what might be called "managerial plan fraud," which coexisted happily with what might be called "operational

134 P. SCRANTON

plan fraud," anchored by work processes. "This is particularly ample in the building industry," noted the Planning Office's chief accountant,

> where much of the work is, in the nature of things, concealed by and covered over with plaster and paint. The regular practice is to perform the work only partly, then cover it over and report its completion according to specifications, obtaining credit for more labor time than was in fact expended. Building firms are driven to this expedient by the tightness of their "wage fund" allocations. At the rates of pay... which they may disburse on a particular project, they could not get decent labor, so they pay higher rates and recoup themselves by doing a less thorough job than they were supposed to.[60]

In 1954, the state Investment Bank began reviewing project estimates and actual charges to assess the "squandering" of construction funds. The team identified 200 million ft in overspending for 1954, then 76 million in 1955, and 84 million in the first nine months of 1956. These were sizable but not vast sums; but the inquiry was "necessarily limited by the impossibility of reviewing more than a fraction of the accounts, and especially by the common resistance displayed by the investor [client], the construction firm, and the Ministry of Construction."[61] The extent of conventional, everyday plan fraud could be neither calculated nor estimated; construction executives worked resolutely to keep investigators in the dark. Consider this the revenge of the managerial and technical bourgeoisie on the planning cadres, in this case a strategy *with* design.

CONSTRUCTION WORKERS: LIVING THE CONTRADICTIONS

Unlike socialism's mythical stalwarts, peasants and factory workers, construction brigades represented to the agencies and enterprises employing them a disorderly rabble—unpredictable, unreliable, untrustworthy. Too many of them were rootless single men, unmoored from family ties or, in thousands of cases, ripped from them by the state. Everywhere what they built was permanent, whereas they were temporary (except in local building co-ops, a more stable setting). To be sure, this negative characterization was not wholly fanciful, but it fed into companies' shabby treatment of construction workers on the job and off. Conversely, propagandists heroized a thin strata of skilled male and diligent female builders as symbolizing the new era—hard working, tidy and resolute, and exemplary in their commitment to building socialism. Those portrayals *were* largely fanciful—depicting women marching to sites in crisp work outfits, when seas of mud and a lack of sanitation actually produced radically different scenes.[62] Roughly 250–300,00 men and women performed Hungary's postwar construction work, 11–14% of non-farm labor.[63] But whether marginalized or lionized, they were more crucial for modernization and industrialization than their share of the workforce might suggest.

The dramatic surge in building after 1945, further invigorated by drives to expand heavy industry and infrastructure, created severe problems for ministries and enterprises. "Large-scale building was started in the country, including in areas where there was no building in the past. Sufficient numbers of workers had to be provided, transported to these areas, accommodated, supplied with food and [with] suitable living conditions." Second, construction involves many skilled trades and in the absence of mechanization, a mass of unskilled workers digging foundations and trenches or hauling, lifting and piling heavy materials. Hence, no "uniform class of workers" existed, while sufficient masons, carpenters, electricians, plumbers, or plasterers were never available. A partial solution was to recruit capable, if often self-trained, specialists from rural districts near major projects.

> A great number of skilled workers and the majority of unskilled ones came from the villages and brought with them their simple, placid views, a limited education, and a certain reserve… They visited their families at least every fortnight and even left the building industry during harvesting and threshing. The majority… continued to lead a double life: they retained their small lands which were cultivated partly by members of the family and partly by themselves. The government did everything possible to put an end to this.[64]

Four other labor groups augmented local talent: enterprises' permanent employees, migratory skilled workers, the declassed and deported barred from all but manual toil, and prisoners, both political and criminal. State security forces separately managed forced laborers, though at times they worked alongside and among enterprise brigades.

On large projects, companies housed their own employees and incoming skilled workers with nearby families wherever possible, much like the soil-drillers discussed previously. But "double-life" locals and the declassed fared much worse, at least in the early years. The "general usage... was to erect temporary, rather primitive, quarters," primitive because their cost was not properly budgeted. A one-time ministry official explained:

> Saving on the estimated operational costs proved a good opportunity to make a profit. Moldy material was used for the erection of temporary buildings and bad doors and windows [were] put in, as they were to be pulled down anyhow... This was the reason for the numerous complaints... The furnishing was very unsatisfactory – it consisted merely of a makeshift wooden bed.

With the organization of construction trusts in 1951, ministerial directives concerning "living quarters" began to be observed. Iron bedsteads "with spring mattresses" arrived and storage units for workers' personal possessions appeared. Next, enterprises hired "social managers" to supervise housing, food, work clothing, etc. on site. At large sites, firms provided three daily meals for eight forints total, but only lunch on smaller jobs (three ft).[65]

A Diósgyőr planning official was unsparing in 1952, however. "The barracks have been newly erected but can only be described as jerry-built and present an extremely squalid aspect, inside and out. The trust supplies bed and bedding and provides abominable meals at the nominal rate of three forints a plate."[66] By the mid-fifties, county-level firms had built hostels for construction teams, some with reading rooms and recreation areas. Despite such improvements, construction workers remained a disappointing, if not ungrateful lot, at least from the ministry's standpoint. They were workers but were not class-aware, perhaps "because they changed their places of work frequently and had no time to make friends with and confide in each other." Lacking common political views, they were "indifferent" to the Party, oriented to independent activity, and thoroughly "anti-Soviet." The unskilled especially showed no interest in socialism; at least half identified not with the national project, but "with [their] village."[67] Closer to the ground, a Győr Party secretary described housing project workers not as "indifferent," but as "hostile." In September 1952, the regional construction trust started six buildings with 44 apartments each, but had fallen "considerably behind schedule" by early 1953. Not only was recruiting workers difficult, given relatively low pay rates, but a sector-wide labor shortage also provided applicants with a seller's market. The firm had to make "concessions," drafting contracts for rural residents who would work through the winter, but return to their farms in the summer. Predictably, these folks paid no attention to the Party and ignored orders to attend seminars and other events to the point where the secretary "has given up announcing them." As a body, they refused to subscribe to the "Peace Loan," a wage deduction that pretended to support international harmony (but really was just another tax). No means "to coerce the workers" was at hand; many "would like nothing better than to be fired," the reporter claimed, but the project needed them. Supervisors had to overlook late arrivals, missing materials and remarks insulting the People's Democracy.[68]

Management had been so desperate that it "did not even require labor books to be shown," bypassing the state's core workforce control device—a pamphlet in which every hiring and dismissal was inscribed. Anyone recorded as fired or quitting without permission was banished to the bottom of the job ladder, except in construction.[69] Perhaps skipping the labor book checks permitted "loafers... gypsies, small landholders, and 'questionable' characters" to join the Győr workforce, but much else was also going badly. Recruiters had filled brigades with "15–16 year old boys [who] find greater pleasure in playing rather than working," especially in an "old cemetery" on site, "where the soil is full of bones and skulls, giving the young boys handy things with which to assault each other and... to tease the girls." Foremen faked output records, helping brigade leaders elevate already-inflated output rates from 83 to 97% of plan ("it looked better that way"). In such circumstances, who could be astonished that walls of three partly-completed buildings collapsed— "two during a wind storm and one when lightly run into by a truck"? According to an RFE analyst, due to the "acute shortage of manpower, this trade is forced to employ the 'bottom' of the working class, rejected by other enterprises, unskilled class-aliens who cannot get other employment or irresponsible youngsters."[70] True enough, but he omitted the forced laborers sent from prisons and camps to construction projects, who soon will be encountered.

Whether from indifference or hostility, construction upsets were pervasive. When foremen did not conspire to assure workers their expected earnings, when norm supervisors ruled, as at another state housing firm, tumult could result. Piece-rate workers "never knew how much they would get"; the calculations were invisible to them. Thus every pay day degenerated into a scandal; the workers were loudly cursing, threatening, and occasionally there was even violence – they would, for instance, topple the chair or the table of the payroll clerk. So it often happened that the payroll clerk was afraid to go out himself to the workshops and asked the manager or the party secretary to go ahead of him and [give] a speech to the workers, which usually cooled them off a little bit.[71]

Given such antagonisms, dedication to task would have been surprising. One summer worker reflected ruefully on his first experience with the building trades:

Once I saw a piece of pipe simply left out of a water connection. The building had to be finished and dedicated and yet a piece of pipe was missing. So instead of applying for it, ordering it, having it approved, the plumber simply put two ends on the pipes and plastered up the space between these two sections. No one noticed it at first and once they started to turn on the water, they started to look for the shortcoming. By then the plumber was far and gone on another job.[72]

Hostile or indifferent? It hardly matters, although incidents like these indicate that construction remained a battleground, not a venue comfortable for Party activists or efficiency monitors.

Until gradually phased out (beginning in 1953–1954), forced labor represented a not negligible segment of state construction work.[73] If the Tisza projects provided homes for declassed engineers and managers, they also were chiefly built by prisoners, according to former Smallholder activist István Rácz, long confined in the dreaded Recsk internment camp.

The hydro-electric works of Tiszapolkány was also another ambitious project; a dam was built there on the Tisza for the production of electricity. Another large undertaking was the combine of Kasincbarczika and one could go one enumerating the many lesser works which were constructed. Of these, Tiszapolkány, Kazincbarczika and the quarry of Recsk were constructed in their entirety by Hungarian prisoners, who were not paid a cent for their labors.[74]

Forced labor in Hungary did not originate with the party state; the Horthy regime mobilized compulsory labor battalions during the war, and, after 1945, the Soviets deported an estimated 300,000 Hungarians to Russian labor camps, most survivors returning by the early 1950s. When the Budapest deportations commenced in 1951, many "bourgeois elements" were initially interned in camps, along with other political "unreliables", belligerent workers (often miners), and purged Party members.[75] Thousands were then seconded to state farms, mines, and to a lesser degree, factories, all of which profited from their free (or nearly free[76]) labor. But those delegated to construction work had different experiences. They might be shipped to a major project and settle in until it was completed or canceled. They could remain in camp and be assigned in teams to jobs within commuting distance. Or they could constitute a sizable force moving among projects as needed, supplementing insufficient free labor. At all points, however, they remained in state custody, a harsh fate.

For instance, in 1951 the Army secured 3,000 forced laborers to erect stone barracks accommodating 5,000 soldiers on a 370 acre site near Kalocsa (Bács county), 140 km south of Budapest. "Even the engineers [we]re internment camp inmates," a reporter noted. Building squads worked 9.5 hours six days a week and a half day on Sunday for wages "as high as one forint per hour" (ca. 60 ft/week or 250 ft/month). Half was "deducted for food"—half a loaf of black bread twice daily, plus soup and vegetables; "meat is given only once a week." However, the guards found the meals provided them inadequate, "and therefore, the soldiers steal the meager rations of the workers." The project also employed locals who had to observe "military law" on site, but at least "they may go home after work." In the capital, the Albertfalva camp lay just across the Danube from factory-lined Csepel Island. Its 1400 inmates worked on housing construction and in riverside factories, including a building materials plant. A thousand lived in a repurposed four-story mill and the rest in a "barrack botched up by the prisoners themselves." As one remembered:

This barrack is terribly primitive... Its walls are about 2 cm [>1″] thick and made of mud stuck on wood. The roof is made of tarred paper. The barrack has been constructed by famished and exhausted convicts... The commander of the prison forced this job on the prisoners, later to account for it as if it had been done by civilians. He pocketed the money paid out for the latter. No wonder that in bad weather the rain inundates the unhappy convicts. [It was] not built by experts but by those who never in their lives had carried either bricks or beams and had never tried to put them together.

Here also the workers were paid, after a fashion. They earned 18 ft/day, from which "they deduct 10 ft daily for food and [worn] out clothes." Two more forints went toward the guards' salaries and most of the rest vanished into "volunteer contributions and offerings." In sum, "a forced laborer was not considered a human being in the eyes of the communist leaders. They had the same opinion about free workers, too," but were careful not to reveal such sentiments.[77]

An unusual 1953 report provides a detailed account of Hungary's forced labor system in December 1952, just before a first-stage disassembly began. The Ministry of Justice then "had about 90,000 prisoners at its disposal," 47,950 at 65 labor camps and worksites and the rest confined to jails. Of those hired out, about one-third worked on construction jobs, accounting for just over five percent of Hungary's construction workers (Table 4.1). The power plants and the Budapest palace transformation mentioned above were included among the 16 sites, as were the Albertfalva and three more military barracks projects. Six southern counties favored for the big machine tractor/tank repair stations lacked construction camps, but nine of the 13 central and northern counties (and Budapest) had one or more. This may reflect the far more agricultural orientation of the southern crescent, by contrast with the north. In the end, forced labor as state practice slipped gradually into the shadows,

Table 4.1 Distribution of forced labor by sector, December 1952

Sector	Number of camps	Number of inmates
Mining	14	7,200
Manufacturing	5	3,600
State farms & TSZs	21	17,300
Construction	16	15,900
Maintenance (RR and Airports)	3	950
Not specified	6	2,900
Total	65	47,950

Source CIAIR, "Forced Labor," 13 October 1953, 1–4 (Secret, CIA-RDP80-00810A002500480010-4). Table compiled from individual camp entries

4 AN UNFINISHED PROJECT: CONSTRUCTING SOCIALIST CONSTRUCTION 141

although in 1954 Rákosi, seeking to keep his purge victims out of sight, slowed releases to a crawl (and was berated for it by Khrushchev).[78]

MEGA-PROJECTS: THE BUDAPEST SUBWAY AND SZTÁLINVÁROS

The capital's second subway line and the steel complex above the Danube were Hungary's two most expensive construction projects during the postwar decade. The underground cost over three billion forints before being canceled in 1954 and Sztálinváros four billion and counting for the plant, town and port, all built in start and stop cycles into the 1960s. Both were not simply white elephants, but white mammoths—immense projects haunted by weak designs, budget overruns, construction glitches, and monumental errors in judgment. An architect later commented: "Although *planning* was a key term in those years, the political leadership seemed to be lacking it. They often made ad hoc decisions instead of being systematic."[79] Both projects honored Stalin by emulating Soviet achievements—the Moscow underground, sections of whose fourth phase opened as the Budapest excavations began, and Magnitogorsk, the Soviet replica of US Steel's Gary Works, whose multi-million ton annual capacity was crucial to victory over Nazi Germany.[80] Budapest surely needed another subway; buses and trucks jammed central city traffic daily. Its one line, opened in 1896, linked the park and zoo in Pest to an administrative and shopping district along the Danube, but did not cross to the Buda side. Hungary did *not* need a giant steel plant, however; it had only minor domestic supplies of iron ore and its vast soft coal reserves could not be used to fire up smelters and foundries. No matter, even if Hungary's entire steel output would only be "about equal to the annual production of one US steel plant of medium size."[81] Cold War anxieties brought commitments to convert Hungary "to a land of iron and steel," the showpiece of which would be Sztálinváros. The mercurial Zoltán Vas, a one-time head of the National Planning Office, asserted in October 1954 that the entire effort was "a megalomaniac swindle." (He was soon demoted.)[82] Having started badly, both mega-projects went downhill.

In 1949, Ernö Gerö, Rákosi's close colleague, known as the "bridge-builder" for his construction zeal, moved from heading the Ministry of Transport to directing the Finance Ministry and chairing the Supreme Economic Council. That year, his Transport successor instructed the State Institute of Underground Architecture to draw up plans for a second subway as a contribution to socialist efficiency: "the fast underground reduces the time people have to spend travelling to their workplace." Construction began in spring 1950.[83] Three agencies cooperated in the initiative: the Subway Designing, Subway Investment and Subway Construction Enterprises, directed by one chief executive. The head of the Statics Group at Design noted that "the sandy subsoil in Budapest prevents the building of elevated trains, whilst a semi-deep subway would be impractical because the streets are too narrow and the [water] mains would be disrupted by the tunnel. The only solution is a deep tunnel." For traffic management, a north-to-south line under the Danube would be ideal, as it would carry industrial workers to the Csepel Island industrial complex. But "strategic considerations" won the day for an east-to-west line to connect the East and South railway stations and "provide large air raid shelters." This design included a "secret tunnel" only for wartime use, linking Pest's East Station through the downtown Kossuth Square stop with Buda's West Station, as well as "a large and elaborate shelter for the Party Headquarters." Soviet control extended to every detail. Eight to ten military engineers reviewed and countersigned blueprints.

> The Designing Bureau received the exact path of the subway tunnel from Russian military engineers. This path had to be followed to the last centimeter, but it was so drawn as to make utter nonsense of the location of stations. It became an almost insoluble task... The whole project was under the Soviet Central Underground Railway Administration in Moscow [which] prepared the outline plan for the subways in the satellite capitals.[84]

The subway program had vertical and horizontal components: creating means of access to platforms and preparing stable underground tunnels between them, at an average depth of 40 m [130']. The Deák Square station in central Pest was especially complicated, not only because of its three levels (intersecting with the old line and with the anticipated North–South one) but also due to military precautions. Designers learned "that the roof of the station must resist the direct impact of 750 kilo [1650 lb.] bombs. They were given Soviet military engineering manuals and blueprints of the Maginot Line and modeled the roof on Maginot Line techniques." Rather than standard roof dimensions 60 cm [2'] thick, "the instruction was to design for 250 cm [8']." Compared to the "intricate and difficult" vertical work, designers regarded "the actual driving of the tunnel" as "comparatively plain sailing."[85] Subsurface workers would

4 AN UNFINISHED PROJECT: CONSTRUCTING SOCIALIST CONSTRUCTION   143

hardly have agreed. Tunnels and platforms were so deep in the ground that "sometimes work has to be done under a pressure of two or three atmospheres." In the absence of a boring machine[86] appropriate for soft or sandy conditions, teams used a retaining shield and manual labor to excavate an eight meter [26′] diameter tunnel at the rate of one meter a day [3.3′], work that was "strenuous and exhausting." After a four hour shift, laborers needed another four hours to recover (Fig. 4.3). Inadequate and unreliable equipment led to accidents and deaths.

> Working conditions… are made unbearable by careless operation of the caisson installations and by inhumane treatment. The ventilation device is very often out of order and workers suffocate in the caissons. Sudden air pressure drops due to the poor operation of valves and compressors are an everyday occurrence… Almost all laborers suffer from caisson disease [which] starts with pains in the feet and arms, then spreads to

Fig. 4.3 Budapest Subway construction, 1952 (Donor: UVATERV. *Source* FOTO: Fortepan—ID 91594, http://www.fortepan.hu/_photo/download/fortepan_91594.jpg, Wikimedia Creative Commons)

all the joints... accompanied by severe headaches, and finally ends in a hemorrhage of the lungs and in heart trouble.[87]

Improper operation of the decompression chambers led to multiple cases of caisson disease ("the bends"),[88] as harried section bosses reduced the pressure adjustment period to "20 or 25 minutes" from the 45 minutes regulations required. Hazard pay that raised monthly earnings from 500 ft to "1200–1600 ft" was necessary; otherwise firms "would not get anyone willing to descend into the caissons." Not a good bargain for those taking the offer, however, as returning to "normal health after working in the caissons" was unlikely.[89] Also, "at least 30 percent of the manual workers were déclassé elements. It was somewhat like the Foreign Legion, nobody asked any questions. There were lawyers, ex-landlords, ex-officers, and all sorts of people."[90]

Supply problems also dogged the subway builders. One of the Party dailies complained early in 1953 about "non-delivery of machinery and equipment" for the project. For instance, a metalworking company had requested a deadline extension for four, 15-ton band coilers ordered in August 1950 and due in August 1952. The giant state machine builder, MAVAG, had shipped only four of 21 pumps due by September 1952, and the freight elevator completion date had been postponed for a third time. "The one elevator finally delivered to the work sites was faulty"; its gearing propelled it at three times the designed speed, "forcing workers in the shaft to depend on buckets and pulleys for another two months." Finally three state metalworking plants had, on average, delivered under half of the tunnel tubing elements required.[91] The Soviets were not much help either. The Design enterprise engineer groused:

> The project received a large quantity of construction steel from Russia. These were prefabricated steel segments and they were found to be disfigured and corroded. The project submitted them for examination to Prof. Gillemót [a metallurgist]. He reported orally that these steel parts had been manufactured between 1933 and 1936 and must have been stored in the open air ever since. [Our director] asked him to put this opinion on paper, but he refused to do so. This quantity of steel is now lying abandoned in the open air on some vacant ground in... southwest Budapest.[92]

A surveyor setting up an apartment house project in that area confirmed the presence of these useless materials, despite ongoing shortages.

4 AN UNFINISHED PROJECT: CONSTRUCTING SOCIALIST CONSTRUCTION   145

I saw enormous quantities of pre-fabricated steel parts, all quite rusty, piled up on vacant lots. On inquiry, these turned out to have been brought there after they were deemed unusable for the underground tube. I estimated the quantity and worked out the cost, and found that the value of this steel, rusting away slowly... was equal to 30,000 two-room flats.[93]

Construction costs rapidly overran estimates, as designers had framed their initial budgets not knowing that "elaborate air raid installations [would] be demanded in a year or two." Between 1950 and 1952, some "15,000 employees were occupied by the project." Zoltán Vas issued a June 1952 report claiming that work was already full year behind schedule everywhere but at the South Station, which had "more favorable subsoil conditions." Once again Soviet components were substandard; iron tunnel lining segments had to be reworked at a cost of 30 million ft. As well, "most of the construction machinery was supplied by the USSR and proved unsatisfactory."[94] Initially, the whole line was expected to cost 2.5 billion ft, but by spring 1953, 3.5 billion had been spent on about three-quarters of the planned elements. Another two billion would be needed to finish the job; in the interim the Soviets "were no longer pressing for results as they once had." Indeed, "it was understood within the office that the Russians no longer thought us reliable and that a bomb-proof railroad connection was not such a good idea."[95]

Cutbacks on heavy industrial spending after Stalin's death hit the subway operation hard.

In the autumn of 53, the periodical allocation of funds was cut by 30 percent. In the spring of 1954, the decision to suspend the project had been taken in principle, and during the summer of 1954, preparations for stopping the work were completed. By the autumn of that year, they switched to a care and maintenance basis.... When [the director and I] were summoned to Rákosi's secretariat to discuss the suspension of the project, Rákosi received [us] in a five-minute audience. He declared that there is no more money for the subway, it is finished, and said that [we] can have one million forints per annum for care and maintenance.

The director replied that 450 million forints a year was the projected maintenance cost for the unfinished line. Rákosi would not budge, but diligent lobbying secured 65 million in 1955 and 140 million in 1956, when the Revolt terminated the program. A senior design engineer judged that the central error was the Russian's insistence on placing the tunnels at so great a depth. "No traffic or other technical consideration demanded a level 40m below the surface. This depth was chosen in view of the arbitrary 750 kilo bomb idea. The technical optimum would have been 15m or so... As a result three billion would have sufficed for the whole project." Subway planning revived in the mid-1960s, avoiding the most crucial errors of its failed predecessor.[96]

In a sense, Sztálinváros was the subway's technical inverse. Being a system, the underground could not be activated until completed; tunnels without stations and escalators had no value. By contrast, the steel complex, being a collection of loosely-linked units, could begin functioning when individual elements were finished. Once one open-hearth furnace became operative, ingots could be poured and shipped. Once a foundry was up and running, molten steel from the furnace could be molded into machine components. Hence, Sztálinváros began operating while construction continued. Indeed, in a peculiar variant on what aerospace engineers termed "concurrency," design modifications drawn from initial practice reshaped later phases of construction.[97] And, once again, location, soil, politics, and the Russians all mattered.

Commandeering billions of forints and intended to double Hungary's iron and steel output, Sztálinváros reflected the planning and politics tangles that animated the subway project, particularly ad hoc decision-making driven by Soviet imperatives. An initial 1946–1947 plan aimed to situate a major steel complex at Mohács along the lower Danube, so as to take advantage of sizable ore deposits across the Yugoslav border (8 km south) and inexpensive water transit. Creating an integrated steel mill is a vast undertaking. The enterprise must secure immense supplies of electrical power, coal, ore, water, and limestone, develop or extend transport networks for hauling millions of tons of inputs and outputs, and construct scores of buildings and facilities: blast furnaces to make pig iron, open hearth furnaces for transforming iron to steel, foundries for pouring ingots, billets or slabs, rolling mills to flatten slabs into sheets and ribbons of steel, a coke works to transform hard coal into furnace fuel (plus pipe systems to capture off-gases for chemical processing), machine shops to build and repair equipment, cranes by the dozen and internal railways by the mile, not to speak of offices, infirmaries, storage yards, and roads. All this was envisioned for Mohács; construction began in 1947. A year later the Stalin-Tito breakup shuttered the project. "The foundation work of the shops and plants was abandoned and left as they were, till finally they were ruined by the weather." The town did benefit unexpectedly, as "18 large apartment houses of four stories each" were consigned to its care. A new site was urgently needed.[98]

The riverside location further north selected "on short notice" proved problematic. Dunapentele in Fejer County, an oversized village (pop. 3500), rested along a level bluff 30–50 m above the Danube, along which sat a "marshy island" that could be remodeled into a reception point for raw materials. No rail line then reached the village; local roads were hardly broad or durable enough to support heavy truck traffic, and of course, few experienced construction workers lurked in the hinterlands. In Budapest, extensive prior development created obstacles to subway building, whereas Dunapentele's relative isolation hampered the steel mill project. ("It turned out to be a very poor place for a such a huge plant.") Everything would have to be brought to the site except the Mohács plans, which were on their way to the USSR: "All the necessary details for the modification of the plans were sent to the Institute of Metallurgic Projects at Leningrad."[99] Difficulties soon multiplied. According to one engineer:

> The transportation of the material from the river to the site of the plant proved to be a very hard problem all the time. Moreover, it seems to me that the final decision concerning the site... had not been preceded by thorough geological research. As it turned out... the high plateau at the Danube consisted of that kind of sandy soil which is so common on the great Hungarian plain... The loose and unsettled sandy soil there is usually very good for certain types of farming, but it's not good for the construction of large plants.[100]

Building the port, rail connections[101] and core plant elements were the first orders of business; creating a town (separate from the original village) and on-site housing for the construction workforce stood next in line. To have a port, one must define a harbor and edge it with docks and facilities for moving cargo. The marshy island was an unpromising site, but fairly standard engineering practices could work a thorough transformation. To create a harbor, three heavy-duty dredgers commenced removing sand from the inlet between the island and the bluff (Fig. 4.4), reportedly 1000 m^3 daily, using it "to build a circular dam around the island" and to raise its surface "above the water level." This meant relocating an estimated 750,000 m^3 of rock and soil—a two-year job working seven days a week. On the land side, facilities construction demanded tons of bricks, offloaded from barges during dam construction. A representative

Fig. 4.4 Construction of the Sztálinváros port, 1952 (Donor: UVATERV. *Source* FOTO: Fortepan—ID 91581, http://www.fortepan.hu/_photo/download/fortepan_91581.jpg, archive copy, Wikimedia Creative Commons)

"sent down from Budapest" for a 1951 production meeting identified a problem, however.

> The speaker brought to the attention of the workers that [in] the unloading of the ship, too many bricks are broken and had become rejects. The dock-workers promised thereupon that they would reduce their rejects to the minimum. This offer, made by the dock-workers, was carried out successfully for weeks. It was discovered only later why there had been no more brick rejects. The explanation was quite simple, namely the rejects were thrown in the water, in such quantities that at the end, the ships coming down the Danube, bringing the necessary raw material for the buildings, could not anchor anymore in the harbor of Dunapentele because the whole harbor was filled with broken bricks.[102]

To stabilize the harbor wall, concrete "caissons" holding 50 m^3 of gravel were to be lowered and secured to one another, but initially they

4 AN UNFINISHED PROJECT: CONSTRUCTING SOCIALIST CONSTRUCTION   149

just sank into the mire and later tended to slide out of position. Nonetheless, work proceeded steadily until "the harbor was officially opened up on one Sunday in 1953."

> The cabinet ministers appeared there and many good Party line speeches were delivered. On the Monday following the festive opening, the concrete wall of the harbor caved in, fell into the river and blocked the place for any approaching boats. Our planning office [had] planned the harbor and the people in charge of this work were immediately arrested. The result was one of those tremendous scandals.

The designers escaped punishment when the chief engineer proved that another office had certified the final plans; then finger pointing in all directions commenced. Contractors claimed the concrete was low quality; the concrete plant documented that this wasn't so. "Everybody worked in a sloppy way and I do believe that workers stole the [cement]; consequently the mixture did not contain the necessary amount." Even with emergency repairs, the harbor "could not be used for about three months."[103]

Supplying the town and steel mill with Danube water was another essential, but in 1951 the pumping plant and distribution system project encountered immediate difficulties related to soil characteristics. "A main waterline was being constructed and a concrete pipeline four kilometers long was installed. When this was finished, the sandy soil yielded beneath the pipeline and broke it in many places." This was not the first (or worst) subsidence misery at the steel mill site. An early 1952 report confirmed that the Planning Office had become "alarmed because of the serious difficulties… in the actual construction. The subsoil does not seem able to support such heavy buildings. Slidings and sinkings have resulted." Thus,

> Minister Ernö Gerö called a meeting at which were present Zoltán Vas, president of the State Planning Office, Kirov, representing the analogous Soviet office, and all the competent university professors and Hungarian geological experts. There was a violent discussion in the course of which reproaches were exchanged about the choice of this site. The first decision taken has been the urgent dispatch of geologists to the scene.[104]

Kirov also pledged to have an expert sent to the site from the USSR. Among other fixes, engineers implemented a Soviet technique for

150   P. SCRANTON

compacting soil by using below-ground explosions; although delays were unavoidable, construction of "heavy buildings" did resume.[105]

The quantities of material required were staggering: 120 million bricks, 200,000 tons of cement, 100,000 m^3 of lumber, 55,000 tons of machinery, 110 electric cranes, 65 km of rail track and 30 km of roadways. Despite top allocation priorities and a four billion forint budget, Construction Trust No. 26, headed by the eminent Johanna Wolff,[106] found deficiencies on every side. Retaining skilled labor was a perennial challenge, despite high wages and stores crammed with food, as was managing over 10,000 young rural laborers who needed close jobsite supervision and tended to drunkenness and fighting on weekends. Their absenteeism amounted to 71,000 working days in the first half of 1951. Everywhere, "the work progresses jerkily and is frequently unsatisfactory." Plans had been drawn "without studying the territory"; brigades started building "before discussing the work thoroughly with the planning enterprise. Then when the work is already in an advanced state, the plan is found to be unfeasible." Since the spring 1950 start date, the core plan had been modified at least six times, while inspection of tasks completed had become nearly impossible:

> The urgent need for work inspection has been repeatedly demonstrated: the surface of the road leading to Adony [20 km north] resembles a rollercoaster, on which is it is impossible to drive at speeds exceeding 60 km an hour [37 mph]; badly prepared concrete, crooked walls, inaccurate surveying on buildings, ill-fitting prefabricated parts at the steelworks and in [the town] all attest to the importance of work inspection.[107]

Rushed work plus inadequate controls led to accidents. Walls collapsed and pillars fragmented, injuring and killing workers; critics attributed failures to "Soviet innovations... being applied there, as everywhere else in Hungary, but not always with good results."[108] A planning engineer added: "It is true that the first official casting in the Foundry was held on 7 November 1951, but the construction was far yet from completion. Because of the tempo dictated by the leaders the work is of a poor quality. The concrete pillars... are cracking and are held together by means of iron belts. The cracks are covered with plaster."[109]

For workers at the construction sites, "chaos reigned." Arriving laborers waited for days to receive job assignments; tools were often

4 AN UNFINISHED PROJECT: CONSTRUCTING SOCIALIST CONSTRUCTION 151

unavailable or inappropriate for tasks, and while wages were high, "payment was often late." Housing, initially in huts and tents, was dreadful, as was sanitation. When spartan barracks were erected, their adjacent halls for men and women seemed to encourage sexual adventures and did result in pregnancies. In addition,

> the food was terrible and the number of portions delivered to the construction site was insufficient. Therefore workers quit work ahead of time to secure their meals in the canteens. Work morale was low; tools and construction material were left lying around the construction sites. There were reports of workers who slept through their nightshift or who did not show up for work at all.[110] The work [on] the first socialist town of Hungary was poorly organized, of low quality, and above all, it was slow.

Moreover, theft was ubiquitous. In winter 1953, managers reported that the wood swiped from construction areas "amounted to 30 cubic meters *per day*."

> Anything and everything was stolen and traded on the black market. In wintertime wood was stolen from construction sites to heat dormitory barracks. In summer, heating material was stolen from the workplace to replenish winter stocks. Bicycles, blankets, clothing, money or food were all treasures worth owning, stealing or selling.[111]

The planning engineer confirmed this: when accompanying a Trust director on an inspection, he discovered that in one of the steelworks' main halls, all the ventilation fans and most of the radiators had somehow "disappeared." His conclusion: "It characterizes the morale of the Stalin Plant workers and technicians that they would tear down the whole plant with more enthusiasm than [that] with which they are building it."[112]

Enough. Eventually Sztálinváros's three components functioned adequately: bringing raw materials in by rail and water, manufacturing steel in quantity, and housing the permanent workforce securely.[113] In stages, the construction squads diminished and the overall budget rose to six billion. However, given the Nagy Cabinet's emphasis on investing in agriculture and consumer goods (1953–1954), construction ceased on the works in January 1954, though not on the town. The harbor was still unfinished as were mechanical facilities to convey incoming materials. The Soviets had pledged to supply large volumes of iron ore from its Krivoy Rog reserves (3000 km distant from the mill); but Moscow reneged in

152   P. SCRANTON

1954, instead selling "this ore to the West in order to acquire foreign exchange." At last the circle closed. Six years after the Tito split, one year after Stalin's death, Yugoslav iron ore began flowing north to Sztálinváros both by rail and by water.[114]

Once Rákosi pushed Nagy aside, construction restarted in 1955, but the management fiddles continued. To reduce inventories and assure meeting the profit plan, materials worth 2.5 million ft were written off as useless during the last quarter of 1955 (although some would be "used at a later date"), because the accounting loss was disregarded in "calculating bonuses." That year as well, "the loss of machinery and other equipment to the amount of about 10 million ft [was] accounted for in the balance sheet of the Construction Trust of Sztálinváros. All equipment being the property of the state, this item was not debited to the profit and loss statement."[115] Thus were materials and machinery made to disappear from the books, just as they disappeared from worksites. the complex never thrived, never made a genuine profit, and ultimately was an economic albatross, having absorbed money, labor, and materials that could have had far more positive effects had they been used otherwise.

CONCLUSION

Constructing socialist construction was not a tidy process. Though Stalinism had a reputation for single-minded centralization (consider "one-man-management"), Hungary's building programs were disorganized, competitive, and borderline anarchic. Creativity and improvisation were widespread, but put to wholly non-socialist uses—"pushing" for unauthorized advantages or resources, hiding "reactionary" staff and "bad kader" workers, manipulating bonus systems, inventing fraudulent accounting techniques, faking work records and repurposing public property for private ends. Determined to control operations, top managers sought and got floods of reports, then hired thousands of bureaucrats to analyze torrents of information, and were little better off for the effort. Plans were poorly connected to execution, were routinely politicized (especially during the years of "war panic," 1950–1952),[116] were perennially incomplete and/or delayed and were consistently subject to "modification," authorized or not. The proliferation of new projects (and its companion, the neglect of maintenance and repair) reliably assured demand for materials, labor, and transport exceeded supply. Hungarian socialism's "shortage economy" was the everyday, surface manifestation of an unending seller's market, founded on the state's obsessive dedication to rapid economic transformation despite weak and unbalanced resource bases and insufficient capital. Yet in the People's Democracy, workers faced a tight-fisted buyer's combine; a seller's market for their labor would have torpedoed the entire project. The scarcity of construction workers stemmed from their lowball earnings, whereas feeble wages stimulated deception and theft, much like compulsory deliveries energized rural illegalities. Labor scarcity also authorized the routine exploitation of forced labor—extra hands at reduced or no cost—and the ready employment of the declassed and the deported. Soviet oversight and interventions could not be dodged, or even critiqued, while Stalin lived, and Russian "innovations" often proved unreliable. Throughout the postwar decade, the dream of mechanization boosting productivity would neither evaporate nor materialize. Hard manual labor characterized construction as it had for centuries; the projects just had become much, much bigger. Finally, the quality of what was built was so often terrible that one marvels at projects that functioned well, even if dams, power plants, or factories were completed late and well over budget.

In a way, that's the nub of the construction contradiction: amid this swamp of shortcomings, stuff did get built and most of it worked, more or less well. Despite the mess and the fraud, by 1956, electric power lines stretched across the nation, a rail and highway network supported billions of trips annually, and hundreds of new schools, community centers, and ugly apartment blocks had sprouted in towns and cities. Housing remained the Achilles heel of postwar building drives, however, left largely to private entrepreneurs using state loans to fund scavenging for informally re-allocated materials, a sheepish validation of the theft economy. Yet acknowledging construction's accomplishments does little to erase the deep malaise, even distress, that permeated its institutions and its workforce. Not working hard, whenever and wherever possible, while cheating when feasible served as unspoken rules of the trade, exemplary elements of a strategy without design hostile to state actors, to building socialism, to the security and surveillance apparatus and especially to the Soviets. In construction at least, the socialist project was crumbling, in shambles, well before the October Revolt.

Notes

1. Rudolf Bićanić, "Economic Growth Under Centralized and Decentralized Planning," *Economic Growth and Cultural Change* 6(1957): 63–74. Bićanić was a Yugoslav economist and critic of Stalinism. See his *Problems of Planning, East and West*, The Hague: Mouton, 1967.
2. RFE Field Report, "The New Economic Policy After Five Months," 10 December 1953, 2–3, HU OSA 300-1-2-41759 (hereafter RFEFR).
3. Béla Balassa, *The Hungarian Experience in Economic Planning*, New Haven: Yale University Press, 1959, 81.
4. MC units could and did build projects sponsored/designed by other ministries, often working on military jobs, for example, but rarely on railway construction.
5. CIA, Office of Research and Reports, "The European Satellite Power Complex, Part I: Hungary," 30 July 1951, 17–18, 20 (Top Secret, CIA-RDP79R01012A000900050001-5); János Gács, "Planning and Adjustment Policy Changes in the Development of the Building Materials Industry," *Eastern European Economics* 21:3(1983): 105–24, Estimates suggested that, by 1950, three people occupied each available Budapest room, down from four in 1946.
6. Resző Nyers, *The Cooperative Movement in Hungary*, Budapest: Pannonia, 1963, 210–30.
7. Trusts were clusters of enterprises either in the same trade (horizontal, e.g. excavation) or in different trades cooperating in a project or an area (vertical).
8. CIA, Economic Intelligence Report RR147, "Housing in the European Satellites, 1949–1958," 17 September 1958, 46–47 (Unclassified, CIA-RDP79R01141A001200050002-0). The State Bank provided loans for about a fifth of home projects; the rest relied on private funds. Contemporary sources on county, co-op and private builders, sparse for these years, are more plentiful after 1957.
9. They were Ajka (aluminum), Kazincbarcika (coal, power and chemicals), Komló (coal), Oroszlány (coal), Tiszapalkonya (chemicals and power), Várpalota (coal and power) and Dunaújváros/Sztálinváros (iron and steel). See P. A. Compton,

"The New Socialist Town of Dunaújváros," *Geography* 50:3(July 1965): 288–91.

10. RFE Background Report, "Building Industry and Construction in Hungary before the Revolution," 15 February 1957, 4–8, HU OSA 300-8-3-3211.

11. Raw materials had their own ministry in the early 1950s, but were brought inside Construction by 1953. See CIAIFD, "Jurisdiction of New Hungarian Ministries," *Allam és Igazgatás* (State and Administration), March 1952 (Restricted, CIA-RDP80-00809A000700090152-2). "Residences" here refers to apartment blocks and "installations" to plumbing, heating, electrical work, painting, etc.

12. RFE, "Building Industry," 14–17.

13. Ibid., 20–21. In the first Nagy years, MC bonuses stopped being paid chiefly for timely completion and depended instead on profitability. Soon, jobs once finished on time with losses were finished late but profitably. Balassa, once an MC business manager, argued that the pursuit of bonuses anchored project administration (*Economic Planning*, 132–38; see also Béla Balassa, "My Life Philosophy," *The American Economist* 33:1 [Spring 1989]: 16–23). CURPH Interview No. 100, 38, HU OSA 414-0-2-127 confirms the shortage of technical staff.

14. László Zoltán, "Situation of the Hungarian Building Industry in the Light of a Survey of Construction Activities in Hajdú-Bihar Megye," *Statisztikai Szemle* (Statistical Review) 23:1(January 1955) (Unclassified, CIA-RDP80-00809A000700250026-4).

15. Quoted in Balassa, *Economic Planning*, 128.

16. RFEFR, "The 'Iparterv' State Planning Company for Industry," 25 March 1953, HU OSA 300-1-2-32499. See also CIAIR, "Organization and Construction Projects of the Ministry of Building," 22 July 1952 (Secret, CIA-RDP82-00457R013000280010-0).

17. RFEFR, "Liquidation of Private Planning Offices," 26 June 1953, HU OSA 300-1-2-34109.

18. CIAIFD, "Jurisdiction"; Balassa, *Economic Planning*, 157.

19. RFE, "Building Industry," 4, 7; Balassa, *Economic Planning*, 157–58.

20. Balassa, *Economic Planning*, 158–59.

21. Ibid., 86–87.

156 P. SCRANTON

22. Ibid., 196.
23. By 1952, MC had drafted a materials allocation priority list of the top 13 projects under way, headed by the Sztálinváros steel town and mills. See CIAIR, "Project Priority List for Scarce Materials," 14 February 1952 (Secret, CIA-RDP82-00457R010200420005-1).
24. Balassa, *Economic Planning*, 82, 188–89.
25. CURPH Interview No. 71-M, 1, HU OSA 414-0-2-70.
26. An experienced draftswoman for a bridge builder described meeting with Szijártó in order to secure a license. "I lost my temper and was rather fresh with him. He asked me whether I knew who I was talking to. I said that of course I was talking to a Communist minister. When he asked what I meant by Communist minister, I said "A velvet chair without knowledge." He started to laugh and told me that nobody ever talked to him with such a big mouth... and gave me the license" (CURPH Interview No. 87-F, 37, HU OSA 414-0-2-87).
27. CIAIR, "Recent and Current Projects of the Hungarian Construction Trusts," 27 June 1952, 2 (Secret, CIA-RDP82-00457R012500040009-4).
28. CURPH Interview No. 38-F, 25–26, HU OSA 414-0-2-33.
29. CURPH Interview No. 225, 1, HU OSA 414-0-2-201. See also RFEFR, "The 'Iparterv' State Planning Company."
30. CURPH Interview No. 245, 4–5, 7, HU OSA 414-0-2-219. A double burden: her father had been the mayor of Szolnok and owned several factories, whereas her spouse had worked in Horthy's foreign office.
31. CURPH Interview No. 458, 16, HU OSA 414-0-2-278.
32. CURPH Interview No. 442, 68–69. HU OSA 414-0-2-263. These locations are all adjacent to the Tisza river valley, which runs north to south through the plains east of Budapest.
33. One CIA informant suggested that some Party secretaries were active recruiters, going to labor camps to extract "civilian and army engineers," telling "them openly that they needed them because of their technical knowledge." See CIAIR, "Planning Institutes and Investment Enterprises," 23 June 1953, 2 (Secret, CIA-RDP80-00810A00150051000801).

34. Canalization is introducing locks and weirs into a waterway to make it navigable. See http://www.hortobagyte.hu/lifeplus_hirek.php?page=6&en (accessed 29 March 2021).
35. CURPH Interview No. 246, 13–14, HU OSA 414-0-2-220.
36. CURPH Interview No. 243, 29–32, HU OSA 414-0-2-217.
37. Ibid. In their 48 hour real-time weeks, engineers were supposed to book 500 engineer hours. Scoring 12,000 EH's in a month met the productivity quota for 24 weeks. The respondent asserted that on his departure in December 1956, he was five years ahead in work credits.
38. Ibid., 62.
39. RFEFR, "Budapest as Seen by Visitors," 21 July 1955, HU OSA 300-1-2-60367. In 1955 Budapest's Elizabeth (Erzsébet) Bridge was the last of eight over the Danube being reconstructed. Work had begun early in 1952 (CIAIFD, "Build Bridges, Highway, Rail Lines," 4 June 1952 [Restricted, CIA-RDP80-00809A000700060566-6]).
40. CIAIR, "Hungarian Power Plants," 20 May 1949 (Secret, CIA-RDP82-00457R002700700002-7); CIAIR, "The Present Status of Electrification in Hungary," 11 February 1949 (Secret, CIA-RDP83-00415R001600090004-0); CIAIFD, "Economic – Building Activity," 20 October 1950 (Confidential, CIA-RDP80-00809A000600350496-3); CIAIFD, "Transportation – Bridges, Rail," 24 November 1950 (Confidential, CIA-RDP80-00809A00060036-516-9); CIAIFD, "Economic-Fuel and Power, Electrical industry," 30 December 1950 (Secret, CIA-RDP80-00809A000600370169-4); CIAIFD, "Education – industrial Training," 24 October 1950 (Confidential, CIA-RDP80-00809A000600350602-4).
41. CIAIR, "Recent and Current Projects," 1, 4. CIA believed that 1,000 of BRCT's Diósgyőr workers were convict laborers—criminals though, rather than political prisoners. For administrative detail on one Diósgyőr project, see CIAIR, "Planning Institutes and Investment Enterprises," 3–4.
42. RFEFR, "Painting Industry in Hungary," 18 April 1952, HU OSA 300-1-2-18423.
43. CURPH Interview 82-M, 27–31, HU OSA 414-0-2-82. This soil tester reported monthly income of 2000 ft, about double that of a skilled factory worker.

44. CURPH Interview 62-M, 2, 37–38, HU OSA 414-0-2-60.
45. CURPH Interview No. 87-F, 54, HU OSA 414-0-2-87.
46. CURPH Interview No. 10-M, 30, HU OSA 414-0-2-3. He added that his superiors never praised good work. "There was perhaps a silent understanding and recognition, but not more than that" (30).
47. RFEFR, "Trouble in Construction of Tractor Stations," 21 July 1953, HU OSA 300-1-2-33515.
48. CURPH Interview No. 457, 14–16, HU OSA 414-0-2-277.
49. RFEFR, "New Bakery for Ozd Lags Far Behind Building Schedule," 22 April 1955, HU OSA 300-1-2-57486. For a Budapest project similarly delayed (due to machinery mis-specifications), see RFEFR, "Sabotage at a Construction Project," 21 April 1953, HU OSA 300-1-2-33712.
50. CURPH Interview No. 136, 64, HU OSA 414-0-2-163.
51. CURPH 442, 56–57.
52. For which see CURPH 120, 58, which reports about a clerk in a "building industry concern" entering fictitious names on his pay list. When he was caught, friends raised funds to repay the firm, but he went to prison anyway.
53. Or worse. In December 1952, the state executed a bridge-building enterprise director for embezzling "hundreds of thousands of forint." RFEFR, "Death Sentence for Embezzlement," 23 May 1953, HU OSA 300-1-2-34921.
54. Balassa, *Economic Planning*, 132.
55. Ibid., 133. Note that 50 ft for an opera ticket would be 6–8% of an office clerk's monthly pay (ca. 600–800 ft.). Few lower level office staff were eligible for bonuses.
56. CURPH 100, 31, 33, 43.
57. Balassa, *Economic Planning*, 134–36.
58. CURPH 458, 16.
59. Balassa, *Economic Planning*, 141–42, 148. Balassa supervised the balance sheets submitted to the large trusts mentioned and often was involved in negotiations between trusts and enterprises (148). Some high-priority projects paid special bonuses for on-time completion, ca. 1950–1952, with payouts reaching 100% of technical and managerial salaries. This ended in 1953 with Nagy's administration (150). Internal struggles were not unusual.

Financial managers could score bonuses by reducing inventories (hoarding), but technical staff lost bonuses when needed materials were unavailable and construction stopped (160–61).

60. CUPRH. 458, 7.

61. Balassa, *Economic Planning*, 191. At the official exchange rate the 1954 overcharges amounted to $17 million; at the "informal" rate, only $6 million; but they could easily have been ten times the sums discovered.

62. See Sándor Horvath, *Stalinism Reloaded: Everyday Life in Stalin-City, Hungary*, Bloomington: Indiana University Press, 2017, Ch. 1. Inverse culturally to exemplary women workers was the persistent story that prostitutes displaced from brothels were assigned to construction projects, noted by Horvath and at CURPH 10-M, 19.

63. CIA Research Aid, "Labor Supply and Employment in Hungary, 1949–1958," January 1959, 6 (Official Use Only, CIA-RDP79S01046A000600100001-4). The non-farm workforce varied from 2.0 to 2.4 million, ca. 1950–1955.

64. RFEFR, "Building Industry and Construction," 21. The writer's urban condescension toward them is palpable.

65. Ibid., 22–25.

66. CIAIR, "Recent and Current Projects," 3.

67. RFEFR, "Building Industry and Construction," 23–25. As there was much construction in the capital, skilled workers there had more permanent housing, but there were also hostels for incomers, notably at Csepel island, south of the center, where a large well-outfitted facility reportedly provided free lodgings (23).

68. RFEFR, "Conditions at the No. 48/1 Construction Trust in Győr," 9 January 1953, HU OSA 300-1-2-29582. The report suggested that having a construction employment contract protected individuals from police harassment, even if they walked away from the job, because information flows among agencies were slow or non-existent.

69. CIA, Provisional Intelligence Report, "Control of the Labor Force and Trade Unionism, 1946–55," 20 July 1955, 25 (Secret, CIA-RDP79-01093A00090010005-4).

70. RFEFR, "Conditions." For details on the operations of the labor book policy, see CURPH Interview No. 151, 67–69, HU OSA 414-0-2-167.

71. CURPH Interview No. 120, 36, HU OSA 44-0-2-147.
72. CURPH Interview No. 205, 21, HU OSA 414-0-2-182.
73. For the jousting between Rákosi and Nagy over releasing prisoners and internees, see Ferenc Váli, *Rift and Revolt in Hungary*, Cambridge: Harvard University Press, 1961, 144–51.
74. CURPH Interview No. 152, 246, HU OSA 414-0-2-168. The Rácz transcript is the longest in the CURPH collection, running well over 500 pages, wholly worth reading. CIA confirmed the use of forced labor in construction work along the Tisza: CIAIR, "Industrial Notes from Hungary," 12 November 1953 (Secret, CIA-RDP81-01036R000100020012-6).
75. An estimated 3,000 of the Tisza workers were among some 10,000 Hungarian POWs repatriated from the USSR in 1951–1952, then interned for forced labor rather than freed. See CIAIFD, "Forced Labor in Hungary," *Neue Zürcher Zeitung*, 26 October 1952 (Restricted, CIA-RDP80-00809A000700100441-9). Men of draft age unsuitable for military service were "employed in the construction of military installations, under army control." The camps were distinct from formal prisons, most of which the AVH ran (CIAIR, "Data on Prisons," 20 January 1953, 1–3 [Secret, CIA-RPD82-00457R016200270005-2]). "Prisoners held in AVH jails are never sent to work" (1).
76. Reportedly, the Ministry of Justice charged some enterprises a nominal wage rate, up to half of which was returned to camp or company administrators for "expenses," the rest of which was supposed to go to internees' families but perhaps did not (CIAIFD, "Forced Labor").
77. RFEFR, "Forced Labor in Albertfalva Factory," 21 October 1952, HU OSA 300-1-2-26675. This informant escaped from the camp just after Christmas 1951, but did not reach West Berlin until August 1952.
78. Váli, *Rift and Revolt*, 150–52.
79. Endre Prakfalvi, "The Plans and Construction of the Underground Railway in Budapest, 1949–1956," *ICOMOS – Hefte des Deustschen Nationalkommittees* 20(1996): 101–107 (Emphasis in original).
80. https://en.wikipedia.org/wiki/Moscow_Metro; https:// en.wikipedia.org/wiki/Magnitogorsk; https://en.wikipedia. org/wiki/Budapest_Metro (all three accessed 26 March

2021); CIAIFD, "Traffic Survey in Connection with Budapest Subway Planning," 19 June 1951 (Confidential, CIA_RDP80-00809A000600390692-1).

81. CIA Provisional Intelligence Report, "The Ferrous Metal Industry of Hungary," 13 March 1957, 1 (Secret, CIA-RDP79-01093A001200020009-5). In 1955, the report asserts, Hungary supplied from "indigenous resources" ten percent of the coke and 23% of the iron ore used in steelmaking.

82. "Hungary Reverts to Basic Industry," *New York Times*, 26 January 1955, 10; "Satellite Events Heralded Change," ibid., 9 February 1955, 10.

83. Prakfalvi, "Plans and Construction," 101.

84. CURPH Interview No. 466, 2–5, HU OSA 414-0-2-284. Subways in Warsaw and Prague were being planned, but Budapest was first in line.

85. Ibid., 3–6.

86. https://www.sciencedirect.com/topics/engineering/tunnel-boring-machine (accessed 26 March 2021).

87. RFEFR, "Inhuman Working Conditions at the Metro Construction in Budapest," 18 October 1951, HU OSA 300-1-2-973; Prakfalvi, "Plans and Construction," 102.

88. https://www.merckmanuals.com/home/injuries-and-poisoning/diving-and-compressed-air-injuries/decompression-sickness (accessed 26 March 2021).

89. RFEFR, "Inhumane Conditions"; RFEFR, "Wages of Caisson Workers at Budapest Metro Construction," 19 October 1951, HU OSA 300-1-2-9226.

90. CURPH 466, 10.

91. CIAIFD, "Supply Shortages Slow Budapest Subway Construction," *Nepszava*, 8 January 1953 (Restricted, CIA-RDP80-00809A000700110202-3).

92. CURPH 466, 7–8. László Gillemót was director of the Iron and Metals Industries Research Institute.

93. CURPH 457, 13.

94. Prakfalvi, "Plans and Construction," 102; CIAIR, "Budapest Subway," 9 August 1954 (Secret, CIA-RDP80-00810A004500900005-1).

95. CURPH 245, 9–13. This interview contains elaborate detail on the project's decline by an observant draftswoman.

162 P. SCRANTON

96. CURPH 466, 6, 8–9; CIA Intelligence Brief, "Resurgence of Subway Construction in the Communist Bloc," 16 February 1966, 4 (Top Secret, CIA-RDP79T01003A003100100001-5).
97. Irving Mayer, "Program Management with Configuration Control," *IEEE Transactions on Aerospace* 1(1963): 467–73.
98. CURPH 246, 2–3.
99. Ibid.; CIAIFD, "Build Danube Port Near Dunapentele," *Nepszava*, 13 March 1951 (Confidential, CIA-RDP80-00809A000600390172-5); CIAIR, "Difficulties at Dunapentele," 2 February 1952 (Secret, CIA-RDP82-00457R010000310009-1); Mark Pittaway, "Creating and Domesticating Hungary's Socialist Industrial Landscape," *Historical Archeology* 39:3(2005): 75–93. Also see RFEFR, "Sztálinváros Being Built After Russian Plans," 28 February 1953, HU OSA 300-1-2-31483.
100. CURPH 246, 2–3.
101. For railways, see CIAIFR, "Reopen Railroad Lines to Traffic," *Közlekedési Közlöny* (Railway Gazette) December 1951 (Restricted, CIA-RDP80-00809A000700050248-0).
102. CURPH Interview No. 477, July 1957, 8–9, HU OSA 414-0-2-290. Reinforced-concrete barges, fabricated 10 km upstream "on the island of Tass," floated down to the site, where they were "filled with gravel" and became components of the harbor wall. Many "were rejected because of faulty construction" (CIAIR, "Steel Combine at Sztálinváros," 21 April 1952, 2 [Secret, CIA-RDP82-00457R01150000270009-0]).
103. CURPH 246, 9.
104. RFEFR, "Hungary: Industry," 5 July 1951, HU OSA 300-1-2-1796; CIAIR, "Difficulties."
105. CIAIR, "Steel Combine at Sztálinváros."
106. http://architectuul.com/architect/johanna-wolf (accessed 29 March 2021). Wolff, early a specialist in reinforced concrete structures, assisted in rebuilding Budapest and in constructing the Inota power plant before leading the Dunapentele project. She was a pioneering female architect, a model Communist woman, and, after 1953, the parliamentary representative from Sztálinváros.

107. CIAIFD, "Progress Report on Stalin Works in Hungary," 14 August 1952, 1–3 (Restricted, CIA-RPD80-00809A000700070530-3); CIAIR, "Steel Combine."
108. RFEFR, "Assistance Denied to Injured Laborers at Sztálinváros," 20 December 1951, HU OSA 300-1-2-12774;, RFEFR, "Conditions in Sztálinváros," 28 February 1952, HU OSA 300-1-2-16292.
109. RFEFR, "The Stalin Iron and Steel Plant in 1952," 11 March 1953, 3, HU OSA 300-1-2-31921. "It is not unusual for cement cross-pieces to cave in under the weight of the roof or for roofs made of cement to fall apart" (CIAIR "Sztálinváros Combine," 6 March 1953, 3 [Secret, CIA-RDP80-00810A000400150003-1]).
110. This despite a 20% bonus for night work. See CIAIR, "Sztálinváros Combine," 6 March 1953, 1.
111. Mark Laszlo-Herbert, "The Construction and Transformation of Socialist Space in the Planned Cities of Stalinstadt and Sztálinváros," unpublished PhD dissertation, University of Toronto, 2016, 93–94, 128–29. This fascinating study uses chiefly Hungarian sources to document the bizarre process of creating, then operating the Danube steel complex, comparing it to a companion new town in the DDR.
112. RFEFR, "The Stalin Iron and Steel Plant in 1952," 4, 7.
113. By mid-1953, 80 identical housing blocks had been erected in the New Town, each 300 m long and 4–5 stories (CIAIR, "Sztálinváros Combine," 6 March 1953, 2).
114. "Laborers… used wheelbarrows to bring up the ore from the barges at anchor." CIAIR, "Arrival of First Shipment of Soviet Iron Ore," 4 May 1954 (Secret, CIA-RDP80-00810A004001110005-9); CIAIR, "Economic Information," 13 October 1954, 2 (Secret, CIA-RDP80-0810A005000800006-5); CIAIR, "Cutback at Sztálinváros," 16 November 1954 (Secret, CIA-RDP80-00810A005300770006-6).
115. Balassa, *Economic Planning*, 161, 165.Balassa was a staff accountant and business manager on the steel mill project and wrote a treatise on its workshop administration in 1955.
116. CUPRH Interview No. 458, 22, HU OSA 414-1-2-278. The Soviets were anxious that US anti-communism would lead to a

Third World War, a concern that American engagement in the Korean War did little to alleviate. See William Lee and Richard Staar, *Soviet Military Policy Since World War II*, Stanford: Hoover Institution Press, 1986, Ch. 1.

CHAPTER 5

Socialist Commerce: Provisioning, Coping, Maneuvering, and Trading

Under the [Stalin-era] system, distribution was highly centralized, it was tightly divorced from production... and, in general, trade played a passive role. Producer goods were distributed by central agencies on an allocational basis, laid down in detail in directive plans. As a rule, only consumer goods were handled by trading enterprises. It was commonly accepted that under socialism, trade should not be allowed to control production, as this would interfere with planned development. Of the five major divisions of material production, trade was considered to be least important, the level of personal earnings in trade was well below the national average, there was a very high labor turnover, and the public rating of employment in trade was near the bottom of the occupational ladder.
—J. Wilczynski, 1973.[1]

The Hungarians you meet personally tell you they don't go out, they can't afford to, or they go out on a great occasion, such as your own visit. And then you look around these places that are filled. They cost money to eat and drink in and you wonder who the people are and you get various answers but the frankest was from a man who said, in a great café on a busy night, "Look around you, everybody here steals." And he explained that "in Hungary today you have to steal, the workers steal what they make at their benches and take [it] home and sell it second-hand in black channels."
—Sy Bourgin, *Time* correspondent, May 1956.[2]

© The Author(s), under exclusive license to Springer Nature Switzerland AG 2022
P. Scranton, *Business Practice in Socialist Hungary, Volume 1*, Palgrave Debates in Business History,
https://doi.org/10.1007/978-3-030-89184-8_5

165

166   P. SCRANTON

Everyone lives from the market and measures the operations of a regime through his stomach.
—Exiled planning chief, 1957.[3]

Developing a socialist system of exchange was not a high priority for the Hungarian state. In orthodox Marxism, only productive labor generated value; being non-productive, trading was secondary. Commerce just moved things around the economic chessboard, although the ways they were moved needed to correspond with socialist principles. Thus in and after 1948, Hungary gradually nationalized private commercial establishments. Shops and stores, restaurants and taverns, wholesalers and warehouses, carting and hauling, repairs and personal services—all came under the supervision of the Ministry of Domestic Trade. In tandem, the Ministry of Foreign Trade absorbed import/export firms, while stock trading and currency exchange (with the West) ceased.[4] However, displacing capitalist practices yielded awkward socialist institutions which failed to meet many social needs and desires—for fresh vegetables, for durable shoes, for a reliable bicycle. In consequence, enterprising Hungarians revived older business forms and improvised new ones. The result was a tidy if complex official commercial system and a parallel, necessary hodge-podge of private actors' lawful, illegal, and frankly criminal practices. This chapter will first visit the state-authorized sector (Provisioning), then will sketch its somewhat dubious counterparts (Coping and Maneuvering). The discussion closes with a brief overview of import/export relations (Trading), which state agencies handled clumsily, despite their crucial economic role.

PROVISIONING

Urban Hungarians had long bought their food, clothing, housewares, and furniture from shops or public markets, and in the larger cities, from department stores. However, before the socialist transformation, rural folks were more often self-provisioners than purchasers. Most had worked others' land for shares of field crops, meanwhile gardening, raising pigs and chickens, baking their own bread, and largely living at arm's length from the money economy. Given poor roads and slow travel, trips to village shops had been infrequent and, in any event, such shops were thinly stocked. Postwar land reform provided a million or more country people with parcels generally insufficient to sustain families. This short-coming led to searches for paid employment, commonly by sending sons to towns. Remittances from their labor ended food shortfalls, covered purchasing tools, seed, or fodder, and paid taxes (new to the once-landless). Reports soon circulated that peasants were buying bread from bakers and wearing "city" clothes, signaling that cash-based commerce had arrived and was displacing older rural practices.[5]

After the 1946 economic stabilization, which introduced a new currency, the forint, commercial sectors revived "relatively rapidly."

> By 1948, there were 72,000 small businesses, 18,000 restaurants, 400 hotels and boarding houses and 8100 large trading enterprises in operation. By this time, however, the state and cooperative trade organs also were functioning, and in 1948, they conducted 15 percent of total domestic trade. The industrial kitchens, consumers' supply cooperatives, and commercial organizations managed by villages... played an important role in supplying the population.

Consumer co-ops sponsored 2600 outlets, and villages supported 2900 general stores, mostly for farmers, plus 1200 taverns. Nearly half of retail purchasing took place in Budapest, the other half equally divided between "provincial cities" and the villages. Most enterprises were tiny. Proprietors ran more than half of the shops by themselves; only nine percent of retailers had three or more workers. Wholesaling was comparable: 8100 enterprises with only 31,000 employees, 60 percent of traders with either one or none. Almost all restaurants were family-run taverns or inns offering very simple fare.[6]

Rákosi's administration, preoccupied with heavy industry, state farms, TSZs, and the Russians, took few decisive steps regarding existing commercial networks, other than nationalizing about 20 department stores. The state did take over wholesaling and reconfigured its acquired import–export firms into product-based agencies for foreign trade in textiles or machinery. Both moves provided key control levers over commerce. Everyday shoppers little noticed such organizational changes. Steadily though, private retailers and service providers closed their shops, having found their taxes hiked, their supply lines thinned, their leases and licenses canceled.[7] Given the unending housing shortage, families eagerly reshaped vacant Budapest stores into apartments with ground-level views of the streetscape.[8] Shoemakers starved for leather joined artisan co-ops (KTSZ) or shifted to factory work. Restaurants and taverns found contracting for wine, beer, and kitchen basics ever more difficult.[9] When owners threw in the towel, state managers took their places or just locked the doors. By 1952, the state operated 22,000 socialized chain retailers (one-quarter of those active in 1948, mostly food shops) and 5900 restaurants (down by two-thirds), alongside 2700 residual "private businesses."[10]

However, the state overreached when eliminating petty capitalists. Foods offered in its chains (Közert) were of low quality, the apparel drab and unsellable. Repairs of clothing, radios, or bicycles became nearly impossible to accomplish, while hundreds of villages lacked a barber. Moreover, "in spite of directives, the construction organs neglected to install commercial and restaurant units on the ground floors of new housing buildings," blunting plans to expand commercial spaces.[11] Thus during 1953–1954, the new leaders encouraged entrepreneurs by authorizing thousands of retail licenses and pledging access to materials for repair work. They also relaxed restrictions on farmers' public market sales and undertook to increase the quality and variety of retail stocks in the villages.[12] By late 1954, visitors to the capital commented brightly about the reappearance of private shops on once-bustling Váci Utca, formerly a center for upscale shopping and dining. Beauty parlors and a fashion and culture bookstore now abutted boutiques for stylish clothing and shoes. In Budapest's residential districts, unused garages hosted hairdressers, fruit sellers, and dressmakers.[13] To be sure, from the commanding heights, these sprouts had little importance; what really mattered to the ministries was industry and agriculture. That judgment was in error, however. The popular welcome of the commercial revival signaled instead that the socialist project had stalled and might slip into reverse.

Seizing retail enterprises was not a subtle process, but it was so spatially scattered as to be hardly visible. Consider the situation of one 26-year-old draftee, discharged from the Army in 1945, who returned to his home town near the border with Austria to start business life as a tavern keeper and restaurant owner. His enterprise thrived initially:

> Right after 1945, I made good money… As time went on, however, my taxes kept on increasing until they became unbearable. I was not able to pay, and one day during 1948, armed policemen entered my business, took a complete inventory, and chased us all out [without compensation]… All undertakings, wholesale and retail stores, and transportation, utilities were

nationalized, and the difficulties of food supply became so [severe] and encompassing that the state of affairs became truly desperate. In 1950, for instance, even meat was rationed.[14]

Elsewhere in villages, direct appropriation was the rule: "The representative of the Ministry of Domestic Trade calls on the owner of the business in the evening and demands the keys to the cash register and the account books. By these acts, the state assumes possession of the business." By fall 1949, all Budapest "oil and gasoline stations, as well as the larger paint stores and pharmacies," had become state property.[15] Seizing thousands of local groceries and village shops and shuttering many of them disrupted shopping patterns (former owners often became managers or clerks, though always at a different site[16]), but this did not precipitate nationwide shortages and rationing. Those were the twin consequences of reparations, Soviet occupation, and the industrialization drive.

The state implemented rationing even as it was exporting thousands of tons of food as reparations. Most was destined for the USSR, but some fed Romanians and Czechs. Leading Budapest processing plants handed over the bulk of their 1951 output: 50 percent of the meats and fruits from the capital's largest cannery, three-quarters of the Tejert Milk Company's butter, 80 percent of Mirelet's frozen foods, and from Globus, 1.6 million kilos of canned ham.[17] As well, a Swedish reporter explained: "The Hungarian Government is responsible for the feeding of the 120,000 Soviet soldiers stationed [here]. The major portion of the canning factories' production goes to the Army." The Soviets did pay for exports to its zone of occupation in Austria (at low prices): from January to June 1950, 5500 tons of livestock, 1840 tons of sugar, 790 tons of rice, 6000 tons of sausages, and 485 tons of vegetables, again largely for military forces. Actually, the Russians exchanged a portion of these shipments for Western currency, fueling Austria's black market.[18] The Party press acknowledged that exports contributed to food troubles, but also blamed a fodder shortage, weak organization of distribution, and "criminal" enemy propaganda. Swedish analysts dismissed such evasions:

The obvious reason for the shortage is that the government is paying for the Five-Year-Plan's machinery with food. The Soviets demand the expansion of Hungarian heavy industry. Last month alone, Hungary had to deliver 500 tons of butter to Switzerland and Belgium for the machine tools imported by the government. Exactly 90 percent of the 10-million-dollar trade agreement concluded with Austria is to be paid in food. In turn Hungary is importing... machinery from Austria for the Manfred Weiss factories, which employ 18,500 workers.[19]

In July 1951, Imre Nagy, a good Party member and Minister of Agriculture, used the Party daily to explain the meat shortage in an entirely reasonable way that ignored export commitments and transactions. A summer 1950 drought shrank fodder crop harvests, he noted. Farmers, faced with the prospect of starving livestock, sold or slaughtered far more animals than normal. "The slaughterhouses, operating in three shifts, could hardly satisfy the demand." Meat prices actually fell due to the oversupply, but shortage followed along dutifully. By spring 1951, the meat excess had been absorbed, but husbandmen had few remaining cattle, pigs, and sheep to market. Tight supplies sent prices soaring, "followed by speculation and illegal slaughtering, resulting in the further decline of the already decimated livestock" herds. Admitting that meat allotments were "small," Nagy urged Hungarians to take heart, as their situation was better than that of "rich England, where much smaller rations are available of salted, frozen or canned meat only." Deftly concealing the USSR and the food-for-machines exchanges while delivering a perfectly-capitalist supply-and-demand account, he suggested that better days were coming. Bumper crops of corn and barley were anticipated; so by late fall, pigs and poultry fattened on this abundance would begin reaching the market, and "the meat situation will improve rapidly."[20] Stock traders know that market predictions are fragile; socialist predictions were no less frail.

Rationing had already triggered a near-walkout at the Kábelgyár cable factory on April 16, workers arguing that "while they were being deprived of their actual needs of bread and meat, the political police guards watching them had enough bread and sausage for lunch." They began "the day by holding debates and discussions as to whether they should go on strike. After being severely threatened, they started work one hour late."[21] A fall 1951 report revealed that, at the city's public markets, the

> greengrocer women... abuse the regime in the most offending way and are not afraid of the consequences. From the long queues of housewives lining up in front of the shops, policemen have to pick out each day a number of women for cursing the regime in rude words. However, it may

be observed very often that the policemen do not like to make such arrests and try to pretend that they didn't hear these remarks.[22]

Hungarians detested rationing. Their constant (and misdirected) complaints to the Ministry of Food "handicapped" its ability to function. Thus in September, the ministry broadcast a clarification—rationing was "not under its jurisdiction," but rather belonged to the Ministry of Domestic Trade, where all grievances should be directed.[23] The state's approach to conserving resources *was* working, but it caused so much friction and resentment that Rákosi's team sought another means to this end. Out of the frying pan…

The result was a three-part scheme: almost all rationing would end, wages would be increased, and prices of food and much else would also rise, though appreciably more than wages. After staff worked during the autumn to determine new levels and ratios, the Council of Ministers shipped the new lists quietly to Budapest's "Athenaeum" printworks a week before the planned 1 December 1951 rollout, for distribution to retailers ahead of time. "On 26 November 1951, a detail of the AVH appeared in the printing shop and closed it hermetically. Not one of the employees… was permitted to leave the building until Saturday evening [1 December]. They had to stay there, to sleep there, and to eat there." That Saturday office and factory workers received their earnings as usual; but instead of being able to shop ("everybody runs to the shops on payday"), they were in for a surprise. In the late afternoon, "Radio Budapest announced that Rákosi would speak at 7:00 pm to the workers. At 6:50 police agents arrived at all state-owned stores and food shops and ordered them to lock up. People doing their Saturday night shopping were astonished and flocked into the streets to hear [the] speech." They learned that except for meat and fats, rationing was over, that wages would be increased 20 percent, and that the "free market" with "free prices" would resume the next day.

The people understood immediately what free prices meant and there was open criticism in the streets as they blamed the government for this "Christmas Gift." The shops were then rushed by workers and housewives; the storekeepers and the government were called "thieves" and "brigands." Popular indignation forced… reopen[ing] the shops at 9:00 pm and people rushed to buy rationed items at [the] old prices until midnight.[24]

172   P. SCRANTON

From a second account:

> When the new prices were posted in the windows of the closed shops, the population was so much excited about them that remarks were openly made against the regime and about the "high standards" in the People's Democracy. A great number of people gathered in front of the big food stores and policemen tried to disperse them, but in vain. The population was so belligerent that police decided not to interfere.[25]

On Sunday, the Party paper printed a Rákosi speech which celebrated the nation's economic accomplishments, then justified the changes, arguing that rationing had fostered "bureaucracy and corruption" and that "speculation had become rampant." Increased prices would eliminate these problems; no longer would farmers feed "cheap bread and flour to the hogs," as "the proper relation between purchasing power and the available supply of commodities" would be restored.[26] On Monday stores reopened, posting the new rates.

> Bread per kilo was listed at 2.80 ft as against the old price of 1.60; lard went up from 17 ft to 35; sugar from 6 ft to 12; butter from 26 ft to 70, etc. Cotton fabrics, such as flannel were unavailable, but listed as 12 ft per meter before 1 December 1951; the price now moved up to 26–28 ft. The people reacted furiously as they computed a 20% increase in wages as against a 40–50% decrease in available goods [for their earnings].[27]

The state had sought to break a dual price system in which open/free markets doubled or tripled official prices for products that had regularly disappeared from shelves. For instance, with a coupon bacon could be had from a state outlet at the old price of 40–50 ft/kg, though supplies were sparse. In market stalls, bacon might sell for 150 ft/kg and at that price, supplies were ample. The day after the ministry unveiled its new bacon price (120 ft), the free market price dropped to 130. For many items, re-pricing reduced such gaps notably (putting quality aside), but the key problem was that workers earning 800–1000 ft/month couldn't afford either price.[28] This hardly distressed the leadership, however, as suppressing consumer demand fit neatly into the imperatives of commercial exporting—meeting Soviet requirements while trading food for capital goods. Cynically, one might suspect that they expected the market could play the villain here, deflecting attention from their own planning sleight-of-hand.

So, imagine that you were an urban shopper in 1952, seeking food and clothing for your family. What were your options? On the food side, a useful starting point may be diet—what most people ate daily in Budapest or Debrecen or Győr (Fig. 5.1). Breakfast, as for many in "rich England," was bread spread with lard. Lunch was had in the office, school, or factory canteen, frequently bread and a hot soup featuring potatoes and seasonal vegetables.[29] Dinner, except on Sundays, was a cold meal—cured sausage or processed meat, cheese, bread, and condiments. With both partners working and two or three families sharing apartments, cooking was difficult, though as this sketch suggests, bread was a principal food and thus, if badly made, a source of controversy.[30] When feasible, Sunday dinners featured fresh meat or poultry, truly a challenge for most, given the price increases.[31]

Now, again, what options did food shoppers have? As a female electrical engineer from Budapest explained: "Food, generally green vegetables and fresh fruit we bought at the big free markets where the peasants brought in their goods. All the other staple food[s], like sugar and flour and meat, etc., we bought at the state stores. We never bought anything on the black

Fig. 5.1 Dunakapu Square Market, Győr. 1950 (Donor: Tamás Konok. *Source* FOTO: Fortepan—ID: 28215. http://www.fortepan.hu/_photo/download/fortepan_43687.jpg, Wikimedia Creative Commons)

market because the black market prices were so high we couldn't afford them."[32] The capital and every sizable town had public markets (ranging from daily down to once a week) where farmers who had met compulsory delivery quotas could lawfully sell surpluses directly to consumers (Fig. 5.2). Buyers reported that prices were somewhat higher than in the Közért stores, but the freshness and quality of eggs, for example, was superior and worth the (illegal) difference. Közerts offered staples (flour, sugar, rice, canned goods) along with some fruits and vegetables at fixed prices, but the latter were usually second rate because the best agricultural products went to export. "The State food stores had not such good quality foodstuffs but they were less expensive. Prices on the free market were higher, but there you were sure to receive fresh food."[33] Közért staff, often criticized for surly service, also had a reputation for

Fig. 5.2 Batthyány Square Market Hall, Budapest District 1, 1952. The hall, built in 1900, could accommodate nearly 700 stalls in its 3000 m^2 of floorspace (Donor: UVATERV. *Source* FOTO: Fortepan—ID 1094. http://www.fortepan. hu/_photo/download/fortepan_3972.jpg, archive copy, Wikimedia Creative Commons)

short-weighting bulk goods (flour, sugar), although this wasn't possible with packaged items.[34] The black market was not a place but a situated connection between seller and buyer for scarce, usually compact goods (watches, nylons, razor blades), few of which were foodstuffs.[35] Finally, a number of privately-owned shops revived in 1953, once Nagy-regime agencies issued licenses. Known as

Maszek stores, they offered specialty foods (and decent produce between market days), but again at prices neither white nor blue collar workers could manage.[36]

Three other options could help satisfy food requirements. In areas where transit routes were favorable, townsmen and women with ample time (often elders) could take buses or short-haul trains to nearby farm districts and quietly purchase goods from private farmers, vintners, and orchard keepers. Second, those with ample budgets could avail themselves of prepared meals at Közert-operated buffets and state-run restaurants.[37] In both cases, one might be observed by AVH informers and be challenged as a "hoarder," particularly during rationing, or as a "grafter." Direct buying from farms rested in a gray area: Were the official prices charged? Had the seller completed compulsory deliveries? Likewise, fine dining, as at Budapest's legendary Gundel (founded 1866), raised suspicions about the sources of funds for such extravagance, even among Party officials who frequented the city's somewhat-faded night spots.[38] For them, however, there was the third option, a special emporium—"the so-called 'Rákosi kitchen' on Apponyi tér [a few blocks from Váci Utca] which sold luxury food and drink to those few who were permitted to enter."[39]

Purchasing clothing could be, if anything, more complicated than buying food, not least because tight budgets meant that saving for clothes meant skimping on food. State retailers sold factory-made garments, of course, but private tailors and dressmakers coexisted with the chains throughout these years. Artisan cooperatives (KTSZ) likewise sewed both made-to-measure and off-the-rack men's and women's styles.[40] For those with family or friends outside the Bloc, IKKA, a personalized import agency, offered a gift parcel service through which clothing and other items could be shipped to Hungarians, the donors paying added transit and customs fees. It seems the vast majority of such packets came from the US, by way of coordinating enterprises in New York City and Cleveland.[41] Given the urban dislocations, many parcels went to rural communities that housed deportees, but farm households also had sustained their links with relatives who emigrated to the States.[42] A once-affluent Budapest woman noted:

> Few peasants ever wear the national costumes [any more], but men, women, and children are dressed like "city folks." The men wear rubber boots, which they have often received from abroad. Many of the farmers who have relatives in the U.S. receive IKKA parcels. [The writer] herself saw how three farmers once received IKKA parcels of 15 and 20 kilograms each.[43]

Clothing in these years was expensive for ordinary workers: for a bland suit of dubious quality (first-rate fabrics being exported) 900 ft, easily a month's wages.[44] Thus IKKA parcels were prized; even if the American clothes didn't fit, they could be altered or traded, or perhaps best, put up for sale at one of the state's commission shops, which re-sold goods from overcoats to damask tablecloths to furniture. New clothing from foreign sources was always in demand and at high prices, which supplemented family earnings. Valuable used articles flowed in to commission (or consignment—*bizományi*) stores, especially from those being declassed, those who needed "to obtain money quickly." Established "under the control and management of the previous 'State Enterprise for Pawn-shops,'" these outlets proliferated in Budapest as the upper and middle classes liquidated personal property and household goods under duress. Naturally, appraisers estimated "the receiving value of goods on commission... as low as possible."

> The goods will very rarely be sold at that shop to which they were given on commission. There exist [special] shops for receiving the goods... and others where the goods will be sold. In this way, the unfortunate customer... will never learn the price at which his goods were sold and he must be satisfied with the estimated value. He will never learn the profit which the selling shop had made [either].

Receiving centers paid "the seller half of the estimated price and the balance after having sold the item." Goods extracted from the city's "fashionable districts" then traveled to suburban sales outlets near "the workers settlements on the outskirts" of Budapest. Through this maneuver, workers could furnish their apartments and outfit their families at affordable prices, compensating somewhat for their meager incomes.[45] The state proclaimed these agencies as being "in the interest of the working class," but finding a better example of capitalist opportunism would pose a challenge.

In state pawnshops, personal items could be pledged for short-term loans. Underpricing on the buying side was routine, as in the consignment stores. For instance, with gold rings and jewelry, appraisers loaned 18 ft per gram of gold, but, once the pawn period expired, re-sold the same gold at 80 ft/g. Moreover, a special regulation forbade giving more than 500 ft for any item. Thus a bracelet whose gold content weighed 50 g would not net 900 ft, but just 500; later, the state would vend the gold for 4000 ft. Such rules served "to push people who are in a tight corner into a more difficult situation."[46] Unsurprisingly, both pawn and consignment shops overflowed with goods during the deportations; they were "in fact so busy that no one today will buy a Persian carpet or rug." One shopper, looking for a used bookcase in a state warehouse,

> came out into the street [and] saw a couple of trucks being loaded. Asking what it was, she got the reply, "Persian rugs. We have 15 [freight] carloads of them in storage and it's tough trying to get rid of them since nobody will buy them." Nobody buys carpets, and nobody seems to buy furniture, so that the prices for both of these items have been considerably depressed.[47]

Savor it: oversupply yields depressed prices and slack markets – another great moment in building socialism.

The Ministry of Domestic Trade, which regulated commerce, included the usual policy departments (finance, planning, labor, accounting) and seven "Practical Departments" organized by sector: food, drugs, clothing, hardware, fuel, catering (restaurants, hotels), and "cultural goods." This last handled "furniture, watches and jewelry, photographic equipment, sporting goods, toys and musical instruments, and 'commission goods' (second hand articles)." Its assistant director for cultural goods in 1956, a 29-year-old single mother, provided an in-depth review of commercial practice since 1949, when she had started at the foot of the organizational ladder after her father's sudden death. Each of her department's "categories" (e.g., furniture) had just one wholesale enterprise and one retail firm, the latter supervising "a chain of shops." Nationally in furniture these numbered 45, joined by 50 commission stores, 200 for toys and sports, 45 for musical instruments, 70 photographic shops and 110

178   P. SCRANTON

jewelers—in all, 550 cultural retailers employing 3,000. Completely separate were the array of village cooperative shops designed to meet rural needs, controlled by local councils but supplied by ministry wholesalers.[48]

In the six cultural sections, outlet managers participated in drafting quarterly plans, sending estimates to the central wholesale firm based on recent sales (and their distribution across product lines) and on "trade gossip" about likely production trends. As in construction, they tended to be holdovers from the capitalist economy.

> The majority of them were old shopkeepers, expert tradesmen, who knew each other from pre-war [times] and maintained close contacts. They had "feel" – in Közért anybody could be a shop manager, anybody can sell lard or flour, but in our trades the old experts had to be retained. You cannot foist a camera on a customer unless you know something about cameras.

From experience, the shopmen could make "a shrewd estimate" of what local summer or fall demand might amount to. "Then they turned around and understated this estimate by as much as they dared to. The reason, of course, was that the lower their plan, compared to the eventual turnover, the larger their bonus." Manipulating proposals to assure bonus payments was universal; in cultural goods, bonuses topped out at 50 percent of salary vs. 20 percent at the Közérts. Routinely, the department's assistant director would modestly boost retailers' bottom-level estimates before presenting them to the ministry planners, who generally concurred, except in special circumstances. For instance, they "may have learnt that there is prospect of a more generous foreign currency allocation for consumer goods imports, in which case they increased the planned turnover figures, as imported stuff sold like hot cakes."[49]

The Council of Ministers, however, framed its growth expectations based on political agendas; thus it always established appreciably higher targets than those from the ministries. The latter "reflected a desire to understate [goals] and thus to secure larger bonuses, while the Council figures were intended to secure wage economies via small or zero bonuses." The National Planning Office regularly backed ministry proposals, but the Council

> could always get its own way if it really wanted to. The most flagrant case was in the textile and clothing trade, where the poor chaps could for two whole years never get more than 80 percent plan fulfillment, and

accordingly never received any bonuses, because of the ridiculous turnover plan targets set by [Ernö] Gerö.[50] They could barely exist on their basic salaries.

Once department targets were confirmed, each cultural section outlet's share had to be apportioned, a process which offered "an incentive for the shop manager to bribe the plan people in his firm so as to secure a smaller target (which he could easily over-fulfill) at the expense of the other... shops." The resulting bonuses were "shared" with the plan officer.[51] Of course.

In the high Stalinist years—the "years of fright"—consumer goods were far from being plan priorities. "There was such a material shortage that one could not have a shoe soled, and... most things were either not to be had at all or only in the wrong season." An upward trend commenced in 1952, accelerated by the Nagy cabinet's commitments to providing manufactured goods to farm households.[52] As rural incomes rose, the ministry reported that country buyers accounted for some 70 percent of retail sales gains, the residual credited to "Budapest and the other main industrial towns." Furniture plans more than trebled in real terms; when comparing the fourth quarters of 1952 and 1956, three-fourths of the advance derived from "the increased standard of living of the peasant population." Jewelry and watch sales had doubled, chiefly because "since 1953–54, we were allowed to import West German and even Swiss watches."[53] This, and rural retailers' often-thin inventories, may account for reports of energetic shopping by farm families after profitable market days.

> Those farmers who manage to sell their goods in Budapest do not keep their money long. Instead they go on shopping sprees. The state textile stores are always overcrowded by peasants, who do not seem to have difficulties making their purchases... One of the reasons for the "peasant invasion" is that there is little if anything to be bought at the village stores... At the state hardware store, [I] once watched two peasants [purchase] two 25-L containers for fat, paying 200 ft per container. They also buy many kitchen utensils... [though] even a small pot costs between 25 and 30 ft.[54]

In 1955, the old restrictions crumbled further once the ministry decreed that state retail firms (but not individual outlets) no longer had to rely solely on their assigned wholesalers. With the reauthorization of private producers (again, Maszek), procurement agents could deal directly with them. "From then on, a retail firm could buy, without anybody's approval, a dozen knitted sweaters or dining chairs from a Maszek artisan and was no longer absolutely dependent on its appropriate state wholesaling firm."[55] Nagy-era changes benefited wholesale buyers as well. For instance, with raw materials for furniture sparse in the early 1950s, they went "humbly" to the factories and responded gratefully even if offered nothing but "pale blue tables and chairs." Later, as supplies for consumer goods' production rose, the wholesale director "would talk very differently. He knew from the executives of the parallel retail firm what sort of qualities and ranges consumers happened to want at the time." Once a factory had ample lumber, buyers could approach sellers as colleagues, "taking off their hands all the supplies that were allocated to them" while providing "better quality" goods in a "wider range" of designs. Coupled with the restoration of installment purchasing for furniture (1954, later extended to other durable goods like cameras), retail commerce seemed on the verge of a vigorous phase. The return of Rákosi's heavy-industry-promoting team obstructed any such trend.[56]

COPING AND MANEUVERING

Coping refers to the adaptive strategies of buyers and sellers dealing with the rigidity and unpredictability of the commercial organizations and environments sketched in the Provisioning section. Maneuvering suggests more active efforts to evade controls and regulations, at times by initiatives that covered the spectrum from deception to fraud to crime. Several brief stories will help set the stage, one about coping told by a variety shop manager and two about maneuvering recounted by a clothing and shoe store director and a KTSZ salesman. First, coping:

> Regarding the Food Distribution Company, for instance, we always had to make a plan for the next three months. Of course, this was purely guesswork. The idea was that according to the plan and estimate which is submitted, the production would follow these demands, but of course it never worked. It very often happened that commodities were manufactured which no branch... ever asked for, and then we were compelled to sell them by all means. For instance, different sorts of textiles, or canned foods, etc. Also there were the export rejects which had to be sold.[57]

There was little to be done. The goods requested didn't arrive; instead, unwanted, unsightly stuff took their place, whether dumped by factories, rejected by foreign clients or intercepted by export inspectors. Plan targets weren't adjusted when unsellable inventory replaced goods customers were known to want; so staff bonus prospects promptly vaporized. However, other responses were available and were anticipated by those on upper echelons. The manager of a modest Pest shop, a "bad kader" 45-year-old with two decades' experience, grumped:

> I was not compensated in the way I should have been for the responsibilities I had to assume in running the store. I received 900 ft a month. The reason for this low pay was understood by everyone, that is that employees of the state stores could illegally take what they wanted, that is, steal. The ministry knew that such stealing was going on and therefore did not want to pay any higher salaries. [It] was done on the following basis: by making no. 3 quality yard goods into no. 1 quality... and the difference between the two prices... would be pocketed. Naturally, we reported that the no. 3 quality goods were sold for the standard price set by the ministry.[58]

Fleecing the public was acceptable to all parties in the trading network, evidently, except the victims, who complained through letters to newspaper editors. Store managers, though, simply had to maneuver within the commercial bureaucracy:

> There was a certain corruption in this matter of making orders from the central office. I had a personal acquaintance in the office who saw to it that I would get saleable material, so that the goods would not stay in the store. For this he would get a certain kickback for sending quality goods which I could sell. If there was a greater traffic in the goods sold, then he would share more in what we were able to make from our sales.[59]

Such deception and fraud extended into illegal entrepreneurship, as illicit middlemen supplied venturesome store directors with goods unobtainable through official channels. One such vendor, arrested in 1955, received a 20-month jail sentence. He had worked as a traveling salesman for a Budapest handicraft cooperative, a "council enterprise"; yes, truly, a traveling salesman in a planned economy. He owned a car, neatly registered to a sportsman friend,[60] used for visiting retailers to solicit orders and assess shortages of articles KTSZ workers could make as special items,

182   P. SCRANTON

outside the plan. "I was able to live exceptionally well under Communism, because of my special job," he asserted. Earnings of "4000 to 5000 ft a month in 1956" funded a comfortable bourgeois lifestyle: his wife tending house rather than doing badly-paid work, meat on the table four or five times a week, custom-made clothes and shoes, and season tickets to the opera. Nevertheless, when arrested, he "was accused of selling [apparel] to managers of state stores who sold the goods," then pocketed a portion of the difference between the illegal purchase and official sales prices of such scarce items, delivering the rest of the illegal revenue to his supplier.

> Very often my private craftsmen and tradesmen friends were able to manufacture the merchandise in demand at a cost which left us a profit despite the fact that the price was set very low.[61]... On my rounds I acquired orders from my [retailing] friends. I also received a share of their profits. This was not exactly a legal thing to do... The state wholesale and retail outlets were [at that time] strictly forbidden to buy merchandise from any other source if [it] was available from government outlets. [Also] it was strictly illegal for un-nationalized private tradesmen and craftsmen to sell their goods through a salesman.

His successful marketing operation met needs state factories and wholesalers ignored, but was wholly unlawful. As appealing his conviction dragged on through 1956, he continued practicing this lucrative trade, as his earnings report testifies, but come the uprising, he and his family wisely fled. Within six months, having settled in New York City, he was "employed by a textile import–export firm."[62] Never having abandoned capitalism, he had migrated to a place where his skills were both appreciated and lawful.

The sites at which coping and maneuvering materialized were diverse, as might be expected. The commercial organizations in play included the state's chain stores, public markets, and restaurants, yet around them circulated a swirl of transactions at the margins: repair work facilitated coping, whereas illegal entrepreneurship and black market exchanges exemplified maneuvering by both buyers and sellers. At a Közért, regular customers who befriended clerks or managers could expect that items much in demand but inadequately supplied might be saved for them. Such under-the-counter sales of paprika or tea helped families cope by adding variety to their daily fare. The same was true at Keravill, the appliance and bicycle/motorcycle stores, where scarce spare parts, especially bicycle and motorbike chains, were reportedly reserved for family and neighbors with connections and some ready cash.

> The State sold motorcycles (Csepel) but the stores only got five or six chains [a month] and there were thousands of motorcycles sold. The store employees' salary was 800 forints and the manager earned 1,000 a month. They would accept a 100 forint commission and sell the chain to the customer.[63]

On another ledger, the use of tie-in sales (to get X, you must also buy Y) helped managers cope with high sales plan targets and unload dead stock cluttering up inventories. Accusations that clerks routinely short-weighed unpackaged goods flew from all directions, yet a few forints skimmed daily gave a much-needed boost to rock-bottom earnings.[64] These coping ventures involved giving to some, what others might have had, or taking from others for one's own benefit. Individualism had in no way ceded its primacy to socialist cooperation.

Repairs were different, as they made a mutually-beneficial connection between those possessing defective goods and those with the skills necessary to revitalize them. Difficulties abounded on all sides, however, concerning materials, spare parts, the spatial distribution of artisans, and the dreaded state price lists. Taking the last first, Béla Csikos-Nagy's Price Office controlled rosters of charges for auto repair, shoe repair, and several hundred thousand other goods and service transactions (e.g., Motor Vehicle Repair in two volumes, 660 pages).[65] Mechanics and artisans repeatedly criticized published rates for repair and maintenance work as too low to cover labor and materials. Altering the manuals was impossible. Fixed prices were one foundation of the ministry's entire commercial system, after all.[66] So in order to stay afloat financially, craftsmen overestimated job requirements, solicited side payments for prompt service, and urged clients to acquire their own replacement parts. Finding someone to accept repair jobs got progressively more difficult as the cohort of skilled veterans aged or emigrated without being fully replaced. Independent craftsmen were last in line when allocating new or refurbished equipment and machines, and given uncertain earnings prospects, few apprentices selected shoemaking or appliance repair as a vocation.

184 P. SCRANTON

Before long, many villages had no one who could fix broken tools, cracked boots, or radios on the fritz. Most lacked tailors and dressmakers, as well as wood- and metalworkers. Sending appliances to KTSZ fix-it shops in Pecs or Debrecen entailed long wait times; returning those under warranty to their original factories was just as slow. Delays stemmed in fair measure from the parts crisis, which ballooned as the calendar pages turned. If the disabled item was from the USSR or another Bloc nation, much less the West, there could be little hope of ordering parts—they often had to be fashioned by duplicating the broken component, perhaps feasible for vehicles but daunting for electrical goods.[67] Hungarian plants tended to make only those parts for which the official prices delivered profits; loss-makers were "overlooked," unavailable. As for materials, craftsmen improvised elaborate schemes in order to acquire them. Peter Cukor, a Holocaust survivor whose family leather business had been nationalized, explained how illegal entrepreneurship facilitated repair work:

> My uncle Mishi... worked in a radio factory in Budapest and was responsible for cutting the back panels of radios out of impregnated cardboard. He managed to lay out the design in such a manner that he had wide strips of the material left over. At night I would go to the factory and Mishi would throw the leftover material over the fence. I collected the stuff and tied it into bundles and then delivered it to various shoemakers... They in turn used it for making insoles. This was a profitable operation [as] we got the material for free and sold it for a high price, but the risk was also high.[68]

A much larger volume of materials, illegal textiles which Maszek middlemen sold to legal artisan garment makers, flowed from joint Russian-Hungarian firms cheating on taxes. Mill directors reported to authorities that they produced ten meters of cloth from each kilo of cotton, but actually wove "14 m of some inferior quality," paid taxes on the ten and sold the other "four meters to the non-Socialist sector through the back door." These firms were supposed to remit 70 percent of all sales to the state as turnover tax,[69] but income from selling the extra four meters was off the books—gravy for the Russian managers who got "the profits of State Capitalism." Thus illegal managerial entrepreneurship fed the private clothing market.

These "black" deals by the Russians were the mainstay of the Maszek trade in Hungary, as Maszek traders, in order to live, were willing to deal without invoices, receipts and certificates. The Hungarian Communist authorities were fully aware of these Russian practices, and organized renewed drives for "certificate discipline"[70] but of course the sole real solution for them would have been the stamping out of the Maszek or quasi-Maszek sector willing to deal with the Russians on a "black basis."... The enterprise either would use the illicit profits... for private enrichment of the managers or for the building up of hidden reserves to offset thefts by employees.

As the early 1950s displacement of private trade narrowed the Maszek pathway, "the major outlet for Russian and 'Socialist' illegal sales became the 'fairs' (itinerant markets)." Domestic Trade tried to obstruct this through creating a state fair firm "to drive out the private peddlers"; this failed completely and they "continued as outlets." (When Nagy reauthorized Maszek activity in 1953, older channels likely revived.) Overall, Soviet managers "displayed a fine contempt" for Hungarian administrators. At one jointly-owned textile factory in Pápa (Veszprem), directed to deliver two million meters of cottons monthly to the state, they instead made a "black deal" with Austrian traders, shipped them the goods, "and obtained raw materials in return," an "ultra-capitalistic" entrepreneurial policy.[71] Hungarian regulators had no leverage to intervene.

Most illegal business was on a much more modest scale. A building trades worker in Szeged (Csongrád) earned about 1400 ft/month, plus a productivity bonus, but needed more funds in order to assist his parents. Thus, "he often had a secondary source of income, after hours jobs. He worked... as a mason on plant construction or even as a driver to earn more money."[72] A Budapest factory worker netting 850 ft/m supplemented his pay "by unloading coal freight cars in the evening hours. I earned between 20 and 25 ft per evening and spent this money immediately on food." He was also well aware of the city markets' unlicensed vendors: "Some people would come from the country to town with some products and would sell them without authorization."[73] A plumber from the Sopron (Györ) gas works enthused about his odd jobs:

We had plenty of opportunities to do black work, after our work in the plant. Everybody needed some installation work, or pipe fitting, or anything like that. We were always called to private homes... Out of the black work we could make as much money as our regular pay was. All the workers were doing the same; this was the main reason why they liked

186   P. SCRANTON

the gas factory and tried to stay there. Everybody used the material of the plant for the private works, the material was simply stolen... The discipline was not too strong... The party secretary was very often drunk.[74]

In Györ city, a mechanic at the huge Wilhelm Pieck railway equipment plant agreed:

> About half of my friends, together with me, worked part-time at odd jobs; this was all on the sly, for this was illegal. This *"Fusi"* work brought in good money if one had special skills. Some went out in the fields to hoe for smallholders, getting 30 ft for half a day's work. Others, like myself, specialized in repair jobs, from motorcycles to watches and everything else... I mainly fixed motorcycles, putting in new parts. [I] got the new parts from smugglers.[75]

At Debrecen (Hadjú-Bihar), a former border guard who tended "three holds of vineyards" lived off the income, selling his wine "for 12 ft [per liter] without the knowledge of the authorities." One county to the west, in Gyöngyöspate (Heves) Miklös Patai had produced wine and fruit brandy for export until his firm's nationalization in 1949. "To compensate for the sudden drop in his family's income, Patai regularly traveled via motorcycle to nearby towns, including Eger, to sell wine secretly to legal distributors, though he worried about being caught by the Secret Police."[76] Naturally, no one reported "black work" or illicit market sales to the tax authorities, making them even more magnetic.

Swiping state property to obtain materials was a common illegality; selling state property directly or using state institutions and information for private dealings was riskier and more complicated, though perhaps more lucrative. Gasoline diverted from state supplies serves as an example. The Rákosi regime gradually took possession of private vehicles and commercial trucks, setting up depots for repair and maintenance. Transport drivers had gas permits that entitled them to fill tanks at depots for 1.5 ft/liter. "It is quite usual for the driver to manipulate the measuring instruments a little, to show that more gas has been used up than is actually the case." The difference, siphoned from the tank, found new users. However, though many "participated in this fraud," the small number of potential buyers ("very few people own a car") drove the sales price of stolen gas down to one ft per liter. As private cars became somewhat more common, the opportunities for "black carriage" grew.[77] To avoid the mess and hazards of siphoning, station attendants could simply vend gas directly, particularly to motorbike owners like Patai. An underpaid Sopron functionary (800 ft/m) recollected: "I was working then (1952) at a gas station and was stealing the gas. I sold it on the black market, especially to my friends from the army. In Hungary, anybody who wanted to live has stolen. Stealing was not considered a sin, because it was against the state."[78]

In 1954, a "bad kader" commercial veteran, recently released from prison, had to leave his new job in the Hotel Astoria's wine cellar because the Budapest AVH identified him as illegally residing with relatives in the city. A sympathetic police major advised him to find a hotel position elsewhere. (Nagy was then rehabilitating detainees, and the AVH no longer bared its teeth at every opportunity.) The Astoria's director made several phone calls and located an opening at Lake Balaton's Rianás restaurant, to which he relocated and from which he moved to the nearby Golden Star Hotel as an administrator. Despite his ragged background, within a year hotel overseers promoted him to general manager, confirming the shortage of experienced executives. From this perch, he surveyed the entrepreneurial buzz permeating the grounds. Unlike state-sponsored vacation lodges for virtuous workers, the Golden Star was a "free" house, welcoming anyone who could afford its high rates: Party leaders, foreign dignitaries, businessmen from the West, and newly-prosperous Maszek traders.

> The porter as well as many of the maids tried to make their own private business. The foreign guests brought along nylon, perlon, and many other items. The maids, waiters, and waitresses, porters and so on sold such imported items. The square before our hotel was all the time like an oriental market. Everybody was doing business there.

Some hotel workers were "déclassé elements. After 1953, many former deportees came to Balatonfüred and lived there in very great poverty." The Golden Star hired a lawyer as its "general handyman" and a Horthy-era air force captain to handle maintenance, but could not find a place for a dismissed cavalry colonel. In the capital, the Astoria's porter had reaped 5,000 to 6,000 ft/m, over half from tips and illegal trade; Golden Star staff sought comparable riches.

> Needless to say that everybody stole as he could. Actually the Communists higher up knew of it exactly... [They] openly admitted that there was

188   P. SCRANTON

a great cheating going on. At one time we had a meeting of the shop committee where many Communists participated. The main topic of the meeting was how the norms could be cheated. The Communists did not protest against the proceedings.[79]

On another front in the service and entertainment trades, a Budapest accountant cited "an interesting case of fraud... in one of the night clubs."

[It] received its liquor supplies, like all the other establishments, from the Central Agency of the Catering Trade. The employees not only sold the drinks at exorbitant prices, but, using less and less of the official supplies, also served drinks from liquor which they had purchased privately from stores. The business was unusually prosperous... The employees took extreme care to keep accurate official accounts and even hired... a chief accountant who, by the way, had been summarily dismissed from his previous job. It was "an enterprise within an enterprise."

The staff shared profits from the illegal liquor, shielding the substitution from agency scrutiny. Suspicious of a busy club buying ever-smaller quantities of liquor, the Central Agency "built in" an informer "under the guise of a waiter assigned to the place." Once he learned of the scheme, the fraud came to light.[80]

Business venturing also surfaced *inside* state commercial agencies. An erstwhile black marketeer followed his main chance in the late 1940s, joining the Party once it gained control. Having secured a post in the Domestic Trade section "entrusted with the prevention and suppression of corruption," he learned what scams did and didn't work. A year later he became section chief of a new division "providing the communities with sport items, musical instruments and furniture," the DT cultural commerce department profiled earlier in this chapter.

It was a pleasant place to work. We purported to be supporters of the regime, [but] we were all wearing masks. We worked at least 10 hours a day, but the effective work was not more than two or three hours. The rest of the time was taken up with all sorts of activities, including doing your own business; especially after 1953, when the private sector of the economy... had been revived. There was much we did to help the independent businesses. This was not legal and was not done openly. But the top management, at least, knew about it and it became an established practice.

Favors directed to Maszek enterprises generated substantial reciprocal "rewards." Plainly "this was institutionalized corruption; often I made more on the side than my regular salary," he boasted. Even so, this self-styled "opportunist" judged that "the illegal practices at our office were actually beneficial to the Hungarian economy." That may have been correct, given the official system's shortcomings.[81]

A official in the Budapest land registry chronicled the course of an illicit vacant property finder's market, as state efforts to expand the city's housing stock began to flounder. In 1953, the Nagy cabinet debuted a home-construction program through which "the worthier citizens received very cheap Government loans and were given the opportunity to acquire cheap building lots." The empty tracts assigned to this project soon were fully allocated "and people were looking around for more cheap real estate." The solution was identifying land the state deemed abandoned, due to its owners' emigration to the West, failure to pay taxes, deportation or death abroad (think war casualties or gulags). Thus

> people began to skin the building lot market. They would go to a desirable spot and try to establish... that this was abandoned land... A new rule was made, stating that absent owners lost their rights... We had to work with them to check the various claims made by the prospective builders. If the lot was really without a live, tax-paying owner, it could be given away at a nominal sum. A new breed of real estate hyena developed who sniffed out absentee owners and followed up the ownership procedure for a considerable fee, which the prospective owner paid.[82]

Whether the hyenas performed productive labor when identifying buildable plots for busy Budapest bureaucrats and Party "worthies" was a question for the theorists. The work paid well and helped address the capital's nagging housing deficit.

Party spokesmen never hesitated to condemn the black market and the frauds and thefts so prevalent in commerce, but these too solved problems, albeit in gritty ways. The black market, like the other "black" commercial forms, materialized in spot transactions, whereas illegal entrepreneurship created ongoing capabilities and relationships, as with the real estate hyenas or the clandestine wine distributors. At the upper end of the price spectrum, employees of wholesale enterprises were renowned for spiriting away motorcycles and washing machines for black marketing—not of course in a public square, but for those who had commissioned their theft. A recycling firm's accountant recollected: "I wanted to install an electric boiler in my bathroom. After hunting for it for long weeks, I was able to get one for 20 percent higher than the regular price through an employee of a state trading house."[83] This was not an isolated case, as a food shop manager affirmed: "Regarding the Black Market, this was going on all the time. Whenever a commodity disappeared from the regular market, you always were sure to find it on the Black Market. There was a very strong Black Market in all textile materials, and also in electrical appliances, for instance, electric stoves."[84]

Covert importing was another pathway to deliver goods to prospective buyers, chiefly items easy to conceal with a high value-to-volume ratio. A Budapest milling machine operator sketched the trade:

> There was a black-market, but only in luxury articles smuggled in from the West. These were nylons, watches, medicine, textiles, etc. They were brought into Hungary by Danube sailors and by sportsmen, or by Hungarian officials who had some opportunity to travel abroad. The black market in these goods was not organized. If a person brought... such goods into Hungary, then he would sell them to friends or acquaintances, or perhaps to colleagues at the office. The price... was comparatively high but these goods were of considerably better quality.[85]

Hungarians judged domestic watches as inferior to those from Austria or West Germany; for the official price, one could purchase a much better device from a smuggler, or secure an adequate timepiece for half what the state stores charged. So too were Hungarian razor blades disdained; elevated prices for Czech or Austrian brands were no obstacle.[86] "There were people who smuggled to Hungary from Czechoslovakia several hundreds of razor blades, fixed on their chests below their shirts with insulating tapes. [They] could be bought in Czechoslovakia for very low prices."[87] An inspector at the city's Ganz Electrical factory detailed a closer-to-home variant:

> There was a black market in tools and electrical equipment. For example, cable wires would frequently be stolen by the workers in the factories and sold to fences. These fences would in turn sell the tools and equipment to private dealers for about 25% to 30% less than their official price. The

dealers would be glad to pay this price because otherwise they were unable to get materials or tools.[88]

Finally, an unexpected source of off-plan commodities were the occupying Russian troops, who in a small-scale version of their leaders' chiseling would buy items priced cheaply in military base canteens and shops and resell them to Hungarians. With their higher salaries, Soviet officers, living off base, unlike enlisted men, purchased "items of luxury" to make available to their neighbors, a practice that sometimes reduced local hostility.[89]

Coping and maneuvering complemented and expanded the options official commerce offered Hungarians. State authorities did labor to limit unlawful and unregulated commerce, arresting and jailing miscreants, but their efforts little availed in a context of plan failures, material and service shortages, and low-quality consumer goods. Thus in the theft economy, inventive, risk-taking entrepreneurs strove to fulfill unmet needs and profit thereby, near and past the edges of legality. Unauthorized procurement through theft was pervasive, exemplified by a remarkable 1952 wave of vanishing government typewriters, reportedly "smuggled by Soviet Army trucks into Romania and Austria."[90] Perhaps the liberalization of travel and trade after 1953 reduced smugglers' incentives by making many black market items readily available. Perhaps the increased availability of consumer durables ended the illegal appropriation of washing machines from state warehouses. Even if so, fixing weak elements in the empire of Domestic Trade hardly compensated for the system's incompleteness, incoherence, and inconsistencies. Broad reforms plus a comprehensive rethinking of commerce might do the job, but such steps were on no-one's agenda.

TRADING

All operative activities of foreign trading are performed… by state-created enterprises… The monopoly of foreign trade is a monopoly *outwards*, that is, all economic activities beyond the frontiers are exclusively performed by institutions and companies qualified for that aim. It is also a monopoly *inwards*, that is, in the circle of the various goods and services, all foreign trade transactions are concentrated in the hands of a single enterprise… [Domestic] distribution is never so concentrated. In foreign trade,

192   P. SCRANTON

however, all goods and services have one exclusive purchasing and selling organization.[91]

The Ministry of Foreign Trade dates from June 1949, when decrees established it as the successor to the postwar Commerce ministry's foreign trade directorate. Seven national enterprises had begun import/export management in fall 1948; the new ministry added ten more IMPEXES, each overseeing a production domain: Nik—heavy machinery and factory installations; Elektroimpex—electrical and precision instrument products; Külforget—textiles and raw materials; Monimpex—wine, spirits and tobacco, and others, including the highly-specialized Mavad—"Dead and live game." (Hungary was famed for its hunting reserves.) These firms made sales deals independently; they licensed exports and could "assume obligations," though all directors reported to the ministry, which the National Economic Council and the Council of Ministers supervised. Importing seems to have been more centralized, especially as deals with the West demanded hard currency or negotiated goods exchanges. Hence an Import Council, created in 1951, "authorize[d] proposed imports," guided by the National Planning Office president. Separate, parallel administrations coordinated intra-Bloc trade or commerce with "Western Countries."[92]

Key initial tasks, as defined by Moscow, included reducing trade with capitalist suppliers and thereby seeking Bloc autarky through substitutions. A ministry official recalled:

> In changing the direction of foreign trade from a westerly to an easterly course, the maximum stress was laid on basic materials and "essentials."... For instance, Hungary's main sources of aniline dyes used to be Switzerland, Germany, the U.K. and the U.S. In conformity with the spirit of autarky, it was attempted to cover as much of these needs from Russia as possible... As a result Hungarian printed textiles completely lost their competitive position.

Sadly, attempts at domestic dye synthesis yielded only "chrome black." Meanwhile, Soviet dyes cost 20 percent more than their Western counterparts, but "their poor quality was a graver matter than their relative dearness." Raw materials imports from the Bloc failed to replace those once purchased from the West and deliveries also proved unreliable. "Despite all the ingenuity of Hungarian technicians, the quality of

Hungarian manufactures deteriorated." Hence, trade agencies had "to offer cut rate exports in odd lots to all comers. This was a source of very heavy loss."[93]

Also costly were delays and errors in manufacturing. Minister of State Ernö Gerö reported in June 1950 that "there are technical and political shortcomings in Hungary's export trade." Producers and exporters were not cooperating effectively and contract deadlines failed to be met. A large order of radios for Bulgaria was completed two months late, and, as the short-term letter of credit had expired, sat in a warehouse until the financing could be renewed. Similarly, the Diósgyör Machine Tool factory shipped on time just one of 15 turret lathes, and Budapest Tool had a lathe delay "because of reworking necessitated by poor workmanship." Factory and agency inspectors screwed up a major sale of Orion's glass-lined thermos bottles by failing to note that the contract specified they be labeled "Made in Hungary." Omitting this led to the entire shipment being returned. Such pratfalls led to the installation of foreign trade "quality inspectors" at plants fulfilling international orders, their salaries paid by the manufacturers.[94]

It was not enough. Export enterprise agents traveled to the Milan Trade Fair in summer 1951, restoring a connection that dated at least to the 1930s, when "Hungary was always one of the foremost exhibitors at Trade and Industrial Fairs and Expositions in Europe." Modern trade fairs appeared in and after World War I as attempts to draw buyers to host cities/nations in an environment of growing export restrictions and as an opportunity for sellers from abroad to coax orders from local firms.[95] Hungary's 1951 exhibit, however, drew "jeers," not applause from the Italian press. The representatives were, for example, "obliged to offer for sale cheap, ugly and vulgar watches, designed for sale to [local] peasants and out of style in the rest of the world for a century." These had to compete with "beautiful and modern Swiss and German watches and clocks," and could not.

> These men, who were old experts in the business of international trade, soon learned for certain what they had suspected before: that their goods were priced out of the market. The prices fixed by the government on the instructions of Moscow were impossibly high... Since it was their duty to attempt to secure orders, they felt that if they could offer their products at competitive prices, they still might accomplish something. Their attempts to secure permission to reduce their prices were turned down.[96]

Two years later, a report on Milan's 31st Fair was more sympathetic but still brutal, expressing "a sense of profound pity, almost of shame" in reviewing the displays.

> The Hungarian exhibit shows a complete bathroom – evidently the latest and most up-to-date now made in that country. The style was crude and the enameling poorly done, in some places being so thin that after a couple of cleanings the bare terra cotta would come forth... One could admire the fine handicrafts and embroidered blouses... For the rest, however little good can be said. A few poor, shoddy scientific instruments were shown, some old chinaware [and] textiles – of designs and weaves similar to those found in the poorest and cheapest of Italian country peddlers' stocks.

Food packaging was just as dated; nothing remained "of the fine sense of line and design that we in the West have always considered to be the hallmark of all that which is Hungarian."[97]

Problems with export transactions kept bubbling up in every category. Budapest's Lang Machine factory delivered four boat motors to a Bloc client in 1951, but only two "were of acceptable quality." Just 14 turret lathes of a 50-unit order shipped on time, and inspectors rejected another 50 as "unfit for export." (Tool builders commonly redirected defective machinery, once repaired, to domestic users.) Sweden had purchased Hungarian textiles for decades, but by 1952, trade relations were sorely strained. Shipments paid for in advance didn't arrive; "time and again" the quality deficiencies of delivered fabrics meant they could not be distributed on "the rather spoilt Swedish market." When a client demanded "indemnification," a Hungarian trade official in Stockholm replied: "You can go straight to Stalin with your complaints!" Hungarotex ignored all protests and "the young and totally inexperienced clerks whom the commercial head of the Hungarian Legation... sends to meet the infuriated Swedes just shrug their shoulders."[98]

The reason why trade representatives in Stockholm were young and inexperienced is not hard to find. Initially, to reach export opportunities, Hungarotex had little choice but to hire "businessmen of the pre-war period" who could restore contacts and who spoke the relevant languages. The state did not trust these capitalist veterans; they were "rarely sent twice to the same country as it is considered undesirable that they should become too intimate with the local inhabitants." This of course undercut the value of language and network skills, but so what? By fall 1952, six of Hungarotex's 14 fabric salesmen "had incurred the displeasure of the ministry" and were no longer employed. Why? Most likely, taking the theft economy across the border, they had embezzled state funds, then slipped away.

[Trade reps] still do very substantial business with and through Belgium, Italy, Switzerland, Austria, Holland and in lesser degrees, England and West Germany. They open bank accounts in their own names in Western banks, and when they have stolen enough money and still have time to escape from the political police, they "resign" and go over to the Western democracies as "political martyrs." They make their most lucrative profits by illegal re-exportations.

Re-exportations were three-corner deals for commodities the U.S. had embargoed for delivery to Bloc nations, frequently handled through intermediaries in Cyprus, Turkey, or Israel. As Hungary was anxious to secure copper, alloy metals, or ball bearings, price was no object and room for skimming readily available—the result: "bad kaders" behaving badly.[99]

Young, inexperienced agents replaced them, but their knowledge base was fragmentary and their language capabilities meager. One observer summarized the sequence:

At first employees of IMPEX enterprises were generally long-established, pre-Communist regime businessmen and banking experts, useful for their experience and knowledge of foreign languages and conditions. However, by 1952, the IMPEX enterprises had hardly any Hungarian representatives abroad because they defected in large numbers. The enterprises were in some cases represented... by Western firms. Later [they] recruited their employees and representatives from the workers' cadres [and] paid high salaries and per diems in order to keep them satisfied.

In addition, family members of those selected were not permitted to depart with the new cohort of agents, a stratagem aimed at reducing flight risks. It seems to have worked: a mid-1954 account claimed that in foreign trade, "no interesting defection has been known for a year."[100] In December 1953, a blistering critique in the Party daily signaled the Nagy leadership's judgment that the handling of external trade was seriously deficient. In July, the state had already merged Foreign Trade with Domestic, but evidently to little effect. "These organizations still have not learned to trade... They make no systematic study of the market. They frequently accept the first trade offer made, even though this may cause difficulties in meeting the demand for certain articles at home." Nilex, the heavy industry enterprise, only assigned "commercial scouts" to Asia after a year of prodding, whereas Electroimpex hadn't sent someone East in two years' time. Agents also promised buyers goods, no Hungarian firm was making and didn't promote the items that were being manufactured. And on and on. Thus, early in 1954, the ministry urged representatives "to survey and report on complaints over defective goods." Quality control inspectors were now to be chosen on technical, not political grounds, and "will accordingly be better paid." Miracle of miracles, "replacement parts production is to be increased," even as import sections received instructions to seek agreements for "luxury consumer items like tea and coffee," often unavailable at home.[101] After such critiques and adjustments, it is hardly astonishing that the ministry convened a week-long self-study conference in July 1954—what *is* astonishing is that a ten-page summary of this quite frank assessment has endured.

Division heads, section chiefs, and special guests (including 30-plus factory directors and chief engineers) gathered on July 19 to hear László Hay, head of foreign trade, present a "general report." Hay emphasized the value of long-term price stability and multi-year contracts, the need to offer buyers easier credit terms, and his interest in deals providing Hungarian goods to several Western countries at once, previously forbidden. Then the problems began rolling out:

Béla Szilágyi, Inter-bloc trade

- Insufficient orders were on hand to assure continuous production of diesel and steam locomotives; layoffs loom, meaning a financial loss and damage to prestige. As well, capitalist nations are shrinking purchases and pressing for credit agreements rather than paying cash. Exports of consumer goods must continue, even if domestic troubles result, in order "to retain the markets thus far secured."
- "A whispering campaign [re] the lack of continuity and availability of spare-parts deliveries for Hungarian-made machinery might greatly harm export trade... the supply of spare parts in proper qualities and quantities [must] be secured."
- The ministry lacks proper staff, especially "linguists." Technical reps have weak "commercial knowledge and have to be educated while on the job abroad."

- A critical failing is "poor coordination between State enterprises, the ministry, the trade commissioners, and the traveling sales representatives,"[102] as well as within the ministry's divisions. Reorganizations are in process.
- Last, " A new working style is needed. 'Slowness' must be liquidated."

Desaő Lantos, Light Industry

- Due to insufficient capital investments, light goods makers were "frequently unable to match old established qualities."
- "Radio sets were exported in spite of inferior quality." Such practices hurt exporting.
- The ministry seeks to increase the export of "items requiring more in labor and less in material." However, factory managements are not clear about how to implement this and need guidance.
- "Hungarian foreign trade has no 'export profile.' The production of export articles is unstable. For instance Ferunion reduced drastically the number of articles available for export because many, such as sheet glass, cannot be produced in sufficient quantities... Hungarian telephone sets are in need of modernization. Electroimpex has no competent sales force abroad."
- Stocks of imported raw materials are low, and current shipments are decreasing.

An agricultural specialist added: "[F]oreign customers cannot depend on Hungarian state enterprises. The latter attempt to sell what they have and have no interest in what the customers want."[103]

The news from the Heavy Industry side was hardly more encouraging. On day three, Deputy Minister Jenő Incze first ticked off the multiple reasons for inadequate sales:

- (1) "Lack of trade craft. Only trade specialists are capable of furnishing competent special information and not the trade commissioners." (2) Weak network of sales reps abroad. (3) Slowness in the submission of offers. (4) Too long delivery times. (5) Bad price policy. (6) Bad commercial terms of payment. (7) Delays in finalizing deals. (8) Inadequate preparation of traveling sales reps (especially, "badly timed visits to customers"). (9) Obsolete types of merchandise. (10) Delivery delays.

- On a more positive plane, though Bloc countries reduced orders for Hungarian capital goods, given cuts in their own industrial spending plans, at least machine tool sales look promising. "Today there are 50 to 60 types of Hungarian-produced machine tools on the world market."
- Hungarian tractors use old designs, but thus "it requires little mechanical know-how to handle them." Our factories can now produce surpluses for export.
- "There is no need to force the sale of items produced in series. There is a greater chance in bidding on individual items [for which] Hungary can rely on a universally trained body of engineers. In such individual items, Hungary is favored by a less competitive market."
- Nowadays, there actually are "twice as many" skilled technicians and engineers as plants can absorb. We should use some of them "as traveling consultants to support salesmen," so as "to offer more services, such as technical assistance, planning, installation, and break-in training."

Jenő Solt, of Technoimpex, the designated exporter of metal- and wood-working machinery and agricultural tools, promptly drove a nail into the notion of promising prospects: "Most of the Hungarian machine tools are obsolete in type. Hungarian tractors can only be sold to places where they have not been sent before. People who bought them before will not buy again."[104]

On the fourth day, the floor opened to a general discussion, including comments from those staffing factories, who shared their frustrations and disappointments.

- Ferenc Mészáros: "The electrical current meters are too bulky and heavy injectors are not [made] of rust-resistant steel; the pumps are getting stuck."
- Edmund Kallós: "The electric current meters are not properly calibrated."
- Electroimpex rep: "The electric industry did not receive money in the past for capital investments because it was classified as light

industry. Now [under Nagy] it receives no money because it is regarded as heavy industry."

- Mr. Somkuti: "The textile export suffers mainly from three evils: a) Pieces are not delivered in standard lengths. (Too many odd sizes); b) Improper packaging; c) Delay in delivery."
- Mr. Maracska (Heavy Industry division head): "The Prototype Committee [assessing innovations] is lacking in courage needed for decisions. A hydraulic locomotive suffered a three-year delay in production because of its indecisiveness."

It might seem that not much more could be said, but Friday's session concluded the main program with painful probes into the ministry's own shortcomings. István Palós, a divisional Party Secretary, "decried the fact that missions are understaffed, appointees have insufficient training, and support is not forthcoming from the ministry." Complaints surfaced that "the young proletarians appointed to foreign trade missions become complacent, lazy and clannish. They do not show sufficient interest to supplement their education." Perhaps in consequence, haughty diplomatic personnel "in many instances, look down on trade commissioners and refer to them privately as... horse dealers." The final session on the following Monday seemed listless; decisive proposals to reconstruct practices and enhance capabilities failed to materialize, replaced by entreaties to maintain "cordial relations" with host country officials and to beware of Western trade missions' "dark schemes."[105]

Ministry leaders recognized that foreign trade was a shambles, even as young agents were being groomed to replace the defectors and the politically unreliable. On one side, trade reps from the enterprises, with limited technical and commercial knowledgeability, sought to make contracts and meet plan quotas, perhaps not all that diligently. On the other hand, manufacturers were ill-disposed to take up special orders to match foreign requirements; such jobs were distractions when their core effort was to exceed quantity targets and maximize bonuses. (Redesigning outputs to ensure international competitiveness was out of the question.) It must have been dreadful to reveal (even if not in public) the fact that those buying Hungarian tractors once, would not do so again. Investigating customers' reports of defects and delays generated no leverage to increase quality and on-time delivery. Worst, the nemeses of planning reared their gnarly heads—coordination failures among internal functions and in the broader business environment—but addressing them was beyond the ministry's compass. A few reforms and initiatives did follow the conference: a Merchants' Trading Bureau to enhance artisan co-ops' access to export orders, a thorough reworking of rules and routines for trade reps and commissioners, and the assignment of technical experts as IMPEX aides in contract talks. But the persistent "inflexibility of the production system" could not be overcome. Even the individual projects, for which some thought Hungary had an advantage, could not be worked into existing industrial plans, except over several years.

> A medium-sized project such as a radio broadcasting station, for example could be accepted only for a two-to-four year delivery, longer for large-scale projects such as power plants, and still longer for equipment requiring sweeping new designs. As a result, by the time of delivery, equipment would no longer be up to date, and very often, would even be obsolete.

The curse of "slowness" was not lifted; and any hope of revitalization surely dimmed with the resurgence of Rákosi in 1955, bringing both a re-emphasis on serving Soviet interests by again prioritizing heavy industry, and the defenestration of the IMPEXES.

> In the spring or summer of 1956, a drastic change took place when all but a very small portion of Hungarian export trade jurisdiction was removed from the IMPEXES. Under a decree published in the official gazette five of the largest plants engaged in the production of export items... were designated to export their own products as in pre-1949 days... The five factories named in the decree set up their own export departments.[106]

Hungary's experiment with transforming commerce into an arm of the socialist project had withered.

CONCLUSION

Socialist commerce was socialist in being wedded to top-down planning, specifying sales targets, and macro-level managing through fixed prices and materials controls. Yet it could neither suppress nor evade markets, much to ideologues' chagrin. Relying on capitalist-era merchants and traders for specialized knowledge was perhaps a temporary necessity, until their replacements could be schooled for the work. But as Trading suggested, exporting meant either taking Soviet direction or facing competing capitalist technologies, finances, and prices—winding up subordinate in either relationship. At home, the illusion of controlling commerce could barely be maintained, given the diffidence of producers and ministerial overseers. Extensive theft and fraud illuminated the inadequacies of Hungary's distribution network and organizational practices—terrible pay for commercial workers brought compensatory stealing or lawless entrepreneurship; greed within and around state agencies spawned self-enrichment schemes; the impossibility of surveillance in rural domains opened spaces for farmers marketing agricultural goods, with or without licenses; poor-quality industrial products drew smugglers who provided profitable foreign substitutes, and toxic factory relations led workers to swipe state property for ready resale, supplying Maszek enterprises. The socialist commercial system was porous, even if pervasive, and the complementary institutions and sites for maneuvering around its shortages, regulations, and deficiencies were sophisticated, if disorganized and often invisible.

Trade was non-productive; exchange was predatory, as buyers and sellers each tried to get more than they gave. But state administration was likewise non-productive, and its managers, facing Soviet exactions, also strove to extract much and provide as little as possible. The vast force of state bureaucrats, who guided, compelled, supervised and sanctioned, added not one nail to a barrel, not one window to a house, not a fencepost to a field. Nor, as is evident with the Ministries of Domestic and Foreign Trade, were these arrays of planners, assessors, accountants, and directors competent in their jobs. One can sympathize with their bottomless misery at always being in the middle, between industry and agriculture, between producers and consumers, between suppliers and users, without celebrating their underwhelming performances. Indeed, by seizing shopkeepers' and tavern-owners' property, by deploying commission and pawn shops, and by manipulating prices and supplies, state actors reinforced the theft economy they hectored citizens to reject, falsely promising that socialism would provide what the people needed. In spurning this deal, one plumber-in-exile perhaps spoke for many: "It is worse to be fed while one's hands and feet are tied, than to stand on one's own feet and look for bread and butter."[107]

NOTES

1. J. Wilczynski, *Profit, Risk and Incentives under Socialist Economic Planning*, London: Palgrave Macmillan, 1973, 174. The other

four divisions of "material production" were industry, construction, agriculture, and transport and communications.

2. RFE Background Report, Sy Bourgin, "Lecture on Hungary," 22 May 1956, 6, HU OSA 300-8-3-2991. (Hereafter RFEBR) Bourgin was Time's Central European correspondent, 1946–1956, and had served in US Army intelligence during World War II.

3. Columbia University Research Project on Hungary Interview No. 100, 43, HU OSA 414-0-2-127. (Hereafter CURPH)

4. Except for illicit dollar exchanges. Dollars were needed to pay for "black market goods smuggled into Hungary." The going rate in 1951 was 40–50 ft/$1.00 (official rate, 11.8/$1), with $100 bills most sought after, as "they eliminate the problem of bulk."(RFE Field Report, "Currency Black Market," 13 June 1951, HU OSA 300-1-2-660). (Hereafter RFEFR)

5. For a classic case study, see Chris Hann, *Tázlár: A Village in Hungary*, Cambridge: Cambridge University Press, 1980, and as well, Idem., "The economistic fallacy and forms of integration under and after socialism," *Economy and Society* 43(2014): 626–49.

6. Imre Fenyö, "On the Development and Future Perspectives of Domestic Trade," *Közgazdasagi Szemle* (Economics Review), April 1965, Joint Publications Research Service [hereafter JPRS] Report 29,990, 10 May 1965, 18–20.

7. CIA Information Report, "Statement of István Antos, Under-Secretary of Finance," 26 January 1949 (Secret, CIA-RDP82-00457R002200770004-3). (Hereafter CIAIR).

8. RFE Field Report, "Impressions of Hungarian Mood, Autumn 1951," 1, HU OSA 300-1-2-13,006.

9. CURPH Interview No. 155, 32, HU OSA 414-0-2-171.

10. Fenyö, "Domestic Trade," 20. A Swiss report estimated that 2/3rds of retailing had been nationalized by spring 1951. See CIAInformation from Foreign Documents, "Communists Meet Many Obstacles," *Neue Zürcher Zeitung*, 15 March 1951 (CIA-RDP80-00809A000600400107-8). (Hereafter CIAIFD).

11. Fenyö, "Domestic Trade," 20.

12. János Rainer, "The New Course in Hungary in 1953," Working Paper 38, Cold War International History Project, Woodrow Wilson Center, Washington, D.C., June 2002.

13. RFEFR, "Budapest a Year Ago and Today," 4 June 1954, HU OSA 300-1-2-47,145; RFEFR, "Recent Visitors' Impressions of Budapest," 12 October 1954, HU OSA 300-1-2-51,124; RFEFR, "More Private Shops Open," 27 November 1954, HU OSA 300-1-2-53,066.
14. CURPH 155, 32, 74.
15. CIAIFD, "Hungary Nationalizes Retail Business," 20 January 1950 (Confidential, CIA-RPD80-00809A000600280375-5).
16. RFEFR, "General Picture of Budapest," 30 June 1953, 1, HU OSA 300-1-2-36,141. Fenyö claimed that many closed retailers had been utterly marginal, housed in outmoded premises, and uneconomical. ("Domestic Trade," 20).
17. CIAIR, "Report of Food Products to Russia and the Satellites as Reparations," 5 April 1951 (Secret, CIA-RDP82-00457R007200370010-8).
18. CIAIFD, "Reports Food Shortage in Hungary," *Svenska Dagbladet*, 28 May 1950, 2 (Restricted, CIA-RDP80-00809A000600320515-4); CIAIFD, "Economic-Foreign Trade," 1 February 1951, 2 (Confidential, CIA-RDP80-00809A000600370698-7); RFEFR, "Hungarian Sugar Sold on Austrian Black Market," 6 June 1951, HU OSA 300-1-2-460; RFEFR, "Illegal Trade Between Hungary and Austria," 25 October 1952, HU OSA 300-1-2-27,056.
19. CIAFD, "Reports Food Shortage," 1. The Weiss plants in Budapest reportedly were focusing on armaments at this time.
20. CIAIFD, "Explaining Serious Meat Shortage," *Szabad Nép*, 1 July 1951 (Confidential, CIA-RDP80-00809A000700010428-4). See also CIAIFD, "Hungary Introduces Rationing," *Nepsava*, 24 December 1950 (Confidential, CIA-RDP80-00809A000600370037-9). The meat situation did improve after 1953. See RFEFR, "Budapest Meat Supply," 1 August 1956, HU OSA 300-1-2-73,610.
21. RFEFR, "Hungary: Resistance, Economic," 15 May 1951, HU OSA 300-1-2-140.
22. RFEFR, "Morale and General Mood," 5 September 1951, HU OSA 300-1-2-6045. The distribution of ration tickets varied according to the physical demands of labor. Thus miners' allocations were 75 percent higher than office workers'. CIAIFD, "Lists

204 P. SCRANTON

Soap, Fats Rations," 23 April 1951 (Confidential, CIA-RDP80-00809A-000600390123-2).

23. CIAIFD, "Defines Certain Responsibilities of Ministries," 22 December 1951, 2 (Restricted, CIA-RDP80-00809A000700030561-4).

24. CIAIR, "Survey of Economic Conditions," 1 April 1952, 2 (Confidential, CIA-RDP8200457R011200560009-1).

25. RFEFR, "Preparatory Measures for the Increase of Food Prices," 8 December 1951, HU OSA 300-1-2-12,388.

26. CIAIFD, "Rákosi Reviews Economic Progress," *Szabad Nép*, 2 December 1951 (Restricted, CIA-RDP80-00809A000700050408-2).

27. CIAIR,"Survey of Economic Conditions," 2. See also RFEFR, "Budapest citizens shocked by bad quality of bread," 10 December 1952, HU OSA 300-1-2-28,631, and "Most Food Prices Go Up in Hungary," *New York Times*, 6 December 1951, 13.

28. RFEFR, "Preparatory Measures"; RFEFR, "Prices after 1 December 1951," 27 December 1951, HU OSA 300-1-2-13,144.

29. Not so for transit and construction workers, many of whom carried lunches to work. At large construction sites, mobile food services provided mid-day meals. See CURPH Interview No. 221, 14–15, HU OSA 414-0-2-197.

30. Rural diets, with the potential for more fresh vegetables, milk, eggs, and fruit, were arguably far more healthy than those of the urban working class. Yet in winter months, peasants depended on potatoes and bread as mainstays, just like their city brethren. At other times, fresh foods vanished into compulsory deliveries or into market exchanges (as households tried to secure cash for taxes, et al.).

31. CURPH Interview No. 45-F, 37. HU OSA 414-0-2-41.

32. CURPH Interview No. 106, 38, HU OSA 414-0-2-133.

33. CURPH Interview No. 45-F, 39, HU OSA 414-0-2-41.

34. CUPRH Interview No. 506, 34, HU OSA 414-0-2-304. "They were unable to steal butter, because it was already wrapped in standard packages. As a result the Közert manager didn't order butter for his shop and thus there was always a butter shortage".

5 SOCIALIST COMMERCE ... 205

35. Peddlers did sell black market goods and unauthorized agricultural products on the fringes of public markets, but this was chancy, as unlicensed selling could be harshly punished.
36. Maszek roughly means "self-employed." Other Maszek firms sold textiles or did outwork for manufacturers. See CURPH Interview No. 85-F, 37, HU OSA 414-0-2-85, and CURPH Interview No. 97-F, 36, HU OSA 414-0-2-98. Clients attributed Maszek stores' high prices to the severe taxes the state imposed on them (CURPH Interview No 94-M, 33, HU OSA 414-0-2-95), but owners were also reputed to be adept at bribing tax officials (CURPH Interview No. 60-F, 35, HU OSA 414-0-2-59).
37. The quality and range of meals at such buffets and dairy restaurants apparently declined after 1948, even at newly opened venues. See RFEFR, "Glimpses of Today's Budapest," 17 May 1952, 2, HU OSA 300-1-2-19,852, and Idem. "Glimpses of Red Budapest," 1 July 1953, 1–2, HU OSA 300-1-2-36,135.
38. A fine 1951 joke captures this: One evening, a restaurant in Budapest was suddenly raided by police. [One man] was eating a most expensive looking meal. Police turned to him and began to ply him with the standard questions: "What is your profession?" "I have none," was his curt reply. "Well, then, how do you live?" "I live on the help I receive from my son." "And what does your son do?" "He is an iron turner [machinist]." Police now got very interested and asked: "Is he a Stakhanovite or a shock worker?" "He is neither," came the cool reply. "Well, does he do overtime work?" "No, he does not." Completely at a loss, police asked, "Well [where] is he working?" "At the Ford Factory in Detroit." (RFEFR, "Jokes," 28 July 1951, HU OSA 300-1-2-3220).
39. CURPH Interview No. 439, 85, HU OSA 414-0-2-260.
40. RFEFR, "Glimpses," 17 May 1952, 5.
41. US Department of State, Foreign Service Dispatch, "IKKA, Hungarian Relief Organization," 20 May 1953 (Confidential, CIA-RDP78-01634R000100110034-2); Idem., "IKKA-Affiliated Relief Agencies in US," 4 June 1957 (Unclassified, CIA-RDP78-01634R000100110019-9). Estimates of the shipments' annual value ranged from $365,000 to $2 million/yr, meaning nobody knew much about the flows.
42. Zachary Levine, "Concealed in the Open: Recipients of Clandestine Jewish Aid in Early 1950s Hungary," AHEA: E-Journal of

the American Hungarian Educators Assn., 5(2012): http://ahea. net/e-journal/volume-5-2012. See also CURPH Interview No. 75-F, 19, HU OSA 414-0-2-74.

43. RFEFR, "Glimpses," 17 May 1952, 3.
44. RFEFR, "Standard of Living," 12 December 1952, 1, HU OSA 300-1-2-28,606. For "good quality cloth," 1400 to 1600 ft/m. (RFEFR, "Miscellaneous Current Prices in Budapest," 26 May 1953, 1, HU OSA 300-1-2-34,933).
45. RFEFR, "Glimpses," 1 July 1953, 6–7. For consumers' views, see CURPH Interview No. 22-F, 24, HU OSA 414-0-2-14 and CURPH Interview No. 41-M, 78, HU OSA 414-0-2-37.
46. Ibid., 7. A detailed, unsavory tale of state manipulations to secure Persian rugs for next to no money from those being declassed appears at page 8. By 1956, state rates for purchasing gold objects rose to 25–30 ft/g. The most artistic items went to export and the ordinary "stuff was melted down and re-cast into wedding rings, which were then sold for 140 ft/g," a profit of 115 ft./g. (CURPH Interview No. 604, 15, HU OSA 414-2-342).
47. RFEFR, "Glimpses," 17 May 1952, 5.
48. CURPH 604, 1–6. Farmers' Consumer Cooperatives had weak hardware assortments, drab clothing, and many items out-of-stock. They predated the socialist period, as ca. 1500 operated in 1938, accounting for 7.5% of retail sales that year (Resző Nyers, *The Cooperative Movement in Hungary*, Budapest: Pannonia, 1963, 52–3.) They were bare bones operations. A busy clerk complained: "We had no cash register and therefore, the sales slips were always in confusion. We had to stay late in the evening to straighten it all out [and] in order to prepare the goods for the next day." (CURPH Interview No. 565, 15, HU OSA 414-0-2-336).
49. CURPH 604, 9–11. Cultural shop managers earned 1800 ft/month and senior sales agents, 950, plus bonus, ca. 1956. Közert clerks were paid as little as 500 ft/month, with little prospect of bonuses (16).
50. Gerö, regarded as Rákosi's closest adviser, served as Minister of State and of Foreign Trade after 1950,. (https://prabook.com/web/erno.gero/1346821, accessed 13 April 2021).
51. CURPH 604, 11–13.

52. For a thorough account of policy changes, see CIA, "Economic Characteristics of the New Course," 29 September 1953 (Secret, CIA-RDP79R01012A003200020003-3).
53. CURPH 604, 5–6. Retail sales increased every year from 1952 into the 1960s (Fenyö,"Domestic Trade," 22).
54. RFEFR, "Glimpses," 17 May 1952, 3.
55. CURPH 604, 13–14.
56. Ibid., 14–15. In Hungary, completing installment payments preceded taking possession of a bedroom set or a washing machine.
57. CURPH Interview No. 95-M, 18, HU OSA 414-0-2-96.
58. CURPH Interview No 486, 2–3, HU OSA 414-0-2-297.
59. Ibid., 6.
60. Members of national sporting teams (fencing, swimming, et al.) and stars in Hungary's beloved soccer leagues received special privileges, including access to international travel, automobiles, spacious apartments, and the like.
61. As state prices for everything had been set centrally, and as state factories had substantial administrative and overhead expenses, their directors declined to make goods whose wholesale prices ensured losses. This left holes in retail sales arrays which artisan co-ops could fill at a profit, given their lower expenses for administration, supervision, et al.
62. CURPH Interview No. 49-M, 1–2, 20–27, HU OSA 414-0-2-45.
63. CURPH Interview No. 46-M, 39, HU OSA 414-0-2-42.
64. CURPH 49-M, 24–25; CURPH Interview No. 55-M, 24, HU OSA 414-0-2-52; CURPH 94-M, 33, CURPH Interview No. 97-F, 38, HU OSA 414-0-2-98; RFEFR, "The Commercial State Enterprise Keravill," 10 April 1953, HU OSA 300-1-2-33,270. For a detailed view of how this worked in the meat trade, see RFEFR, "Budapest Meat Supply,"1–9, 1 August 1956, HU OSA 300-1-2-73,610.
65. CIAIFD, "Official Hungarian Price Lists," 23 February 1954, (Confidential, CIA-RDP80-00809A000700160266-8). Volume 1 covered 18 vehicle brands, including Buick, Ford, Chrysler and Hudson; Volume 2, eleven more. An appendix listed "106 additional models"; their repair charges were to duplicate those for designated reference vehicles in the main volumes.

66. The price manuals were revised after the 1956 Revolt, but this did not alter their constraining influence on commerce.
67. CURPH 74, 20. Skoda, the great Czech vehicle enterprise, reportedly made parts in quantity, but getting them to Miskolc was another story. See Valentina Fava, *The Socialist People's Car: Automobiles, Shortages, and Consent on the Czechoslovak Road to Mass Production*, Amsterdam: Amsterdam University Press, 2013.
68. Levine, "Concealed in the Open," 6. Insoles covered the flat interior of a shoe and were usually glued to a leather or rubber outer sole. See https://www.shoeguide.org/shoe_anatomy/ (accessed 16 April 2021).
69. For turnover taxes, see J. Wilczynski, *Socialist Economic Reforms and Development*, London: Macmillan, 1972, 221–26.
70. Certificates confirmed that goods being used or sold had been lawfully purchased from state manufacturers or wholesalers. Blank certificate forms were prized.
71. CURPH Interview No, 448, 11–13, HU OSA 414-0-2-270. Respondent was a senior official in textile and leather wholesaling, 1950–56.
72. CURPH Interview No. 10-M, 29, HU OSA 414-0-2-3.
73. CURPH Interview No. 2-M, 20–21, HU OSA 414-0-2-24.
74. CURPH Interview No. 232, 21–22, HU OSA 414-0-2-207.
75. CURPH Interview No. 221, 24, HU OSA 414-0-2-197.
76. CURPH Interview No. 46-M, 22–23, HU OSA 414-0-2-42; Levine, "Concealed in the Open," 5.
77. RFEFR, "Gasoline Cheaper,"19 July 1956, HU OSA 300-1-2-73,293; CURPH Interview No. 20-M, 25, HU OSA 414-0-2-14.
78. CURPH Interview No. 217, 19, HU OSA 414-1-2-193.
79. CURPH Interview No. 208, 29–37, HU OSA 414-0-2-185.
80. CURPH Interview No. 151, 98–99, HU OSA 414-2-0-167.
81. CURPH Interview No. 414, 10–12, HU OSA 414-0-2-245.
82. CURPH Interview No. 245, 16–17, HU OSA 414-0-2-245.
83. CURPH 151, 72.
84. CURPH Interview No. 95-M, 18–19, HU OSA 414-0-2-96.
85. CURPH Interview No. 32-M, 45, HU OSA 414-0-2-27. For detailed comments from a long-term black market participant, see CURPH Interview No. 83-F, 29, HU OSA 414-0-2-83.

86. CURPH Interview No. 6-F, 18, HU OSA 414-0-2-68; CURPH Interview No. 58-F, 20, HU OSA 414-0-2-55.
87. CURPH Interview No. 150, 4, HU OSA 414-0-2-175. See also RFEFR, "Shortage in Razor Blades," 3 August 1951, HU OSA 300-1-2-3602, and RFEFR, "Hungarian Can't Look Sharp on Native Blades," 18 April 1956, HU OSA 300-1-2-70,126. German blades cost five times as much as local ones, but were much sharper due to better quality steel.
88. CURPH Interview No. 29-M, 27, HU OSA 414-0-2-23.
89. CURPH Interview No. 44-M, 32, HU OSA 414-0-2-40; CURPH 6-F, 23.
90. RFEFR, "Thefts of Typewriters," 21 May 1952, HU OSA 300-1-2-20,002.
91. Stephen Szászy, "State Trading Activities in Hungary," *Vanderbilt Law Review* 20(1967): 393–428, quote at 395.
92. CIAIFD, M. Kudryashov and N. Pohov, "Organization and Regulation of Foreign Trade in Hungary," *Vneshnaya Torgovyla*, December 1951, (Restricted, CIA-RDP8000809A000700070276-7); CIAIR, "State-Owned Foreign-Trade Companies in Hungary," 2 December 1950 (Confidential, CIA-RDP80-00809A000600380340-2).
93. CURPH Interview No. 449, 7–8, HU OSA 414-0-2-270. Respondent worked in the ministry's department of trade planning and control, focusing on "textile, rubber and leather raw material imports" (5).
94. CIAIFD, "Reports Shortcomings in Export Production," *Nepszava*, 20 June 1950 (Confidential, CIA-RDP80-00809A000600340684-5); RFEFR, "Institute Supervises Exports," 29 November 1951, HU OSA 300-1-2-118,334.
95. The Milan Trade Fair commenced in 1920 to allow Italy and other European countries to display their products in an environment of rising trade barriers. By the 1960s, it had grown into a 10-day April event hosting 35,000 manufacturers from scores of countries. See RFEFR, "Hungarian Officials at the Milan Fair," 12 June 1951, HU OSA 300-1-2-589; Albert Carrera and Lidia Torra, "Why Did Modern Trade Fairs Appear?" CORE Research Papers in Economics, http://www.econ.upf.edu/docs/papers/downloads/874.pdf (Accessed 22 April 2021).
96. "Hungarian Officials," 12 June 1951.

210   P. SCRANTON

97. RFEFR, "The Thirty First Milan Fair," 25 April 1953, HU OSA 300-1-2-33,912.
98. CIAIFD, László Kőváry, "Scores Poor Quality of Export Products," *Nepszava*, 6 January 1952 (Restricted, CIA-RDP80-00809A000700050242-6); RFEFR, "Go To Stalin With Complaints," 4 June 1952, HU OSA 300-1-2-20,669. Kőváry was director of planning at the Foreign Trade ministry.
99. CIAIR, "Hungarotex," 26 September 1952 (Secret,CIA-RDP82-00457R014000370001-9); CIAIR, "Organization of Foreign Trade Ministry," 20 May 1953 (Secret, CIA-RDP80-00810A001300040003-0); CIAIFD, "Hungary Smuggles Strategic Goods From Near East," 2 July 1953 (Restricted, CIA-RDP80-00809A000700120004-2); CURPH Interview No. 452, 5–6, HU OSA 414-0-2-273. Representatives were not sent to Bloc countries, where orders were mostly bulk purchases forwarded from Moscow. On embargoes, see R. T. Naylor, *Economic Warfare: Sanctions, Embargo Busting and Their Human Cost*, Boston: Northeastern University Press, 2001. For detail on Hungarian strategies to evade embargoes, see CURPH Interview No. 202b, 17–19, HU OSA 414-0-2-179.
100. CIAIR, "Import–Export Enterprises in Hungary," 17 November 1955 (Confidential, CIA-RDP82-00046R000300060004-8); RFEFR, "Hungarian Businessman Comments," 25 May 1954, HU OSA 330-1-2-46,710.
101. CIAIR, "Ministry of Foreign and Internal Trade," 30 October 1953 (Secret, CIA-RDP80-00810A002600960001-7); CIAIFD, "Hungarian Foreign Trade Deficiencies," *Szabad Nép*, 29 December 1953 (unclassified, CIA-RDP80-00809A000700190198-1); CIAIR, "New Economic Program as it Affects Foreign Trade," 15 February 1954 (Secret, CIA-RDP80-00810A003600190001-1).
102. Trade commissioners had the authority to sign agreements; sales reps did not. Commissioners regularly had fewer languages and technical skills that sales agents, however.
103. CIAIR, "Conference of Hungarian Commercial Attachés and Trade Commissioners," 26 October 1954, 1–4 (Secret, CIA-RDP80-00810A005200460003-4).
104. Ibid., 5–6; CIAIR, "Import–Export Enterprises," 2.
105. CIAIR,:"Conference," 7–8.

106. CIAIR, "Merchants' Trading Bureau," 14 February 1955 (Secret, CIA-RDP80-00810A005900600010-3); CIAIR, "Standard Instructions to Foreign Trade Delegations," 11 February 1955 (Secret, CIA-RDP80-00810A005900360004-7); CIAIR, "General Principles of Hungarian Foreign Trade," 23 December 1957 (Confidential, CIA-RDP80T00246A039200300001-3). The five companies were a leading pharmaceutical and chemicals firm; the electrical equipment giant, Egyesült Izzó; the Csepel bicycle and sewing machine factory; the nation's largest telecommunications company, and a medical and precision equipment firm. ("General," 4).

107. CURPH Interview No. 54-M, 50, HU OSA 414-0-2-51.

CHAPTER 6

Hungary's Socialist Industrialization: A Snare and a Delusion

In production, the emphasis lays on quantity with no one paying attention to quality. This necessarily followed from the system of norms and premium incentives. Wages were so low that no one could allow himself the luxury of disregarding the additional sums that the premiums represented. As a result there evolved, in time, a gigantic conspiracy, where the workers produced a great amount of low-rate or worthless goods, the inspectors put their stamps of approval on them, and the commercial establishments accepted and passed them on to the consumer.
—István Rácz, 1957.[1]

In 1950, a raincoat design was introduced similar to the British trench coat, and from 1950 to 1955, this was the only type produced. It was cheaper to continue production of one design, and there was no price incentive to the production of other models. The most serious aspect was that it also paid to produce only one size of raincoat, the price differential for larger sizes being insufficient to cover the additional material cost and for smaller sizes, to cover the additional labor cost. Unfortunate persons of more or less than average stature were thus quite unable to buy a raincoat to fit them.
—G.F. Ray, 1960.[2]

Where nobody can trust anybody... there on one hand will develop spontaneously a wonderful highwayman's code of honor [and] on the other hand complete amorality will be the rule. [A] shop-foreman in the shipyards of

© The Author(s), under exclusive license to Springer Nature Switzerland AG 2022
P. Scranton, *Business Practice in Socialist Hungary, Volume 1*, Palgrave Debates in Business History,
https://doi.org/10.1007/978-3-030-89184-8_6

213

Obuda explained [it] to me... in the following words: "Listen to me, Joe, they are the biggest asses when they say the sabotage is organized. Everybody is doing sabotage. I am an old Social-Democrat. Do you know what it means—"spontaneous sabotage" (öntevékeny szabotázs)? And in addition, it's very useful and lucrative. Copper is needed for the ships destined for the Soviet Union? Plated sheets will be good enough for them! The copper will be sold to the small foundries. I do it and my colleagues do it, often without saying a word to each other.
—Budapest worker, 1957.[3]

Never a brilliant idea, transforming Hungary into a socialist "nation of iron and steel" through massive investments in heavy industry and infrastructure, revealed itself in practice as a truly terrible scheme. It was a snare because industrialization necessitated vast spending for plant, machinery, and infrastructure that continued for decades, blocking funds for sectors critical to national well-being, notably agriculture and consumer goods. It was a delusion because Hungary did not possess the fundamental material, power, and human resources to fuel a major expansion of manufacturing capabilities, especially in metals and chemicals. To turn the industrialization project into reality, the nation had to import millions of tons of materials, export sufficient goods to pay for them, and renew or construct modern transport and power grids, although demand for investment capital perennially overmatched supply.

Before the war, Hungary had manufactured and successfully exported machinery, electrical goods, pharmaceuticals, wine, and processed foods (salami, sugar, canned goods)—trade often underwritten by German capital and Budapest banks. However, it had negligible capacity in basic metals, its principal ore reserves being bauxite, not iron or copper. Moreover, reducing bauxite industrially to aluminum demanded far more electric power than the nation could provide. Hungary's modest petroleum reserves could not supply extensive chemical or fuel distilling plants, nor was the production of artificial fertilizer far advanced. Like Poland, Hungary did have coal resources, but chiefly of low-BTU varieties, rather than the hard coal processed elsewhere into hot-burning coke for smelters and blast furnaces.[4] Nevertheless, propelled by the Soviet example, by Russian "advisers," and by Cold War ambitions and anxieties, the Rákosi regime implemented two multiyear investment and production plans (1947–1949, 1950–1954) top-heavy with funding for "heavy industry"—metals, chemicals, mining, power, machinery, and transport.

Expansion in these sectors was of course a boost to construction and building materials enterprises. Allocations for "light industry," including ceramics, textiles and apparel, fabricated electrical or metal goods, food processing, leatherwork and furniture, lagged far behind (as did funding for agriculture).[5] Handicraft trades like tailoring, dressmaking, cabinet work, or tile stove building were effectively ignored, as were auxiliary industrial activities like subcontracting, repairs, and waste reclamation. This chapter will assess segments of these industrial domains—heavy, light, craft, and auxiliary—one by one.

Several baseline conditions of manufacturing, some particular to Hungary, should be appreciated at the outset. In industry as in construction, good outcomes depend fundamentally on the *materials* flowing through processes. Machine reliability, user requirements, access to capital and labor, and timely logistics all matter substantively, to be sure. But when incoming materials are inferior, undersupplied or simply unavailable, first-class technologies, eager buyers, and fat bank accounts can rarely remedy the deficiency, particularly in an economy of allocations, not markets. *Shoddy inputs propagate* through production networks, polluting downstream practices; industrial actors cope by learning indifference or more actively, by fakery, falsification, deception, and evasion, as noted in the first epigraph. In Hungary, low-end cotton fiber made poor yarn, which yielded shabby woven or knitted fabrics for clothing that itself was neither durable nor comfortable. So too for low-iron-content ores, second-rate fruit, high-sulfur petroleum, or unseasoned timber, whose compulsory (or unavoidable) use reduced the quality of intermediate or final goods. In socialism's first decade, deficiencies in industrial inputs were consistently referenced in managerial, workforce, and consumer complaints, but not remedied.

A second fundamental issue was the pervasive influence of Soviet military, ministry, engineering, and managerial personnel, more so in heavy industry and infrastructure than perhaps anywhere else outside the military. Postwar Russian looting and reparations paralleled the seizure of German-owned factories (and some German-Hungarian ones), which Soviet directors operated, exporting goods to the USSR at favorable prices and exchange rates. In October 1952, the Russians arranged that Hungary purchase most of the former Nazi plants, reinvesting some of their proceeds into four fields they monopolized going forward: aluminum, petroleum, civil aviation, and Danube shipping.[6] In addition, the USSR remained a leading materials supplier to Hungary and an exacting buyer of industrial goods made to detailed specifications that rigorous inspections enforced. Hungarian workers well knew that the Soviets acquired their nation's best-quality outputs, leaving rejects and seconds for domestic use; at times, their resentment made Russia-destined goods targets for fraud, as the third epigraph suggests.

Next, because raw materials and power supplies were thin, Hungary had to secure key inputs from the Bloc and the West—iron ore, non-ferrous metals, cotton, precision machinery and lubricants, for instance. This dependence seriously constrained ministries and enterprises. Without adequate reserves of Western currencies, state agencies had to nego-tiate goods-for-goods exchanges—salami and textiles bartered for Swiss instruments or West German machinery. This in turn meant fabricating internationally-competitive outputs to match capitalist needs. As well, it required regularly accepting terms of trade (contract prices and exchange rates) unfavorable to Hungarian firms, because state agents proffered export goods below factory cost in order to close deals. Loss-leading transactions sparked state subsidies to erase enterprises' balance sheet losses (often 100% or more of a transaction's stated value). Of course, such subsidies prevented alternative uses of the funds, but what one might call the "materials imperative" ruled. At the same time, Hungarian agents struggled to evade US-led embargoes on "strategic materials," notably complex machinery, non-ferrous or alloy metals, and precision devices.[7] This meant buying, say, Chilean copper (at well above world prices) through a Swiss intermediary, routing it to Beirut, reshipping it in Magyar vessels through the Bosphorus and eventually west and north along the Danube via Bulgaria's Black Sea ports. None of this was cheap, quick, or efficient, but other options were scarce.[8] Just as troubling, mate-rials secured through Bloc exchanges all-too-often arrived after delays, fracturing production schedules, and/or in lower-than-specified qualities, fouling machinery and ruining export prospects for the resulting second-rate goods. When state agencies fraudulently certified defective shipments, the recipients' inspectors alertly rejected and returned them. Budapest distributors then disposed of such "dead" goods at fire-sale prices through Közérts or to producers (think small electric motors) who otherwise could not acquire items directed solely to export channels.

Fourth, these problematic and frustrating conditions fostered dishonest, opportunistic, yet pragmatic behavior throughout Hungarian manufacturing. In the perennial sellers' market that directive planning created, neither domestic nor foreign suppliers were under any particular obligation to meet quantity and quality contract terms or shipping deadlines. Clients had neither accessible alternative sellers nor, actually, the authority to change supply agreements. Enterprises in all sectors thus made do with what did arrive—turning out cutting tools that failed after hours, not days, metal castings whose composition did not meet specifications, or brittle shoe leather that deteriorated rapidly in use. Moreover, given the quantitative benchmarks anchoring output plans, delivering badly-made products did not obstruct bonus harvests. Last, given the essential role bonuses played in supplementing staff incomes, production shortfalls that threatened premiums triggered creative accounting and reporting routines commonly known as "plan fraud." Thus did industrial structure and practice sustain and deepen the theft economy, as managerial maneuvers ran side-by-side with workshop earnings fiddles, off-the-books entrepreneurship (using state resources), and plain old stealing (often to supply Maszek craftsmen). Hungarians' endless spare parts moaning harmonized with these jagged tunes, for making components contributed little to reaching tonnage targets and absorbed materials that could be put to better use in fabricating entire Diesel engines, bicycles, or radios that counted toward plan quotas.[9] Worse, parts' mandatory sales prices, set in the 1948 lists, regularly stood below production expenses, another reason for enterprises avoiding them. Spares turned out by users or by Maszek shops employing substandard or substitute materials cost far more than book prices and rarely proved durable.

Taken together, Hungary's inadequate resource and power bases, its obligatory responsiveness to Soviet "guidance," its reliance on foreign trade for large volume inputs and essential specialties, and its plan-based obsession with quantity targets hardly constituted a promising environment for industrialization. Other settled practices added further impediments. The state required full employment, thus enterprises were overstaffed, especially with administrators drafting stacks of reports the ministries required. The Party pressed for activists' and loyalists' appointment to key offices, whether they had professional or technical credentials or not (mostly not). Meanwhile the state employed informers and the AVH to root out "unreliables" and "reactionaries," though chief engineers and managers contested such purges, often resolutely. The National Planning Office sets implausible goals for production, cost reduction, and materials conservation, which led to rushed work, unwise shortcuts, deferred maintenance (to reduce machine downtime), rising defects and rejects, and lax inspection (to cover faults). Thus, in addition to shoddy inputs propagating through the material dimensions of the production system, *shoddy practices propagated* through its organizational structures as well. Yes, of course, a great deal of stuff was nevertheless made and used, eventually more than before 1939, but not as planned, not as expected, and not as hoped for in building a socialist Hungary.

Later sections of this chapter will informally follow the movement of a basic material through its production phases—for instance in heavy industry, iron from ore to pig to molten steel to hardened forms like slabs and sheets, sent on to casting or machined into components to be assembled, tested, and delivered—thereby creating final goods like lathes, bicycles, trucks, or tools. In appreciating the complications that accompanied these extended sequences of transfer and transformation, one can begin to understand the many contingencies that hazarded-effective industrial production, the vigilance, cooperation, and coordination needed to assure successful operations, and the multiple points at which accident, incompetence, or mischief could wreak havoc with the entire process.

Second, due to space constraints, only a few sectors can be reviewed here in each industrial domain, though sources abound for many others. For instance, the discussion of heavy industry includes iron/steel and machinery, but not chemicals, aluminum, electrical power or armaments; textiles and printing appear in light industry, but not shoes, radios, or appliances; carpentry and box-making in handicrafts, but not tailoring and upholstering; repairs in auxiliaries, but not subcontracting or hauling. Omitting these sectors prevents bloating; those covered are offered as exemplary not typical, because no sector can stand for its domain as whole, given the diversity of processes, technologies, and personnel in each.

THE CORE: HEAVY INDUSTRY

The principal origin space for heavy industrial throughput is iron and steel work. Most blast furnace iron is refined into molten steel, which cools into billets that become sheets, plates, rods, and castings, foundations for almost every type of machinery and tools, as well as for construction beams, concrete reinforcements, housewares, farm implements, and transportation equipment. Germany, the US, and the USSR, followed by France, the UK, Japan, Sweden, and Italy were the industrial world's steelmakers in the interwar years, not Hungary. The shrunken Magyar lands did enclose several modest iron and steel enterprises, primarily producing for domestic use: Manfred Weiss in Budapest, Rima at Ózd, and Hungarian Royal Iron and Steel at Diósgyőr (founded 1770), the latter two located in Borsod county east of the capital.[10] Socialist Cold War planners slated existing works for dramatic expansion and envisioned a new, million-ton-capacity/year plant (Sztálinváros). Before long, Hungary could double or treble its steel capabilities, contributing to the Bloc's triumph over American imperialism and Western capitalism alike.

This program did not work as expected. A 1951 US assessment noted:

> Hungary's iron and steel industry is dependent on a constant flow of imports of raw materials. Coke is produced for domestic use from Hungarian coal, but the ferrous metals industry is dependent upon imports for metallurgical requirements. A low-quality iron ore is mined in Hungary, but a large proportion of that consumed must be procured abroad, principally from the USSR... [Purchasing] iron and steel scrap from abroad is basic, but there is a world-wide scrap shortage.[11]

The sector's trade relations were also problematic. Only 15% of iron ore came from Hungarian deposits, 85% from distant Russian mines, most traveling by rail. Overall, steelmaking

> is operating under many serious handicaps. Raw materials received from the USSR have not been satisfactory. Iron ore, for example, although containing a high percentage of iron... has required sintering, or agglomerating before it can be used in blast furnaces.... Both the mining and the steel industries are handicapped by worn and obsolescent equipment and machinery and there is a lack of modern industrial techniques and skill. The industries are poorly organized, and the Ministry of Heavy Industry is constantly attempting to regroup and reorganize them... to reduce operating losses.[12]

Were this not trouble enough, Soviet ore supplies failed to meet quality expectations. "The red iron ore received from the USSR [which] was supposed to have an iron content of 60–65%, usually had an iron content of only 50–52%. Not only were the Soviets cheating Hungary by delivering an ore 10% inferior to the quality agreed upon, but the deliveries were almost always delayed."[13] Meanwhile, the USSR was extracting 20% of the iron and steel Hungary produced: "railroad rails...

reinforced concrete iron... locomotive wheels, rail cars, [and] locomotive parts," as well as machinery. Understandably, Soviet engineers and technicians populated most metallurgical plants, giving "instructions which have to be executed, rather than advice."[14] Sometimes that went badly, as at Diósgyőr in 1951, when an open hearth exploded during "the introduction of Soviet methods," reportedly killing twelve and injuring 20 workers. Budapest officials arrested "the local staff of engineers, mostly German [DDR] experts," but investigators determined that furnace workers had not been properly trained in the cycle-time-saving procedures.[15]

Pig iron processed in blast furnaces from ore, and scrap iron salvaged from wastes and discards, were two core inputs to open hearth (Martin) steelmaking. Enduring problems affected both. When in summer 1952, the Ministry of Metallurgy announced another set of missed plan targets, a Party paper, *Szabad Nép*, blamed the disappointing results on "disorder in the works" and "the efforts of some workers to save time by omitting important steps in steel production." Diósgyőr's blast furnaces had failed to coordinate output transfer schedules. Thus several batches of molten pig iron arrived simultaneously at the open hearths. "As a result, the pig-iron-filled ladles were left blocking the tracks," delaying foundry deliveries. A more serious deficiency surfaced at Ózd: "The quality of metallurgical output is another issue that has been receiving too little attention. In June [1952] only 7.4% of the pig iron which Ózd... sent to the steelworks conformed in grade to plan specifications, and only 10.1% of the lot sent in July was satisfactory."[16] A 90% rate of below-grade pig, likely derived from low-iron-content ores, would yield thousands of tons of limited-use, below-grade steel, unless makers ignored the shortcomings and just shipped it to fabricators.

Pig iron represented about half of the charge for open hearths; scrap metal the other half. As of 1950, Hungarian steelmakers required 350,000 tons of pig and 400,000 tons of scrap annually, but recovery practices inside their mills recycled enough metal that only 200,000 additional tons had to be secured. Whereas "70,000 tons can be procured in Hungary," the other two-thirds, 130,000 tons, required importing.[17] This necessity created three stress points. Yet another critical material had to be purchased abroad, probably through barter or for hard currency. Second, scrap's metallic composition was unpredictable,[18] adding uncertainty to the characteristics of the steel being made. Third, if Hungary's steel output was to expand, more blast furnaces were surely needed, but then so was more scrap; and the state could not easily fund ever-larger foreign purchases. Blasted and twisted metal left over from World War II had already been absorbed; across Europe scrap was becoming scarcer and costlier. Thus intensified home front searches were imperative. The People's State had mobilized scrap drives at least since April 1949, when the Manfred Weiss workforce, 6500 strong, received congratulations for having "collected 230 carloads" in and around its Budapest plant. Other factories, including MAVAG, Hungarian Iron and Steel, Goldberger Textiles, and the Ganz shipyard and electrical works, gathered "lesser amounts," resulting in a 300-carload total.[19] By 1950–1951, however, such easy pickings were gone. The state proposed excavating a huge dump at the Ózd works, where metal mixed with slag had been buried "under layers of earth." Analysts estimated that 50,000 tons could be extracted there, with another 20,000 tons likely to be found near Diósgyőr's coal tar "distillery." "A thorough search of residential areas should be made" as well for every 50–60 kg of scrap recovered and mixed with a similar amount of pig, 100 kg of steel could be produced.[20]

A Council of Ministers December 1950 economic resolution decreed that the Minister of Domestic Trade "shall organize a waste-material-collecting agency, which shall reach every house," aiming to increase by 50% the 1951 volume of "scrap iron, nonferrous materials, leather, paper [and] rags," appealing "primarily to youth" to "strengthen socialist industry" by executing collections "enthusiastically."[21] And they did. However, a Sopron (Győr) observer claimed in late 1951 that the "collection drive is very badly organized," with children gathering scrap, not to build socialism, but "to get paid for it... In order to get more money, [they] unscrew door handles, tear down electric wires, and devastate public property." One-fourth grader climbed a telegraph pole and liberated spools of copper wire kept there for repairs; others, having cashed in their day's haul, broke into the scrap storage sheds, swiped the contents, then re-sold "their loot to other [collecting] points in the same town."[22] An accountant at the Tolnya county MEH (Trash and Garbage Collection Trust, "a nationalized version of the rag-and-bone-merchant's trade," Fig. 6.1) confirmed such practices. In 1951,

> Young Pioneers (Úttőrők) in uniform descended on towns and villages, they rang the bells in every house and declared that they were willing to collect from attic to cellar everything that was refuse: they [actually] collected everything they could lay their hands on: brass knobs were

Fig. 6.1 MEH scrapyard with Mercedes truck tire being repaired, 1951 (Donor: Építész. *Source* FOTO: Fortepan—ID 15,086, http://www.fortepan.hu/_photo/download/fortepan_23439.jpg Wikimedia Creative Commons)

dismantled from doors,... iron door mats were stolen, etc., and amidst deprecations of the lady of the house, everything was piled on pushcarts and transported to the collecting station; there the boys were paid for what they collected on a per kilogram fixed rate basis. Rates were as follows: one kg iron[23] – 10 fillers; one kg brass or copper – 4 to 5 forints; one kg rags – 45 fillers; scrap paper – 50 fillers per kg; clean paper – one forint per kg.[24]

Recycling the already-recycled through theft, as at Sopron, was common: "The boys would turn in what they had collected, and during the night they would steal it, because the [storage] station was not locked,

6 HUNGARY'S SOCIALIST INDUSTRIALIZATION: A SNARE ... 223

and the next day they would bring it in again and collect the money for it again; sometimes they would sell the same material three or four times." Eventually when the great Sztálinvárosfurnaces commenced operation, their "raw material supplies were furnished by the MEH in the form of cast-off stove pipes, irons, exploded radiators, and steam boilers out of use for several decades."[25]

Scrap gathering gradually became more systematic but if anything, more predatory, as official collectors with quotas to meet replaced greedy Young Pioneers. The MEH unit at Kaposvár (Somogy) actually overreached during its May 1951 campaign, fulfilling a 50-carload target five times over. In response, Budapest officials raised the monthly assignment first to 70, then to 80 carloads, but to no avail. In the first drive, "all the houses of the district were literally cleaned out of whatever scrap iron there was"; meeting a higher goal was now hopeless. In some Kaposvár districts, "only two or three percent of the planned amount was collected." Frustrated MEH agents commenced purchasing used equipment ("motors of old makes") and even "machinery in a quite good state, and which could still be repaired." Market-conscious managers soon discovered that they could sell those motors and machines quite profitably to enterprises seeking repairable equipment. For instance, Sztálinváros directors purchased a defunct steam locomotive MEH bought in Ringakovacs village and converted its boilers "for heating the workers' lodgings... Naturally, MEH made a fortune out of this deal." Such canny repurposing met no plan targets, however; and Budapest sent a control commission to discover "the reason for this economic sabotage." Failing to "understand that... it was quite impossible to find scrap materials [in] the prescribed quantities," the visiting team simply ordered another, even more intensive campaign for summer 1952.[26]

By 1954, at least in Debrecen (Hadjú-Bihar), collectors obtained household scrap "more or less by force," deciding which articles "must be handed in... regardless of whether they are still in use." A fiddle comparable to that in Kaposvár arose. Given that roughly 20% of the household items gathered could "be sold as second hand goods," the unit separated these from the tonnage piles and marketed them at prices 30% below official used goods rates. Factory regulations had established delivery quotas for waste materials ("without payment"), but MEH bought additional quantities for cash, paying plant managers directly, "as if received from private individuals." One might expect such a revenue stream could increase the volume of usable material designated as scrap, benefitting the unit and the factory manager, if not the nation. Similar deceptions and thefts at times came from unanticipated directions: "A Soviet major from the airport near Debrecen once called the MEH office and offered to sell some scrap. He delivered in person several truckloads of new aluminum airplane parts and was paid the normal price of aluminum scrap."[27] Several truckloads—how very helpful to the scrap drive and to the major, though surely unauthorized by the Soviet Air Force. A more subtle fraud arose in Budapest amid the scrap iron famine of 1953. Earlier, the yards' truck drivers' "main earnings came from thefts of metal scrap, which they sold to the official scrap services or to tradesmen." But as oversight and supplies grew tighter, they devised new tactics. Being paid per hundred kilos for the iron they hauled offered an opportunity. As outgoing, but not returning vehicles were weighed,

> the workers loaded a truck with 60 hundredweights, passed the two weight controls, but at the railroad station unloaded 20 hundredweights only. They returned with the rest, added 20 hundredweights, and went back to the station, repeating this three times, and unloading the whole shipment at the last tour. They theoretically had delivered 180 hundredweights, when in fact only 100 hundredweights were shipped... When the iron shortage became even greater, the workers loaded 20 hundredweights of stones in the bottom of the truck and heaped iron scrap on top.[28]

Over and again, even as the state formalized the trade, scrap represented money-in-waiting, a stimulus for illicit trade and creative entrepreneurship. Weak coordination of accounting by the yards and the railways perfectly concealed the fraud.

Once steelworkers loaded pig iron and scrap, of whatever quality, into open hearths, hot gases blended them at temperatures above 1600 °C. Refractory bricks lined furnace interiors to deflect the heat loads and protect both the outer walls and the workforces. Yet as with other materials, Hungary's firebricks and the mortars that cemented them did not perform as planned. Produced locally, "they were of poor quality because they were made of inferior materials," a MAVAG engineer explained.

> The bricks could not withstand the high temperature and the binding materials could not resist the pressure of the liquid steel in the furnaces. The bricks cracked, causing the steel to flow under the furnaces and all around them. There had been 15 published cases of cracking, and many more unpublished cases. During 1951, there were 15 fatal accidents and 40

injuries serious enough to require hospitalization. The management tried to put the blame for all these mishaps on the workers.[29]

One of MAVAG's 1951 failures occurred when "a substantial quantity of molten steel was lost through a hole in the No. 9 furnace." This was "due to a faulty repair," managers claimed when accounting for "the serious production lag," but they omitted to mention that the fault likely lay as much in the refractories as in the repair.[30] At Ózd that year, a series of physical failures and worker errors also caused substantial delays and suspicions of sabotage.

> Recently, molten steel escaped from an open door of Martin steel furnace No. 6 and covered the floor. More than once, a 30-ton ladle has been set in place to receive the charge of a 40-ton furnace, with the result than 10 tons of steel overflowed. During one week, furnace tap plugs broke four times. The entire 160–180 ton charge was lost, and the furnace had to be recharged. Tens and hundreds of tons of steel are lost due to carelessness and lack of responsibility and there is no one to take the blame.[31]

On another occasion, Diósgyőr workers slowed down the open hearths, claiming they had "too few ladles to remove the slag from the pig iron. Actually, the temporary slag dump was overflowing, and since no one had prepared a new one, it was impossible to empty the slag ladles."[32] Passive resistance, anyone? Perhaps steelworks executives were not far off base in viewing workers as sources of trouble, but the Ministry judged the managers "guilty because they have failed to mobilize their employees for compliance" with plant procedures and regulations. As so often,

> lack of discipline...results in lower production and higher waste. In [MAVAG's] Martin Steelworks at Diósgyőr, instructions given for the handling of ingot molds are neglected. As a consequence the quality of the pig iron is poor and the volume of waste is rising. It is not uncommon for pig iron to adhere to the ingot mold. In the Diósgyőr open hearth plant alone, there are 600 such molds.[33]

More damaging to output targets were the tactics work teams used in attempts to achieve them, one of which was to ignore "preventive maintenance. Instead of observing the rules of proper care, the workers keep their furnaces in operation for longer periods of time in order to [reach] their quotas. As a consequence stoppages occur." On occasion,

226   P. SCRANTON

several suddenly-idled furnaces had to be relined and rebuilt simultaneously, overwhelming repair staffs and extending down times. Division chief József Simkó argued in 1951 that

> the workers in the MAVAG factories were indifferent toward their work and avoided attending union or Party meetings whenever they could. They had been asked so often for greater effort and greater sacrifices that even the offer of special overtime pay did not interest them. MAVAG workers were convinced that, no matter what they did or what they were promised, they would be the losers in the end... It was impossible to gain their good will.

The Russians only added to the disarray. Supervising Diósgyőr production of railway equipment for the USSR, they had no qualms about ordering changes in shop practices.

> The Soviets were very demanding. In January 1952, they insisted that 100 to 200 kg of steel above the standard quantity be poured into locomotive wheel casting molds. As a result, hardened excess steel had to be removed [from the molds] with disc saws. This created another problem because the equipment necessary for this task had been imported from the West and was [now] unavailable because of the embargo.[34]

Expanding heavy industry's capacity was an uneven process; it was far simpler to build factory sheds and install fabricating tools than it was to augment steel production. "It usually takes a long time to carry out capital investments in the iron and steel industry. Also the cost of plant capital for a given percentage of increased output is much higher... than in any other industry. It is also more difficult to obtain a sizable increase [in steel output]... by reorganizing the production."[35] Half of steel mill products (rails, reinforcing rods) went directly to end users; only the other half was available for downstream processing. As fabricating capabilities grew faster than mill outputs, the likelihood of material shortfalls increased for machinery and tool makers, makers of construction beams or girders, and engine, vehicle, and locomotive builders.[36] By 1954, the scrap famine had become "so acute" that only two of Ózd's ten open hearths could function, "although some 11,000 persons continued to be employed." Engineers thus commenced what might be termed "desperation recycling," sending work gangs of 300 to mine a 50 m-high [164'] slag mountain a few hundred meters outside the plant, so as to salvage "residual iron."

> [Lumps of slag] were broken into pieces and loaded into railway cars to be transported to the steel mills. In dragging the slag to the level ground at the foot of the hill, the men worked with the aid of wire cables and pulleys. The smaller slag pieces were broken up by big iron balls, about three meters in diameter, which were lifted by cranes and then released to fall on the pieces of slag. Holes were drilled into the larger pieces and dynamite inserted; [they] were then lowered by cranes into a deep pit with a thick iron cover and the dynamite was detonated by electricity... [The results were] passed through a magnetic sieve, so that pebble-sized bits of slag might be reclaimed.[37]

Gradually, Moscow realized that iron and steel production throughout the Bloc was not only technically disappointing, but also that ambitious Party appointees with inadequate experience had managed heavy industrial enterprises badly. Thus the Soviets called an April 1955 conference to announce a "complete reorganization of technical direction," bringing in "experts" from Poland, Czechoslovakia, and Hungary for consultations. The chair, a deputy director of the Soviet Research Institute for Iron and Steel, promptly admitted that the practice "of replacing existing technicians by men chosen primarily for political rather than technical qualifications had serious disadvantages." These men could not guide "the sound development of the industry."

> On the other hand, the deposed technicians had been driven into a role of passive resistance. Orders issued from above were followed blindly and to the letter, although the experienced technicians often knew that they were not only impracticable but actually harmful to the industry. Nobody dared criticize for fear of accusations of disobedience and sabotage. The desire of the new men to prove their ability led to unrealistic planning, nonsensical attempts at overproduction, wholesale falsification of statistics, and competition and rivalry between individual iron and steel works. Under these circumstances, the real technicians and the workers lost all pride in their work.

This foolishness "must cease"; crucially, "an end must be put to the practice of false statistics," as, for instance, including rejects in output totals. "True statistics, even if they show a setback, are of infinitely

228   P. SCRANTON

greater value than false ones reflecting unreal progress."[38] With Stalin interred and reformist Nikita Khrushchev serving as Party First Secretary, economic performance and technical competence had become priorities in a quest both to improve Soviet citizens' standards of living and to lift the fog of repression and fear. Three years earlier, such a meeting and such rhetoric would have been unthinkable.

Shifts in behavior followed the Moscow gathering quite rapidly; some had been in process beforehand. Previously, Russian officials had treated visiting Bloc engineers with disdain, showing them "very little" and deflecting their comments. "Today [summer 1955], the Soviets are prepared to discuss their more secret processes and are intensely interested in the reactions and options of visiting technicians." Indeed, they invited Béla Simon, a Hungarian steel expert, to Magnitogorsk to "inspect" alloying practices for "a new titanium steel, the manufacture of which the Soviets have hitherto kept a jealously-guarded secret." Even better, "the quality of the iron ore imported into Hungary from the USSR has greatly improved. It comes from Krivoy Rog, is carefully selected and is no longer mixed with dust." The long-anticipated "improved steel production" finally resulted. Personnel and information issues had drawn attention earlier in 1955: a Russian team investigating Hungary's metallurgical sectors was "repeatedly exasperated by the false statistics given them by the 'political' directors, and by the latter's lack of any real technical knowledge." A transformation soon commenced through which "command of the Hungarian iron and steel industry has been gradually passing back into the hands of the older, experienced engineers. Political upstarts... have been removed."

> This development has led to immediate improvements...The former rivalry between Diósgyőr and Sztálinváros, which had harmful effects on the industry as a whole prior to January 1955, has ended. These works are no longer headed by men motivated by personal and political considerations. Today the works are in the hands of former colleagues and friends, members of an exclusive small circle of "old guard" iron and steel engineers, far more concerned to assist than to compete with one another.

Now in the ascendant, steel technicians revealed their undercover efforts toward "ousting the political newcomers," reflected in "their refusal to cooperate with the new men and their passive resistance through disinterested subservience." Disinterested subservience—what an elegant expression of coping strategies requiring neither planning nor coordination. Another sign of a shift toward validating expertise was the reinstatement of many "political undesirables," this was not a wholly-excellent thing, however, for among those restored to influential posts was one engineer, "pushed very much into the background as a result of his former fanatical Nazi sympathies, [who] is today head of the Martin Furnace Department at Diósgyőr."[39] This rising tide didn't discriminate; it lifted former fascists, as well as aging Social Democrats and non-politicals, all in the service of a socialist industrialization in which none of them believed.

Despite this comedy of errors (or tragedy of hubris), steel emerged from Hungary's furnaces, foundries and workshops, to become machinery and vehicles (or door hinges, hand tools, and small motors, on the light industry side). The Heavy Industry Center (NIK) coordinated the three principal steel mills, two of which also made final goods, and the major steel-consuming plants, like Budapest's Ganz & Co—electromechanical products, bridges, railroad cars, and shipbuilding—and Györ's Magyar Waggon (as of 1953, the Wilhelm Pieck Works)—railway rolling stock, bridges, and diesel engines for vehicles. Among the five, Ózd did no fabricating, whereas Manfred Weiss (as of 1951, the Matyas Rákosi Works), lacking blast furnaces, melted pig and scrap in open hearths for its own products—agricultural machinery, tools, bicycles, sewing machines, and motorcycles (including motors). Diósgyőr's MAVAG covered the entire spectrum—converting ore to steel for castings, sheet, and ball bearings, while also creating bridge beams and girders, locomotives, and farm machinery.[40] These diverse production orientations suggest that the material and spatial features of Hungarian steelmaking which planners inherited constrained their options for allocating tasks and optimizing investments. Ministries recognized that broad output ranges and batch production of each motor or girder type absorbed time and resources that could be efficiently targeted by simplification and specialization—fewer models in fewer plants. Dreams of mass production animated heavy industry planners seeking to "allocate the production of any one line to only one factory." In theory, this "only plant policy" optimized machinery, reduced duplication, and enabled enterprises to introduce shortcuts that would curtail waste and expense. In practice, unintended consequences multiplied.

230   P. SCRANTON

Numerous bottlenecks result from this policy, owing to the absence of any alternative source of supply should one factory's production be interrupted. For example, the Csepel [Vehicle] Works is entirely dependent on the Hungarian Steel Goods Factory for laminated [leaf] springs and on the Small Spring Factory for spiral springs. When at the beginning of 1953, the latter's deliveries of springs were of unsatisfactory quality, the Csepel Works nearly had to cease production.[41]

Rather than try to unwind specialized reassignments, ministries responded to underwhelming performance by serial reorganizations. Having access to neither physical nor financial resources adequate to devise backup supply chains, they could do little more than reconfigure lines of authority on paper.

Addressing steel-consuming enterprise practices will commence with pre-1956 activity at the Ganz Works in Budapest, before traveling to a few smaller machinery building firms. Thanks to reports made just as socialist nationalizations were in process, Ganz's production values and equipment holdings can be reconstructed. In the first half of 1948, its divisions shipped goods worth 209 million ft [$18M, at official exchange rates], 40% of which came from its railway units and 20% from electrical work. The Ózd, MAVAG-Diósgyőr, and Manfred Weiss plants reported raw steel output at 361,000 tons over the same six months, again half for direct use and the rest for fabrication.[42] Machining that steel at Ganz occupied thousands of skilled workers and over 500 heavy tools, most pre-war if not obsolete (Table 6.1).

As this census indicates, few new tools had arrived since 1945, mostly lathes, half being belt-driven "cone" models with overhead power transmission, rather than "modern" tools with individual, variable-speed electric drives, the postwar Western standard. Almost three quarters of its "tool park" dated to the 1930s or before (382 of 533), a fifth rated as "obsolete."

The tiny number of grinding tools also suggests that Ganz practices lagged the technological edge. For much precision work, grinding was steadily superseding cutting, but unluckily, Hungary had minimal supplies of the abrasives key to quality wheel-making. Discs produced domestically wore out rapidly, whereas more durable imported wheels were costly and difficult to secure. A 1949 US report stated: "Hungary has no known production of abrasive grains," though its needs were estimated at 550 tons/year. "Grains" were tiny sharp bits of Al_2O_3 or SiC glued and

Table 6.1 Machine tools at Ganz Railway, Machinery, Electrical, and Shipbuilding, 1948

	Modern/New	Modern/Used	Old/Working	Obsolete	Total
Lathes	27	58	160	32	277
Planers	1	8	25	6	40
Milling Machines	5	23	15	3	46
Drills	7	20	50	38	115
Grinders	0	1	5	0	6
Presses	0	1	43	5	49
Total	40	111	298	84	533
	7%	21%	56%	16%	

Source CIA, "Data from the Work Plan," Table 3. Modern/New refers to postwar additions, Modern/Used to tools installed during the war (mostly German), and Old to pre-1939 machinery

shaped into grinding wheels. State agents tried in 1948 to place orders with US firms, but these were declined; after the 1951 embargo, processes needing first-rate abrasives were not feasible in Hungary. Only second-quality wheels could be produced; they eroded in five hours or less, undercutting machinery builders.[43] This conundrum spotlights another materials deficiency which substantially affected Hungary's machinery builders—being unable to match Western and Soviet expectations about precision undermined exports and reduced tool values.[44]

Steam locomotives were the principal output at the Ganz railway shops, in 1948 largely for Russian reparations. Between January and June, the plant delivered 53 Type 424 engines to the Soviets (Fig. 6.2) and 105 smaller Type 50s, both built to broad-gauge specifications and designed for freight hauling. "The amount paid to Ganz for each [424] was US$40,000 whereas the price for which they would normally sell on the open market would be $90,000," a loss to Hungary of $50,000 per unit. Similarly, the Type 50s brought $47,000 each in ruble credits, but their market price neared $95,000, more than twice as much. All together, the state had to absorb nearly $7.5 million in unreimbursed manufacturing costs, or more accurately, had to transfer that sum to Ganz to offset its balance sheet deficiencies. It was surely good news to no-one in Budapest that the Soviets had commanded provision of 130 more Type 50s by 1952.[45] MAVAG's locomotive works fared even worse. Required to supply 180 engines as "indemnity" goods, the enterprise found that

Fig. 6.2 Ganz 424 steam locomotive and tender, 1963 (Donor: Gyula Simon. *Source* FOTO: Fortepan—ID No. 70604. https://commons.wikimedia.org/w/index.php?search=MAV+424+locomotive&title=Special:MediaSearch&go=Go&type=image. Wikimedia Creative Commons)

after acceptance, the Russians assessed many of them as "sub-standard production, refusing to pay for them, but actually never returning them to Hungary."[46]

Despite these stresses, Ganz engineers revived a prewar project to develop an electrically-powered "lightweight" freight locomotive as a contribution to nationwide railway electrification. An earlier version, designed by Kalman Kando, Ganz's managing director, had serious reliability problems; its electric-drive transmission axle frequently bent or broke "after not more than 5000 km" of service. The second Kando model would provide direct traction to each of the wheels "without a driveshaft," delivering 3200 horsepower, sufficient for freight hauling. A prototype tested in 1951 seemed technically promising, but had a crucial market limitation: "These locomotives cannot be used anywhere else in the world, because there are no railroad lines anywhere else depending on 16,000 V, 50 cycle alternating current." In consequence, Ganz would build only about 30 V–41s for domestic use, until 1964, when MAV converted electric traction to 25,000 V, 50 cycles, ending its isolation from international markets.[47]

As a chief producer of key export goods, Ganz had priority access to scarce materials. One worker explained: "There was no copper. But when the Ganz factory had to manufacture cranes for the Soviet Union and Poland, it received copper to be used exclusively for those cranes. For the Hungarian cranes, ordinary aluminum was used, which could corrode after a few months."[48] Nonetheless, issues regularly arose concerning both the availability and the quality of incoming materials. One welder at the locomotive works complained: "The ratio of rejects was high, because the material was bad. Also the workers had to work too fast, otherwise they did not earn enough."[49] Consequently, the engine division reached only 80% of plan goals (February 1952); and its iron foundry rejects neared 10% (in the steel foundry, six percent), though the goal was one or two percent. Although Ganz's railway equipment and heavy machinery for the USSR, other Bloc countries and Argentina continued to be highly-regarded, production kept stalling due to late components deliveries, "as a result of which there has been a large falling off in production."[50]

In the meantime, the Ganz electrical works had hit a reef; plan failures became so severe that the ministry dismissed the technical director and plant manager (replaced by the Party secretary and a production chief) and demanded "the strictest economy of materials... especially as to copper." Yet, "instead of first-class raw materials, various scraps have to be employed, whereby the reliability of the product is endangered."[51] Exactly so. When Ganz Electric delivered 460 motors to "the Soviet receiving commission" in January 1952, "the commission rejected 270 [of them] because the switch axles were made of substitute material." Four large motors also failed inspection—the bearings supporting the axles were not sourced from Sweden's SKF works, as specified.[52] Whether in materials or components, substitutions imperiled sales and reputations, if detected. By the mid-50s, Ganz Electric's once-heralded workforce had become resentful, not least because poor materials and subsequent rejections had reduced their earnings. An inspector of electrical exports reported that

> the workers very often damaged the [finished] machines or put them out of order. This was often the case with electrical installations. Here, the repairs required a considerable length of time. I, myself, have witnessed several such cases in our factory. The industrial workers were the ones who

234   P. SCRANTON

dared to express their dissatisfaction the most... There were some officials [however] who were more concerned with the welfare of the people than with state interests. For example, there was a superintendent in our factory who sometimes would order good machines to be dismantled and repaired although they were in perfect condition. This was only to give work to the men, who otherwise would have been idle.[53]

The railway equipment division also faced serious challenges by 1954. Exporting 90% of its output had authorized its acquisition of imported machine tools—"a large number... from Switzerland and Czechoslovakia," which "greatly improved" production technologies. Such capacities enabled monthly deliveries valued at 60–65M forints [$5.5M], but the qualifications of its 6000 shop and office workers had declined. "The world-famous skilled workers and technicians of Ganz have been dispersed all over the country, being either officially transferred or dismissed on some pretext or other." As in construction, many fired technicians found places "on the staff of the Ministry of Metallurgy and Machine Industries and in the various planning bodies." By 1953 "only ten percent of the old specialists" were still employed and "plant organization" was haphazard.[54] Inadequate supplies and low-quality inputs caused endless headaches, as did ineffectual shop work practices. Cutting tools presented "a grave problem" for machinists, as the embargo had blocked sales of hardened British tools and domestic replacements proved unreliable.[55]

The factory suffers from both a shortage of raw materials and the defective quality of steels, insulating materials and paints. Faulty blueprints and incorrect work pieces have also given much trouble. Recently deliveries to the USSR have been held up by bearing metal swelling and jamming and by breakages of piston rings. Finished parts of railroad carriages frequently have to be scrapped on account of loose metal finding its way between plates and on account of unequal thickness of plates. Seventy to eighty percent of cylinder blocks for diesel engines have had to be scrapped during the last three years.[56]

In 1954, the material implications of this disarray wrecked two major contracts: 26 sets of four-car diesel passenger railcars for Argentina (Fig. 6.3) and 20 six-unit models for the Soviets.[57] The four-car version placed the engines in/under the first unit and seated passengers in all four, with space for standees in commuter transit. The larger design had diesel locomotives at each end with four passenger cars in between. For

Fig. 6.3 Ganz four-unit railcar at Henderson, Argentina, on its final run before retirement, 1977 (Photographer: Carlos Pérez Darnaud. *Source* Plataforma 14, https://upload.wikimedia.org/wikipedia/commons/3/33/Tren_estacion_h enderson.jpg Wikimedia Creative Commons)

the Argentines, Ganz had delivered 22 sets by November 1954, the rest to be shipped by spring 1955. Discouraging reports came back to Budapest, however. While being "anxious to place further orders... the railroad authorities [were] adamant in their demands for improvement in the quality of materials and labor." Parts built into the trains that were "not up to specifications" must be replaced before future contracts could be considered.[58] Overall, repairs had been required on 18 of the railcar sets, causing delays in putting them into service. What had happened?

First, due to the scarcity of copper and nickel-molybdenum alloy steels, Ganz designers replaced "copper-asbestos gaskets in the diesel engines [with] a sheet iron-asbestos surrounded by a thin copper frame. This contraption is most unsatisfactory and caused a number of breakdowns." Second, special steels should have been used to fabricate "the clutch discs of the speed gear box," but the Ministry transferred production to a plant without prior experience, resulting in steel "with too many impurities." Third, railcar springs developed cracks, some breaking, due to "careless heat treatment," as did springs inside fuel oil pumps. Shop practices were deplorable. Machine work on the clutch discs lacked accuracy; some had fewer than ten percent of their teeth cut correctly. Cases enclosing the diesels' main bearings were not properly assembled; hence "the bearings became loose without being noticed and caused damage to the engines." Finally, the on-site Ganz representative failed to report these and other shortcomings to Budapest officials. Fearing "unpopularity with the staff at home," he instead blamed "the ignorance of the local staff." Eventually, Ganz management "reluctantly admitted" their responsibility for all defects and deficiencies and working relationships with the Argentine railways gradually recovered.[59]

The Soviets were tougher customers. At the outset, although their six-unit sets cost five to eight million forints each [\$425 K–\$700 K], depending on specifications, the Russians refused to cover Ganz's production estimates. Actually, "they may have offered even less than half," a proposal which Budapest "accepted without much argument." During manufacturing, Moscow announced an engineering design change, "demand[ing] that the body of the coaches should be build 60 mm higher," which added costs that they shrugged off. Then the hammer blow. Having received the first group of completed trains,

> the Soviets accepted only eight and cancelled the rest of the order, on grounds of faulty workmanship. They maintained that the welding was poor, which the Ganz engineers admitted, and that the electro-pneumatic bogeys[60] were badly constructed. The Russians had nevertheless approved the construction designs… The 12 trains which were rejected are now lying unassembled at the factory. It will be difficult to dispose of them since they are designed for the Soviet broad-gauge railways.

Despite the damage and waste, the Ganz rail plant reportedly still had sufficient orders from Czechoslovakia and from Budapest's streetcar authority to keep its 7000 workers busy.[61] Perhaps so, but its situation was far from rosy.

In a report filed almost simultaneously with the Soviet debacle, a sharply-critical visitor, having toured the plant, affirmed that Ganz was no longer the technical and market force it had been in the 1930s. A new model of its four-car diesel railcar was being service-tested on the state railways. "However, it is very often returned to the Ganz workshops for innovations and further experimental work. This train is approximately ten years old in design." That summer, the main factory worked at under 50% of capacity, constructing ten to twelve diesel coaches (for Poland) as well as a dozen tank cars (for the USSR). Like others, this visitor thought Ganz's "diesel-powered coaches give the impression of being made of second-rate material," including "inferior glass windows." Although the new product division was busy fabricating a prototype 2000 hp diesel locomotive, "the factory in general made an unfavorable impression and many workers appeared to be idle." The conclusion: "it is improbable that present products from this factory can match the excellent products of pre-war days."[62] Millions of forints in investments and hundreds of millions in contracts could not sustain what had been a world-class railway engineering enterprise, not in a poorly-coordinated industrial nexus, where low quality and/or scarce materials combined with the dispersion of a capable workforce and the hostility of the replacements, to undermine plans for Ganz to again be an export powerhouse. If ruinous Soviet prices forced massive state subsidies, if substitutions, repairs, and redesigns made production dynamics unstable, and if its products repeatedly disappointed clients in the West, Ganz could not meet such expectations.

Ongoing technical and operational shortcomings may also be found among users of heavy industry's basic outputs. Exploring two salient issues will round out reviewing the first socialist decade—problems with product quality and the ubiquity of sabotage, fraud and theft. On the first count, steel produced by the Diósgyőr works failed to meet requirements when fabricated at nearby machinery building shops. A 1954 critique charged: "The forged axles supplied… are frequently deficient, the material being streaky and containing embedded particles of slag. In some cases there are cracks. These faults are discovered only during and after machining, and in many cases 20% to 50% of the axles are rejected."[63] Budapest's Red Star Tractor Works groused that "there is a great deal of trouble caused by the inferior quality of some of the materials" received. For instance, incoming "steel bars are not uniform in hardness," which varies even "within one and the same bar." Without further heat-treatment, machining them would yield unreliable components. The capital's Lang Machine Works likewise argued that production of diesel engines, boilers, and steam turbines "is not efficient because of…

the poor quality of domestic steel" supplied by foundries using material from Hungarian open hearths.[64]

Farm machinery builders fared the worst. According to an agricultural machine designer, "they were getting the poorest raw materials – the war industries got the best, then came the machine-tool makers, vehicle builders, and so on, and the farm machinery industry was at the end of the materials queue." At one point, assigned as an expediter (or "pusher") to secure materials for fabricating a "special plow," this designer endured one frustration after another.

> The steel for the plow-share was ordered from Diósgyör, and they, without any prior warning, simply delivered a different specification. This then had to be cold-rolled in the Obuda shipyard, where there was 30% breakage. The units then had to be sent back to Diósgyör for hardening. The hardening furnace was too small, and the plates got bent. They had to be sent back to Obuda for re-rolling, but Diósgyör then refused to take them back again. A battle ensued and eventually a Deputy Minister had to intervene with threats. Finally the plow-shares had to travel to Mosonmagyaróvár for assembly. The whole long battle yielded seven of these plows![65]

Two Diósgyör-to-Budapest round-trips and a third westward from Diósgyör to a town near the Austrian border meant the plates traveled over a thousand kilometers, adding costs and wasting time, largely because steelmakers, caring little for farm equipment orders, ignored design specifications and shipped the wrong raw materials. A toolmaker at the Mosonmagyaróvár plant exposed the connection between material delays and quality deficiencies.

> This system operation with tremendous waste. We were short on time, our monthly planning was always out of joint, and we did not get our raw materials when we needed them... To fill our production norms we simplified the work processes and lowered the quality... The checkers were told to pass through many second rate products.[66]

Even when proper iron or steel is available, things can go askew in foundry casting—pouring molten metal into hardened sand molds to make components with complicated shapes difficult or impossible to achieve through metal-cutting. At times, interior or surface holes appear when hot gases aren't fully expelled; warping happens through uneven

6 HUNGARY'S SOCIALIST INDUSTRIALIZATION: A SNARE ...   239

cooling; molds can leak (runouts) or fuse sand and metal; and if temperatures are too low, castings can crack or the metal can fail to fill all the mold's nooks and crannies.[67] Casting is a grimy process, but it has to be done with care and precision to provide users with quality metalwares. This was not often the case in 1950s Hungary. Even the Party press recognized "the shortcomings under which Hungarian foundries are working." Indeed, it "very often publishe[d] outright revelations or bitter complaints about such conditions."

> The alarmingly low quality of casting in all Hungarian foundries has been one of the major bottlenecks of Hungarian [heavy] industry in recent years. *Szabad Nép* of 15 July 1953 pointed out that, while the rate of defective castings on the average amounts to 6–8 percent, in some foundries it reaches 20 percent. *Szabad Nép* of 15 September 1953 stated that very little had been achieved in the fight against defective castings. The ratio... was intolerably high in the foundry of the important Lang Machine factory throughout 1953... In some cases [it] amounted to 50–60 percent in the Rákosi Works.[68]

An inspector of castings at the Wilhelm Pieck Works (Györ, formerly Magyar Waggon) confirmed this sorry situation. His shop shipped components to "all factories manufacturing vehicles," each item being twice checked: "We made sure only good pieces left the plant." Two problems surfaced. A very high proportion of the foundry's products failed in-house inspections, and the contracting enterprises rejected others which had passed, filing claims for compensation—claims which may have been tactical so as to reduce their own running costs.

> The percentage of defective products was amazingly high; 23 to 25 percent of our total production [failed] the first inspection (meanwhile I have found that the comparable percentage in the US is 0.5 percent and in West Germany 3 to 5 percent)... Of the 75 percent then shipped, perhaps 35 to 45 percent was rejected by the manufacturer of the end product. I was then sent out regularly to investigate and determine... just how much of the liability was with us... As a rule of thumb, I usually accepted half of their claim... which kept both them and us quite satisfied and avoided litigation. Frequently the rejects were used [by the buyers] in producing trucks for domestic use... Other times we took the defective castings back and resold them to a truck maintenance company, called Autóbontó, which kept the domestic truck fleets in operation.

240   P. SCRANTON

The vehicle makers flunked castings that couldn't meet export requirements. Thus Pieck's adjusters worked with multiple firms repurposing "half-finished products… refused by manufacturers of export equipment." The volume of rejects was astounding; Budapest's Csepel plant, one of Pieck's five biggest clients, "alone" registered "about 140 to 150,000 forints in claims *every other week* [ca. US$320 K/yr]."[69] Low-quality materials and poor foundry practices generated endless waste, intensified by the Cold War materials blockade the US championed.

In 1953, the Lang Machine Works struggled when embargoed inputs could not be purchased and substitutions failed to meet requirements. As a result, "the quality of the products has deteriorated during the past six months. Special solutions had to be found in every branch due to the lack of first-grade material." For instance, in sugar plant machinery, "instead of the necessary copper pipes, steel pipes are used." With Western supplies of "high-grade cobalt steel" blocked, "the plant had to construct a milling machine made of domestic hard steel," and fabricated an aluminum condenser for a food processing enterprise, "instead of the usual steel one." As well, "there is much trouble [with] the Russian argon-gas welding method used with aluminum and rustproof materials, since the boiler manufacturing shop cannot get any foreign rustproof electrodes." In each case severing links with Western suppliers forced design adaptations that reduced product utility and reliability.[70]

Such product deficiencies provide a bridge to the practice of sabotage and fraud in heavy industry. Sabotage enters the picture here because badly-paid and poorly-fed-and-housed workers rarely could express their resentments through theft; swiping chunks of steel or machine parts was pointless. Instead, hindering production beckoned—though dangerous when caught or informed on. The Party press repeatedly announced drives to combat the evils of capitalist-sponsored wrecking, though "sabotage" angst becomes harder to credit when simply missing plan targets or incurring export rejections triggered employee arrests and jail time, as did railway accidents and construction delays. Yet even in the high Stalinist years, industrial workers' rejection of the new setup was evident. A dismissed economist explained that in 1950–51, although "the strongest opposition came from the peasants" who "sabotaged or slowed down deliveries," animating an "anti-regime atmosphere," factory hands

> showed the same behavior. They slowed down their work, made faulty products, stole from the factories daily, cheated the state with their wages

6 HUNGARY'S SOCIALIST INDUSTRIALIZATION: A SNARE ... 241

and did not attend Communist meetings. The people were asked in vain to express their opinion. Nobody said anything and this passivity showed that nobody agreed with the regime... This resistance was very effective.[71]

Despite the exaggeration ("nobody agreed with the regime"), this account captures the tenor of the times in heavy metal. For instance, an equipment factory department making machine screws

had been falsifying its figures. It was only regularly producing large-sized screws, while the output of small screws, being unfavorable in terms of overall production norms, was entirely neglected. As a result only 50% of the target was produced. To justify this obvious production slump, some of the machinery was damaged. As a result of this "practice" the largest proportion of big screws remained in the warehouse, while the lack of smaller sized created difficulties.

Once the cover-up was exposed, the perpetrators were suspended and slated for trial, but this scheme was hardly major-league sabotage—dynamiting dams or derailing trains.[72] An identical strategy appeared at Budapest's Cutting Tool Factory: "Underproduction in small cutting tools and overproduction of large sizes." The "continual scramble to fulfill the plan and thereby increase pay-packets" lay at the root of this maneuver, which resulted in warehousing "large tools... for lack of demand," while appeals for small cutters "cannot be satisfied."[73]

Rejection also manifested itself in positive shop-floor initiatives (the inverse of sabotage), signaling workers' anti-regime sentiments in unexpected ways—solidarity toward targets of state coercion for damaging machinery or "making seconds." An example: When state Price Administrators resisted political interference in fall 1948, as the Party assumed control, a staffer refusing to "falsify statistical data" fell into the hands of the AVH. He spent the next five years in a series of prisons, emerging from the Recsk quarries in 1953 to catch on as a lathe trainee in a Budapest machinery plant. Word of his past soon got round.

From that time on, there was hardly a single worker in the section who did not lend him a hand at every opportunity. One worker would adjust [his] machine; another would share his mid-morning snack. A few days later, one of the foremen asked [him] why he was doing that particular type of work – with that machine, at the moment – since he could not earn very much at it. Within an hour, [he] received another work assignment with

242   P. SCRANTON

which already, on the fourth day, he was able to improve his output [and earnings] by 160 percent.

Before long, Personnel learned of this favorable treatment and forced his departure, but the workers' message remained. Inside a year, guided by a top Ministry of Housing accountant, this "reactionary" snared a glass factory clerical job in Tokod (Komárom county), where, due to general staff incompetence, he "could do anything he desired." After he straightened out production scheduling and improved accounting and legal agreements, the Ministry commenced seconding him to "organize the work systems of other factories." When in 1956 the Price Administration sought to re-hire him, he declined, to the delight of his factory colleagues. After so much turmoil, his "life had never been so beautiful."[74]

If sabotage was elusive and mostly concealed, fraud was common, though just as carefully concealed. Usually, manufacturing fraud arose either in the shops or in the offices, in the former centered on faking production and hiking earnings and in the latter devoted to maneuvering around plan targets and collecting bonuses. A shopfloor case from Duclos Mining Machinery (Budapest) shows how collusion between machinists and supervisors could benefit both, extracting unearned wages in exchange for payoffs.

> When I was a skilled worker for one year already, I got a raise [from ca. 1000 ft/mo] to where I could make two thousand forints per month, but this was only possible by giving three to four hundred forints monthly to a time-analyzer of the shop for giving me additional working time on account of pretended additional work, due to the alleged fact that I had... faulty material. For example, it was told that [the workpiece] was greater in diameter than it should have been.[75]

At the former Siemens generator and motor plant, management increased production quotas "every four or five months." Thus to keep earnings stable, the shop men "work[ed] like mad."

> The high norms do not even allow them time to smoke a cigarette. As a result of haste, the machines often go out of order and there is very little time given to fix them. Therefore, it is very difficult for the workers to meet the norms. Very often workers resort to trickery in order to show that they fulfilled their quotas. They present the same piece of work twice to the inspector, but if they are caught they are severely punished.[76]

Faking output was evidently easier at Ganz, where electro-technicians regularly received a monthly bonus (250 ft), "because they could report great endeavor whereas they actually did only a little."[77]

Office fraud ranged from the trivial to the comprehensive, the latter termed "plan fraud." Similar to construction schemes, machinery plant engineers and draftsmen could manipulate quantity norms to exceed bonus thresholds. At Mosonmagyaróvár's farm equipment plant, "if one prepared a blueprint of a tool-construction problem, one never erased mistakes, but simply started a new blueprint. In the end one submitted all the spoiled plans together with the completed one and got a premium for all."[78] Local, modest, and unassuming, such fiddles were easily replicated. Assertive plan fraud is a more expansive defection from socialist rectitude: two heavy industry examples, in petroleum refining and in metalworking. A junior chemical engineer at Komárom's *Almásfüzítő* refinery reported earning 3000 ft/month in 1953, 1800 as his base pay and 1200 more in bonus (67% of base). To achieve this and keep the bonuses coming, the technical staff duped their Soviet supervisors (who never came out from Budapest), as well as Hungarian technical overseers, neither of whom knew much about operations. "It would not have done them any good to try and interfere in the plant, because each refinery is unique; you cannot check and control it until you know it well enough. The local engineers would just lead you around by the nose." As a result, they "let us have our own way."

> "Having our own way" meant primarily the production of the right plan fulfillment statistics. If we fell behind in a particular period, we were not prepared to forego our bonus, but started to cook the stock records instead. We would overstate the stock figures to an extent sufficient to make up for the shortfall of delivered production, and even if they came out to check, they could never prove that the stock is not there – wherever they sought it, the missing quantity was always supposed to have been pumped into some other tank. Having produced 90 [%] and reported 100, we could always request X days stoppage for repairs and maintenance. We would use X - N days for repairs and produce the missing 10 [%] during the N days.

Problems arose, however, when the Ministry began reducing the number of days allotted for suspensions. The cuts left sufficient days for maintenance, "but not for repairs *and* clandestine production. Hence the equipment deteriorated very quickly."[79] Of course, sustaining bonus payouts was the staff's priority; sacrificing premiums in order to preserve the enterprise's capital assets was never chosen. As for fuels and lubricants:

> It is best not to talk about the quality of our products at all. Only the quantity mattered... We were cursed by the users, but we always said, we cannot help it, we are working to rule... Besides, since the Hungarian motor fleet was old, quality requirements were not so high as they were in the West... If a large user noticed that their truck fleet was deteriorating quickly because of the poor quality of the lubricants, there was nothing they could do. They were glad to get any.[80]

In metalworking, plan fraud could assume the shell-game form just sketched, but there was also a "more profitable" variant, as Györgyi Karolyi, the State Planning Office's chief accountant documented. On the first count, firms facing a plan deficit could take input materials (steel rods), cut them to proper lengths for use (say, as cotter pins for locomotive wheels), but then halt the fabrication process. Accountants then declared these just-started items to be finished goods worth X ft each, a sum added to monthly output totals, assuring bonuses. To balance the books, that actually-unfinished batch had to be completed in the next month "for free," while the regular quota also had to be met. Hence, "this type of fraud is limited to tiding over temporary troughs in performance by mortgaging, as it were, future temporary peaks." The more elaborate game involved systematically inflating the labor cost of semi-finished components, then making many more than needed, so as to inflate total production values and reach bonus benchmarks.

> [The firm] will carry out an enormous lot of such simple operations, overstating the labor content of each, and never dreaming of turning more than a fraction of the "semis" into finished products. After a while it will be noticed [by superiors] that the firm is carrying a huge quantity of "semis" in its inventory, or the manager or chief accountant may himself point out the fact to the Directorate or Ministry, complaining about the interest cost of carrying these semi-finished stocks for which he has no use. [Earlier,] he was obliged to produce them, but the plan was revised... and he now wishes to be relieved of this "idle inventory."

Now comes the skillful deception. Once the ministry agrees to disposing of the warehoused "semis," the maker offers them at their "true labor cost," not the inflated one on the books; and through the magic of accounting, the fraud is validated.

> The firm's *output account* had been credited with [say] 1.90 ft [each] in the first place. It is **not** now debited with the shortfall between 1.90 and the sale price of [say] 0.80 ft, Instead, the *profit-and-loss account* is debited with the "loss," but generally speaking the profit-and-loss account is of no interest to anyone – the main bonus is tied to output.

As no reconciliation of the two accounts was undertaken (again a coordination failure), the disparity between them went unnoticed, plan targets were met, bonuses were paid, and another metal-using firm secured cheap semi-finished materials.[81] Perfect.

With some exceptions, theft in heavy industry centered on illegal entrepreneurship. At a Budapest tractor plant in the early 1950s, "the workers were very ingenious in finding extra sources of income. For instance, they used the machinery belonging to the firm to make articles for sale or for themselves." One machinist recollected:

> A friend of mine, an iron turner and philosopher, had finished gymnasia and was a sort of semi-proletarian because his father had owned a butcher-shop. At this time one could not buy buttons in Budapest and so my friend decided to make buttons. He used the firm's machinery to make a machine which could make buttons and hired an agent to sell them all over the country. He earned about 4–5,000 ft/month with this trade, as well as 2000 ft in the firm. This sort of thing was fairly typical.[82]

Comparable appropriations took place at a Györ county farm machinery plant, where the head of the tool storeroom routinely undertook "after-hours work, using scrap from the plant." His supervisor, a Party member, had approved this activity, but the landscape changed.

> Economic necessity often forces workers in plants to fabricate gadgets out of waste materials. Everywhere... one can ask a shop foreman and do this after work hours. In Hungary, if one is politically disliked, such an act can be branded a crime whenever this is convenient for the authorities. I once made a gadget out of waste materials with the written permission of our section manager. By the time I was finished, our section manager had been replaced and this looked like a good opportunity to accuse him and me

of theft. I was dragged to police headquarters and urged to work as an informer…

Instead he left for the West.[83] By contrast, an unvarnished case of workplace theft surfaced in Budapest's Lang Machine Works not long before the Revolt. Over the course of several months, "several hundred light bulbs… disappeared from their sockets," to the consternation of management. Since the culprits could not be identified, the firm determined to take "energetic measures," remodeling its illumination system with new sockets and "bulbs fitted with bayonet holders, which cannot be used in private households."[84] That may have fixed the bulb drain, but deeper problems remained unaffected. A 1954 report summarized the heavy industry drive's central defects.

> The industrialization of Hungary was planned in the most thoughtless and irresponsible manner… The planning was undertaken on the Soviet pattern but what applies to the USSR does not always apply to Hungary. The greatest mistakes were that the plans were drawn up without due consideration for two of the most important factors: available raw materials and fuel. No improvement can be expected in the future because neither the Russians nor the other satellites are in a position to fill in the gaps.[85]

THE PERIPHERY: LIGHT INDUSTRY, HANDICRAFTS AND AUXILIARIES

The First Five Year Plan's investment goals, repeatedly raised after its first draft (1948), peaked at 80 billion forints in the February 1951 version [US$7B], half devoted to industrial expansion, only 13% to agriculture and much of the rest to infrastructure spending. About 90% of the industrial allocation "was concentrated into the so-called heavy industrial branches,"[86] leaving just 4B ft [$350M] for renewal or modernization of peripheral domains: light industry, handicrafts, and auxiliary activities, principally maintenance and repair services. Some textile mills could secure new machinery, and several dozen factories arose in provincial towns (an element in spatial decentralization), but light industry's consumer goods enterprises had no leverage on capital allocation decisions. Productivity gains were negligible; in general, workforces expanded faster than output. The crafts faced secular decline after 1948; with their shops confiscated, thousands "retired" to working from home or just entered factories. This decay stunted repair services. Reportedly by 1952, the Budapest metropole supported roughly fifty shoemakers for over 1.6 million residents.[87] Repair work in industry and agriculture was comparably challenging, not least (1) because maintenance added nothing directly to planned output, while demanding resource expenditures, (2) because the availability of materials, spare parts, and experienced workers was uncertain, and (3) because factory maintenance units were frequently drafted into production roles as plan deadlines neared. Nonetheless, marginalized businesses shared at least three things with more favored enterprises in steel, metalworking, and chemicals—overly-ambitious plan targets, persistent uncertainty, and diffident, if not hostile workforces.

Textile manufacturing anchored one wing of Hungary's consumer trades, food processing the other. Budapest hosted most of the leading fabric plants, refitted after 1945 both to provide reparations shipments and to meet a portion of domestic demand. Early in the Five Year Plan, however, noticeable shortcomings drew the Party's attention. Textile Trade Union secretary Károly Döbrentey reported that, at the Budapest Spinning Works and elsewhere, a third or more of individual work quotas went unmet, "a typical phenomenon in the entire textile industry." Poor maintenance brought spinning-frame breakdowns, but more salient was management's inability to curb "a heavy increase in absenteeism." Nationally, 250,000 textile work days had been lost to no-shows in 1950, "a full year's work for 1000 workers." Late arrivals had become chronic. For this reason, "at the Lorinc Works, 37 of the 66 spinning machines were idle at the shift change on December 5." Despite its "outstanding plant" award, the city's Wool Spinning and Weaving Works "continues to make defective products." Its yarn lacked "uniformity" and snapped during weaving—a fault that neglected maintenance magnified. At Goldberger, Hungary's most prominent fabric printers, "the machines ha[d] not been overhauled since 1945," undermining efforts to boost output. With 4000 workers and an international reputation, Goldberger keyed textile exports, but "the quality of raw material as well as the finished products varied greatly."[88] Management installed output incentives, a technician explained:

> [T]here were premia, distinctive titles for the fastest workers and for the inventors of new, faster processes. Innovations often were not reported; instead the factory used the process to speed up production, because that way all the workers received more in premiums than the inventor would

have gotten [as a bonus]. The drive for speed damaged very much the quality of the products. In my field for instance, we produced thicker yarn than required because that goes faster [in the frame]. This way we surpassed the norm in [yarn] length and received high premiums. If the undue thickness was detected, we were fined, but that was still less than the premium.[89]

A 1951 Soviet engineering evaluation of textile practice was harsh: "There is still no satisfactory provision for planned preliminary maintenance, especially regarding important machine parts, materials, and necessities." Repairs were badly done, but inspectors certified them anyway. These "poorly-repaired machines operate faultily until the next scheduled repair." When maintenance programs *were* laid down, workers ignored them: "Machines are not cleaned, dusted or oiled as prescribed." Moreover, stoppages were all too common, often because enough yarn-carrying bobbins for weaving had not been prepared. Changeovers in doffing full yarn spindles and replacing them with empties were also slow; spinners tying in ends for the next run then rushed the job so much that frames quickly suffered broken threads on as many as a quarter of their spindles. "It takes each of the women time to restart these spindles." As for technology, cotton finishing departments operated "antiquated and run down" equipment, whereas wool establishments' machinery was merely "outdated." Quality control was useless, chiefly because, "to speed up plan implementation,... entire series of operations are omitted, which is detrimental to the quality of the product." The ministries were also useless, generating neither the inspection standards nor the technological norms which could end the deception and "secretiveness which prevail in the factories." The analyst, a good Party man, made the usual (and equally useless) recommendations—greater workforce discipline, improved management practices, and visits from Stakhanovite exemplars to inspire both.[90]

Russian concern about quality outputs was well placed. For instance, the Györ woolen mill's raw materials all came from the USSR and three quarters of its output ("first-quality products") returned there. Fabrics "of inferior quality" stayed in Hungary.[91] Yet a Budapest trade official judged that Soviet supply practices caused the underperformance, because Hungary was pressed to buy fiber through "Russia's re-export trade."

Russia would buy, for instance, wool and cotton on the world market, and re-sell [it] to Hungary, either at higher prices, or at identical prices but extracting for re-export the *parcels of poorest quality*. This was particularly the case in wool... The cotton spinning and weaving mills would be started up at a pace corresponding to the annual plan, and in a few months' time would learn that there was no cotton for them to go on with. *The major qualitative difficulty arose from taking Russian cotton as equivalent to "cotton."* In fact, Russian cotton is chronically immature [short fibers] and contains a heavy admixture of seed shells.[92]

Resentment of the USSR percolated through the manufacturing sector, but rarely did spinning or weaving mills provide platforms for upheavals. Rather, textile workers deployed that "disinterested subservience" encountered earlier. In one accountant's view,

Passive resistance took many forms, for instance, at Szeged they were installing a large textile concern which was equipped with machines imported from Russia. The installation of the machines was supervised by a textile engineer friend of mine... He told me of the following conversation between two workers. "A: Look, Comrade, there is a big 'eight' there in this wheel (workers' slang to say that the axis was improper [creating a wobble]), though it is the product of Soviet industry, which is leading in the world. B: Never mind, what can a small 'eight' matter to such a big country." – And they went on installing the faulty wheel.[93]

Theft could become an issue when a mill's production was wholly devoted to exports, meaning that none of its products reached domestic consumers. At a Budapest factory using Italian nylon yarn to knit women's hosiery, "some of the women can't resist temptation and steal some of the valuable Nylons." Management reacted foolishly to the disappearances.

One day, last Summer [1953], after work the management locked everyone in the factory and conducted an "intimate" search of all workers for stolen stockings. This abnormal and undignified procedure, which lasted for several hours, caused such an uproar that the workers did not appear the next day in the factory. The Ministry had to step in to negotiate and blame was put on the directrice of the factory, but finally nothing happened to her.[94]

Though textile mills were rarely hotbeds of rejection, print shops could be volatile, particularly given printers' Social-Democratic allegiances, perennially combative unions, and bitterness at the confiscation of their collective property—Budapest buildings, pension, and unemployment funds, "in short everything that the printers had built up and reaped during the last 30 or 40 years."[95] A female typesetter from Debrecen recalled: "We were always dissatisfied and discussed it, not only among one another, but also with the manager and director. There were loud [arguments] about the norms. The printers turned over the case, which [took days] to be reset. The person who did it was fined 50 ft [$4]." The "case" was a large block of hand-set type, painstakingly composed then locked in place for the press. Smashing a case once was a classic strike gesture in craft shops, but here a protest (strikes were banned), which management punished, barely. She added:

> The people always sabotaged, but nobody ever admitted [it]. Somehow, we always found the ways and means to manage to hinder production. It cost quite a lot of money to the company. People were desperate, because some of them could never make more in the norms than 100%... In the last few years, the opposition continuously strengthened... But the Party became also wilder. For instance, one day a young girl in the shop answered, when she was called to go to the Party meeting, "To Hell with the Party," and she was immediately dismissed.[96]

A press technician at the Government Printing Office said the "Communists knew that the workers were reactionary, yet tolerated them because of their skills." Indeed, on-the-job printers actively demonstrated their "dissatisfaction with the norms."

> The workers did their [tasks] very sloppily, not only in order to achieve more in the shortest possible time, but also with the intention of doing harm to the Communists. Open strikes were quite out of the question. The AVH would have taken away everyone involved immediately. There was, however, much delay in acquiring necessary tools. For example, if some tool or part was needed, it would sometimes take two or three weeks to get it. This was done very subtly. Probably the white collar workers were in on these delays.[97]

Another Budapest shop contingent *performed* its passive dissent. When obliged to join May Day or other political parades, they marched "in complete quiet... as if it had been a funeral," rather than "cheering or clapping as they were ordered to do by blaring loudspeakers." During the 23 October 1956 demonstration, these printers undertook a special, illegal job—just as the Revolt began. Having acquired a mimeographed copy of university students' initial Fourteen Demands, they realized that many more were needed.

> After I... saw the meeting get underway, I hurried back to the printing shop and talked to one of my friends, asking him to print as many as they could. We went ahead right away with the printing and we printed approximately 50,000 leaflets. When I received the leaflets I went back... and gave them to the students, who were happy to distribute them. But then we went over to another printing shop, an even larger one, where we had good friends who dared to do something, and they printed even more...[98]

In quieter times, opportunities for solidarity (to fraudulently boost earnings) confirmed printers' refusal to embrace Rákosi's socialism. A Györ shop estimator, for example, used his position for "great benefit to all of us, because by consistently over-estimating labor and materials costs intentionally, it was possible for us to overfill our quotas and remain a lead plant, which meant bonuses for all." More individualistic was a printer at Globus (800 workers) who could not support his family on the 1300 ft he earned. When the Nagy cabinet re-authorized Maszek enterprises, he began home-based, spare-time work for a custom bookbinder, putting in long hours but pocketing more than double his usual monthly pay.[99]

Printing and publishing firms offered few targets for theft, other than paper and pencils, perhaps; but at electrical and metalwares plants, much could be carried away, if one could figure out a scheme. *Egyesült Izzólámpa* (known as Izzó, founded in 1896 as Tungsram) was the world's third largest producer of electric light bulbs when nationalized in 1945 and had long been Hungary's principal source for radio vacuum tubes. It provided so many occasions for sins against the people's economy that management spotlighted thefts prevented.

> At the factory gate there was a big showcase with stolen and recovered radio tubes, transformers, and other products of our plant; the names of thieves and their punishments were also listed. Checking the employees after work was a thorough and major operation. Men and women left the plant in single file in separate lanes. Plant security guards looked over

everyone and sent approximately every sixth man or woman to a little room to be frisked. These sergeants were very thorough, but I am sure that still a lot was stolen.

And indeed it was. The company spent 300,000 ft for a theft detection system, which did little good, and sponsored a show trial of two men caught stealing equipment, which wholly backfired. "The experts who were called in testified that the goods stolen were rejects, and all the way down the line, everyone tried to help these two. The whole plant refused to condemn them and in the end they got off quite easily." One other factor encouraged persistent theft: "the fact that the first-class products... disappeared into exports." Regulations reserved second-class goods for state agencies, so that individuals could purchase only third-grade and faulty items. Hence "it was inevitable that a thriving black market operated, in the cafés and taverns in the vicinity of the plant, in first-class tubes. Prices there were about half of official prices for third-class merchandise."[100] Electrical factories used scarce copper; workers routinely stole bits of it for sale to small shops or repairmen. Thus, as in Izzó, during shift changes at Budapest's former Siemens plant, security agents randomly selected workers who were "stopped and carefully searched, even to the extent of having to undress completely." Still, "despite rigid controls, workers succeed in stealing small amounts of copper by hiding them in hand packages, which [we]re not subject to control."[101]

Small tools reserved for enterprises were likewise difficult for households or workshops to acquire lawfully. Many buyers sought such goods, once liberated from factories, like files for shaping wood or metal. One employee's pilferage

method was to tie a file to his leg. Workers were usually searched for stolen goods at the gate of the plant. However, the guards had no time to feel for anything hidden in the lower part of a person's trousers. [One day, though] as he passed the guards, a file accidentally dropped from his trousers and the string... did not break, so the file was dragged along on the ground behind him. The noise of the file caught the attention of the guards and one of them started walking after the worker. At that very moment, several workers surrounded the man with the file, so as to hide him from the eyes of the guards and other workers stopped near the guards and asked them to look in the other direction and ignore the incident. The guards understood... and cooperated.[102]

The purchasers of stolen industrial goods were artisans whose access to materials and parts was hindered by low priorities or completely blocked by regulations (as with copper). Still, as handicraft co-op members or as independent Maszek entrepreneurs, they met needs invisible to planners yet often urgent for citizens.

Craftwork co-ops [KTSZs], promoted diligently by the Rákosi administration, increased from below 400 in 1949 to nearly 1750 by 1952, declining to about 1400 due to mergers (1956). Membership swelled from 11,000 to 144,000 across that span. The state's goal was to induce economies of scale in KTSZ workshops employing 100+ persons and producing "consumers' articles in small series" (batches). This did not go well, "as a result of the regulations on the supply of materials." Lacking inputs, workshops sought subcontracting orders "on behalf of large state enterprises," firms that could provide raw materials directly. Such arrangements "became rather widespread"; it was foolish to try making consumer items on one's own—clothing, housewares, leather goods—without assured input flows.[103] Thus, KTSZs routinely helped big industrial firms meet plan targets, especially by fabricating needed components on time, instead of providing goods and services for workers and farmers.

Persuasion, propaganda, coercion, and state regulations, combined in various proportions, pressed craftworkers and small manufactories to associate with KTSZs. A machinist recalled:

Between 1945 and 1949, I worked as a self-employed electric technician, fixing radios, electrical switches and controls, rewiring electric motors, etc. By 1949, the government had raised raw material prices so high that I could not afford to buy them, nor could I afford to pay the taxes, which were increased to a prohibitive level. As it happened, no self-employed person was prohibited from staying in business for himself, but economically he was forced out in the end. In 1949, I took a job as a tool-constructor and tool designer in an agricultural machinery plant.[104]

During these years, the proprietor of a small shop making cardboard boxes for the state tobacco enterprise (and for retailers) sought to evade state control. When all firms having 20 or more employees fell under regulation, he kept 19 on the job and sent orders out to the others, who worked from home. After nationalizing larger box-makers (1948), officials required that the Tobacco Monopoly cease purchasing cartons from this Maszek shop, terminating his best account. The next year, finance officers rejected the firm's tax returns, then tripled the sum due. Seeing no path forward, in January 1950, he requested his company be nationalized. The ministry "refused this and assured me that the State is in need of such qualified craftsmen as I was and I should not have any more fears about the survival of my business." This was pure dissimulation; within weeks auditors arrived to pore over his books; police soon accused him of black market dealings. Finally, "two men appeared in my office and requested me to leave everything there, immediately. In this simple way, I lost everything." As an unemployable class enemy, this factory owner began outwork knitting on a hand-powered machine, making export goods for Budapest's main wool products plant.[105] Neither the electrician nor the box-maker entered a co-op, though they did remain economic actors in unanticipated ways.

A cabinet maker in Nograd County, just north of the capital, did join a KTSZ and contributed a vivid commentary on its operations. He traveled a route similar to those above, experiencing serial tax hikes and suffocating rules, until a 1951 Party secretary summoned his village's "independent tradesmen" to a town hall meeting. No more would their capitalistic behavior be acceptable; production cooperatives were coming and protesting "orders from Budapest" would not be tolerated.

> This... meant that I had to give in all of my tools and equipment, all my capital, but I did not become the owner of the cooperative. I had to work there with my own tools, but the money we [made] went to the state. It was simple robbery – a robbery from the small people... All I had was a very small shop which I had built up... and I had started out as a real proletarian.

The new enterprise commenced as a "mixed co-op," including building workers, mechanics, "and even barbers." Four reorganizations followed in six years. By 1956, of the 30 area bricklayers, carpenters and joiners drafted into the first KTSZ, only six remained. "Many people left the cooperative because they got fed up. They went to Budapest and took jobs there with the different factories." KTSZ leaders also awarded memberships to new people without apprenticeships or training, following a few weeks work in construction—a terrible practice.[106]

Management "was even more confused and changed just as often." After the last restructuring, the carpentry group got a carpenter as its chief. "He was a likeable person, too"; but as he wasn't a manager, screwups followed. "In a cooperative it was necessary to keep books; and the orders coming from Budapest prescribed what kind of books should be kept. He did not know anything about bookkeeping. Then one day a commission appeared at our premises and wanted to see the books. There were no books and he was accused of sabotage." Arrest and a trial ensued, and though the poor man was eventually amnestied, his reputation was ruined. No replacement manager arrived; "anarchy" reigned at the coop—"everybody did as he liked." Eventually the local council compelled the group to hire a bookkeeper to deal with paperwork; but actually, "we had many bookkeepers, since few of them lasted for any length of time." Naturally, with fragmentary records, payments to artisan members were small and spotty, a few hundred forints every now and then. Little wonder that members took on "black work" directly from local households and businesses, performing it on weekends and, especially for indoor jobs, in the winter.

> Then, finally, Imre Nagy came and he issued a new order concerning the productive cooperatives. [E]very member should get a monthly salary and at the end of the year if any profit is left, the profit should be distributed among the members. From this time on, we got a regular salary in the same way as the other workers got it. At the beginning it was 600 ft/month, but later it was increased several times. In 1956, I was getting 1100 ft.[107]

Such improvements paled vis-a-vis the perennial problem of getting materials for contract jobs. First, triplicate forms had to be filled out for every item needed.

> It was sheer nonsense what happened then. The requisition forms were sent down to the lumber yard. Then for a long time we did not get any material. Finally, when we received it, it was the wrong type. If I asked for two-inch boards, I certainly received one-inch boards, and so on. It was an everyday occurrence that we started a job on a Monday or Tuesday afternoon [and] we had to break it off because we had no raw materials. Then a week later, we received the lumber, so we could work for a few days again. Then we had to stop and take up another job or be idle for a few days because the lumber was not delivered again.

Bad supply practices had real consequences. When building a warehouse for the state railway, the co-op requested the "four-inch" roofing beams specified in the blueprints, but the state lumberyard sent two-inch beams instead. "So we [carpenters] used the poor ones. After our job, the roofers came and put the tiles on. The building was hardly finished when one of the beams broke and the roof collapsed. This is how the cooperative did its job."[108]

Maszek firms, banned or operating underground from 1949 to 1953, represented independent businesses of the smallest sort—sole proprietorships or firms with very few workers (depending on shifting regulations). An engineer dismissed from a Budapest communications job in 1948 took up illegal subcontracting, building small transformers for a state electrical enterprise focused on other, more important products.

> Most of the raw materials were provided by the firm ordering the transformers. All [other] material was obtainable on the black market, and usually at prices below the official ones. This was due to the fact that the black marketeers would purchase the material from workers who had stolen it from the factories, or still had an old stock.... It was imperative that I deliver all transformers ordered from me on time. This was possible only by purchasing... on the black market.

When submitting bills, he had to provide a certificate that taxes had been paid on prior contracts, but having no permit, this was impossible. So he submitted a document showing taxes paid, which cooperative plant officials accepted, even though the those taxes "were levied on my house." Dodging employment regulations and remaining invisible as an enterprise was handled through outwork relationships. "I had my workshop in my own yard. The individual parts of the transformers were prepared for me by skilled workers, whom I paid 12 to 16 forints per hour [more than double factory rates]. I myself only combined these parts in the last stage. I handed out work to evade conspicuousness, so that even my closest neighbors knew nothing about my activities."[109]

Several years later, an engineer at a Budapest laboratory instrument plant reported severe product quality deficiencies, which nicely facilitated illegal entrepreneurship on his part. "The factory manufactured an electronic machine measuring so-called pH concentrations... by the thousands. But they were all out of order and the indicators were going wild, even without a chemical reaction." Management shelved for a few weeks any devices sent back for recalibration, then returned them "with a 1000 ft bill for repair services, yet in the very same condition." Recognizing what needed to be fixed, the engineer cuts a deal with university officials to become a "special consultant" and commenced rebuilding the meters. "The university could make out a bill, while a private person couldn't. [He] went to the university laboratory, fixed the meters, and charged whatever he thought was a fair price. The university added their overhead, approximately 20 to 30%, the the meter was repaired in a week. He charged about 400 ft per machine and cleared 1000 ft per month," until the 1956 revolt upended a useful, if flagrantly unlawful collusion that well served firms trying to determine pH accurately.[110]

An electrical contractor, forced out of business in 1952 by high and rising taxes, returned to Maszek activity two years later when the Nagy cabinet lowered the legal barriers.

> [I] received my raw material from the state. For one month's work, I got one-half a kilo of copper, which was insufficient to do the necessary electrical jobs. I did not want to use any stolen raw material because of the great risk involved. I had at that time some hidden raw material from my old business. So I sold it. Even in this case I had to make out false bills to the customers... then I ran out of raw material and it was impossible to carry out business... The policy of the government was to ruin the independent business man through indirect ways.

After nine months, he turned in his license and reapplied to his former workplace, which welcomed him. Yet while in business, his qualms about theft did not extend to tools. "It is true that stealing went on on a large scale. For example, I could not get a certain type of drills. I rang up one of my former workers who was now working in a factory and told him to get me one of those drills. When I met him, he gave me a pack full of drills in the value of at least 600 forints. As he explained: 'I ruin the factory rather than support this system.'"[111] The ironies here were dual: first, that violations of socialist order proved essential to filling economic gaps initiated by those who created and defended that order, and second, that workers' rejection of the socialist project was likewise essential to providing the materials and tools needed for gap-filling.

Another substantial error was the perennial neglect of repair and maintenance (R&M), distributed across agriculture, industry, construction, and transportation. Scattered across this and prior chapters, accounts of shoddy maintenance, deferred or inept repairs, and their effects have repeatedly surfaced. Frequently concerning machinery failures and scarce

258   P. SCRANTON

or unobtainable spare parts, these deficiencies also extended to buildings crumbling through maintenance defaults, orchards or vineyards ruined through inattention to pruning, and water or electrical system breakdowns. As well, repair services for individuals were elusive. In 1955, a *New York Times* correspondent noted:

> One... difficulty [is] getting anything repaired. The Government has tried to meet this need by allowing individual artisans and small shops to resume their activities, but they operate under difficulties and a cloud of suspicion. Because of the haste with which builders try to "fulfill their plans," the need of repairs is constant. In a newly-built hotel in the steel town of Stalinvaros, the tap came off in my hands when I washed.[112]

Differential emphases on repair and maintenance may be detected along three lines, however, in: (1) sectors where failure would cripple operations and thus where R&M had a high priority; (2) sectors where neglect would reduce but not wreck performance, leading to repeated calls for better practices; and (3) areas in which state actors were indifferent to the costs of deferral, which lay outside their accounts and responsibilities. This last cluster included R&M for private homes and farmsteads, for personal possessions (appliances to shoes), and for bodies' everyday needs (hairdressers, barbers, razor blades, soap). Hence illegal entrepreneurs, "black" workers, and Maszek firms delivered such goods and services while Party theorists grumbled about capitalist residues. As for the second group, throughout manufacturing, skimping on R&M hampered production and reduced quality, drawing attention once the cumulative consequences of meeting targets while ignoring overhauls inhibited reaching quotas and landing bonuses. In agriculture, comparable faulty practices affected not only farm machinery reliability at MTSs but also TSZ and state farm crop yields when workers applied fertilizers irregularly or skipped weeding common fields altogether. In this section, however, attention will be paid solely to the first category, in part because this study has neglected those domains where R&M could *not* be neglected, namely electric power and transportation.

The Ministry of Heavy Industry was initially charged with managing electricity production and distribution through the Electric Power Trust, which experienced four reorganizations between 1949 and 1955. One constant amid these shifts was detailed managerial planning by plants supplying the nation's three grids, each of which annually "submitted their routine inspection, repair, innovation, and maintenance needs for the following year." Trust staff collated these statements, eliminated duplications, and adjusted the "expenses for repair, service and maintenance" in relation "to the value of equipment (which was not to exceed 15–20% of value)." Once allocations arrived, the contradiction between plan and performance sharpened, as each power plant manager now had to focus on meeting output expectations.

> The plant manager's chief difficulty was lack of money, workers, and materials ([only] 50 percent of the needed spare or component parts were available)... He never paid attention to the amount the Ministry allotted for each item, but left it to his bookkeeper to "cover up" by juggling the figures to show the prescribed inspection [and] repairs for the book auditor from the Ministry... The planned production had to be fulfilled no matter how much the inspection, repair and service, or improvement and development suffered.

The Electric Power Trust always reduced plant-level requests for "repairs and improvements," even when urgent. Managers responded to inadequate funding by, for example, "not changing oil in the transformers and turbogenerators as prescribed," then running them below capacity so as to keep temperatures down. They also installed calorimeters in the boiler system "to save coal" and lower expenses. Inspection of the forty different pump models plants relied upon was complex and hampered by parts problems. "Shortages such as these were the reason why all inspectors, no matter how skilled, shied away from investigating the correct use of appropriations, [so long as] the plant was running smoothly."[113]

Boilers were the heart of the system, the plant's "most sensitive equipment"; their maintenance called for a 42-man team, which collaborated with management to systematically defraud the Power Trust. Regulations officially allotted eight weeks for overhauling each boiler,

> [but a] special boiler crew geared for the highest efficiency could service a boiler in four weeks. The saving in money, which was kept secret, was divided among the boiler service crew and the plant management. The reason [they] kept the time and money savings secret was because previously a few persons who had invented time-saving procedures had received only a small token award, while the savings actually amounted to many thousands of forints. Most of the time was saved by the plant chemical

260   P. SCRANTON

engineer who used an unidentified formula which dissolved boiler water residue [scale].

Material incentives delivered efficiencies and innovations, hidden so that their benefits could be directly, if criminally, enjoyed by all, rather than being captured by the state for a "token" payment. Management ignored maintenance for equipment other than boilers. Engineering log entries falsely confirmed "service accomplished" on transformers and turbines; "the money allotted for their service was drawn from the bank" by financial officers, then "used to carry out necessary repairs" detailed in the original budget, but "disallowed" by the Trust. Breakdowns did occur, "traced to the lack of maintenance." Thus engineers shunned "positions of responsibility for fear of severe reprisals." In practice, year after year, "it was practically impossible under a given budget to fulfill the production norms unless one circumvented the prescribed rules and regulations."[114] A related problem undermining effective power production was the poor quality of Hungarian soft coals "of very low caloric value" which also had to be "transported over long distances," incurring expense and exposed to delays.[115]

Budapest was one district in which major machinery repairs were well-organized, if not always well-executed, as the Ministry of Heavy Industry sponsored a center for overhauling gasoline and diesel motors, steam engines and "machines driven by such motors," as well as repairing and building electrical generators. The plant also had " a shop with different kinds of lathes" for parts making. Even after Stalin's death, management had kept "unreliables" in manual labor slots; but this changed by 1955, when "a few so-called reactionary anti-people men" were promoted to leadership posts.

That last year, 1956, we were able to meet the production norm and everyone was able to receive a few hundred more forints in premiums. [However,] the quality of work was poor. Motors for flour mills were repaired but very quickly they were returned for repair again because they did not hold up. Many of them were returned within a week but stood in our plants for numerous weeks... Our planing machine and so-called milling machines were 15 to 40 years old in the shop. These machines could not do a good job. Furthermore we did not have materials with which to do a good job. The steel was not of quality.[116]

Thus the talents of reactionaries, adequate for meeting targets and nailing down bonuses, could not overcome the long-term failure to replace obsolete tools, which, combined with using second-rate materials, yielded shoddy repair of factory power units, thereby undermining other enterprises' production programs. The propagation of error persisted.

Hungary did build sturdy trucks; keeping them on the road was the job of vehicle repair centers, the largest of which (800 workers) was of course located in the capital. Like the electric power system, Central Truck Repair, supervised by the Ministry of Transport, also experienced multiple reorganizations, three in the four years after 1948. First, the ministry transferred bodywork to another firm, so Central could focus on engines. Then planners added several small parts makers, but later again separated parts-making from repairs after the Cinkota vehicle components plant opened (ca. 1952) in the eastern suburbs.

> This [factory] was the prototype of incompetence and inefficiency. It was supposed to render car parts imports from the West superfluous. [But] its machines existed mainly on paper, hence it was reduced to craft methods, it was hardly mechanized at all. It had no costing system; the authorities said let it just start producing. As a result it began to incur frightful deficits. Its management was changed four times, but to no avail.

Matters were little better at Central Repair, as the shortcomings of Party men in leadership positions could not be remedied; the Party secretary protected them resolutely. Worker morale collapsed as ministerial decrees increased output norms annually, once by 18%, flattening earnings. Higher-ups "never admitted that the revision of norms was a way of reducing wages. It was contended to be a way of increasing labor productivity... The workers themselves cursed about it terribly."[117] At vehicle repairs' Sopron branch (Györ), parts were rarely accessible.

> We repaired government vehicles, buses, trucks, cabs, but there was never any material for repair. We used second-hand parts and always patched up the old equipment. We called it the abuse of technology; often we were out of screws and we were [just] told: "The problem can and must be solved." All the [shop] equipment was outdated and old; it was taken away from former Maszek garages and repair shops. We had no new equipment at all... If one complained, one was either told that there was no allocation for this improvement or that it was planned and budgeted for [the future].[118]

262   P. SCRANTON

With the 1953 Nagy openings, Maszek vehicle repair shops revived and thrived; a senior economist at the National Bank was observant. Unlike most citizens, top-level state managers had access to passenger cars, as did soccer, theater, and film stars. Western brands were much sought after but when repairs proved necessary, state agencies were supposed to take charge of the jobs, unfortunately. By 1956, they simply could not compete with Maszek entrepreneurs,

> even in prices, because the private sector could cheat on taxes, had less overhead and was more flexible with time. At the nationalized factories, the repair of a car took weeks, partly due to a lack of parts. The private sector auto mechanics, on the other hand, smuggled spare parts from Vienna. Their earnings were very high. Just to give you an example, I earned 3000 ft/month, the president of the bank had 5,000, a minister had about 5,000, whereas a private sector auto mechanic... could earn 10–20-30 thousand ft a month. [First Deputy Minister of Finance Janos] Vörös said to me: "I don't mind if they earn twice as much as a minister, but when I discover that they earn four times as much, then something is wrong."[119]

Yes indeed, something was wrong with Hungary's industrialization, top to bottom, start to finish, actually many, many things.

CONCLUSION

Even if a Maszek auto mechanic earning 30,000 ft a month was an urban legend, that a First Deputy Minister entertained it exemplifies how out of kilter Hungary's industrial practices had become. Factory workers continued to scrape by on 1100 ft pay packets that just covered food, rent, and transit, but not clothing, household goods, or repairs. The theft economy's planners undercompensated them for building industrial socialism; and they responded by stealing and cheating when possible or with indifferent efforts on the job when not. Creative manipulation of plan regulations—gaming the system through plan fraud—became a key means to augment earnings, and could even engender opportunistic solidarity between managers, engineers, and workers, as just noted at electrical power plants. Widespread integration of bonus pay into employees' expectations lies at the foundation of what, at this chapter's outset, István Rácz termed "a gigantic conspiracy, where the workers produced a great amount of low-rate or worthless goods, the inspectors put their stamps of approval on them, and the commercial establishments accepted and passed them on to the consumer."[120] In steel, textiles, and elsewhere, plant directors' inability to compel suppliers to observe specifications and delivery deadlines yielded both unanticipated shutdowns and deficiencies in product quality. Delays disrupted production schedules, whereas poor quality materials and components percolated dismally through downstream manufacturing stages, wrecking export contracts through returned shipments and revenue losses. Soviet supplies, demands, and oversight exacerbated anti-USSR sentiments at all levels, provoked by domineering management practices, predatory pricing, deliveries of shoddy materials, appropriation of first-quality goods in multiple trades, and arbitrary rejections of exported products deemed substandard.

Unquestionably, Hungary's heavy industrial enterprises turned out generally-serviceable bridge trusses, machinery, and vehicles, though DDR purchasers did complain repeatedly about trucks idled "because of lacking spare parts," and buses needing major overhauls after three months service.[121] Consumers could rely on goods such as housewares and processed foods as sturdy or safe, if often in short supply, but had only contempt for state-produced clothing or shoes that cost too much and wore out too quickly. Upper-income cadres happily sustained the livelihoods of custom shoemakers, tailors, and women's wear designers (capitalist residues), while workers made do with replacing a couple of work shirts each year or found at a commission store a US-donated men's suit a dressmaker could transform into a women's suit for office wear.[122]

Among enterprise directors and their clients, industrialization's core defect after a decade of socialist construction was the persistence of omni-directional uncertainty. Capitalist production depends profoundly on reliable relations of contract, trust, or reciprocity to carry forward projects and reduce free-floating uncertainty to calculable (and insurable) risk. Material incentives and the prospect of sanctions intersect with settled interpersonal and interfirm relationships to assure performance, if not profit.[123] These recursive practices rarely proved feasible during the socialist development of industrial Hungary. Instead, disruptions, defaults, and defections erupted repeatedly, upending shopfloor routines and undermining plan targets—political interference, forced dismissals and/or arrests, Soviet interventions, production suspensions due to machine breakdown, late supply deliveries, no coal or no power, accidents stemming from sloppy maintenance or staff indifference, refusals and returns of goods shipped, unexpected design or contract changes, plus workforce absenteeism, incompetence, or sabotage.

This industrial melee, initially managed by politically-reliable Party members with few technical or organizational credentials, fostered enterprise environments in which engineers and skilled workers sought to avoid responsibility for outcomes and to avoid promotion. Better to lurk in the shadows, try to protect one's position, and perhaps work to create evidence documenting plan fulfillment, thereby deflecting ministerial investigations. Industrial capitalism took shape through iteration and indirection, through learning by failing, through both contests and alliances with state actors and agencies—step-wise approximations that may represent the broadest articulation of "strategy without design." By contrast, Hungary's drive toward socialist industrialization had, if anything, *an excess of designs and designers and a surfeit of strategies and strategists.* Alongside programs from ministries and planners, countless unauthorized individuals and enterprises introduced competing designs and strategies, few of which served socialist goals—tricks to boost outputs and reap bonuses, materials substitutions to complete products despite shortages, process improvisations to speed output (whatever the quality) or alternatively, sloppy work to hike the rejects level, opportunistic schemes to deceive ministries, directors, pay clerks or foremen, blame-shifting and responsibility dodging, diverse tactics for theft, fraud, embezzlement and illicit entrepreneurship, hiring "reactionaries," or even sabotaging export goods so they might be distributed domestically. In a profound contradiction, those in command of the nation could not control situated practices and local rejections (a failure repeatedly ignored or denied); force and fear proved insufficient for creating widespread commitments to a socialist future, indeed were destructive to any such project. Perhaps because socialist practice had to be *built*, and built in a Cold War hurry under Soviet tutelage, rather than promoted recursively through incentives, education and experiment, Hungary's grand construction project stalled and stumbled, until in Fall 1956, it shattered.

This declension was widely recognized, inside the regime, by dissidents, and in the West. Late in 1954, Zoltán Vas, the veteran Communist politician and head of the Council of Ministers Secretariat under Nagy, bluntly criticized the heavy industry surge: "The Second Congress of the Hungarian Workers Party in 1951 made a grave mistake in resolving to make Hungary 'a country of iron and steel'... Excessive industrialization required us to forego more food and clothing, and most important of all, the expansion of agricultural production." Rejecting his analysis, the re-ascendant Rákosi team soon demoted him to a peripheral job.[124] A trade analyst affirmed in 1956 that Hungarian manufacturing costs were so high that exports had become increasingly uncompetitive. In addition,

> as regards the quality of the output, Hungarian industry is unable to compete not only because of negligence [in production] but also certainly because of worker sabotage. The Egeysült Izzó factory in Budapest sent a shipment of bulbs to Romania, but the Romanians returned the whole delivery because the bulbs lacked filaments. Some months ago Hungary sold a delivery of men's shirts to Belgium. These were returned too, as the factory had fastened the shirts with rusty pins so that [they] had rust stains on them. They sent another delivery... in which shirts of size 42 had been equipped with size 38 collars and vice versa.[125]

All the while, U.S. analysts had been sifting information suggesting that, by November 1954, "high-level dissension has developed within the Party," while "popular apathy has grown and overt resentment has increased."[126] Resistance was "unorganized, passive. Takes [the] form of non-cooperation – absenteeism, shoddy workmanship, withdrawal from collectives, resistance to quotas, etc."[127] A more extended review concluded: "Hungary is almost certainly the most troubled of all the European states subject to the USSR. Its population is overwhelmingly hostile to the Communist government, and is apathetic and uncooperative toward the economic program." In manufacturing, generalized resentment surfaced as "deliberate misunderstanding of instructions, low quality production, high damage and reject rates, and other kinds of subtle sabotage." Meanwhile black market traders "obtain much of their merchandise as a result of widespread pilfering by workers." At last, the snare crushed the delusion:

> Over the long term Hungary's basic economic problem is that of maintaining its industrial plant [while] importing a large part of the raw materials essential to the operation of that plant. These imports can be paid for by proceeds from the export of an agricultural surplus or, alternatively, but less probably manufactured products... [However,] prospects are poor for achieving a significant surplus under Communist agrarian policy.[128]

Rapid industrialization had plunged Hungarian manufacturing into cycles of overinvestment and underperformance with little potential for

266   P. SCRANTON

a growth breakout, even as the costs of keeping this badly-designed establishment running could not be covered by exporting its low-quality products. State subsidies might keep the machinery going; but the whole project resembled planned industrial socialism only in form, not in practice. How could anything but more trouble lie ahead?

NOTES

1. CURPH Interview No. 152, 18, HU OSA 414-1-2-168. Mr. Rácz was a Smallholders Party representative in the postwar Parliament, then a forced laborer (1950–1953), before working in manufacturing after his release.
2. G.F. Ray, "Industrial Planning in Hungary," *Scottish Journal of Political Economy* 7:1(1960): 134–46, quote at 141.
3. CURPH Interview No. 442, 56, 120, HU OSA 414-1-2-263.
4. CIA, Information Report, "Estimated Coal Consumption of Hungarian Industries for 1949," 29 June 1949 (Secret, CIA-RDP82-00457R002900140012-6). (Hereafter CIAIR).
5. Béla Balassa, *The Hungarian Experience in Economic Planning*, New Haven: Yale University Press, 1959, 27–35. As noted earlier, after postwar rebuilding, housing was not a high priority; and while providing loans, the state left much of this work to private enterprises.
6. CIAIR, "Soviet Economic Enterprises in Hungary," 27 May 1955 (Secret, CIA-RDP82-00046R000500150009-1).
7. Ian Jackson, *The Economic Cold War: America, Britain and East–West Trade, 1948–63*, New York: Palgrave Macmillan, 2001.
8. CURPH Interview No. 202b, 17–19, HU OSA 414-0-2-179. The Soviets, for example, were not generous in offering non-ferrous and alloy metals to Hungary.
9. Ministries did create special plants for spare parts production for vehicles and agricultural machinery, but the diversity of models and profusion of parts, along with inadequate assessment of what items failed most often, limited their usefulness. In addition, both parts plants and repair centers reportedly sought unauthorized subcontracts to manufacture goods demand for which had overtaxed factories charged with producing them. Such jobs were more profitable than making parts, payment for which was determined by the frozen rates of the 1948 price manuals.

10. CIAIR, "Hungarian Heavy Industry," 30 December 1949 (Secret, CIA-RDP83-00415R003300080008-8); Weiss evidently did not have blast furnaces, but re-melted billets received from domestic mills or imported.

11. CIA, Office of Research and Reports, *The European Satellite Power Complex, Hungary*, 30 July 1951, 43 (Top Secret, CIA-RDP79R01012A000900050001-5).

12. Ibid., 46.

13. CIAIR, "The MAVAG Metallurgical Works near Miskolc," 8 January 1954, 3–4 (Confidential, CIA-RDP82-00046R000300150009-3).

14. CIAIR, "Steel Production in Hungary," 26 January 1953 (Secret, CIA-RDP82-00457R015900060009-5); and CIAIR, "Steel Production in Hungary," 14 July 1953 (Secret, CIA-RDP80-0810A001600790001-7).

15. RFEFR, "Accident in Diósgyőr Steelworks," 1 September 1951, HU OSA 300-1-2-5855.

16. CIA, Information from Foreign Documents, "Metallurgical Workers Fail to Fulfill Pledges," *Szabad Nép*, 14 August 1952 (Restricted, CIA-RPD80-00809A00070010368-1) (Hereafter CIAIFD).

17. CIAIR, "Iron and Steel Production in Hungary," 26 October 1950 (Confidential, CIA-RDP82-00457R006100180009-0). The text suggests that rolling mills were the main source of internal scrap.

18. See Carl Zimring, *Cash for Your Trash: Scrap Recycling in America*, New Brunswick, NJ: Rutgers University Press, 2005.

19. CIAIFD, "Scrap Drive Successful," *Szabad Nép*, 7 April 1949 (Restricted, CIA-RDP80-00809A000600220862-1).

20. CIAIFD, "Decree Scrap Metal Collection Week," *Szabad Nép*, 12 May 1951 (Confidential, CIA-RDP80-00809A000600400525-4).

21. CIA Provisional Intelligence Report, "Supplies of Iron and Steel Scrap in the Soviet Bloc," 10 December 1952 (Confidential, CIA-RDP79-01093A000300030003-0); CIAIFD, "Hungarian Council of Ministers Issues Resolution," 31 December 1950, 5 (Confidential, CIA-RDP80-00809A000600370905-6).

22. RFEFR, "Scrap," 19 March 1952, HU OSA 300-1-2-17148.

23. NB: 100 fillers = 1 forint; 11.5 forints = US$1.00 (official rate). At this conversion, about one US cent was paid for one kg of iron vs. 40–50 cents per kg of copper or brass, which helps explain the theft of brass items.

24. CURPH Interview No. 151, 52–53, HU OSA 414-0-2-167. Young Pioneers was a school-based organization aiming at cultivating socialist values at all grade levels; its leaders surely scorned the capitalist cupidity on display here.

25. Ibid., 53–54. Through 1956, following the 1953 construction halt, Sztálinváros did not contribute significantly to national steel production (See CIAIR, "Work at Sztálinváros," 10 May 1954 [Secret, CIA-RDP81-01036R000200050065-7]).

26. RFEFR, "State Enterprise MEH," 28 October 1952, HU OSA 300-1-2-27140.

27. CIAIR, "MEH Scrap Collecting Enterprise, Debrecen," 29 March 1954 (Secret, CIA-RDP80-00810A003801070011-0). 60 hundredweights = 6 tons.

28. RFEFR, "Shortage of Iron and Metal Scrap in the Factories," 25 March 1955, 2, HU OSA 300-1-2-56594.

29. CIAIR, "MAVAG Metallurgical Works," 4. For background on the shortcomings of Hungary's ceramics industry, see CIAIR, "Technical and Economic Report Regarding the Ceramics and Refractory Industries," 16 February 1953, 1–6 (Confidential, CIA-RDP82-00047R000200470003-4), which stresses that "inferior clays" and inadequate power supplies yielded unreliable products (3).

30. CIAIFD, "Conference Reveals Problems in Hungarian Metallurgical Industry," *Szabad Nép*, 16 October 1951 (CIA-RDP80-00809A000700040001-4).

31. CIAIFD, "Blames Management, Party for Production Lags," *Szabad Nép*, 4 November 1951 (CIA-RDP80-00809A000700040123-9).

32. CIAIFD, "Metallurgical Workers," 14 August, 1952.

33. CIAIFD, "Conference." Ingot molds receive liquid iron from blast furnace ladle pours; billets are iron blocks extracted from molds once they cool. Molds are usually prepped with a refractory or graphite coating to prevent adhesion of the billet, but in molds that have scars or cracks on interior surfaces, they may fail

to loosen when opened, demanding time to separate the billet and the mold sections.

34. CIAIR, "MAVAG Metallurgical Works," 2, 5.
35. "Engineering industry" is a European term for what in the US is called metalworking.
36. CIAIFD, János Sebestyén, "Hungarian Heavy Industry in the Three-Year Plan," *Gep* [Machine], February 1949 (Restricted, CIA-RDP80-00809A000700030328-8). In basic steel, adding more open hearths is useless unless blast furnace pig iron capacity increases proportionately, which cannot happen unless ore processing and preparation facilities also are augmented, which by turn necessitates extension of materials handling operations. Putting lathes in a shed depends on having power sources and an appropriate workforce, but is otherwise a simpler task.
37. RFEFR, "Raw Materials Lack Forces Steel Mills to Salvage Iron from Slag Heaps," 14 May 1954, HU OSA 300-1-2-46048.
38. CIAIR, "The Rationalization of the Soviet Bloc Iron and Steel Industry," 18 July 1955, 1–2 (Secret, CIA-RDP80-00810A007400370003-0). The Soviet Institute also was concerned with steel production planning.
39. Ibid., 3.
40. CIAIR, "Hungarian Heavy Industry," 2–4. NIK also oversaw ten steel-using fabricators creating machinery, machine tools, and equipment.
41. CIAIR, "Mechanical Engineering," 14 October 1954 (Secret, CIA-RDP80-00810A005000670007-9).
42. CIA, "Data from the Work Plan of the Technical Department, Hungarian Heavy Industry Center, 1 May–31 December 1948," Table 3: Machine Tools in Use by Five Major Heavy Industry Enterprises, April 1948, 8–16, 27 February 1950 (Secret, CIA RDP80-00809A000600140038-5); and *NIK Statisztika*, June 1948, Heavy Industry Center, Budapest (Secret, CIA RDP80-00809A000600270638-3).
43. See CIAIR, "Shortage of Abrasives in Hungary," 20 January 1953 (Secret, CIA-RDP82-00475R016000210007-8); and CIA, Intelligence Memorandum No. 185, "The Abrasive Industry of Eastern Europe and the USSR," 17 June 1949 (Secret, CIA-RDP78-01617A000500260002-3).

44. In the Bloc, Czechoslovakia and the USSR had substantial reserves of abrasive materials, but these were not sufficient to meet their own needs and thus were not exported (CIA, "Abrasive Industry," 3).
45. CIAIR, "Hungarian Delivery of Locomotives as Reparations to the USSR," 13 July 1948 (Secret, CIA-RDP82-00457R001600800006-40.
46. RFEFR, "Production in the MAVAG Locomotive Factory," 30 August 1951, HU OSA 300-1-2-5655.
47. CIAIFD, Imre Erdős, "Manufacture of Electric Motors in Hungary," *Magyar Technika* (Hungarian Technology), August 1950 (Confidential, CIA-RDP80-00809A00060037027704); CIA, "The New Type Kando Electric Locomotive," 23 January 1951, (Secret, CIA-RDP83-00415R006300160003-1); Imre Jákli, "History of the Electric Locomotives in Hungary," http://www2.chem.elte.hu/gigant_club/mav/electric_story. html (accessed 2 June 2021); https://en.wikipedia.org/wiki/ MAV_Class_V40 (accessed 31 May 2021); and https://en. wikipedia.org/wiki/KálmánKandó (accessed 31 May 2021). For more on electrical outputs, see Gyorgy Fischer, "Results and Experience Gained During 1950 in Manufacture of Electric Motors," *Magyar Technika*, January 1951 (Confidential, CIA-RDP80-00809A000700040061-8).
48. CURPH Interview No. 20-M, 23, HU OSA 414-0-2014. Informant was a toolmaker and electrical maintenance worker at Ganz.
49. CURPH Interview No. 2-M, 22, HU OSA 414-0-2-24.
50. CIAIR, "The Ganz Works in the Hungarian Five-Year Plan," 28 August 1952 (Secret, CIA-RDP82-00457R013500320006-5).
51. Ibid.
52. CIAIR, "Economic Information on Hungary," 28 October 1952, 8 (Confidential, CIA-RDP80-00809A000600150056-3). SKF (*Svenska Kullagerfabriken*; 'Swedish Ball Bearing Factory') was Europe's most-accomplished bearing manufacturer (https://en.wikipedia.org/wiki/SKF, accessed 1 June 2021). For more on ball bearing issues, see RFEFR, "Two New Ball-Bearing Factories in Hungary," 13 May 1953, HU OSA 300-1-2-34533; CIAIR, "G. Lang Machine Works, Ltd.," 8 February 1954 (Secret, CIA-RDP80-00809A000600050238-3);

CIAIR, "Ball Bearing Factory, Debrecen," 31 March 1954 (Secret, Cia-RDP80-00810A003801140001-3); and CIAIR, "Red Star Tractor Works (Budapest)," 1954, 9 (Secret, CIA-RDP80S0154R005400010005-2).

53. CURPH Interview No. 29-M, 27, 31, 35, HU OSA 414-0-2-23. Confirmation of motor sabotage at Ganz may be found at RFEFR, "Conditions in the Shipbuilding Industry," 1 August 1951, HU OSA 300-1-2-3457.

54. CIAIFD, József Kárpáti, "Problems of the Hungarian Railroad Car Industry," *Gep* (Machine}, April 1953, 3 (Confidential, CIA-RDP80-00809A000700170367-5).

55. RFEFR, "Ganz Making Automotrices for Export," 27 March 1954, HU OSA 300-1-2-45043. See also RFEFR, "A Westerner Looks at the Inside of a Hungarian Factory," 1 December 1952, HU OSA 300-1-2-28265, and CIAIR, "Hungary: Cutting Tool Industry," 16 August 1954 (Secret, CIA-RDP80S0154R005900100002-0).

56. CIAIR, "Ganz Railway Car and Machine Shop, Budapest," 9 March 1954 (Secret, CIA-RDP80-00810A003601120006-2). Re: "bearing metal"—here too, the cutoff of imported bearings forced reliance on local products which failed to meet performance requirements.

57. The CIA report on the contract I judge to have been with Argentina has excised references to the receiving nation. However, online searches of Wikimedia Commons and Google Images show non-Bloc Ganz traincars only in Argentina, a prewar client. The report notes that "both countries' prosperity is based on agricultural economy." Hungary sought to "import wheat" in partial payment; and Argentina was (and remains) a major wheat exporter.

58. CIAIR, "Faulty Manufacture of Hungarian Diesel Trains," 19 November 1954 (Secret, CIA-RDP80-00810A005300780005-6).

59. Ibid.

60. Bogies or trucks are wheel and axle assemblies beneath railcars which guide them along the tracks.

61. CIAIR, "Export of Trains from Ganz Railcar Factory," 16 September 1955 (Secret, CIA-RDP80-00810A008000200002-2).

62. CIAIR, "The Ganz Railroad Works," 13 September 1955 (Secret, CIA-RDP80-00810A007900280003-5).
63. CIAIR, "Diósgyör Engineering Works (Dimavag)," 14 October 1954, 3 (Secret, CIA-RDP80-00810A005100010006-1).
64. CIAIR, "Red Star Tractor Works," 4; CIAIR, "G. Lang Machine Works, Ltd."
65. CURPH Interview No. 603, 13, 17, HU OSA 414-0-2-337.
66. CURPH Interview No. 242, 18–19, HU OAS 414-1-2-216.
67. https://www.thomasnet.com/articles/custom-manufacturing-fabricating/types-of-casting-defects-and-how-to-prevent-them/ (accessed 4 June 2021).
68. RFEFR, "Production Difficulties at Sopron Foundry," 15 April 1954, HU OSA 300-1-2-45670.
69. CURPH Interview No. 253, 3–4, HU OSA 414-0-2-226 (Emphasis added).
70. CIAIR, "Lang Machine Factory," 2 June 1953 (Secret, CIA-RDP80-00809A001300770008-5).
71. CURPH Interview No. 39-M, 36, HU OSA 414-0-2-34.
72. RFEFR, "Screw-up in a Screw Factory," 11 May 1954, HU OSA 300-1-2-44590. Feverish Munich and New York exile journalists labeled many a rail collision or boiler explosion as sabotage, but although the CIA dutifully recorded these assessments, analysts omitted them from summary reports as "unverified."
73. CIAIR, "Cutting Tool Factory Enterprise," 16 August 1954, 3 (Secret, CIA-RDP80S01540R005900100002-0).
74. CURPH Interview No. 551, 30–35, HU OSA 414-0-2-324.
75. CURPH Interview No. 154, 15–16, HU OSA 414-0-2-170.
76. RFEFR, "Conditions at the Budapest Siemens Electrical Equipment Factory," 12 May 1952, HU OSA 300-1-2-19752.
77. CURPH Interview No. 15-M, 27, HU OSA 414-0-2-8. For comparable deceptions in an agricultural machinery plant, see CURPH Interview No. 242, 49, HU OSA 414-0-2-216.
78. CUPRH 242, 21.
79. CURPH Interview No. 241, 11–12, HU OSA 414-0-2-215.
80. Ibid., 15.
81. CURPH Interview No. 458, 4–7, HU OSA 414-0-2-278.
82. CURPH Interview No. 564, 24, HU OSA 414-0-2-335.
83. CURPH 242, 3, 30.

84. RFEFR, "Budapest Lang Factory Confronted with Large Scale Thefts of Electric Bulbs," 29 January 1955, HU OSA 300-1-2-54203.
85. RFEFR, "Hungarian Industry Collapsing," 26 November 1954, HU OSA 300-1-2-52971. Despite the report's rhetoric, Hungarian industry was not collapsing, though it was far from thriving. The report's diagnosis of the planning failure, however, was on point.
86. Ivan Berend and György Ránki, *The Hungarian Economy in the Twentieth Century*, London: Croom Helm, 1985, 202–04.
87. CIAIR, "Living Conditions," 4 February 1953, 6 (Secret, CIA-RPD80-00809A000600030449-1).
88. CIAIFD, "Industrial Shortcomings in Hungary," 22 December 1950, 3–5 (Confidential, CIA-RDP80-00809A000600370853-4).
89. CURPH Interview No. 133, 28–29, HU OSA 414-0-2-160.
90. CIAIFD, Z. J. Altuhov, "Survey of Reserves, Weaknesses in Hungary's Textile Industry," *Magyar Technika*, June 1951 (Restricted, CIA-RDP80-00890A000700030402-0).
91. CIAIR, "The Grab Textile Works at Györ," 10 September 1952 (Secret, CIA-RDP82-00457R013600250003-5).
92. CURPH Interview No. 449, 8–10, HU OAS 414-0-2-270 (emphasis added). Problems with low-quality Soviet cotton were evident already in 1948 (CIAIR, "Soviet-Hungarian Cotton Negotiations," 28 June 1948 (Secret, CIA-RDP8200457R001600520004-7).
93. CURPH Interview No. 151, 138–39, HU OSA 414-0-2-167.
94. RFEFR, "The Sock in the Stocking," 2 June 1953, HU OSA 300-1-2-35139.
95. RFEFR, "Persecution of Hungarian Printers," 24 March 1952, HU OAS 300-1-2-17316.
96. CURPH Interview No. 80-F, 28–29, HU OSA 414-0-2-80.
97. CURPH Interview No. 59-M, 25, 29, HU OSA 414-0-2-56.
98. CURPH Interview No. 88-M, 4, 37, HU OSA 414-0-2-88.
99. CURPH Interview No. 515, 7, HU OSA 414-0-2-314; CURPH Interview No. 485, 4–5, HU OSA 414-0-2-296.
100. CURPH Interview No. 512, 13–14, HU OSA 414-020-311; https://en.wikipedia.org/wiki/Tungsram, accessed 14 June 2021.

101. RFEFR, "Conditions at the Budapest Siemens Electric Equipment Factory," 16 May 1952, 3, HU OSA 300-1-2-19752. Siemens arrived in Budapest in 1904; the USSR operated its plant for six years after 1945, until transferring to the Hungarian state in 1951 (Our history in Hungary—Digital Asset Management—Siemens, accessed 14 June 2021).
102. CURPH Interview No. 33-M, 32, HU OSA 414-0-2-28.
103. Rezső Nyers, *The Cooperative Movement in Hungary*, Budapest: Pannoia, 1963, 61–64.
104. CURPH 242, 17.
105. CURPH Interview No. 477, 3–10, HU OAS 414-0-2-290.
106. CURPH Interview No. 525, 21–23, HU OSA 414-0-2-319.
107. Ibid., 25–28.
108. Ibid., 29–30. Lumber dimensions are given in inches in the translated interview, but were surely reported in centimeters originally.
109. RFEFR, "Ways of Beating the Communist System," 5 August 1953, HU OSA 300-1-2-37578.
110. CURPH Interview No. 129, 17–18, HU OSA 414-1-2-156.
111. CURPH Interview No. 243, 45–48, HU OSA 414-0-2-217.
112. John MacCormac, "Once Gay Budapest Now Dull," *New York Times*, 6 November 1955, 27.
113. CIAIR, "Survey of the Hungarian Electric Power Industry," 1 May 1958, 19–20 (Confidential, CIA-RDP80T00246A042100120001-0). Information in this study covers the period from 1947 to early 1957.
114. Ibid., 22. See also RFEFR, "Power Production in Hungary," 14 May 1957, HU OSA 300-8-3-3239. Heavy industry consumed ca. 60% of all electrical power (RFEFR, 3). Station and transmission breakdowns numbered 1139 in 1953 and 571 in 1954 (4).
115. CIAIR, "Hungarian Power Developments," 13 October 1955, 2 (Confidential, CIA-RDP80-00926A007800740001-6).
116. CURPH Interview No. 420, 26–30, HU OSA 414-0-2-250.
117. CURPH Interview No. 452, 7–15, HU OSA 414-0-2-273.
118. CURPH Interview No. 233, 8, HU OSA 414-0-2-208.
119. CUPRH Interview No. 528, 14, HU OSA 414-0-2-322.
120. CURPH 152, 18.

121. RFEFR, "Trucks From Hungary," 8 October 1953, HU OSA 300-1-2-39652; RFEFR, "Hungarian Buses Constantly Breaking Down," 22 March 1956, HU OSA 300-1-2-70126.
122. RFEFR, "Effect of the New Course," 18 June 1954, 1–2, HU OSA 300-1-2-47627.
123. See Daniel H. G. Raff and Philip Scranton, eds., *The Emergence of Routines: Entrepreneurship, Organization and Business History*, New York: Oxford University Press, 2017.
124. CIAIFD, Zoltán Vas, "The New Economic Policy in Hungary," *Szabad Nép*, 27 October 1954 (Restricted, CIA-RDP80-00809A000700230069-9); "Hungary Reverts to Basic Industry," *New York Times*, 26 January 1955, 10.
125. RFEFR, "Hungary Reported on the Verge of Economic Collapse," 26 September 1956, HU OSA 300-1-2-75175.
126. CIA, Office of Current Intelligence, "Nature and Potential of the Opposition in Hungary," 5 November 1954, 1 (Secret, CIA-RDP80R01443R000300140021-2).
127. CIA NSC Briefing, "Current Situation in Hungary," 8 November 1954 (Secret, CIA-RDP80R01443R000300140022-1).
128. CIA, National Intelligence Estimate 12.5–55, "Current Situation and Probable Developments in Hungary," 29 March 1955, 2, 4, 6 (Secret, CIA-RDP79R01012A005400040004-6).

CHAPTER 7

The Revolt: Spontaneity, Repression, and Reaction

In October, I spent a few days of my vacation in Budapest. There nothing could be seen of the coming events, except I knew the university students will stage a demonstration. I left Budapest on October 20 and returned to my job in a factory at [Mosonmagyar]Óvár. There we learnt through the way of radios what happened in Budapest. Later on, cars arrived from different cities and people arrived and distributed pamphlets... Later on, Red Cross trucks came from Austria and Vienna. Then work stopped in the shop... not because of political demonstrations but because of lack of raw materials.
—Machinist, Györ county, 1957[1]

Nothing unusual happened even on October 23. Only on the morning of October 24, when I woke up in the workers' barracks and switched on the so-called Molotov Box [a central radio broadcast unit] did I hear the sound of gunfire over the radio. The radio also announced that counter-revolutionary bands had started a revolt in Budapest, but that the situation was under control... But we became suspicious when we noticed that the government kept prolonging the time limit for all insurgents to lay down their arms.
—Miner, in Pecs, Baranya county, 1957[2]

Ludas Matyi (front page cartoon, 27 October 1960): "Why doesn't Daddy get up ?" ask the children, while their peasant father sleeps peacefully. "He doesn't have to hurry. He works in the cooperative."

© The Author(s), under exclusive license to Springer Nature Switzerland AG 2022
P. Scranton, *Business Practice in Socialist Hungary, Volume 1*, Palgrave Debates in Business History,
https://doi.org/10.1007/978-3-030-89184-8_7

278   P. SCRANTON

Absences are frequent: "On such a lovely day one would expect all 137 members of the cooperative farm at Fony to be out in the fields," wrote *Észak-Magyarország* [Miskolc daily] on 1 November 1960. "But no. The majority of members are resting at home, pottering about in their vineyards, or out hunting for day jobs."
—RFE Evaluation and Analysis Department, 1961[3]

On 20 March 1957, CIA Director Allen Dulles alerted the Agency's Legislative Counsel that members of the US Congress might soon be asking "questions about our advance intelligence on the Hungarian rebellion." Within a week, researchers prepared a 40-page report, summarizing and quoting Agency Bulletins, press articles, and informants' comments from March to mid-November 1956, concluding that "all objective chronologies, analyses and eye-witness accounts… testify to its completely spontaneous nature." The revolt's "momentum and intensity… surprised not only Western observers but the Soviets and even the Hungarians themselves."[4] True enough, yet for months actors within and beyond Hungary had recognized emergent instabilities throughout the Bloc. After Nikita Khrushchev's February "secret speech" to the 20th Party Congress denouncing Stalin's crimes, resignations, and dismissals of hardliners accumulated and public disturbances mounted, notably in Soviet Georgia (pro-Stalin) and Poland (anti-). The Moscow revelations further split the Hungarian Party; meetings in ministries and factories alike featured "shouting and hysterical outbursts by disillusioned members who claimed to have been betrayed by the Party's teachings." "High-level factionalism" continued through the spring; then the Posznan riots in late June set the stage for unseating Warsaw's Stalinists, many of whom were pushed aside during an October confrontation with Moscow that paralleled (and encouraged) the Budapest protests.[5]

Initiatives among students and intellectuals supporting Polish resistance to Soviet dominion and calling for Rákosi's dismissal began by summer 1956, despite the state's palliative efforts: the release of prisoners, removal of barbed wire at the Austrian border, some price reductions, and pledges of greater investment in agriculture. The result: "Nothing Rákosi did or said seemed to have any effect." He resigned in July, replaced as First Party Secretary by long-term assistant Ernö Gerö, then retreated to the USSR as tensions mounted. On 14 October, Gerö traveled to Belgrade, ostensibly following up on improved relations between Tito and Khrushchev[6]; but Yugoslav analyst Vlajko Begović wrote from

7 THE REVOLT: SPONTANEITY, REPRESSION, AND REACTION   279

Budapest the same day: "People refuse to live in the old way. Conditions for an uprising have been created. Who will lead it when the working class is disoriented, [while] the Party lags behind events and has lost authority over the masses?" Two days later, Györ students tabled a demand that Soviet troops leave Hungary. As news of Poland's vigor percolated into university districts, support demonstrations materialized in Szeged, Debrecen, and Budapest, where mass meetings on 22 October generated assertive lists of issues needing swift attention.[7] Rákosi and his pals should be tried; Nagy must head the state; workers should have the right to strike; the economy ought be organized more fairly; closing internment and forced labor camps was imperative. Enthusiasm for Polish advances crystallized into agreement on a procession the next day to a statue honoring General József Bem, who had fought for both Polish and Hungarian independence over a century earlier.[8]

> The peaceful demonstration of students and workers at General Bem's statue in the afternoon... was followed by mass meetings in Stalin and Parliament Squares. The demands of the students, writers, and unions were read to cheering crowds. Waving Polish and Hungarian national flags, they roared: "Send the Red Army Home." "We want free and secret elections." And "Death to Rákosi." But at the same time they carried gigantic posters of Lenin.[9]

Just back from Belgrade, Gerö took to the radio to denounce the crowds as "nationalists" seeking to slash ties with "the glorious Communist Party of the Soviet Union." Within an hour, Stalin's statue toppled from its pedestal (Fig. 7.1), as another Yugoslav journalist looked on.

> This is an expression of bitterness, hysteria, and absolute hatred, so that any analysis would be a myth. Thousands of people are united in storming the high pedestal, and everybody is here along with his hatred. Some of them brought an acetylene torch in a truck and jets of blue and red fire are directed against Stalin's pants, into the pants of the man in bronze who is the personification of an era. However, he stands in Stalinist silence, dignified and even horrible while sparks are bursting at his chest and acetylene jets are flaming those gentle and well-known strong arms of his.[10]

In the meantime, the AVH fired on demonstrators besieging the state radio building, pressing that their demands be broadcast to the nation. The AVH fled as demonstrators stormed the building, occupying it along

Fig. 7.1 Stalin's head on a Budapest square, 24 October 1956 (Photographer: Robert Hofbauer. *Source* FOTO: Fortepan—ID 93004, https://commons.wikimedia.org/wiki/File:1956_a_budapesti_Szt%C3%A1lin-szobor_elgurult_feje_fortepan_93004.jpg, Wikimedia Creative Commons)

with the nearby Party newspaper offices. Overnight, Soviet Army tanks went into action, contested by rebels armed with weapons seized from the secret police, from regular police, and most disturbingly, from Hungarian Army units, many of which refused to fire on their fellow citizens and some of which actually targeted Soviet forces.

An uprising had indeed commenced, and before long, Imre Nagy found himself again in charge of Hungary's chaos. This baffled the Yugoslav observer, a dedicated Titoist:

> I... remain alone with my anxiety. Why are the workers unreservedly helping the people who are fighting for a capitalist Hungary?... I am at pains to establish in a politically-justifiably way my own attitude toward these events which, when observed with mere human eyes, are in my opinion a great tragedy for Hungary. What is the basis of the "people's democracy" in Hungary? What was it that kept this system in existence

7 THE REVOLT: SPONTANEITY, REPRESSION, AND REACTION   281

when a Party which numbered about 800,000 members has disintegrated in a few hours?... What sort of socialism was it which can today be defended only by the political police? What kind of revolutionary and socialist government is this which cannot remain in power without Soviet troops?[11]

The *New York Times* correspondent, by contrast, viewed the rising as a plausible, if dreadful consequence of terrible decisions. "Nagy succeeded to an unenviable heritage since his predecessors had made Communism odious in Hungary... Hungarian communism had been compromised by the attempt to maintain itself in power with the aid of Russian arms."[12]

Holding its ideological line, Moscow blamed the whole "counter-revolutionary" upheaval on plotting imperialists and "Fascist thugs": "This enemy adventure had obviously been in preparation for some time. The forces of foreign reaction have been systematically inciting anti-democratic elements for action against the lawful authority."[13] If so, the outside instigators' "system" was highly-developed, as revolts multiplied across the nation as news from Budapest spread. Steel mill workers rebelled and shut down production at Ózd, Diósgyör, and Sztálinváros; workers' councils pushed Party directors aside in factories from Györ to Debrecen to Miskolc; citizen militias assaulted AVH barracks, at the price of hundreds of dead and wounded; the Hungarian Army fragmented and border guards vanished.[14] Affirming nationalism symbolically, rebels cut socialist emblems out of their national flags, demolished red stars affixed to public buildings, and inscribed "Russians Go Home!" on walls, windows, and even wrecked vehicles, often in proper Cyrillic (Fig. 7.2). Here, finally, strategy *with* design surfaced, but having become legible to state actors (rather than being concealed in diffuse rejection and opportunistic resistance),[15] it was soon crushed, perhaps suggesting that passive resistance, diffident subservience, and pervasive illegality had been more viable strategies.

As might be anticipated, the revolt was full of surprises for all parties involved. Most tragically, thousands of dissident (and many exiled) Hungarians expected that the West would intervene forcefully to take advantage of the cracks in the Eastern Front. Not a chance; France and Britain were embroiled in the Suez confrontation and John Foster Dulles, as Secretary of State, notified the Kremlin that the U.S. judged Hungary and Poland as not worth the risk of nuclear confrontation: "We do not consider these states as potential military allies." Rebels

Fig. 7.2 "Russians Go Home!" In a Budapest shop window, October 1956 (Photographer: Gyula Nagy. *Source* FOTO: Fortepan—ID 24794, http://www.fortepan.hu/_photo/download/fortepan_40202.jpg, archive copy, Wikimedia Creative Commons)

were amazed at the cooperation they received from the "regular" police and the Army, and at the disarray inside the AVH's abandoned headquarters. Teams reviewing files found comprehensive disorganization in information management, including stacks of unfiled reports and disregarded orders. "All in all this huge Byzantine organization was already decaying and falling apart on its own, the Revolt furnishing the last push needed for its disintegration."[16] The rapid dismemberment of governance and economic organizations stunned Party leaders and Soviet "advisors". Inside a week, roughly "2,100 local revolutionary councils and workers' councils" formed in over 1100 communities, displacing factory managers and city officials by the busload.[17] At Budapest's Izzó plant, a temporary council assumed "leadership of the enterprise" and expelled the plant director and chief administrator for having "applied Stalinist, Rákocist, and arbitrary principles." Others lacking "the necessary professional skill" for their managerial posts returned to the labor

Fig. 7.3 Soviet Tank clearing a Budapest street Barricade (Photographer: unknown. *Source* Central Intelligence Agency, https://www.flickr.com/photos/ciagov/8113980088/in/set-72157631830870415/, Wikimedia Creative Commons)

ranks, replaced by technically-competent staff. The council suspended Izzó's much-despised Personnel Office, which assessed political reliability. Dismissed as well were the norm-setting and work-distribution units, thus correcting an "exaggerated bureaucratic apparatus." The new leaders also invited each department to select delegates for a permanent workers council, concluding their manifesto thus: "Let us prove that we are better managers… Let us have democratic socialist elections. Let us start to work."[18]

Such admirable ambitions could not survive the advance of Soviet tank divisions, commencing before dawn Sunday 4 November (Fig. 7.3). Though sporadic fighting continued for days in the capital and especially in provincial industrial areas, the outcome was never in doubt. An estimated 700 Soviets and 2500 Hungarians lost their lives (60% in Budapest), with 1500 Russians and 20,000 locals wounded. Over half of the Magyar dead were industrial workers, the majority of whom were killed in Budapest's 8th and 9th Districts, just outside the city center. In the aftermath, an estimated 200,000 Hungarians chose exile, streaming westward in the winter months despite increasingly-vigilant border patrols. The Soviets anointed János Kádár as Chair of the Council of Ministers. He had become Party First Secretary in October as Rákosi's heirs fled to the USSR, and now replaced Nagy, temporarily sheltered in the Yugoslav embassy.

Reprisals were immediate and harsh, running through 1957: tens of thousands dismissed from jobs and/or arrested; 26,000 tried (with over 90% convicted); 13,000 interned and several hundred executed, including Nagy in 1958, a last cruelty.[19] In the meantime, the regime created a new socialist workers' party [MSZMP] to replace the Stalin-era Workers' Party, whose membership had collapsed from 800,000 to 100,000. Many "convenience" Communists had burnt the Party cards that once assured jobs they now abandoned or from which they were being dismissed. Thus was the Rákosi regime's crisis of political reliability re-convened; the Party's loyal remnants were not numerous enough to manage the state and oversee the economy; and as in the late Forties, brigades of the competent had left Hungary, however unwillingly. Recruitment of new and restoration of old members was the Party's winter 56–57 priority; by March, MSZMP ranks neared 200,000, although its open arms surely welcomed back thousands of careerists.[20]

The economic damage was substantial, well beyond the destruction in Budapest; but deep cracks had predated the Revolt. As a U.S. analyst noted: "The problems of the Hungarian economy were not created [in 1956], but were existent as far back as 1952,... caused not only by over-rapid industrialization but by uneconomic use of Hungarian resources and wrong directions in investments. Industrial production almost broke down in 1953 and they have been trying to redirect it [ever since]."[21] A general strike called in late October continued by fits and starts into 1957, notably in crucial provincial metalworking and coal mining districts.[22] As coal was fundamental to power generation, a 40% drop in electricity output in January 1957 (vs. January 1956) compelled a 25% reduction in manufacturing (57 vs. 56), concentrated in heavy industry (which consumed over half of industrial power). The irony buried in this result was that, although 90% of miners were available for work, much of the work they were doing wasn't mining, because "3,000 more shifts [than planned] have had to be introduced for maintenance work" neglected

7 THE REVOLT: SPONTANEITY, REPRESSION, AND REACTION   285

since the previous summer.[23] Joint analysis of the physical ruin and stalled production gauged the Hungarian economy's net losses at 21–22 billion forints (ca. US$1B), 20–25% of annual output. Emergency loans from the USSR and Bloc nations (3.5B ft) barely touched the shortfall, but were swiftly spent to buy raw materials, particularly for consumer goods sectors.[24]

Compounding these losses was workers' active or passive wrecking of industrial facilities. At Sztálinváros,

> When the Soviet Army occupied the plant [in] November 1956, workers and engineers dispersed. The blast furnace remained untended for three days, and its temperature dropped so much that it will not [soon] be serviceable, according to expert opinion. The Soviet advisors and staff who had been attached to the plant disappeared two days before the outbreak of the revolt and are not known to have returned.

Moreover, during the revolt, the plant's security force "disbanded, and confusion reigned until the militia, reinforced by the Soviet garrison, former AVH members, and loyal Communists, regained control of the combine in April 1957. In the interim, individuals had entered and left the area, introducing and removing objects at will."[25] Just think—"the blast furnace remained untended for three days"—a statement of techno-logical and political rejection performed as inaction while facing Soviet occupiers clueless about how to extract cooling pig iron to avoid it hard-ening in a furnace, forcing a total rebuild. Then, with reasserting state power moving at a snail's pace, six months passed before a mélange of Kádár backers "regained control" of the Stalinist regime's million-ton steel complex. Brutal.

Rural districts had been relatively quiet during the upheaval, although given that regular channels of commerce had frozen, suburban farmers (and bakers) had spontaneously provisioned Budapest and other cities, some selling foodstuffs, others donating them (Fig. 7.4). Realizing that after the invasion, continued supplies could not be coerced, the Kádár administration placated farm households by confirming the end of forced deliveries, which Nagy had initiated, and accepting (for a time) the recent mass withdrawals from TSZs. By the end of 1956, the number of co-ops shrank from nearly 4,000 to just above 2,000, "cultivating a mere 6.1 percent of the country's arable land." Persistent appeals during

Fig. 7.4 Food deliveries in Budapest's District 13, November 1956 (Donor: Gyula Nagy. *Source* FOTO: Fortepan—ID 24837, http://www.fortepan.hu/_photo/download/fortepan_40245.jpg, archive copy, Wikimedia Creative Commons)

1957 helped restore almost all the collapsed TSZs, but total membership reached "only one-third of the March 1956 figure." As well, "the government found it wise to allow the free marketing of farm produce to continue and to issue a decree providing for compensation of damage suffered by peasants as a result of earlier collectivization drives." These were temporizing moves; renewed drives for TSZ formation lay ahead, once stabilization had been achieved. The first signals of a roll-back came in April 1957, with an in-kind land tax "on all holdings exceeding two hectares [5 acres]; and on June 23, the buying of wheat, at a fixed price, was made a government monopoly."[26] Pressure on farm households resumed.

Industrial workers, paladins of the revolt, fared much worse. Norm-setting returned at levels more intense than before; Party review of political credentials revived, as did demands to boost production, even as failures to meet quotas brought reduced earnings in many plants.

One new incentive did arise, however: profit-sharing—a tactical substitute for quantity-based bonuses. "Profit shares are paid to workers at the end of the fiscal year if their firm surpasses the profit margin laid down for it in the plan. Profits thus distributed may not, however, exceed one month's average earnings."[27] In enterprises meeting the criteria, this policy typically added two weeks pay to most workers' annual wage, but the ministries excluded some plants, notably Izzó. A labor journalist explained:

> Factory leaders and leaders of the Ministries alike failed to reveal the bitter truth to the workers... [T]he workers of Egyesült Izzó were the first ones in the fall of 1956 to become connected with the strikes and the last ones to give up and return to work. Regular production did not even start until the following April. The resultant aggregate losses amounted to 100 million forints. This is a staggering amount.

More recent deficiencies reinforced barring Izzó from profit-sharing. Rejects in 1957 alone cost the firm 3.5 million forints, while an efficiency drive improved bulb manufacturing performance by only one percent. Idle shop time added another 400,000 ft in costs unsupported by output. Moreover, "machinery is frequently kept running without production [and] lights are also left burning unnecessarily." Although condemned by Kádár in a January 1958 speech at Izzó, the theft economy spirit also continued to thrive:

> Another serious problem that was overlooked by all is the problem of public property, for pilferage amounts to several hundred thousand forints each year. Alcohol is used in the course of manufacturing processes, yet approximately 10 percent of the alcohol on hand disappears, having a total value of one-half million forints. This amount does not include the value of alcohol drunk on the premises by the workers themselves... One month ago a group of thieves were exposed who stole everything that could be moved... the cost of the damage created by them [was] close to 100,000 forints.

Although production data for early 1958 showed definite gains, "it is not believed for one moment that the new situation will change the bitter feelings harbored by workers."[28] It did not.

Stabilization of the new state apparatus signaled restoration of a closet Stalinism. Purges and reprisals receded, succeeded by reframing the AVH as an Interior Ministry division, reviving the prominence of heavy industry investment, and renewing, in winter 1958–59, the drive for agricultural collectivization. Though modest increases in allocations for rural improvements and consumer goods manufacturing did appear, the old commitments to prioritize exports, increase both quantity and quality, launch "socialist competitions" and set high quotas resumed, with much the same results as before. Norms went unmet, wages drooped, and competitions' "results were disappointing," manufacturing's perennial problems remained in place. A 1960 survey reported:

> There were delays in the supply of materials, machinery was antiquated, labor was inefficiently organized, norms were slack and there were not enough incentives. Production had risen because more people were being employed, but productivity was stagnant. The Minister of Labor complained: "In many enterprises, slack discipline has led to a loss of eight to ten percent of working time. Owing to the inadequate preparation of labor processes, a further five to ten percent of time is spent in waiting for materials, tools, blueprints, and other things."

Workers may have thought otherwise, that these conditions represented not "inefficient organization," but "efficient disorganization," something they had spent years refining.[29] An outside observer in 1961 concurred with the Kádár ministry's judgment that "many factors" were impeding its drive for quality and profit.

> Industry has a serious backlog in retooling and modernization... Industrial techniques are backward; the official press never stops criticizing industry for its inefficiency. Production processes are poorly coordinated, mass production being, on the whole, still foreign to Hungarian industry. There is little standardization, too many types are produced by too many firms with all the waste in manpower and materials such overlapping involves.

Overall, practices "that would cause a capitalist factory to go out of business within a fortnight are rampant... to say nothing of pilfering, racketeering, and the grosser type of embezzlement."[30]

What then might stand as the Revolt's legacy for Kádár-era enterprises, for farmers, and for workers in industry, construction or commerce? Three items stand out. First, it is pointless to confront Soviet power, no matter how fragile and incompetent Hungarian state managers might be. The invasion confirmed that no path existed by which Hungary could exit the Bloc to join Austria in Central European neutrality. Second, as hope for an independent socialism faded, planners had to confront both their profound failure to make the Soviet-dependent system work adequately and the continuing nature of the constraints that yielded that disappointment. In time, tentative notions about broad-based reform gradually emerged, as wider circles of policy makers, academics, administrators, and managers struggled to generate growth in the early 1960s. Third, farmers quietly appreciated that they held some leverage over Budapest, whereas workers had none (or next to none). Out of sight but axial to feeding the nation, rural households soon resigned themselves to joining producer cooperatives while striving to sustain the primacy of family interests over those of the TSZs. This the state had to accept. Factory, shop, and project workers resigned themselves as well, to ongoing performance pressures, continued poor earnings, and the need to augment incomes by whatever means came to hand. The theft economy was neither disturbed nor displaced by Soviet tanks, but if anything, was vitalized by them. The failed revolt confirmed two fundamental premises for a post-56 Hungary: that the people deeply mistrusted the regime and that the regime had too few tools at its command to build socialism beyond its institutions of control.

In 1960, Marika Robert, a magazine writer and 1950 Czech immigrant to Canada, returned to Prague and Budapest to gauge the effects of Communist rule on her former homes. In an article for the national weekly *Macleans*, she reported discovering that Western notions of "the people behind the Iron Curtain as overworked slaves" were wildly inaccurate:

> Even though work is being put on a pedestal there, it has few worshippers. A Communist is not supposed to work for money; he works for the glory of it. As far as I can judge by the people I met… since good work does not mean material advantages, and no one can be fired for doing a bad job, the people behind the Iron Curtain work less and play more than they do in North America.

State officials criticized such practices (sloth and slack) as withholding effort so as to undermine the socialist project, but as this study has indicated, they might better be described as just means for coping with chaos and contradiction. One tactic in that approach to everyday business life was accepting the theft economy—the state steals from us and we return the favor.

Everyone behind the Curtain steals. The butcher puts his finger on the scale when he weighs the meat; if you buy three meters of some material you are lucky if you get two and three quarters: the miners stuff their pockets with coal; nurses take home absorbent cotton, druggists alcohol; factory workers smuggle out from the plant everything from tools to half-made products. Theft is so common that the thieves aren't tried any more in public courts. They are punished at their working place by losing their Christmas bonus or other privileges. On the stage, of course, all this is exaggerated and a worker will be shown presenting his wife with a locomotive for her birthday.[31]

One tragedy of the Revolt, then, was that, whereas it destroyed visions of a national future outside Soviet control, it proved largely inconsequential for socio-economic practice. Enterprise management and laboring lives went on much as before. Yet while people recovered their sense of humor, their aptitude for entertainment, and their need for social contact, nothing worked terribly well and cynicism deepened. All in all, the center had held—but for whom?

NOTES

1. CURPH Interview No. 204, 6–7, HU OSA 414-0-2-181.
2. CURPH Interview No. 36-M, 4, HU OSA 414-0-2-31.
3. RFE Background Report, "Hungary, 1957–1961, Part II," May 1961, 242–43, HU OSA 300-8-3-2294. *Ludas* was a Budapest satirical periodical which started in 1945 and continued publishing into the 1990s.
4. CIA Memorandum, "CIA Awareness of Pre-Hungarian Revolution Developments," 27 March 1957, 1 (Secret, CIA-RDP80B01676R00400170001-1).
5. Ibid., 7, 11. For in-depth analysis of Polish and Hungarian dynamics, see Mark Kramer, "The Soviet Union and the 1956 Crises in Hungary and Poland," *Journal of Contemporary History* 33:2(1998): 163–214. The "secret speech" became public rather quickly, as a copy reportedly reached Israeli security services who forwarded it to CIA. Having verified and translated the text, the Agency shared it with the Department of State, which released it to the *New York Times* in late May (Harrison Salisbury, "Khrushchev Talk on Stalin Bares Details of Rule Based on Terror," *New York Times*, 5 June 1956, 1, 12–16, full text at 13–16).

7 THE REVOLT: SPONTANEITY, REPRESSION, AND REACTION   291

6. "Yugoslavs Renew Ties with Hungary," *New York Times*, 24 October 1956, 8.
7. CIA, Senior Research Staff, "Communism in Eastern Europe: Post-Stalin Developments in the Satellites," SRS-7, Part 11/B, 23 April 1958, 10–19 (Confidential, CIA-RDP80-01445R000100080001-9).
8. See https://www.britannica.com/biography/Jozef-Zacharias z-Bem (accessed 28 June 2021).
9. CIA, "Post-Stalin," 23.
10. Dobrica Ćosić, "Seven Days in Budapest: A Yugoslav Writer Witnesses the Hungarian Revolution," 13 (RFE Background Report, 2 September 1957, HU OSA 300-8-3-9160).
11. Ćosić, "Seven Days," 17. See also Latinka Perović, "Dobrica Ćosić and Josip Broz Tito—A Political and Intellectual Relationship," in *Titoism, Self-Determination, Nationalism, Cultural Memory, Volume Two: Tito's Yugoslavia, Stories Untold*, Gorana Ognjenović and Jasna Jozelic, eds., New York: Palgrave Macmillan, 2016, 105–64.
12. John MacCormac, "Hungary Now in Doubt," *New York Times*, 4 November 1956, 196.
13. Quoted from "Moscow Radio's Report," *New York Times*, 25 October 1956, 7.
14. CURPH Interviews: No. 94-M, 5–14, HU OSA 414-0-2-95; No. 217, 5–11, HU OSA 414-0-2-293 (Györ); No. 204, 6–18, HU OSA 414-0-2-181 (Mosonmagyaróvár); No. 36-M, 4–16, HU OSA 414-0-2-31 (Pecs); No. 72-M, 5–13, HU OSA 414-020-71 (Barayna); No. 93-M, 4–9, HU OSA 414-0-2-94 (Székesfehérvár).
15. For legibility, see James Scott, *Seeing Like a State: How Certain Schemes to Improve the Human Condition Have Failed*, New Haven: Yale University Press, 1999.
16. CURPH Interview No. 526, 39, HU OSA 414-0-2-320. The respondent was a historian sent to evaluate AVH Budapest central office records. For rebel incursions in Györ, which revealed names and locations of AVH informers, see RFEFR, "Hungary, Incl. Budapest, October 29 and 30," 10 November 1956, HU OSA 300-1-2-76438.
17. Wikipedia, "Hungarian Revolution of 1956," https://en.wikipe dia.org/wiki/Hungarian_Revolution_of_1956 (accessed 29 June 2021). A careful, scholarly synthesis, closely attending to the

historiography (over 150 endnotes, followed by an extensive bibliography).

18. Ćosić, "Seven Days," 32–33. See also Bill Lomax, ed., *The Hungarian Workers' Councils in 1956*, London: East European Monographs, 1990.

19. Wikipedia, "Hungarian Revolution." For a day-by-day scholarly reprise and analysis, see Ferenc Váli, *Rift and Revolt in Hungary: Nationalism vs. Communism*, Cambridge: Harvard University Press, 1961, Chaps. 19–29.

20. CIA, "Post-Stalin Developments," SRS-7, II-B, April 1958, 43, 51–52. Fresh purges and arrests surfaced in summer 1957, affecting perhaps 6,000 people.

21. CIA Services Division, "Satellite Committee Meeting, 7 May 1958," 1 (Secret, CIA-RDP61S00527A000200190030-3).

22. Attila Szakolczai, "The Main Provincial Centres of the 1956 Revolution: Györ and Miskolc," *Europe-Asia Studies* 58(2006): 1311–1326. See also CIA, "Post-Stalin Developments," SRS-7, II-B, 34–38.

23. RFE Background Report, "The Economic Situation in Hungary," 4 April 1957, 1–2, HU OSA 300-8-3-3245.

24. RFEFR, "Hungary, 1957–61," 210; CIA, "Services Division," 2.

25. CIAIR, "Danube Steel Works, Dunapentele," 15 November 1957, 7–8 (Secret, CIA-RDP80T00246A038500750001-2). Only one of the planned blast furnaces had become operative by 1956.

26. Jörg Hoensch, A *History of Modern Hungary, 1867–1994*, London: Longman, 1995, 229; CIA, "Post-Stalin Developments," SRS-7, II-B, 44, 48.

27. RFEFR, "Hungary, 1957–61," 219–20.

28. "No Share of Profits at Egyesült Izzó," *Népszava*, 13 May 1958, Joint Publications Research Service Report No. 277, Review of the Hungarian Central Press, 17 September 1958, 113–15. For Kádár, see CIA, "Post-Stalin Developments," SRS-7, II-B, 67.

29. RFEFR, "Hungary, 1957–61," 213.

30. Ibid., 219.

31. https://archive.macleans.ca/article/1960/12/17/marika-roberts-astonishing-account-of-the-lighter-side-of-life-behind-the-iron-curtain-the-communist (accessed 12 April 2021).

CHAPTER 8

Afterword

[In late 1962,] Mrs. Lajos Jakus [reports] the indescribable chaos prevailing in the railroad car manufacturing shop of the Wilhelm Pieck Factory of Győr during the end of the year rush... The head of the planning section fights with the [operations] manager about freeing some tracks for the assembly of cars. The painters' section leader protests angrily against the impossible tasks demanded of his men, but finally promises to attempt the impossible. At the plant Party committee office, three [workers] complain that on account of lack of funds, they cannot do overtime to install electrical equipment... Other mechanics and carpenters scold a cooperating enterprise for failure to deliver parts in time. Passenger cars for the MAV [State Railway] have been ready since August, but cannot be delivered because of defective generators from the Ottó Bláthy Electronic Instrument Factory, or regulators never delivered by the General Mechanical Machine Factory.... In the course of the rush, the accident rate increased by 20%, the Party secretary of the railroad shop contracted a neuritis of the spine [and] the manager of the machine shop lost 8 kilograms in weight. All this shows not only that cooperation between the individual enterprises works by fits and starts, but also that internal leadership is wobbly.
—*Kisalfold* [Győr daily newspaper], 2 December 1962[1]

In 1957, the Soviet-backed Kádár administration faced a host of difficult challenges, none more serious than getting its "building socialism" project back on the rails. With thousands dead, tens of thousands arrested,

© The Author(s), under exclusive license to Springer Nature Switzerland AG 2022
P. Scranton, *Business Practice in Socialist Hungary, Volume 1*, Palgrave Debates in Business History,
https://doi.org/10.1007/978-3-030-89184-8_8

293

and hundreds of thousands exiled, this was hardly a magnetic proposition, but it could not be deferred. Reprisals had to cease, physical damage and destruction had to be repaired, lost expertise had to be replenished, and the "hidden reserves" of the people's energies had to be mobilized to move the economy forward with speed. The first three of these did materialize, more or less steadily, but the fourth—not so much. The second volume of *Business Practice in Socialist Hungary*, subtitled "From Chaos to Contradiction," will document and analyze the dynamics through which the regime pursued "stabilization" in society and economy through the close of the 1960s. As the epigraph documents, "Chaos" filled the years following the Revolt, highlighted by the ongoing disarray in plan implementation. "Contradiction" refers to the irresolvable tensions and conflicts that accompanied almost every push toward socialist development in the 1960s, including workers' withholding of effort, farmers' patient manipulation of agricultural policies, and pervasive delay, deception, theft, and fraud in agencies and institutions at all scales. Kádár's famous inversion of a classic call to crush opponents fit the situation perfectly. He announced in 1959: "He who is not against us is with us."[2] The phrasing confirmed that the Party state understood that it faced "command without control." Kádár had the monopoly of force, yet could not force the emergence of growth, cooperation, coordination, productivity, or efficiency. Rather than coercing fealty and staging enthusiasm, the regime simply celebrated mass indifference, advertised as a form of unity, however shallow. In the Stalinist years, Hungarians had relied on coping behaviors to manage uncertainty. Now it was the state's turn to cope with a recalcitrant and dissatisfied populace. The result: ordinary people responded positively to the regime's restraints on the police, hiring preferences that valued competence, openings for foreign travel, and a sustained expansion of the range and supply of consumer goods. They also mocked Kádár in endless jokes and skits, which the Prime Minister reportedly enjoyed retelling, unlike the Rákosi team. But as the epigraph suggests, no solution to deep problems in production was devised.

It is this peculiar landscape that the second volume of this study will explore in depth.

After a contextualizing introduction, subsequent chapters will investigate patterns of individual and enterprise initiatives, 1957–1966, in the same domains addressed in Volume One: Agriculture, Construction, Commerce, and Manufacturing. Each operated through complex structures and extensive network relationships that morphed during this decade, often in unexpected ways. The chapters will address official plans, prescriptions, and practices, drawing on actors' reports about achievements and shortcomings. Failures in coordination and in observance of rules and contracts exacerbated the nation's foundational deficiencies and vulnerabilities, overshadowing gradual improvements in living standards and a relaxation of political tensions. These everyday frustrations produced insistent calls for revising core planning practices, priorities, and incentives, as did enterprises' continuing inability to meet plan targets.

Consequently the reformist New Economic Mechanism debuted on 1 January 1968, after four years of proposals and negotiations had prepared the way for this national experiment in decentralizing authority and accountability. Regrettably, Hungarian workers and farmers, managers and engineers, were largely excluded from the economic redesign process, which economists and planners directed. Volume Two's final substantive chapter will assess the NEM's implementation and impact into the early 1970s, when its opponents successfully blunted the reform's momentum and largely restored central command and control. Once the first oil crisis arrived in 1973 and Hungary's trade deficits soared, already-rising cycles of foreign debt and government borrowing ballooned. Unable to define their role in either the Bloc or the global economy, the Party state and its enterprises stumbled toward collapse. The Conclusion to Volume Two, "Never Quite Socialist?" will underscore the comprehensive insufficiency of the transition to socialism Stalin's deputies promoted in the late 1940s. This is all the more striking given that the state's overall command over businesses was paired with persistently inadequate resources and was inhibited by priorities ceded to superior Soviet interests. Hence, a key legacy of Party and administrative errors was Hungarians' perennial lack of trust in the state, in its plans, programs, and promises, and thus an absence of faith in or commitment to the socialist project as an entirety. Possible implications of this failure for Hungary's later economic and political travails will be sketched at the close.

For those wishing to encounter the second installment of this socialist soap opera, stay tuned. If all goes smoothly, Volume Two will be released during 2023, also from Palgrave Macmillan in its Debates in Business History book series.

Notes

1. *Kisalföld* (Győr daily), 2 December 1962, 3, JPRS 17451, 4 February 1963, 11–12.
2. "10,000,000 Hungarians Can't Be Wrong," *New York Times*, 27 December, 1964, 140. Instead of: "He who is not with us, is against us."

NOTE ON SOURCES

The American Cold War state generated many of the archival sources on which this monograph is based. *Business Practice in Socialist Hungary* is the result of asking what some years ago seemed a simple question: Inside the communist Bloc, how did post-World War II enterprises manage business practice while trying to "build socialism"? Business and economic historians had diligently explored the ways in which twentieth-century capitalist enterprises functioned and specialists had documented Soviet farm and factory operations, but few scholars inquired about the workings of enterprises in other "actually existing socialisms," particularly those in the Soviet-dominated European Bloc. In preliminary research for a project with Patrick Fridenson, I sought historical and contemporaneous accounts of business practice in Poland, Hungary, Czechoslovakia, and the People's Republic of China, ca. 1945–1970, as all four commenced a transition from capitalism and war (or civil war) to socialism in the shadow of the USSR.[1] The literature in English was enormous: scores of macroeconomic studies, analyses of sectors and industries (steel, cement, agriculture), policy and planning critiques, reviews of foreign trade, and translations of theoretical works drafted by prominent socialist economists. Yet such books and journal articles rarely provided a post-1945 glimpse "inside the firm" or "on the farm." Perspectives and dynamics had been sketched from a high altitude—movement on the ground was barely visible.

© The Editor(s) (if applicable) and The Author(s), under exclusive
license to Springer Nature Switzerland AG 2022
P. Scranton, *Business Practice in Socialist Hungary, Volume 1*, Palgrave
Debates in Business History,
https://doi.org/10.1007/978-3-030-89184-8

298 NOTE ON SOURCES

Answering my initial question was much harder because I was fluent in none of the relevant languages, although massive databases had begun to make relevant technical, economic, and local publications available online. Even were "translate this page" services reliable, it would be quite a surprise were I able to identify the most salient pages to render into English from, say, a Budapest foundry industry journal. At this juncture, the Cold War came to my rescue, in several ways. During my research on socialist enterprise in the PRC, I profited from the online subscription archive that Newsbank maintains for reports circulated by the Joint Publications Research Service (JPRS), US Commerce Department, 1957–1992. JPRS employed several thousand (part-time) translators to create, for use by US officials, English versions of publicly-available, policy-relevant materials from scores of nations—predominantly Cold War antagonists like the USSR, PRC, Soviet Bloc states, Cuba, North Korea, and North Vietnam. Newsbank included newspaper articles, government reports, essays from scholarly and technical journals, speeches, decrees, and radio broadcasts, totaling about 1.7 million files in the database. For Volume One, JPRS sources were less crucial than for its successor, "From Chaos to Contradiction," as most of what has been discussed here happened before the translation service commenced operations.

However, another Cold War actor, CIA, offered a diverse array of windows into socialist enterprises. Until 1957, when JPRS took over the task, CIA gathered and translated "Information from Foreign Documents or Radio Broadcasts," publications circulated to US officials. For Hungary, these IFDs often featured harshly critical newspaper accounts of administrative shortcomings, even in the Party papers, as well as embarrassing technical reports on industrial missteps and assessments of agricultural fiascoes. As well, CIA also solicited, assessed, and shared "Information Reports" which flowed from contacts within target nations, as well as from travelers or exiles, reports classified as Confidential, Secret, or Top Secret. IRs often concerned enterprises, agencies, and ministries, focusing on their organization, personnel, and resources, as well as on the difficulties they encountered. In addition, CIA's Office of Research and Reports produced documentary syntheses, status reviews, and policy recommendations, released as Research Aids, Provisional Intelligence Reports, Economic Intelligence Reports, Intelligence Memoranda, Intelligence Briefs, etc., as well as urgent analyses triggered by foreign policy challenges and crises. Systematically declassified through internal review channels, usually 25 or more years after their origin, such documents are available to researchers. (As needed, CIA staff "sanitized" them to avoid disclosing information about informants.[2]) Access to declassified files increased dramatically when CIA opened its Electronic Reading Room, providing online retrieval for about one million digitized documents through keyword searching, at https://www.cia.gov/readingroom/home. (The US Department of State also offers a Virtual Reading Room - https://foia.state.gov/Search/Search.aspx.) Thousands of such IFDs, IRs, and Reports have been invaluable to the construction of this study.

The records of another Cold War entity, Radio Free Europe, long an arm of US intelligence services, yielded rich detail about everyday life in socialist Hungary, along with its opportunities and frustrations. Over 140,000 RFE field reports and Background Reports and Surveys on Hungary and the other Bloc nations rest in the Open Society Archivum, Budapest, digitized and available for online consultation and research use without constraints. (See https://catalog.osaarchivum.org/?utf8=%E2%9C%93&q=RFE.) Like CIA, RFE staff continuously evaluated the quality of information it received, noting collateral confirmations as well as dismissing tales judged as fanciful or created to impress interviewers. The OSA conserves another online collection crucial to "Creating the Theft Economy," over 350 interviews of '56-Revolt exiles conducted in 1957 by the Columbia University Research Project on Hungary (CURPH), under a Ford Foundation grant. Individual interviews ranged from 20 to over 200 single-spaced pages, using an extensive, standard questionnaire created by Columbia social scientists. The respondents came from every strata of Hungarian society: farmers, factory workers, truck drivers, repair and maintenance staff, engineers and technicians, managers and planners, journalists, playwrights, film-makers, and Ministry officials ranging up to the Vice Director of the National Bank. For decades these sources "simply gathered dust in the manuscripts archive of Columbia University,"[3] until during the 1990s, OSA arranged for their digitization. Their detailed vistas on Communism "under construction" thus became accessible. Though this 20,000 page mass can seem forbidding, the vitality shines through. (See https://catalog.osaarchivum.org/?f%5Bdigital_collection%5D%5B%5D=CURPH+Interviews+with+1956+Hungarian+Refugees.)

Finally, English-language scholarly publications in book and article form have been invaluable. Above all, an essential introduction to the intricacies and deceptions anchoring the "Theft Economy" is grounded in

300 NOTE ON SOURCES

a remarkable analysis by an exiled administrator from Hungary's construction ministries: Béla Balassa, *The Hungarian Experience in Economic Planning: A Theoretical and Empirical Study*, New Haven: Yale University Press, 1959. What CIA informants, RFE contacts, and CURPH interviewees discussed as Hungary's absurdities, Balassa analyzed as the unsurprising consequences of initially eager, then desperate policy implementation. A brilliant achievement, it has been largely forgotten. Balassa, a Johns Hopkins professor and long-term contributor to World Bank trade research, routinely drafted articles cited by thousands of economists; but after 60 years, *Hungarian Experience* has barely cracked 100 citations, at least according to Google Scholar.[4] It remains essential reading.

NOTES

1. The PRC research led to a monograph: *Enterprise, Organization and Technology in China: A Socialist Experiment, 1950–1970*, New York: Palgrave Macmillan, 2019.
2. One feature of early Reports was a closing section which rated and evaluated the sources of information on which they were based, a truly valuable feature. CIA Research was committed to getting the most reliable information available to its policy-making clients, so regularly marked lower-quality material as "unconfirmed" or "unverified."
3. András Lénárt, "Emigration from Hungary in 1956," *Hungarian Historical Review* 3&4(2012) https://hunghist.org/index.php/83-articles/121-2012-3-4-lenart (accessed 10 July 2021).
4. https://scholar.google.com/scholar?hl=en&as_sdt=0%2C22&q=Bela+Balassa+%22Hungarian+Experience%22&oq (accessed 13 July 2021).

INDEX

A

Abrasives, 230, 231

Accounting, 7, 22, 78, 89, 114–116, 133, 140, 152, 177, 206, 217, 224, 225, 242, 245

Agriculture

collectivization, 13, 36, 288

compulsory deliveries, 40, 76–78, 81, 85, 86, 153, 175

cooperatives (TSZs), 3, 40

dairies, 59

drought, 84, 170

fertilizer, 27, 65, 75, 88–90, 214

fodder, 30, 93, 170

great plains, 7

household plots, 89, 96

livestock, 8, 22, 30, 31, 57, 59, 60, 74, 78, 85, 89, 94, 95, 169, 170

machine tractor stations (MTS), 58, 61, 66, 67, 69–75, 85, 88, 94, 113, 128, 129, 258

orchards, 3, 57, 74, 75, 80, 112, 258

private farms, 59, 74, 112

state farms, 26, 36, 58, 59, 63, 66, 67, 69, 80, 85, 91, 113

tractors, 7, 30, 36, 56, 57, 59, 61, 67, 70, 71, 73, 74, 90, 128, 199

vineyards, 3, 57, 59, 74, 81, 82, 92, 258, 278

Aluminum/Bauxite, 34, 38, 39, 214, 215, 218, 224, 233, 240

Anarchy, 117, 255

Anti-Semitism, 11, 12

Arrow cross, 11, 12, 27, 28

Artisans/craftsmen, 183, 253, 258

cooperatives (KTSZ), 38, 168, 175, 180, 181, 184, 253, 254

Austria, 4, 9, 82, 129, 168–170, 190, 195, 277, 289

Vienna, 6, 9, 37, 262, 277

AVO/AVH (state security), 27, 28, 40, 42, 79, 121, 131, 171, 175, 187, 217, 241, 250, 279, 281, 282, 285, 287

© The Editor(s) (if applicable) and The Author(s), under exclusive license to Springer Nature Switzerland AG 2022
P. Scranton, *Business Practice in Socialist Hungary, Volume 1*, Palgrave Debates in Business History,
https://doi.org/10.1007/978-3-030-89184-8

301

302 INDEX

B
Bad kaders (unreliables), 120, 195
Balassa, Béla, 26, 29, 46–48, 91, 108,
    112, 118, 119, 131, 154–156,
    158, 159, 163, 266
Banking, 6, 23, 195
Bank, National, of Hungary, 19, 86
Baranya (county), 70, 71, 75, 277
Békés (county), 73, 77, 86, 92
Beria, Lavrentiy, 28, 40, 49, 75
Bethlen, Count István, 11, 17, 18
Bonuses, 72, 73, 114, 119, 130–133,
    178, 179, 199, 217, 242–245,
    251, 258, 261, 264, 287
Bookkeeping, 255
Borsod, 9, 59, 87, 121, 125, 129,
    219
Bribery, 22, 76, 84, 119, 130
Brick and tile industry, 118
    refractories, 224, 225
Bridges, 30, 121, 124, 125, 229
Bureaucracy, 2, 22, 79, 181

C
Chia, Robert, 57, 79, 99, 105
Clothing, 22, 29, 38, 39, 44, 76,
    131, 136, 151, 166, 168, 173,
    175–178, 180, 184, 215, 253,
    262–264
Coal, 30, 32, 39, 124, 141, 146, 185,
    214, 219, 221, 260, 263, 284,
    290
Commasation, 91
Commerce
    commission & resale, 37, 176, 183,
        201
    cultural, 188
    illegal, 181, 182, 189, 245, 256,
        258
    import-export, 37, 43
    retail, 180
    wholesale, 38, 166

Construction
    deficiencies, 150
    design, 121, 131, 145, 236
    housing, 139, 147
    industrial, 117
    management, 152
    materials, 38, 112, 131
    plan changes/modifications, 133
    planning, 24, 128, 134
    private, 113, 117
    standardization, 114, 288
    subway, 141–145
Consumers
    cooperatives, 38
    prices, 38
Coping, 57, 58, 166, 180, 182, 183,
    191, 229, 289
Cotton, 8, 29, 34, 41, 62–64, 172,
    184, 185, 215, 216, 248, 249,
    290
Csepel (Budapest), 44, 139, 142,
    183, 230, 240
Csongrád, 9, 73, 80, 185
Czechoslovakia, 2, 4, 190, 227, 234,
    236

D
Danube (river), 7, 10, 19, 21, 30, 34,
    37, 114, 124, 129, 139, 141,
    142, 146–149, 190, 215, 216
Debrecen (city), 9, 79, 80, 82, 84,
    173, 184, 186, 223, 224, 250,
    279, 281
Decrees, 24, 26, 40, 81, 91, 119,
    192, 261
Deportations, 29, 139, 177
Depression, Great, 11
Diósgyőr (city), 125, 136, 219, 220,
    225, 226, 228–230

E

Education, 2, 35, 44, 115, 116, 135, 199, 264
Egyesült Izzólámpa/Izzó (Budapest), 251
Electrification
  power plants, 140, 153, 200, 262
  power trust, 258, 259
Embezzlement, 22, 29, 264
Engineers, 31, 34, 44, 115, 123, 124, 132, 138, 142, 146, 149, 196, 198, 220, 228, 232, 243, 262, 264
  community of, 122
Entrepreneurship, 181, 182, 184, 189, 201, 217, 224, 245, 264
Erdei, Ferenc, 62, 63, 108

F

Fejer (county), 147
Five Year Plan (1950–1954), 25, 38, 39, 88, 112, 247
Food
  processing, 8, 84, 240, 247
  stores (Közért), 172, 174
  supply, 26, 169
Fraud
  plan, 114, 133, 134, 217, 243, 244, 262

G

Ganz Electrical Works, 124, 233
Germany
  DDR (East), 220
  FRG (West), 190, 195, 239
  Nazi, 141
Gerö, Ernö, 27, 141, 149, 179, 193, 206, 278, 279
Gömbös, Gyula, 11, 18
Györ, 1, 61, 65, 71, 73, 93, 96, 136, 137, 173, 185, 186, 221, 229, 239, 245, 248, 251, 261, 277, 279, 281

H

Hadjú-Bihar, 9, 83, 84, 223
Handicrafts, 194, 218, 246
Hegedűs, András, 15, 41, 42, 97, 104
Holocaust, 12, 35, 184
Holt, Robin, 57, 79, 99, 105
Horthy, Miklós, 10–12, 17, 18, 30, 31, 120, 138, 156
Housing
  apartments, 22, 118, 120, 136, 167, 173, 176
  hotels, 167
  workers' barracks, 277

I

Improvisation, 2, 23, 152, 264
Iron ore, 4, 141, 151, 152, 216, 219

K

Kádár, János, 14, 284, 285, 287, 288, 292
Khrushchev, Nikita, 141, 228, 278, 290
Kornai, János, 26, 47
Kulak, 74, 75, 85, 86, 92, 103, 105
Kun, Béla, 9, 10

L

Land reform, 67, 74, 89, 90, 166
Lang Machine Works, 237, 240, 246

M

Machinery
  agricultural, 3, 6, 20, 21, 36, 56, 59, 67, 198, 229, 238, 240, 253, 258

304 INDEX

construction, 145
metalworking, 144
Machine tools, 170, 198, 231, 234
Maintenance, 20, 22, 32, 115, 124,
 145, 152, 183, 186, 187, 217,
 239, 243, 246–248, 257–260,
 263, 270
Malenkov, Gyorgy, 75
Manfred Weiss, 67, 170, 219, 221,
 229, 230
Manufacturing
 bicycles, 217, 218, 229
 electrical, 8, 21, 124
 engines & motors, 237, 260
 heavy industry, 214, 218, 226
 light industry, 24, 215
 materials, 6, 36, 39, 214–216, 240
 shipyards, 221, 238
Marketing, 182, 190, 201, 286
Markets
 black, 20, 29, 44, 76, 80, 85, 130,
  151, 169, 174, 175, 182, 187,
  189–191, 205, 208, 252, 254,
  256, 265
 free, 22, 78, 85, 89, 171–174
 public (food), 41, 166, 168, 170,
  174, 182
Maszek (enterprises), 189, 201, 251
Ministries
 Agriculture, 26, 34, 62
 Construction, 120
 Council of Ministers, 24, 25, 42,
  62, 111, 114, 171, 178, 192,
  221, 264, 284
 Finance, 24, 115, 141
 Heavy Industry, 25, 37, 125, 219,
  258, 260, 264, 288
 Trade, Domestic & Foreign, 24
 Transportation, 112
Miskolc (city), 9, 34, 37, 281

N
Nagy, Imre, 21, 40–42, 55, 58, 59,
 66, 75, 81, 83, 87, 93, 96, 97,
 151, 152, 170, 179, 187, 189,
 195, 199, 251, 255, 257, 262,
 264, 279, 280, 284, 285
Nationalization, 3, 23, 38, 186, 230
New Course, 21, 40–42, 98
Nyers, Resző, 15, 96, 97, 107, 109,
 110, 154, 206, 274

O
Ózd (city), 219–221, 225, 226, 229,
 230, 281

P
Pecs (city), 73, 83, 184, 277
Pest (county), 19, 37, 72, 141, 142
Petroleum refining, 243
Pieck, Wilhelm, Railway Equipment
 Co, 3, 186, 229, 239
Planning
 errors, 146
 National Office, 24, 40, 178, 217
 problems, 115
 process, 25
Poland, 2, 214, 227, 233, 237, 278,
 279, 281
Printing industry, 9, 38, 218
Productivity, 69, 70, 73, 153, 185,
 246, 261, 288

Q
Quality
 control, 196, 248
 materials, 240, 263
 product, 237, 256, 263
Quotas/norms, 59, 61, 72, 73, 76,
 81, 84, 85, 87, 88, 118,
 123–126, 174, 188, 199, 213,

INDEX 305

217, 223, 225, 238, 241–243, 247, 248, 250, 251, 258, 260, 261, 265, 286, 288

R

Rácz, István, 138, 213, 262
Railway equipment, 226, 233, 234
Rákosi, Mátyás, 21–23, 27, 29, 35, 39, 40, 42, 81, 83, 87, 90, 96, 97, 141, 145, 152, 167, 171, 172, 180, 186, 200, 214, 229, 239, 251, 253, 265, 278, 279, 284
Rationing, 169–172, 175
Reactionaries/unreliable, 120, 121, 134, 139, 143, 153, 192, 199, 217, 234, 237, 260, 261, 264
Recsk (quarries), 138, 241
Red Star Tractor (Budapest), 71, 237
Rejection/resistance, 13, 27, 35, 42, 57, 97, 134, 225, 227, 228, 233, 240, 241, 249, 250, 257, 263–265, 278, 281, 285
Reorganizations, 13, 114, 197, 230, 254, 258, 261
only plant policy, 229
Repairs, 36, 39, 67, 125, 149, 166, 168, 183, 215, 218, 221, 233, 235, 237, 243, 248, 257–262
Research institutes, 26, 62
Restaurants/taverns, 59, 82, 166–168, 175, 177, 182, 187, 252
Romania, 4, 191, 265

S

Sabotage, 55, 58, 69, 214, 225, 227, 237, 240–242, 264, 265
Scrap industry, 219, 221
Siemens, 33, 242, 252
Skoblykov, Andrei, 34, 62, 63

Smallholder (landowner), 71, 74, 186
Smallholders (party), 20, 23
Smuggling, 22
Soil, 6, 7, 56, 63, 69, 71, 78, 87, 93, 94, 98, 112, 125, 146, 147, 149, 150
Solidarity, 241, 251, 262
Somogy (county), 79, 223
Soviet Union (USSR)
and Hungarian enterprises, 35
control in Hungary, 30
experts, 35
Military (Red Army), 3, 10, 20, 21, 31, 32, 142, 215
rejections (of exports), 233, 240, 263
reparations, 21, 33, 169
Sovietization, 21
trade with, 33
Spare parts, 1, 3, 20, 31, 71, 82, 121, 183, 196, 217, 247, 258, 262
Stakhanovite, 248
Stalin, Joseph, 14, 21, 28, 31, 40, 90, 129, 141, 145, 151–153, 228, 260, 278–280
Standard of living, 20
State railways (MAV), 36, 113
Steel industry
accidents, 150
foundries, 146, 238
furnaces, 146, 220, 224, 229
pig iron, 146, 220, 224
Strategy, 58, 91, 117, 134, 153, 241, 281
Subcontracting, 131, 215, 218, 256
Subsidies, 93, 216, 237, 266
Supreme Economic Council, 23, 141
Switzerland, 169, 192, 195, 234
Szabolcs-Szatmár (county), 85
Szálasi, Ferenc, 11
Szeged (city), 9, 10, 37, 73, 128, 185, 249, 279

306 INDEX

Szolnok (county), 63, 81, 84, 90, 115
Sztálinváros, 114, 118, 141, 146, 148, 151, 152, 219, 223, 228, 281, 285

T
Taxation, 60, 92
Textile & apparel industry
   exports, 182, 247
   Goldberger (Budapest), 221, 247
Theft/stealing
   by managers/engineers, 65, 66
   by the state, 58, 66, 85, 191, 195, 201, 289
   by workers, 20
Tisza (river/region), 122, 124, 129, 138
Trade
   agencies (IMPEXES), 192, 193, 200
   exchange rates, 216
   import-export, 43, 167, 182
   representatives, 194, 197
Trianon, Treaty of, 4

U
USSR
   army, 20
   occupation, 12
   reparations, 21, 31, 169, 215

V
Vas (county), 82

Vas, Zoltán, 42, 141, 145, 149, 264
Vehicle industry (trucks, buses, et al.)
   parts, 66, 73, 184, 261
   repairs, 261
Veszprem (county), 130, 185

W
War
   First World, 4, 7, 17, 193
   Korean, 39, 164
   Second World, 3, 11, 36, 221
Wine, 1, 71, 78, 82, 83, 95, 131, 168, 186, 187, 189, 192, 214
Workers
   commercial, 201
   construction, 131, 134, 136, 140, 147, 153
   factory, 35, 42, 134, 171, 185, 262, 290
   farm, 60
   forced labor, 135, 137–140, 153, 279
   temporary, 59
   training/apprentices, 254
   transport, 186
Working People's Party (communist), 264

Y
Yugoslavia, 4, 12, 17, 129

Z
Zala (county), 3, 94

9783030891831